Lyric Generations

PUBLISHING FOR THE WORLD
125 Years
THE JOHNS HOPKINS UNIVERSITY PRESS

G. GABRIELLE STARR

Lyric Generations

Poetry and the Novel
in the Long Eighteenth Century

The Johns Hopkins University Press
Baltimore and London

Publication of this book has been aided by a grant from the
Abraham and Rebecca Stein Faculty Publication Fund of New York
University, Department of English, and by the generous assistance
of the Chester Kerr Endowment.

The Johns Hopkins University Press
2715 North Charles Street
Baltimore, Maryland 21218-4363
www.press.jhu.edu

Library of Congress Cataloging-in-Publication Data
Starr, Gabrielle, 1974–
   Lyric generations : poetry and the novel in the long eighteenth
century / Gabrielle Starr.
      p. cm.
Includes bibliographical references and index.
   ISBN 0-8018-7379-7 (alk. paper)
   1. English fiction — 18th century — History and criticism.
2. English poetry — 18th century — History and criticism.
3. Literary form — History — 18th century. 4. Lyric poetry —
History and criticism. I. Title.
PR851.S63 2003
820.9′005 — dc21   2003006816

A catalog record for this book is available from the British Library.

For Barbara and Daviss Starr
and the generations who worked hard
for an uncertain future

Contents

§ Acknowledgments

A version of Chapter 1 appeared as "Clarissa's Relics and Lyric Community," *Studies in Eighteenth-Century Culture* 30 (2001): 127–51; parts of Chapter 2 appeared as "Love's Proper Musick: Lyric Inflection in Behn's Epistles," in *Aphra Behn: Identity, Alterity, Ambiguity*, ed. Mary-Ann O'Donnell (Paris: L'Harmattan, 2000), 111–24, and as "Rereading 'Prose Fiction': Lyric Convention in Aphra Behn and Eliza Haywood," *Eighteenth-Century Fiction* 12, no. 1 (1999): 1–18. Thanks to the publishers of these pieces for kind permission to reprint.

I owe deep thanks to some of the best teachers I could have wished for: Leo Damrosch, Philip Fisher, James Engell, Henry Louis Gates, Jr., Helen Vendler, Elaine Scarry, Derek Pearsall, and Dalia Judovitz. I learned more than I can say from colleagues, too: Christopher R. Miller, Amy Mae King, Kevin Gilmartin, Ernesto Gilman, Monica L. Miller, Christian Schlesinger, Sianne Ngai, Marna Miller, Terri Hume Oliver, Mac Pigman, Nicholas Dames, Mary Poovey, Kevis Goodman, Jesse Matz, John Guillory, Marilyn Gaull, John Waters, Elizabeth McHenry, Martin Harries, Philip Brian Harper, Virginia Jackson, Cathy Jurca, and Cindy Weinstein. To the Monday-night club: libations for all! Special thanks to Ernesto for titular aid. Barbara Estrada gave invaluable moral and research assistance. Cheryl Hutt, Russ Carmony, and Kristen Elias helped (against great odds) to keep me sane.

This work has been supported by the generosity of Matthew Santirocco, Mary Carruthers, the Mellon Foundation, the Robert T. Jones, Jr., Memorial Trust, John Ledyard, and Susan Davis. My deep gratitude to Roy Ritchie and the librarians of the Henry Huntington Library: I can't think of a better place to work. I also am grateful to the Houghton Library, the minders of Child Library, Bobst Library, and the British Library. Heartfelt thanks to the anonymous readers at the Johns Hopkins University Press, who saved me from some mistakes and helped me see my work in new ways, and to Trevor Lipscombe, for believing in the project. Carol Ehrlich is a brilliant editor; my thanks. Special thanks to Daria Navon and John Harpole. Without Mom, Dad, George, Reggie, and even Chloe, none of this would have worked.

 Lyric Generations

§ Introduction

From the Restoration through the end of the eighteenth century, the lyric was transformed by a history ostensibly not its own: lyric was rewritten through the structures, strategies, and spaces of the novel. Literary historians for much of the twentieth century conceived of the poetry of the period as "preromantic," tracing lyric from Donne, Herbert, and other early-seventeenth-century poets through Milton and a small canon of poems in the mid–eighteenth century. These histories approach the eighteenth century almost as a wasteland, with a few oases named Thomson, Collins, Gray, or Warton. Such literary cartography has been challenged in recent years because of its historical insufficiencies and its retrospective insistence on the aesthetic standards of romanticism: certain of what the lyric is and should be, critics have sometimes overlooked what the lyric was — hymns as well as odes, fragments embedded in longer poems as well as sonnets, drinking songs as well as ballads.[1] However, even with a sharpened awareness of the various shapes of lyric verse, a larger problem of literary history remains: moving toward an accurate or complete history of lyric requires new answers not only to questions of canon but also to questions of genre. Literary historians must confront a fact basic to eighteenth-century attitudes toward lyric: many if not most of the greatest literary figures of the century — Dryden, Swift, Fielding, Richardson, Johnson, Austen, Burney — either did not write lyric poems or wrote only few. The complexities surrounding this fact do not involve questions internal to poetic genres but complicate accepted generic boundaries: any account of the intricacies of generic production in the eighteenth century must grapple with the consequences of the emergence of the novel.

Eighteenth-century British literature challenges orthodox approaches to genre history. The logic of genre — the grouping of like texts together as they develop, are reconfigured or reclaimed over time — may all too easily promote the conflation of genre history with the idea of genre itself. For critics like Bloom, Hartman, or Abrams, for example, the history of romantic lyric becomes something just shy of a history of poetry, a story of a set of disciplined transmissions, complex reflections, and transformations within a tradition passing from Virgil to Milton to Wordsworth. Recent revisions of this history have broadened the scholarly picture of lyric to include works that were not only outside the canon but outside the concept of poetic tradition.[2] This new literary history remains incomplete, and part of moving toward completion lies in rethinking genre relations. Genre itself invokes a law of contamination, as Derrida puts it, and if there is one thing scholars may learn from the history of the novel, it is the insufficiency of any approach that assumes a strict equation between "genre" and a history of its own forms.[3] This much can be induced from the texts that have become part of the critical history of the novel: conduct books, sentimental and rakish comedy, "she" tragedy, pastoral and heroic romance, ballads, newspapers, letters, diaries, paintings by Hogarth, essays by Steele. Eighteenth-century literary history is steeped in seeming generic heterodoxies ranging from the literary influence of newspapers and political tracts to the cross-pollination of high literary species. *Lyric Generations* is a genre history that seeks to do justice both to the claims of generic identity and to the complexity of historical change.

Michael McKeon argues that genre "cannot be divorced . . . from the understanding of genres in history. . . . The theory of genre must be a dialectical theory of genre."[4] For the history of the novel, this means that no model of generic displacement is sufficient. Novel does not replace romance; romance persists, and the two genres occupy competing positions in epistemological, ideological, and aesthetic debates over "questions of truth" and "questions of virtue." These debates are of enormous consequence, both in terms of "how external social order is related to . . . internal, moral state[s]" and how eighteenth-century subjects come to knowledge, how they can claim to know the truth of themselves and others (McKeon, 20). These contests do not exclusively concern novel and romance; they are about the power of forms and the varying value of modes of representation, and as such concern the competing claims and possibilities of lyric, too. Lyric matters from the start, first as an unstable genre whose political, religious, and literary status would undergo major changes (and significant losses) in the years following the Civil Wars.[5] Lyrics would also take part in the generic transformations of novel and romance: lyric was important to romance from its beginnings as a metrical form through its pastoral incarnations; it was also in the name of romance (of Childe Roland, Childe Harold, or la belle dame sans merci) that romantic poets would make claims for the surpassing imaginative value of poetry in a literary world marked by novels. It is in this context that Wordsworth, in the 1802 Preface to *Lyrical Ballads*, situates lyric as the alternative to the "frantic novels," which, along with other objects of debased taste, have driven Milton into "neglect."[6] The competitions over right representation go to basic textures of language, differences between poetry and prose, and concepts of form dependent upon them. As literature became separated from the other belles lettres, literary form and in particular the status, value, and problem of prose or poetry as marker of literary form became increasingly central; in *Lyric Generations* I suggest one way generic movement is conditioned by the forms of presentation as well as by discourses concerning logical and ideological content.

§ Even for Thomas Percy, the antiquarian whose efforts at recovering lost lyrics were a powerful influence on romanticism, the novel had an important place. It is largely through the path laid out by Percy, Warton, and other scholar-poets that the line of lyric was plotted in the course familiar to modern scholars. To use the words of Walter Jackson Bate, the romantic era was a "renaissance of the Renaissance": the recovery of Donne, Spenser, and their contemporaries combined with the discovery of a native poetic tradition reaching back to Chaucer to spark romantic creativity.[7] Wordsworth, Coleridge, Leigh Hunt, and others turned toward Percy's *Reliques of Ancient English Poetry* (1765) for subject and form.[8] What has always been remarkable about the Percy phenomenon, however, is that his revival of the past as ballads inflected by romance was shaped for and influenced by contemporary literary standards. Percy's extensive revisions of mutilated ballads were among the most influential pieces in the *Reliques*.[9]

With "The Child of Elle" Percy remakes a nine-stanza fragment into a poem of some two hundred lines. In his revised version, Percy's heroine, Emmeline, is in love with a man whom her family despises; she is engaged by force to "a carlish knyght" and becomes desperate. Emmeline elopes in the wake of her parents' anger but is eventually reconciled. Very little of this sentimental tale is present in the original fragment. There, we have only an unnamed maiden relaying her father's threats to her lover; the Child's bravado in response; his charging off with her to meet her father and brothers; her father's challenge; and the Child's begging the lady to alight while he takes care of business. There is no back story, no resolution, no appeal to moral justification: only challenge and conflict. To this core, Percy adds an intriguing set of perceptions and events. Because the heroine must justify her elopement to her parents (as perhaps Percy must to his readers), she argues that legitimate disgust — not unbridled desire — gets in the way of filial duty. She ascribes her elopement to horror of her unwanted suitor:

> Pardon, my lorde and father deare,
>> This faire yong knyght and mee:
> Trust me, but for this carlish knyght,
>> I never had fled from thee.[10]

Emmeline worries that eloping "shold tint [her] maiden fame" (67); to allay these fears, the Child of Elle promises to take Emmeline to stay with his mother until they are wed. Threatened with violence (to will if not body), she makes an impassioned plea to familial love:

> Oft have you called your Emmeline
>> Your darling and your joye;
> O let not your harsh resolves
>> Your Emmeline destroye.   (ll. 177–80)

The ballad as revised by Percy begins to sound something like the story of another elopement, albeit one with no happy ending. What "completes" the fragmentary ballad with which Percy began is remarkably like the stuff of Richardson's *Clarissa*, published some fifteen years earlier.

Clarissa leaves her father's house with a quarrelsome suitor who enjoys giving violent answer to challenges issued by her relatives (much like the Child of Elle). Clarissa does not flee her home because of un-bridled desire (or even by choice), but, as she repeatedly claims, any passion she may reveal emerges because her father threatens her with the "odious Solmes." Knowing that her perceived preference for one suitor suggests a lack of delicacy, Clarissa, like Emmeline, argues that it is aversion to one lover, not inclination toward another, that is her motiva-tion. Clarissa also fears, rightly, that her own destruction will be the result of her family's cruelty and makes almost interminable pleas to parents who used to call her "my best child, my own Clarissa Harlowe" (Letter 16 [hereafter, L], 89). Clarissa's sentimental pleas to her family's love and pride, supplicant yet threatening the dire consequences of re-fusal, are at least an ancestral voice echoing in Emmeline's past. This echo sounds louder when we consider that when the Child of Elle offers his mother's protection to his eloping mistress as a way of assuaging her fears for her honor — an odd detail to include in the skeletal narrative of a ballad — he is behaving like a more sinister lover who has gone before him: Lovelace pretends to offer Clarissa the protection of his aunt as a guarantee of his honorable intentions.

Emmeline's dilemma as a young woman seeking the freedom of marital choice suggests on its own no particular connection to Richardson's novel, but her peculiar circumstances — the offer of feminine asylum, her sentimental treatment of her father, her insistence on familial connection in the face of isolation, her rhetoric of persuasion, the moral concerns involved in her explanations and pleas — not only are absent in the ballad original but are all present in the story of the most famous literary elopement of the eighteenth century. It is not that Percy must be seen as borrowing from Richardson (although Percy quoted *Pamela* in his letters and admired Richardson's work).[11] What matters is that the ballad is fleshed out with events integral to *Clarissa*, in terms not only of plot, but also of character and moral aims, two of the things on which Richardson prided himself most. If Percy asks "what is missing from this fragmentary lyric," a historically accurate answer is, "some of the things we find in novels." The problems that the breaks in one genre pose can be answered by another.

A supplementary and even revisionary relation between lyric and novel was fundamental in eighteenth-century Britain. In the prehistory of *Clarissa*, for example, stock elements of romance, ballads, and Restoration drama — willful children, parental blocks to love, imprisonment — mutated into something new: a tale of the emergence and destruction of a sense of self, of a language of self-expression, and of a community of feeling and right. *Clarissa* responded to and helped create new generic conventions; it satisfied and raised readerly expectation. Percy's revisions were equally engaged in responding to and shaping literary expectations in the years after the novel began to reconfigure literary life. Whatever sources contributed to Percy's work, comparison with *Clarissa* helps clarify one thing about the expectations at the heart of his ballad. While Clarissa's pleas to her father as his disgraced favorite fail ("for you are my own dear papa. . . . And though I am an unworthy child — yet I *am* your child"), Emmeline's succeed.[12] "The Child of Elle" provides a happy and anachronistically (for a ballad with medieval aspirations) sentimental ending of the kind Richardson refused, in effect satisfying the demands Richardson's readers insistently, but fruitlessly, made. In reading ballad against novel we may reconstruct the residue of a generic dialogue concerning readerly expectation and generic possibility. Both genres and both works engaged similar events, similar moral dilemmas, and similar sentiments, all of which were self-conscious innovations in contemporary practice. Where they diverged, then, is significant; Percy's work in revising his ballad brought stark poetic narrative into the age of sensibility, and if perhaps he drew on sources more recent than the Middle Ages, it serves to emphasize the new needs his lyrics had to address in a new age. Novel and lyric would make similar matter perform different cultural work, and as I argue over the course of this book, the practitioners of each form would learn part of that work from the other. "The Child of Elle," one of Wordsworth's favorites among the Percy ballads (see n. 8, above), goes from fragment to lyric by making the impersonal narration of Britain's poetic past speak to the vital energy of its novel present.

Literatures of sensibility and romanticism brought genres into vibrant relationship: the influence of *Clarissa* and Rousseau's *Nouvelle Héloïse* on romantic poets like Blake; that of St. Pierre's novel *Paul et Virginie* on Wordsworth or Helen Maria Williams; the suture of sonnet and narrative in the novels of Charlotte Smith or Anne Radcliffe; the combinations of romance and lyric in works by Walter Scott, Byron, or Keats; the melding of drama and lyric in Wordsworth's *Borderers*; the very idea of the *Lyrical Ballads* themselves. The small example of Percy's revisions, then, is suggestive: if ballads provided plot elements to writers of plays and novels, exchange could work in the opposite direction. (Percy noted in his edition of Shenstone's works that one of Shenstone's poems was based on an episode in *Pamela*.)[13] Novels, especially powerful and popular works like Richardson's, changed the scene; literary productions from ballads to odes entered a world newly marked by a large-scale reorganization and destabilization of literary genres.[14] As Mikhail Bakhtin puts it, "In the presence of the novel, all other genres somehow have a different resonance."[15] The novel thrived on the reuse and reform of precedent genres; it offers a model for the changes literary forms would undergo in a culture where visual, aural, and written media competed for attention and drove cultural change.[16] The emergence of the novel meant the emergence of new possibilities for negotiating this new world.

Instead of looking at the "rise" of the novel in terms of its "cause," I here look at its effects. Novels offered the most extensive ground for the literary exploration of individual experience in the century, and accordingly their greatest effect on romantic poetry can be found in the construction of lyric as a mode deeply implicated by subjective relations. Novels open up a range of emotions to serious literary treatment and redefine literary intimacy in accord with their own principles of representation. First, novels teach that we may better know individuals — their desires, their patterns of feeling and thought, the contours of their moral judgments and lapses — by knowing what goes on within the home, between brother and sister, father and son, mother and child. Intimacy becomes redefined in part by domesticity and domestic encounters, and literary encounters (between and among readers, poets, and narrators or characters) are shaped anew.

Understanding the strength and specificity of the contribution of novels to the futures of literature involves exploring novelistic forms as ways of defining discursive positions. I begin with that bugbear of literary history, formal realism. In Watt's formulation, formal realism is a set of conventions of mimesis surrounding objects of description (ordinary people; historically plausible times and places) and the manner of representation (letters, diaries, etc.): but beyond questions of mimesis, these techniques work to establish a relationship between the world of readers and the world of the read, a discursive problem with rhetorical solutions. Despite recent challenges to its status as generic principle,[17] formal realism understood in this sense involves a rhetorical stance with broad roots in novels from Haywood and Manley to Defoe, Richardson, and Burney. These novelists employed a variety of strategies to perform the rhetorical function at the heart of novel fiction: to tell us *how* novels are to be read, how their worlds are to be mapped onto ours, whether politically, emotionally, or morally. Indeed, although critics normally associate only the names, historical places, letters, editors, and first-person narrators of early novels with formal realism, as I will show, affective practices honed by amatory fiction are central to novelistic rhetorical concerns, to bringing novels into a lived world. So-called formal realism disciplines these affective practices, and as I argue in the latter half of this book, the understanding of the relationship between readers and texts at the heart of the success of the novel is also key in romantic lyrics.

Lyric expression in the long eighteenth century is cross-implicated by and in the languages of emotion in early novels. Novels exhibit two concurrent movements: one in which lyric conventions were reorganized and adapted in concord with emerging theories of aesthetics, another in which private experience and the inner world were given new shape and a new set of literary markers. Richardson, Behn, Haywood, and other early novelists consistently used patterns taken from the amatory lyric, lament, epithalamium, elegy, and Pindaric ode as primary models for constructing shared emotional experience between characters and from character to reader. The story of lyric is equally complex. During this period, problems around shared experience, the value of individual emotions, and the position of the feeling subject emerged as crucial challenges for poets, challenges novelists seem more successfully to have resolved. On one hand, empiricist ideas of subjectivity — the contention that the world beyond the self is the object of individual perception and of uncertainty — could seem to hem in individual selves; on the other, radical changes in British life — a new nation of Britons, an expanding empire — enforced pressures toward imagined community.[18] In this context, any mode that tended to focus on individual experience in isolation would encounter resistance. Accordingly, lyric gave way to the verse epistle as the dominant form of Augustan poetry.[19] With its concentration on two civilized people speaking a common language of morality and discipline, the verse epistle produces a fiction of community to counter "the haunting fear that one's own consciousness is all there is, and that the world and other people may be no more than figments of the solitary mind" (Dowling, *Epistolary Moment*, 11). Poetic discourse takes place in a community of speakers, of friends exchanging letters in public and private.

This move toward community is fundamental to the poetry of the eighteenth century. Augustian lyricism produced poems like Pope's imitations of Horace, Thomson's poems on liberty, or Swift's verses to Stella, poems that participated in an uneasy "tension of the personal against the public," as Richard Feingold argues. This tension pushed lyric into unusual places: "When we speak, as we sometimes do, of the decline of lyric expression in Augustan art, we are missing its presence in works whose shape, though not nominally lyrical, is yet ultimately adequate to the impress of . . . personal pressure."[20] In effect, lyric would expand, under cover as it were, appearing in satires like "The Vanity of Human Wishes," long poems like *The Seasons* or *Night Thoughts*, and epistles like "Eloisa to Abelard."[21]

The movement of lyric into other forms was far-reaching; some of the most daring and consequential generic appropriations of lyric would occur in prose. This process was connected to and prepared for by Renaissance genre critics who, following Longinus, were concerned with "pure poetry," "a rarity that can reveal itself only occasionally in a long poem but, because the great soul is not completely fettered by the forms of discourse, may appear in works that are not basically poetic in intention."[22] Poetry was found in parts of the Bible that had been thought to be prose; poetry could also be written in prose, as in Shaftesbury's *Moralists* or Macpherson's Ossian poems. Critics writing in the mid–eighteenth century were intrigued by such blurring of generic lines. Henry Home, Lord Kames, argued that "literary compositions run into each other, precisely like colours: in their strong tints they are easily distinguished; but are susceptible of so much variety, and take on so many different forms, that we never can say where one species ends and another begins."[23] Even Joseph Warton, who felt prose to be an inferior vehicle for high feelings and imaginative invention, seems caught in the spell when he suggests a remarkable test for the highest kind of poetry: "Drop entirely the measures and numbers, and transpose and invert the order of the words, and in this unadorned manner . . . peruse the passage. If there be really in it a true poetical spirit, all your inversion and transpositions will not disguise and extinguish it; but it will retain its lustre, like a diamond unset."[24] A novel like *Clarissa*, as I will show, may hold decidedly poetic moments in the midst of otherwise prosaic matter — with no violation of contemporary generic decorum and great consequences for literary history.

The movement between poetry and prose was enhanced by critical strains that reveal concerns shared by both forms. Verisimilitude, a term usually associated with the developing novel, is also key in eighteenth-century criticism of poetry. In words similar to those of Johnson on the novel (*Rambler*, 4), James Beattie writes of poems: "Yet we should neither expect nor desire, that every human invention, where the end is only to please, should be an exact transcript of real existence. It is enough, that the mind acquiesce in it as probable, or plausible, or such as we think might happen . . . : — or, to speak more accurately, it is enough, that it be consistent either, first, with general experience; or, secondly, with popular opinion; or thirdly, that it be consistent with itself, and connected with probable circumstances."[25]

One might expect such rules to be important to descriptive poems like *The Seasons*, but they apply to lyric genres as well. Johnson complains of Cowley's *Mistress* that it fails as poetry because he can't believe the speaker to be in love, for "the basis of all excellence is truth: he that professes love ought to feel its power."[26] Such discourse of poetic verisimilitude leads to autobiographical criticism on one hand and the romantic nature lyric on the other — defined in part, as M. H. Abrams does, by the presentation of "a determinate speaker in a particularized and usually localized outdoor setting."[27] The movement toward carefully documented physical context is at work in both poetry and novels, refined toward temporal accuracy and careful dating (especially in the novel of letters, but also in poems like "Lines Composed a Few Miles Above Tintern Abbey, on Revisiting the Banks of the Wye During a Tour. July 3, 1798" as well as in terms of domesticity and the individual (*Clarissa* on one hand, "We Are Seven" on the other). John Sitter writes, "While the problems of the poets and the novelists would seem to oppose each other . . . the roads leading to what Joseph Warton called 'Pure poetry' and what Richardson called 'sentiment' are paved . . . with similar intentions and exact similar tolls."[28] The broad cultural revaluation of emotional life and individuality brings literary forms close together, encourages shared solutions to shared problems.

For Bakhtin and Brean Hammond, this is "novelization": "a movement towards the domestic, the contemporaneous, towards a greater degree of what one is thrown back upon terming 'realism.'"[29] Hammond traces the concern for verisimilitude that marks the novel genre to a literary context that includes drama, mock-heroic poetry, and other genres in the years following the Restoration. Following Bakhtin, Hammond focuses on comic tendencies: novelization is about bringing genres like epic into contact with everyday reality through laughter. But "novelization" is not modal in such a sense. It is true that novels (like *Tom Jones* or *Roderick Random*) often bring epic into humorous and even "disrespectful" contact with the world of its readers (Hammond, 107). In this Bakhtinian formulation, the world of epic is "untouchable, located in an unchangeable past that is called to memory but that we have no genuine capacity to inhabit," while "the novelist [and his or her genre are] in a contemporaneous, non-hierarchical relationship to the material reality s/he represents" (107–8).

Even if that is true of epic, however, novels have constitutive relationships with genres like lyric, which often manifest a deep concern with the proximity (and failures of proximity) between genre and life; these relationships are part of "novelization" as well. Amatory lyrics like those of Donne are about the precarious relationship between convention and perception or genre and life: metaphysical conceits like the compass of "A Valediction: Forbidding Mourning" or the bracelets of hair in "The Funerall" and "The Relique" function to reveal this problem of representation. The yoking of disparate images by violence, the aspect of the metaphysical conceit Johnson found so outrageous, is an attempt to bring life and art together at whatever generic cost. This study concerns the position of novels with regard to what may be defined as continually evolving constructions of the relationship between convention and readerly reality; as such it both builds on Bakhtin's conception of the effects of the novel as genre and questions the terms with which Bakhtin began.

In this book I insist on a careful examination of poetic and novelistic modes. If the epistle, as Dowling argues, takes over from the lyric as dominant Augustan poetic mode, it is, if not dominant in, fundamental to the emerging novel; this is not a coincidence of literary history, for it is largely in the epistolary novel that we find important connections with the lyric. In works like Richardson's *Clarissa*, "writing to the moment" equates writing and emotion: life always exceeds the speed of the pen (as we learn in *Tristram Shandy*), and the writer falls inevitably behind.[30] The matter most important to writing becomes response and interpretation, not action or event, and the letter writer's perception of and response to the world around her occupy both the scene of writing and its substance.[31] For this reason, *Clarissa* is the starting point of this study. Richardson's greatest novel focuses on a dilemma shared by writers of letters and lyrics alike: the epistolary writer is isolated as a feeling subject, imprisoned at the very least by the force and uniqueness of emotion, and attempts to use the letter as a tool to build a true consensus and community.

Clarissa writes to her family, earnestly attempting to evoke in them a sense of her distress; she fails. The problem in the letters that make up *Clarissa* is that limits of subjectivity—here the difference between the absolute presence of emotion in one body and in one mind, and its absolute absence in another—are the necessary starting points of communication. From the impasse they create comes the necessity of speech. In this epistolary world, limits of subjectivity appear as limits of sensation, and the letter emerges as an attempt to cross these bounds. It carries the burden of conveying or carrying affect as well as describing it. Richardson attempts thus to create a kind of intimacy based on imaginative communication, and his work is foundational because of the problems he is compelled to address. His scenes of estrangement lay the ground for romantic poems of isolation (like "Ode to a Nightingale"), offering a prototypical vision, which, combined with other genres and influences, enables a more complete understanding of the kind of communication that isolation, paradoxically, produces in poetry like "Tintern Abbey" and *Poems on the Naming of Places*.

If novel and lyric are interdependent, one might expect significant changes in response to altering conditions to occur at similar points in their histories. They do: epistolary novels begin to disappear at about the same moment that the verse epistle gives way to colloquy. Donald Davie argues that letters are at the heart of the diction of eighteenth-century poetry, providing the basis of polite language from which correctness and purity in diction are produced.[32] The romantic era, for him, registers the falling away of this base: "poets . . . could be guided no longer, in their choice of language, by the conversational images of . . . readers, [because] . . . the literary forms which depended upon [polite diction], the familiar letter and the epistolary novel, fall suddenly below the level of serious art" (25). Davie indicates a set of parallel phenomena: if the verse epistle briefly takes over the lyric, eventually to be replaced in turn, the epistolary heyday in the novel also comes to an end at about the same time. Jane Austen's rewriting of the epistolary *First Impressions* (c. 1796) as *Pride and Prejudice* (1813) marks — symbolically — the outer bound. Dowling argues that the verse epistle collapses, by way of solipsism and isolation, into the lyrics of Chatterton, Cowper, or Gray; perhaps more fully, the epistle reopens into the romantic colloquy. The letter in the novel also opens into free indirect discourse, the method used by Burney, Austen, and others to provide access to inner life. Free indirect discourse supplies the kind of picture of interiority letters can give, but without the limitations of a letter's single vision; similarly, romantic poetry often subsumes epistolary dialogue into the imagined space of colloquy ("This Lime-Tree Bower," *The Prelude*, "To Joanna"). In both poetry and prose, the letter gives way to doubled spaces and thoughts: consciousness is doubled as address (to Nature, to absent friends like Coleridge or Dorothy Wordsworth), as narration (the double vision of narrators in free indirect discourse), and as memory (for Wordsworth, Keats, and Austen alike).

In writing the history of these changes in the following chapters I do not think of lyric in qualitative terms — as it is invoked, for example, in the idea of the lyrical novel.[33] Instead, I approach lyric as a changing body of conventions linked to a particular mode and a particular group of literary kinds (sonnets, odes, elegies, etc.). Finding lyric thus in the novel has meant demystifying or at least defamiliarizing prose. The so-called plain style associated with formal realism is in fact heavily coded, relying on literary tradition more than many have hitherto thought.[34] The mystique of simplicity is deeply ingrained in conceptions of prose for many of us, despite the historical evidence to the contrary (euphuism or *preciosité*, for example). As Wlad Godzich and Jeffrey Kittay point out, in the modern world prose comes to occupy the discursive position of unformed "matter," while verse seems to be the essence of "form."[35] In turn, novels seem loose, baggy monsters, while sonnets are *sonnets:* the form is summed up in the word. In the chapters to follow, I insist on drawing attention to the forms of prose, revealing its structures and patterns, patterns visible if we read prose as an aesthetic object.

In the first chapter I read *Clarissa* in the context of a set of its poetic antecedents in order to highlight formal and thematic connections between epistle and lyric. Chapter 2 undertakes a brief history of the interaction of lyric and epistle in the late seventeenth and early eighteenth centuries, beginning with an account of lyric insertions in romance and focusing on novels by Behn and Haywood. There are other strains of interaction, and the chapter pursues the connection between lyric and epistle in Pope's "Eloisa to Abelard" and "Epistle to Dr. Arbuthnot." The third chapter traces ideological pressures that alter lyric voice and style in Thomson, Gray, Collins, and Winchilsea, with broad reference to the ode and locodescriptive poetry. I offer an analysis of the large-scale features of poetry of the self in the midcentury, pointing out the difficulties surrounding personal speech in a variety of poetic genres. Concerns over how to make personal experience available — meaningful, affective, comprehensible, communicable — would find a different set of answers in novels than in poetry.

If, as I will show, landscapes of emotion for prominent midcentury poets would become alien, distant prospects where entry is harshly regulated and often denied (to poetic persona and reader alike), novelists would construct their fictions to facilitate and direct the reader's entrance and exit. Chapter 4 demonstrates how rhetorical, chiastic practices of early novels offer a way of organizing and promoting contact between real and fictional worlds. Chiastic sites are those places in the texts where readers are asked to map experiences of the world of dates, times, places, and letters onto the world of the fictional — to cross the boundaries of imagination and reality. By arguing in terms of chiasmus, I offer an addendum and alternative to the idea of mimesis; I argue that early novel realisms work by showing readers ways to move from the real as the space of reading to the fictional as the space of imagining.[36]

Chapter 5 explores the variety of manners in which lyric and novel interrelated in imaginative worlds regulated by chiasmus, pointing out that movement between one genre and another was not always felicitous or straightforward. I examine works by Fielding, Smollett, Richardson, Frances Brooke, Charlotte Smith, and others to demonstrate the ways in which lyric worked to mark the boundaries that relate interior experience to communal life, and how, using lyric in combination with strategies from *ekphrasis* to free indirect discourse, novelists were able to create fictions of consciousness to focus readers' movements from the world of reading to the worlds of novels.

The final chapter relates the rhetorical and representational patterns of novels to developments in romantic lyrics. Readings of Wordsworth's poetry and criticism as well as poems by Cowper, Smith, Coleridge, and Keats reveal novelistic modes and topoi as they were adapted to suit a variety of subgenres from georgic to ode, placing emphasis on domesticity, scenes of encounter, and enclosure. Throughout this literary history, I put forward a concept of genre that refuses insularity. Neither lyric nor novel may write its own history, enforcing on the past the generic shape of the present. Any history of genre must be a history of genres, as McKeon claims — of their interaction and mutual revision.

In Coleridge's "Kubla Khan," "A mighty fountain" becomes a "sacred river" flowing into the sea, but the river is no mere dormant thing; it carries "Ancestral voices prophesying war." This river, disappearing into the void only to reappear as song, is itself an echo of an ancestral voice: Milton's "Lycidas." Milton draws upon the myth of the nymph Arethusa who fled a river god by diving into the Ionian Sea; she travels to Sicily and there emerges from the earth as a vibrant fountain. In Milton's poem, the gentle poetry of Arethusa's waters is driven from the scene by a "dread voice" (l. 132) and can only return with the renewal of the pastoral strain: "And call the vales, and bid them hither cast / Their bells and flowerets of a thousand hues" (ll. 134–35). This story of the muse's strain, gone under sea and ground and hidden until it joyously bursts forth as pastoral, is like the doctrinal version of the history of the lyric from the 1640s until the last decade of the eighteenth century. This is more a myth of romantic poetry than its history, however, for many more authors and texts would intervene in the history of lyric than Milton, Cowper, or Gray. Romantic self-fashioning was deeply invested in the story of a poetic past, which in its doctrinal form would exclude "the frantic novel, sickly and stupid German Tragedies, and deluges of idle and extravagant stories in verse," relying on national bards like Shakespeare and Milton, not novelists and bourgeois printers like Richardson.[37] But literary history cannot be ruled by mythologies: if, like the river Arethuse, lyric goes underground during the eighteenth century, it bubbles forth, fountainlike, in a new place.

One

Clarissa and the Lyric

When Ian Watt claimed that *Clarissa* (1747–1748) was a ground-breaking exploration of private experience, he also made it clear that the letter, used as a window on inner life, was the signal principle of Richardson's coup. Critics have since paid fruitful attention to the history of the structural and formal principles of epistolary expression.[1] Letters are only rudimentary frames for whatever they carry — instructions for one's executor, lies to one's lover, pleas to cruel parents, guilt to friends. What is at stake in Richardson's representations of consciousness (most often of suffering, sympathy, or sin) is the relationship of experience to communication: the problems involved in attempts to represent one's experience affectively, to give it a shape that makes others acknowledge its intensity and share some of its force. Clarissa's crisis develops from her emotional and physical isolation. She is deprived of direct communication, shut off from father and mother, friends, all those closest to her. Believing that if "they did but know [her] heart" all would be well, Clarissa attempts to create a complete correspondence with her family — as Lovelace's false etymology would have it, a union of hearts.[2] She seeks consensus — feeling-with, a concord of heart and mind — but as the novel progresses, at moments of emotional intensity, true correspondence seems impossible. Letters fragment and are replaced by relics: the ten papers she writes in near-madness after being raped, meditations composed in sorrow, the emblematic self-elegy engraved on her coffin. These impassioned inscriptions participate in lyric models of emotional consensus taken from religious poetry like the Book of Job and George Herbert's *Temple*. Epistolary correspondence converges with or gives way to lyric attempts at community, and the novel is opened up to the lyric mode.

Richardson situates lyric within the novel's range of possibility, suggesting not only that the history of genre that scholars apply to understanding the birth of the novel needs revision but also that the story of the lyric involves a more complex tradition than is usually granted it. Making this case with regard to *Clarissa* requires an abbreviated discussion of the relations between texts and practices that contribute to the eighteenth-century history of genre as well as detailed accounts of Richardson's aesthetic choices. My concerns here are two: *Clarissa* challenges generic orthodoxies; both in examining that challenge and in exploring Richardson's adaptation and modification of lyric, we are given access to a new way of analyzing the emotional richness of the novel genre.

While most analyses of the language of emotion in *Clarissa* have focused on the influence of drama or epistolary works, the emotional repertoire available to Richardson was more varied.[3] Jocelyn Harris points out that Richardson published Sidney's sonnets in 1724 and knew (and quoted) Herrick, Herbert, and Donne as well.[4] In fact, there was a wide range of available models for emotional intensity, models limited or affected by genre in complicated ways. First, generic and modal distinctions functioned on shifting axes. In addition to the classical drama-epic-lyric triptych, biblical models were important. Lyric was subdivided by lament, hymn, epithalamium, or thanksgiving in the biblical scheme (largely relying on the Psalms, the Song of Songs, and Job), while in other formulations, pastoral, Anacreontic, ode, or elegy were central. In all schools, there was debate over even the most fundamental characteristics of style within a genre or mode. Genres seemed made for expansion and renewal. Even distinctions between prose and poetry were complicated by developments in biblical scholarship that revealed poetry in sections of the Bible long read as prose (chief among these the greater part of Job), and contemporaries spoke of religious enthusiasts' writing as a type of poetry.[5] Literary criticism both reflected and shaped the possibilities for such formal and generic mingling. Not only are compendia like Bysshe's *Art of English Poetry* (1702) organized by theme or emotion instead of by genre, but criticism tended to revolve around exempla, as any perusal of Johnson, Kames, Blair, or Dryden will show. There were a set of recognizable kinds, but they could be endlessly assorted and recombined; novelists took the advantages this offered.

§ Reading novels historically sometimes means reading them backward. The social upheavals and rich generic experimentation that fostered the novel have roots in the Renaissance and revolution: as Nigel

Smith argues, the literature of the revolution is marked by "the 'buzz' of a destabilized society," and it is this buzz that we hear in the literary productions of the following years.[6] Religious lyric was a crucial part of this early modern textual heritage. I focus on three culturally important sources (though there are others): Donne, Herbert, and the Book of Job.[7] John Wesley's 1740s adaptations of Herbert for the hymnal brought a version of Herbert's sensibility to entire congregations — offering the poet's anguish or joy to men and women whose voices could merge with his, making his experience in a sense their own. Wesley's was not the first attempt to popularize Herbert, and an earlier anonymous hymnal, *Select Hymns, Taken out of Mr. Herbert's Temple, and Turn'd into the Common Metre* (1697), was, "before the hymns of Isaac Watts[,] . . . one of the most widely used collections of religious song 'either in private families, or Christian-assemblies.' "[8] Herbert was recommended for women readers by John Dunton's *Athenian Mercury* (1693) and Richard Allestree's *Ladies Calling* (1673), two important precursor texts in the history of the novel. He was singled out for children's reading in Thomas White's *Little Book for Little Children* (1702) and in a catechism for children and servants, Thomas Willis's *Key of Knowledg* (1650).[9] Donne was also alive to eighteenth-century readers, though less popular than Herbert. Not only were his sermons read throughout the century, his pious death (as recorded by Walton) legendary, and his satires famously translated by Pope, but an edition of his lyrics was published in 1719 by Tonson, and he was well-enough regarded to be advertised prominently in a popular miscellany.[10] As Anne Williams argues, poets like these made "a lyric voice of the minutest psychological verisimilitude . . . familiar" to eighteenth-century England (*Prophetic Strain*, 51), either through private reading or through public devotions, and their poetry was available through multiple generic routes.

Job was also central to early modern religious lyric. While twentieth-century critics are apt to read Job as a protonovel, Richardson's contemporaries saw it in another light. As Jonathan Lamb describes, Augustan critics were divided as to whether Job were allegory (the position of Warburton) or historical fact (that of Lowth et al.); the possibilities for interpretation are not confined, however, to theology. While Lowth classes Job as a dramatic text, he reads individual utterances within it differently. As Job exclaims, "My harpe also is tuned to mourning, and my organe into the voyce of them that weepe" (30:31).[11] Job plays an important role both in the developing rhetoric of sublimity and in what would become the rhetoric of the lyric.[12]

At the most emotionally intense moments of *Clarissa* there are traces of these lyric traditions. Clarissa's aesthetic practice manipulates the imagery and ideas of Herbert, Donne, and the Job poet, using a repertoire these poets made their own: a drama of anguish and the internal; utterances closed down or marked off by silence and absence; intimacy thwarted and reduced to the tokens of its loss; and a self constructed at the intersection of these lines. In this chapter I trace the connections between *Clarissa* and four kinds (loosely speaking) or instances of religious lyric, first establishing Richardson's use of the lyric model offered by the book of Job, a key text in seventeenth- and eighteenth-century religious poetry.[13] I then focus on lyrics by Donne that emphasize the problematics of the self-elegy, and poems by Herbert whose structural, rhetorical, and thematic characteristics make them particularly close kin to *Clarissa:* his Jobian laments (constructed in terms of fragmentation and self-division), lyrics of lapsed communication, variations on shaped verse, and emblem poems (taken, as Herbert does, to unify conflicting aspects of personal experience). In turning to religious lyric, Richardson turned toward a form concerned with melding public and private experience; these lyrics provide models of emotional consensus imagined, lost, and ultimately reconstructed.[14]

§ Richardson's plot is simple: barely eighteen, Clarissa Harlowe is tricked away from her father's house by Robert Lovelace, an infamous rake whose weak conscience cannot stand up to his appetites or his monomania. He keeps Clarissa prisoner in a brothel, then drugs and rapes her. Clarissa's suffering is revealed in Jobian terms.[15] He is the "admired exclaimer" whom she often quotes: " 'O! that I were as in months past, as in the days when God preserved me! When his candle shined upon my head, and when by his light I walked through darkness! As I was in the days of my *childhood* — when the Almighty was yet with me; when *I was in my father's house:* when I washed my steps with butter, and the rock poured me out rivers of oil!' " (L 359, 114) Clarissa's identification with Job goes even beyond her final moments: in the tableau she constructs to adorn her coffin, she quotes, slightly altered, from Job's third chapter, and Job dominates the meditations she writes in her sorrow. Clarissa's elegiac verses are all taken from Job and the Psalms, two key models for lyric in the eighteenth century.

Of the many contemporary paraphrases of Job, the majority are lyric, focusing on Job's lament.[16] Clarissa's use of Job follows this pattern: in her trials, Clarissa copies and rereads his lament, finding in it a vocabulary and pattern of expression suiting her own troubled heart. Clarissa writes four "meditations"; save one, they are transcriptions of biblical verses that rely exclusively on lyric sources: Job and the Psalms (one, in letter 399, combines Psalms with Ecclesiasticus).[17] Richardson combines these meditations "written" by Clarissa in an almost apocryphal text, *Meditations Collected from the Sacred Books; and Adapted to the Different Stages of A Deep Distress; Gloriously surmounted by Patience, Piety, and Resignation* (1750). Although Richardson printed the collection, he refused to publish it beyond a small circle of friends, reserving it for those who had been bereaved or were themselves in stages of deep distress.

In restricting the circulation of the *Meditations* as a separate work to readers in crisis, Richardson focuses on an emotional congruity between readers and heroine or text.[18] Clarissa, both in the novel and in her preface to the *Meditations*, emphasizes the foundational importance of emotion in her use of Job: "Indeed, at the first of my calamity, I had great grief, and, at times, had great impatience in my grief . . . : So that I could not help transcribing, as my first Meditation, the Curses of Job on the day of his birth."[19] She writes in accord with an emotional plot line, so that if "perhaps too many of the first Meditations are *passionate exclamations,*" then, "by degrees, more chearful prospects [i.e., of death] opening upon my benighted mind, I looked forward to the promises of divine pardon and reconciliation, which are every where to be met with in the Sacred Books . . . then the Meditations carry a more comfortable appearance," and "at length, my pen, as well as my voice, could break out into *Praises* and *Thanksgivings*" (171, emphasis original).

In adapting the words of Job or the Psalms to her distress, Clarissa is carrying out the reciprocal projects of lyric reader and writer as understood by contemporary theorists of religious poetry. Like the singer of a hymn, Clarissa enters the "I" of the poet (Job or David) and makes it her own, experiencing a profound emotional consensus, sharing her griefs and his in one boundless moment. The eighteenth century marks the point at which this kind of affective claim for lyric is codified in criticism.[20] Robert Lowth's *Lectures on the Sacred Poetry of the Hebrews* (Latin 1753, English 1787), a landmark text in this history, chronicles the emotional terms of biblical poetry. He begins by arguing that "the origin and first use of poetical language are undoubtedly to be traced into the vehement affections of the mind."[21] Hebrew poetry is both morally and aesthetically important for Lowth because of its "extraordinary forms of expression, which are indeed possessed of great force and efficacy in this respect especially, that they in some degree imitate or represent the present habit and state of the soul."[22]

Earlier in the century, the idea of imitating the inner self appears as an essential part of the concept of religious lyric put forward by popular hymn writer Isaac Watts. In his preface to the *Horae Lyricae* (1706), he lauds Job's emphasis on personal experience: "How mournful and de-jected is the language of his own sorrows: Terrors are turned upon him, they pursue his soul as the wind, and his welfare passes away as a cloud; his bones are pierced within him, and his soul is poured out; he goes mourning without the sun, a brother to dragons, a companion to owls; while his harp and organ are turned into the voice of them that weep."[23] For Watts, this kind of representation of emotion is so fundamental that it should be a model for the Christian poet: "our wonder and our love, our pity, delight, and sorrow, with the long train of hopes and fears, must needs be under the command of a harmonious pen whose every line makes a part of the reader's faith, and is the very life or death of his soul" (156). What is key in Watts's analysis is the way in which a poet's expres-sion of experience may lead readers to align ourselves with it, to experi-ence a powerful form of emotional consensus. His own "Poems Sacred to Virtue" (included in the *Horae Lyricae*) "were formed when the frame and humour of my soul was just suited to the subject of my verse. The image of my heart is painted in them, and if they meet with a reader whose soul is akin to mine, perhaps they may agreeably entertain him" (159). This is the complex of emotional response expected by Clarissa and Richardson in regard to the *Meditations*.

Job's and Clarissa's use of lyric paradigms of emotional responsive-ness differ strongly from those visible in the preponderance of early-eighteenth-century poetry. Personal poetry about one's own emotions was not common in the first half of the century (a point to be more fully explored in Chapter 3). However, as Lowth notes, "in Hebrew poetry . . . the free spirit is hurried along. . . . Frequently, instead of disguising the secret feelings of the author, it lays them quite open to public view, and, the veil being, as it were, suddenly removed, all the affections and emo-tions of the soul, its sudden impulses, its hasty sallies and irregularities, are conspicuously displayed" (Elledge, *Eighteenth-Century Critical Essays*, 2:691). Hebrew poetry like Job offers to reveal the self denuded, moving, so that its language (of hastiness, disruption, distress) becomes part of a complex of shared emotion, a lyric model of the experience of reading and writing.

Richardson's decision to model some of the most pivotal language of his novel on the language of Job takes on new importance in this respect. As with the *Meditations*, the ten fragments that Clarissa scribbles in near-madness after she has been raped involve an intensely lyric use of biblical language. A passage from Job 29 is the model (with a shift in person) for her fifth paper: "How art thou now humbled in the dust, thou proud Clarissa Harlowe! Thou that never steppedst out of thy father's house, but to be admired! Who wert wont to turn thine eye, sparkling with healthful life, and self-assurance, to different objects at once, as thou passedst, as if . . . to plume thyself upon the expected applauses of all that beheld thee! Thou that usedst to go to rest satisfied with the adulations paid thee in the past day, and couldst put off everything but thy vanity! — " (891).

In Job 29, Job's suffering casts him back to his own days of grace:

> When I went out to the gate, through the citie, when I prepared my
>   seate in the street
> The yong men saw me, and hid themselves: and the aged arose, and
>   stood up.
> The princes refrained talking, and laid their hand on their mouth.
> The Nobles held their peace, and their tongue cleaved to the roofe of
>   their mouth.   (7–10)

> I put on righteousnesse, and it clothed me: my judgement was as a
>   robe and a diademe.   (14)

> Unto me men gave eare, and waited, and kept silence at my counsell.
> After my words they spake not againe, and my speach dropped upon
>   them,
> And they waited for me as for the raine.   (21–23)

Both lamentations are composed in similar terms: the reference to the glad clothing of the past, a shared emphasis on the body, the adorations of the crowd, and the absence of community.[24]

Richardson underlines the peculiarity of Clarissa's language by giving the fragments a unique provenance: "Dorcas tells me that what she writes she tears, and throws the paper in fragments under the table, either as not knowing what she does, or disliking it: then gets up, wrings her hands, weeps, and shifts her seat all round the room: then returns to her table, sits down, and writes again" (L 261, 889). As Lovelace describes them, these are "poetical flights" (L 261, 894), and within them we find neither Clarissa's normative language nor the novel's normative epistolary discourse. They are expressive of intensive anguish and so moving they draw even the author of Clarissa's griefs into sympathy with them, as Lovelace complains. In line with Watts's description of Job or the *Horae Lyricae*, these passages work to create emotional consensus.

If the postrape papers borrow the language of a lyric model in Job, they also draw on characteristics of lyrics more contemporary. Each paper carries the fiction of being a tiny, discrete document. Punctuation works to enforce cadence, dividing sentences almost as line breaks and caesurae function in verse. Papers 5 and 7 are written with irregular line lengths that could not be farther from the disciplined justification of printed prose. Trochees and spondees litter the page, distancing the language from the smoother, less differentiated tones of plain prose. Richardson attempts regulated disorder, something that imitates the processes of a mind where "thought, and grief, and confusion came crowding so thick" that all seems utterly lost:

> — And can you, my dear honored papa, resolve for ever to reprobate your poor child? — But I am sure you would not, if you knew what she has suffered since her unhappy — And will nobody plead for your poor suffering girl? — No one good body? — Why, then, dearest sir, let it be an act of your own innate goodness, which I have so much experienced, and so much abused — I don't presume to think you should receive me — no, indeed — my name is — I don't know what my name is! — I never dare to wish to come into your family again! — But your heavy curse, my dear papa — Yes, I *will* call you papa, and help yourself as you can — for you are my own dear papa, whether you will or not — And though I am an unworthy child — yet I *am* your child. (890)

This language is highly rhetorical, an index of the burden of emotion it is expected to carry; like any stylized language, it had to be invented, no matter how plain (to take the descriptor usually associated with Richardson's style).[25] Indeed, as Nigel Smith points out, so-called plain style tended toward highly affective rhetoric and even could be modified to "elevat[e] features like rhyme and song."[26] Perhaps it is such complex plainness that drew Richardson to Herbert ("My God, My King"): the language Clarissa uses with her father, that of a recalcitrant child attempting to do her duty but laboring under his displeasure, is remarkably close to that of Herbert's "Longing," also a Jobian lament:

> My throat, my soul is hoarse;
> My heart is withered like a ground
>   Which thou dost curse.
>   My thoughts turn round,
> And make me giddy; Lord I fall,
>   Yet call.   (ll. 7–12)

> Thou tarriest, while I die,
> And fall to nothing: thou dost reign,
> And rule on high,
> While I remain
> In bitter grief: yet I am styled
> Thy child.   (ll. 55–60)[27]

There are evident similarities in diction and self-positioning between this poem and Clarissa's paper: they share an emphasis on fragmentation, the possibilities of grace, and an insistence on the naming of father and child.[28] These similarities might be coincidental: Lawrence Stone notes that the elevation of the father-child bond to a quasi-religious status is one of the characteristics of family life in Puritan England.[29] Clarissa's use of such language is an indication of the later prevalence of this attitude, but the particular issues that surround her writing link this speech firmly to lyric tradition.[30]

The social dimension of religious lyric is crucial to its adaptation in novel form. Herbert's poetry not only layers the language of religious lyric with that of familial hierarchy but, as Michael Schoenfeldt shows, with the "hierarchical authority" of politics.[31] As Helen Vendler points out, "Aesthetically speaking, it is what a lyric *does with* its borrowed social languages — i.e., how it casts them into new permutational and combinational forms — that is important."[32] What I wish to underline here is that both Herbert's and Clarissa's reconstructions of the Job lyric emphasize the social contours of intimacy. For Herbert, the potential austerity of God's relationship to mankind is made personal by subsumption in a father-child model; for Clarissa, the language of authority and of absent grace (her father's "innate goodness") is made intimate by the powerful, if abject, statement with which she closes: "Yes, I *will* call you papa, and help yourself as you can — for you are my own dear papa, whether you will or not — And though I am an unworthy child — yet I *am* your child." The centripetal force of the speaker's voice pulls against the tendency of power to distance, to sterilize, and to estrange. Clarissa's insistence on the edges of isolation always returns to the contact between isolated experience and power, from the political (Clarissa is constantly the "rebel child") to the familial. Herbert's lyric matters because it embodies these formative relations.

Clarissa's convergence with Herbert's lyrics is founded on a concern with ways fragments can be made to speak (fragments of experience or of the self; divisions born of trauma or of conflicting desires and principles):

both Richardson and Herbert are interested in discovering how self-alienation can become the building block of an aesthetic, even lyric whole (this last claim will be most clear in the discussion of emblems with which I close). In Clarissa's mad papers and in Herbert's poems, the speaker's and writer's minds are wracked to such a vast extent (Herbert's phrase from "The Temper") that a coherent sense of self is on the verge of dissolution. In "Longing," the threatened absence of grace exerts incredible pressure:

> My heart is withered like a ground
>> Which thou dost curse.
>> My thoughts turn round,
> And make me giddy; Lord, I fall,
>>> Yet call.   (ll. 8–12)

The promise of grace is balanced against internal fragmentation:

> Lord JESU, hear my heart,
> Which hath been broken now so long,
>> That ev'ry part
>> Hath got a tongue!   (ll. 73–76)

Clarissa's experience of division is the result of rape (and the drugs used against her). As she says in her first mad paper:

> I sat down to say a great deal — my heart was full — I did not know what to say first — and thought, and grief, and confusion, and (Oh my poor head!) I cannot tell what — And thought, and grief, and confusion came crowding so thick upon me; *one* would be first, *another* would be first; so I can write nothing at all — only that, whatever they have done to me, I cannot tell; but I am no longer what I was in any one thing. — In any one thing did I say? Yes, but I am; for I am still, and I ever will be,
>
>> Your true —
>> (890)

This paper, "*Torn in two pieces*," shows a strategy similar to Herbert's — the attempt to reconstruct a fragmented self by reinstating a set of lapsed relations ("I am your child" in paper 2; "I am still your true" here). Richardson, as well as Herbert, explores a dilemma close to the heart of seventeenth-century religious lyric.[33] The first and second papers evoke the same scene that underlies Herbert's lyric project, from "The Altar" to "Longing," "Denial," or "Obedience," and these papers follow the patterns of connection visible in Herbert's poems. There is a linkage between ideas and strategies apparently so strong that when Richardson thinks of one (silence, fragmentation), he is drawn to the other (naming, grace). The fluid relationships of "Longing" are also those of Clarissa's scraps of sense. These two versions of lyric seek to restore a battered self: what is at stake, what must be saved at all cost, is the ability of the expressive voice to provoke a response, to receive validation through an answer. Individual experience holds the potential of a solipsistic nightmare — solitude without redemption, suffering without witness.

While Herbert counts on Christ's mediation between himself and his father, Clarissa has no such hope. For her, the task of reconstructing herself in fragmentation and isolation is carried out via borrowed discourses. She writes herself into discourses available to her (allegory, fable, etc.) that offer stable, if painful, positions. Each of Clarissa's papers can be said to represent emotion and an approach to experience by linking them with a particular style and language (similar to the way in which Herbert chooses a particular form for each poem's emotional and ideational content).[34] In paper 2, the language of lament is sewn to the father-child dynamic. In paper 3, reminiscence is drawn as fable. Paper 7 gives a prophet's allegorical vision; paper 8 shows affinities with outcries at betrayed love.

This concern with formal variety is key. Clarissa is a victim of mental disorder and confusion, by her own testimony; by that of Lovelace, or of an astute reader, there is more to her expression than that: "After all, Belford, I have just skimmed over these transcriptions of Dorcas; and I see there is method and good sense in some of them, wild as others of them are" (L 261, 894). Like the character she quotes in paper 10, she knows a hack from a handsaw. We are accustomed, especially since Wordsworth, to see in poetic composition the disciplining, or at least regulation, of emotion by rule. In Herbert's lyrics, emotion and idea require their own formal shapes in order to emerge on the page. Whether it is "The Pulley," "The Flower," or "Easter Wings," almost all of the poems in *The Temple* show a unique verse pattern. This kind of attention to form is precisely what makes the loose, baggy monster of the novel seem insurmountably distant from its more controlled cousin.

The sprawling dimensions of Richardson's masterpiece encourage us to stop with the truism that this enormous novel could not be more distinct from Herbert's compact lyrics. However, given the context of poetic discourse in the eighteenth century, there is reason to reconsider. The New Critical conception of a poem as a discrete object, a formal creation bounded at top and bottom by the blankness of a page, is by no means definitive; it certainly does not define a normative reading experience at a given historical moment (it was not designed to do so). While in the eighteenth century poems were of course read as individual works (works that could be favorites, extracted for miscellanies, quoted in letter or sermon), they were often encountered, and even designed to be encountered, as members of series. Formal groupings like the sonnet sequence coexisted with collections like *The Temple* or Cowley's *Mistress* (which also appears in *Clarissa*); although one would not read such a collection at one sitting, these texts enforce the idea that each individual poem is part of a larger whole, a specific context that enriches and informs it. This is more than merely to say that all poems have a context beyond their first and final lines: in the case of *The Mistress*, each poem emerges as an aspect of a given experience, a mood or time that itself can be isolated and given aesthetic being, but that is given a new level of meaning, both as statement and as representation, by its connection to its fellows.[35]

Eighteenth-century readers and writers were becoming accustomed to encountering lyric in nonlyric forms and with a relaxation of formal regularity: the embedded invitations and pastorals of *The Seasons* or the lamentations of *Night Thoughts*, for example. The British Pindaric, in its post-Cowleyan irregularity, also substitutes disorder for regulation and discipline. Fragmentariness like that of Clarissa's mad papers then suggests the power and passion of poetry, not an aesthetic or generic failure. Parts and pieces also took on new importance and prose was newly opened to lyric by discoveries in biblical poetics. As discussed above, for Lowth, the emotional disarray of Hebrew poetry, "its hasty sallies and irregularities" (Elledge, *Critical Essays*, 2:691), marks it as poetry in contradistinction to the grammatical discipline of more earthbound prose. While scholars and practitioners had long argued that rhyme was not necessary to poetry, Lowth's theory of parallelism introduced a new concept. In his lectures, Lowth argues that the principle that distinguishes verse from prose in the Bible is semantic doubling: the words of the first half of a line are repeated, with some variation of intensity or diction, in the second. Meter has some importance, but not consistently so. In a dramatic revolution in critical practice, verse had been found embedded in a prose form.

When Robert Alter undertook an analysis of this verse phenomenon more recently, he was aware that readers still found it strange. He begins his defense of biblical poetry with a statement by Barbara Herrnstein

Smith: "Meter serves . . . as a frame for the poem, separating it from a 'ground' of less highly structured speech and sounds."[36] However, meter is inconsistent in biblical verse, and indeed, since poetic systems of meter postdate biblical compositions, Alter instead focuses on the idea of "ground": "the continuously present frame of formal structure of which Barbara Smith speaks is quite conspicuous here. To be sure, there are also certain elements of symmetry and repetition in the surrounding prose, but, set against the tight formal organization of these lines, the narrative text all around is surely perceived by reader and listener as a 'ground' of nonpoetic discourse" (6). Smith does not suggest that this ground surrounding poetic discourse is as immediate as the frame narrative of Job or the preponderance of *Clarissa*, but the idea is useful. Richardson goes to great lengths to separate the language of the mad papers from that of the rest of his novel: formally, these items look different on the page; rhetorically, they sound different; within the fiction, they have a different history. They may not have the "tight formal organization" of semantic parallelism, but they do evince a formal particularity, and in eighteenth-century terms, nothing precludes their lyricism.[37] Indeed, the fragmentation and excerpting of lyrics is key to commonplace books as well as to personal devotional writing.[38]

The series of "poetical" fragments (Lovelace's term), which let us inside Clarissa's tortured consciousness, should be read with such formal and cultural considerations in mind. None of these fragments *is* a lyric, but the strategies Richardson deploys in them are those of lyric traditions. In choosing the language of Job, a language whose emotive and poetic credentials were of the highest order, Richardson makes a gesture toward the lyric that should not be ignored. Keymer has argued that "the mad papers . . . open the way to new modes of composition. . . . Like the rape itself, the fragmentation which accompanies it prepares Clarissa for the redefinition of self and experience in a new literary form, marking the point of a shift from realism to abstraction, and from epistolary narrative to meditation" ("Meditations," 93–94). That new mode also evolves into a lyric one, calling on language, imagery, and structures that mark lyric expression.[39] In her mad papers, Clarissa reaches out. She needs to organize her experience so that it makes *affective* sense: "despite the fact that she has just been raped, she makes an imaginative leap from self to other, which is the more extraordinary because it comes at precisely the moment of her greatest extremity and disintegration. In an instant when her own physical state is ghastly, the words 'If you could be sorry for yourself, I would be sorry too' are an epiphany about Lovelace's self-hatred"

(Kauffman, *Discourses of Desire*, 154). They also represent a kind of lyric epiphany: the moment when fragments appear as the brilliant remains of wholeness shattered; the moment where the possibility of a vision shared does not give way even before its rupture and decay — like Wordsworth's wanton destruction in "Nutting" or Coleridge's unfulfilled desire in "Dejection" — the utterance of someone who has crossed the depths, and remembers both vision and disillusion.

§   While Richardson uses lyric models for emotional consensus, in most accounts of *Clarissa*, the emotive potential of letters takes pride of place. Linda Kauffman attempts to trace some of the characteristics of *Clarissa* to the flexibility of the letter: from love to business to recommendation, letters may encompass almost any subject, offering a rudimentary frame for whatever content they may carry. She quotes Derrida (from *La Carte Postale*): "La lettre, l'épître, qui n'est pas un genre mais tous les genres, la littérature même" (1). Over the literary history of the epistle, however, one affective mode becomes of central importance to the novel. Drawing on Bakhtin, Kauffman suggests that novels work "to restore some other genre, genres that, in their own unmediated and pure form, have lost their own base in reality.... The specific genre that novelistic prose seeks to restore, the genre for which it is a surrogate, is that of amorous epistolary discourse" (45). The fertile epistolary tradition nourishes the kinds of statements and images of emotion crucial to the novel tradition; however, I disagree as to the mode of this expression. If the letter form is an open one, particular characteristics of expression — those of the love letter or the letter of business, for example — tend to borrow style and mode from other, parent discourses. One of these is lyric.[40] The demands Richardson places on the epistle lead him toward a paradigm of communication highly developed in a range of seventeenth-century poems that, like *Clarissa*'s letters, emphasize the violation of ideal modes of communication, ideals of emotional consensus.

   Clarissa, whatever else it is about, is an intensive exploration of a communicative nightmare: the seeming impossibility of sharing emotional experience. Clarissa's dangerous isolation is the exaggeration of everyone's isolation, the separation between one subject and another. Her letters are tools of mediation, working to overcome the gaps between hearts and minds. In the prototypical twentieth-century formulation, Watt writes that "letters are the most direct material evidence for the inner life of their writers that exist" (*Rise of the Novel*, 191). In response to the preponderance of this view in criticism of *Clarissa*, Keymer has issued a caveat to its readers and critics, reminding those who are tempted to read letters as more or less transparent records of consciousness that all self-presentation is ultimately artful. While Richardson and his characters may seem invested in the supposed intimacy and truthfulness of the familiar letter, there is a larger tension and skepticism surrounding the epistolary form in the novel and its century.[41] Letters approximate consciousness in *Clarissa*, but they are not the real thing: true intimacy is more asymptotic than attainable. Even for those characters who believe in their own sincerity, although the letter always pushes toward the ideal of free and truthful communication, it always threatens to run short. We are alone and fallen, and writing seems only to confirm that isolation. The letter is burdened with the hope of transparency; without such a window, given only the mediation of language, with its inadequacies and its inherent possibilities for fraudulent use, we seem imprisoned in our own bodies, confined by our own emotion and experience.

Here the lyric paradigm of Herbert's poetry becomes again important, for here is a structural relationship (in addition to one of quotation and adaptation) between *Clarissa*'s letters and Herbert's lyric project. If Clarissa's letters work toward a myth of the transparency of the soul against which she measures each moment of writing, Herbert has his own version of the ideal subject by which his attempts are scaled. When Herbert even considers the possibility of true mutuality, he hits a humbling boundary. The participation in an absolutely free communion with God is the end of his devotions and of his poetry, as in "Clasping of Hands":

> Lord, I am thine, and thou art mine:
> So mine thou art, that something more
> I may presume thee mine, than thine.
> For thou didst suffer to restore
> Not thee, but me, and to be mine:
> And with advantage mine the more,
> Since thou in death wast none of thine,
> Yet then as mine didst me restore.
> O be mine still! still make me thine!
> Or rather make no Thine and Mine!   (ll. 11–20)

When God seems absent, when Herbert's cries seem to go unheard, all that he desires is encapsulated in that final plea, a desire for a union so thorough that there is no outside, no singularity. Key to Herbert's separation from and union with God is Christ, and it is on Christ's position that

the paradox of this stanza rests. The speaker's inability to come to terms
with Christ's sacrifice is a marker of his distance from complete communion and of the apparent denial of grace. Witness "The Reprisal":

> I have considered it, and find
> There is no dealing with thy mighty passion:
> For though I die for thee, I am behind:
>   My sins deserve the condemnation.   (ll. 1–4)
>
> Ah! was it not enough that thou
> By thy eternal glory didst outgo me?
> Couldst thou not grief's sad conquests me allow,
> But in all vict'ries overthrow me?   (ll. 9–12)

Whatever Herbert's suffering, Christ's passion has prefigured and sur-
passed it. Powers of sympathy pale in comparison: Christ need not suffer
with; he has already suffered for. Any attempt by the poet to offer a
medium for shared emotion is already overthrown by Christ's inimitable
example. He is the ideal lyric subject, and it is against this that Herbert
struggles.

Herbert's inability to attain the kind of complete identity of emotion
that constitutes Christ's passion (the doctrinal fact that Christ suffers for
believers, that his suffering encompasses theirs) is a lyric as well as a
religious dilemma. This problem of consensus is represented in *The
Temple* in terms of silence. In many of his lyrics, as in Clarissa's letters,
Herbert's voice seems to go unheard. "Denial" evokes Herbert's distress
at appeals to God that seem to fall into a void:

> O that thou shouldst give dust a tongue
>   To cry to thee,
> And then not hear it crying! all day long
> My heart was in my knee,
>   But no hearing.
>
> Therefore my soul lay out of sight,
>   Untuned, unstrung:
> My feeble spirit, unable to look right,
> Like a nipped blossom, hung
>   Discontented.   (ll. 16–25)

Thematically and linguistically, this is almost a foretaste of Clarissa's
dilemma. Denied the response and protection of her own father, she
hangs "like a half-broken-stalked lily," at the mercy of Lovelace, her
betrayer (L 256, 881).

What is particularly compelling about both Herbert's and Clarissa's constructions of denial — the absence of complete consensus, intimacy, and correspondence (in Lovelace's terms, again, a union of hearts) — is that it leads each to similar strategies of self-presentation. Surrounded by silence, Herbert's verse emerges as a physical counter, a record and indication of his search for consensus, as in the famous smoothness of "Denial"'s ending stanza, where the last line is finally in tune with the others:

> O cheer and tune my heartless breast,
>> Defer no time;
> That so thy favours granting my request,
>> They and my mind may chime,
>> And mend my rhyme.

Herbert attempts to make use of the material potential of verse (sound); but in addition to using the sensual properties of the poem, he often attempts to use verse as a token, a physical link between himself and God. "Obedience" offers the most explicit instance of this strategy. There, Herbert emphasizes the poem's character as a written document: "On it my heart doth bleed / As many lines as there doth need / To pass itself and all it hath to thee" (ll. 6–8). The poem is expected to function as a physical intermediary between poet and God. Herbert explicitly figures the poem as a deed or contract (l. 10), but it is more than this; ink appears as writing from the heart, to borrow Richardson's phrase.[42] As with Herbert's shaped verse, the poem's physical presence as much as its meaning is key to its effectiveness (or at least to the demands placed on it).

These moves are kin to what Janet Altman terms epistolarity, or "the use of the letter's formal properties to create meaning."[43] Epistolarity often involves a constructive emphasis on the surface of the page, with its ink, illegible script, or even blots caused by tears, as with the drop that falls on a note from Mrs. Harlowe to her beleaguered daughter: "This answer I received in an open slip of paper, but it was wet in one place. I kissed the place; for I am sure it was blistered, as I may say, with a mother's tear! — The dear lady must (I hope she must) have written it reluctantly" (L 54, 230). Herbert's use of such techniques shows how the demand for a lyric consensus, interrupted or foreclosed, pushes toward an epistolary condition. *Clarissa* is located at this juncture. Faced with the foreclosure of lyric consensus, Clarissa and Herbert come to occupy the same imaginative and a similar formal condition. Herbert's letters to God, I imagine, succeed no more (or no less) than any of his other prayers. Clarissa, however, has the disadvantage of merely writing to mortals; they are perhaps harder to reach. For her, community seems impossible, existence almost unbearable; in *Clarissa* the only alternative appears to be death. Possessed by the fear of total isolation, Clarissa makes a prophetic offer: "if there were no other way [to reconcile with her family], I would most willingly be buried alive" (L 30, 141, 142).

The tableau of emblems and verses that covers Clarissa's coffin offers the next best thing. The last letters she sends to her family, imploring forgiveness and a final blessing, receive insults in return; it is only after she realizes that these efforts are useless that she resigns herself to a self-elegy, the only kind she now can reasonably expect. Before, Clarissa's desire to believe in the immediacy of letters drew her to futile attempts to use them to connect with her family. Now, she knows better: "I wish not now, at the writing of this, to see even my cousin Morden. . . . *God will have no rivals in the hearts of those he sanctifies.* By various methods he deadens all other sensations, or rather absorbs them all in the love of Him" (L 367, 1338; emphasis original). Her coffin self-elegy (a term soon to be justified) is the culmination of her concerns over transparency and consensus (again, feeling-with, an emotional union), as Richardson makes clear when he figures her family's encounter with it.[44]

Strewn with flowers and covered with devices, the coffin is brought home to Harlowe Place. Each of her relatives is drawn into its spell — her mother and father can barely look, all the rest are stricken: "Her uncles looked and turned away, looked and turned away, very often upon the emblems, in silent sorrow. Mrs. Hervey [her aunt] would have read to them the inscription — These words she did read, *Here the wicked cease from troubling:* but could read no further. Her tears fell in large drops upon the plate she was contemplating, and yet she was desirous of gratifying a curiosity that mingled impatience with her grief because she could *not* gratify it, although she often wiped her eyes as they flowed" (L 500, 1399).

This is the scene Richardson has promised for more than a thousand pages. In being overcome by grief, Clarissa's relatives begin to settle the debt of understanding they have let mount since the novel's beginning.[45] Their remorse emerges not merely in response to Clarissa's death but in response to her final work of art. This is the inaugural moment, remarkably late in this novel of letters, when the words Clarissa addresses to her family receive the response they deserve. They respond not just to the finality of death but to the power of the lyric mode.

For Richardson, communication and emotional mutuality are clearly at stake — the very reactions of the Harlowe family receive stunted expression. Of Clarissa's father, he writes, "His grief was too deep for utterance, till he saw his son coming in; and then, fetching a heavy groan, Never, said he, was sorrow like my sorrow! — Oh son! son! — in a reproaching accent, his face turned from him" (L 500, 1399), and while Mrs. Hervey would like to read the verses on the coffin, her tears put an end to even that. Richardson emphasizes the limits governing emotional communication and experience. The isolation of a human being in pain is figured by gaps in communication — halting speech, tears that get in the way of seeing and understanding, faces stricken and turned away.

Drawing on the emblem tradition, Clarissa produces her own well-wrought urn; she wraps her body in words, disposing devices and images around her in a careful pattern meant to move viewers and to demand interpretation.[46] The devices engraved on the coffin are not simply monumental; they are images and ideas infused with the pain of a young mind, placed as defense and elegy, as message and conundrum, beauty and marks that elicit pain. Clarissa's coffin is a fusion of lyric strategies. If we compare her final utterance to Job, to Donne's "Extasie" or his self-elegies, where he too wraps his body in words as it approaches death, or to Herbert's virtuosic manipulations of emblems, where traditional signs become reshaped and stamped with his sensibility, each of these reveals yet another vital link, both thematic and formal, between Richardson's work and lyric traditions.

Even if the coffin testifies to a somewhat adolescent desire to make-them-sorry-when-I'm-gone, it goes beyond that in its insistence on artistry.[47] In designing this piece, Clarissa borrows again from her primary lyrical model, Job. In addition to quoting the poem, her choice of monument echoes Job's desires:

> Oh! that my wordes were now written, oh that they were printed in a
>   booke!
> That they were graven with an iron pen and lead, in the rocke for
>   euer.   (Job 19:23–24)

She achieves both parts of this wish. The quotation from Job on the coffin is only a single line (itself a commonplace in the century); more important is the relationship signified by the monument. She is quoting an act (or a desire) whose essence is delayed confrontation.[48] Lamb argues for the conservative nature of Richardson's use of Job, suggesting that *Clarissa* ignores Job's outrage against God and His arbitrary power and recuperates Job's vehemence with her Christian temperament. In neglecting Clarissa's funerary monument and the scene it produces, however, Lamb may overstate the case. She is not Job, but rather his reader: she has learned from his mistakes. Clarissa's outrage is not against God and divine will but against the systematic abuse she receives from her family; the imagined encounter to which Job clings becomes the actual retribution enacted in the text. Job's projected satisfaction in the court of futurity becomes the reader's satisfaction now, and the combination of conflict and monument produces it for us.

Richardson presents a double tableau in which object and affect carry equal weight. In insisting on this doubleness, Richardson's design goes beyond that of Job's wish or the pattern of other epitaphs. Engraved on the coffin, buried with her, the tableau is addressed to those who will see it before it is committed to earth: an epitaph of the "Halt, traveler" variety is not usually carefully addressed to a particular audience, but merely to whoever may pass. Clarissa's pointed communiqué, already steeped within the lyric context of the Jobian lament, takes part in another generic model. The pattern of confrontation and the specificity of address in Clarissa's memorial scene parallel those of the (amatory) self-elegy. The combination of the funerary verses with the emotional response of guilty loved ones is closely akin to the often violent mechanics of the genre, especially as Donne approaches it.

It takes a certain kind of imagination to leap beyond death into the work of art. Among the fifty-four poems of the *Songs and Sonets*, no fewer than thirteen involve such a movement of the imagination.[49] Some simply twist Petrarchan conventions about dying of love or being killed by a kiss, but others, from "The Canonization" to "The Relique," seriously consider the landscape death leaves behind. Donne's self-elegies demonstrate a structural dependence on the idea of communication, with its possibilities, limits, and ultimate foreclosure. These are *Clarissa*'s dilemmas, and her constructions mimic Donne's. I am not arguing for direct influence — even though this is possible — so much as for patterns of representation, an imaginative condition and set of conventions linked to the lyric mode. I will use Donne (himself a proponent of epistolary intimacy) to illustrate the structural similarity between the letter, as Richardson uses it, and one kind of lyric, emphasizing the position of communication and the problems of intimacy or consensus as Donne and *Clarissa* pose them.

Let me first sketch Donne's pattern. Beyond imagining his body bereft of life and motion or contemplating the human community of which he is deprived, Donne consistently dramatizes the gap between

human subjects that, though it is always present, death makes irrevocable. For Donne, the idea of death tends to be closely related to the
insularity of intimacy. In "The Canonization," "A Valediction: of My
Name, in the Window," "The Funerall," and "The Relique," the story is
much the same: it is the threatened end to emotional union, more than
any other single attribute, that is death's true index.[50] A perfect emotional union is figured in relation to two imaginative thresholds: death
and speech. The immediacy of true intimacy gives way, over the course
of most of these poems, to the necessity of mediation, and speech or
other symbolic exchange steps in to approximate lost intimacy. (These
are, as I have suggested, the issues surrounding Clarissa's use of letters
and her coffin-lyric.)

Donne's self-elegies typically involve a precise imaginative condition: "The Canonization" makes an excellent model. First there is a
figure of extraordinary intimacy:

> The Phoenix ridle hath more wit
> By us, we two being one, are it.
> So to one neutrall thing both sexes fit.   (ll. 23–25)

Donne immediately imagines death (bodily death as the closure and
threat to union or the afterlife as the ultimate space of consummation):

> Wee dye and rise the same, and prove
> Mysterious by this love.   (ll. 26–27)

Typically, he follows this by introducing someone excluded from communion whose only access to shared sensibility is mediated by language:

> And if not peece of Chronicle wee prove,
>   We'll build in sonets pretty roomes;
>   As well a well wrought urne becomes
> The greatest ashes, as halfe-acre tombes,
>   And by these hymnes, all shall approve
>   Us *Canoniz'd* for Love:
>
> And thus invoke us.   (ll. 31–37)

Death intervenes, and poetry forms the mediating communication that
offers an inferior possibility of union to those who come behind. With
small variation, the other self-elegies follow a similar pattern. There are
two key points. First, the union of the lovers is measured against death as
limiting or enabling factor, on the one hand, and against an excluded

observer on the other. There must always be an outside. Second, the mediated intimacy language is to provide is lyric — the "pretty roomes" of sonnets. The exclusion of a third person in these poems is effected not merely by bodily separation (there is no physical intimacy available to this other) but by the specter of death. The observer, appearing as the "lover, such as wee" in "The Extasie" (l.73), is condemned to encounter shared sensibility or consensus only as it can be mediated through language; we hear the "dialogue of one" (l. 74), and from it, "Part farre purer than [we] came" (l. 28).[51] Lyric is a substitute form of intimacy.

"A Valediction: of My Name, in the Window" crystallizes these conditions, and it is here that a connection to *Clarissa* is most clear. This poem, like the stricter self-elegies, effects an imaginative leap beyond death in the context of utter union. A pane of glass, both reflective and transparent, figures a form of intimacy that seems immediate:

> 'Tis much that glasse should bee
> As all confessing, and through-shine as I,
>   'Tis more, that it shewes thee to thee,
>   And cleare reflects thee to thine eye.
> But all such rules, loves magique can undoe
>   Here you see me, and I am you.   (ll. 7–12)

Donne starts with an ideal of transparent subjectivity (stated, but suspiciously unproven), with the poem as sheerest intermediary; it is figured as a clear rendering of the self, "all confessing," and through-shining. This is a model of lyric intimacy and its illusions: in the first stanza the page of the poem and the pane of the window, on which Donne's name and words are engraved, are given as approximations of one another.

This is also the myth the familiar letter offers of the transparency of soul, a view to which Donne adhered: "I make account that this writing of letters, when it is with any seriousness, is a kind of extasie, and a departure and secession and suspension of the soul, which doth then communicate it self to two bodies: and as I would every day provide for my soul's last convoy, though I know not when I shall die: so for the extasies in letters, I often times deliver myself over in writing."[52] Donne had quite a reputation as a master of epistolary style in the seventeenth century;[53] in this passage he offers an ideal form of epistolary intimacy. However, as Christopher Ricks notes, given the kinds of letters and poems Donne wrote, he was clearly none too happy to give himself over in writing or any other way.[54] As with *Clarissa* (where something always gets in the way of perfect epistolary communication), Donne offers an asymptotic ideal of intimacy. In "My Name, in the Window," the glass, figuring two people at once, is a limit too; you may see through it, but the closer you get you see only yourself. Part of this is because of the severity of the limiting conditions of intimacy.[55] Death cannot be mediated; the other ultimate separation, that between one human and another, seems no less insurmountable.

Both Donne's comment on letters and "A Valediction: of My Name, in the Window" share the same complex of issues as in the self-elegies proper: the soul's transparency is imaginatively linked to images of death and the idea of mediated communication. Here, he moves to death and remembrance, and Donne offers the name in the window as a memento mori:

> It, as a given deaths head keepe,
> Lovers mortalitie to preach,
> Or thinke this ragged bony name to bee
> My ruinous Anatomie.
>
> Then, as all my soules bee
> Emparadis'd in you, (in whom alone
> I understand, and grow and see,)
> The rafters of my body, bone
> Being still with you, the Muscle Sinew, and Veine,
> Which tile this house, will come againe.   (ll. 21–30)

The speaker's mistress plays the structural role of the audience/observer in the other poems. Instead of the complete intimacy of "The Extasie," union is here threatened by distance and the fallibilities of the heart. With an internal threat to consensus, mediation is necessary not only to an outsider encountering the poem but also to the speaker and mistress themselves. This threat is responsible for the violence of these stanzas, with their savage introduction of the flesh. Words here are a substitute for the body: a name, etched starkly into the window, becomes a skeleton. It is on words as tokens that a resurrection, a coming again, may be sustained: this is the only possibility for intimacy Donne can ultimately offer.[56]

"My Name, in the Window" shares the structure of Clarissa's self-elegy. Clarissa's version illustrates a crisis central to this novel's epistolary structure and to the lyric: consensus or mutuality somehow disturbed or disrupted. Five characteristics of Clarissa's self-elegy can be mapped back to Donne. (1) An ideal union destroyed or threatened: the longed-for union of the heart that Clarissa struggles to attain through letters, no longer possible with her family, is now only attainable with God. (2) The persistence of the outside: Clarissa's relatives are denied that consensual ideal by their own folly, placed irrevocably outside, like the Donnean observer. (3) Violent emotional confrontation: as with the savage appearance of flesh and bone in Donne, the lid of Clarissa's coffin and the body that lies beneath it force each member of her family to undergo a devastating experience. Those left behind are offered her words wrapped around her body, a shocking confrontation in line with those enacted by Donne in the self-elegies (or with Job's image).[57] (4) Mediated communication: like Donne's readers, Clarissa's relatives are offered a substitute for intimacy in the coffin, a substitute that points out its inferiority to the real thing (the beauty of concord while she was alive). In both cases the graven words and images mediate between the speaker's body and the loved ones. (5) A doubling of identities or violent confusion of them: the coffin's lid demands that each member of Clarissa's family situate him- or herself with regard to the demands of pain and grief, that she or he confront an image of the self broken, disturbing, guilty, burdened.

The emblems and verses voice Clarissa's presence; while showing the viewer his or her own image, the elegy overstrikes it with that of the author. In this context, there is a new resonance to those lines from "My Name, in the Window." Lines 7–8 render Clarissa's (now obsolete) ideal:

> 'Tis much that glasse should bee
> As all confessing, and through-shine as I.

The next two encapsulate her relatives' self-recognition as they confront the results and emblems of their own cruelty:

> 'Tis more, that it shewes thee to thee,
> And cleare reflects thee to thine eye.

The closing couplet brings the essence of the elegiac moment, where the two images, that of self and other, are drawn together:

> But all such rules, loves magique can undoe
> Here you see me, and I am you.

For the viewer, the ragged anatomy that is the speaker's name, the letters scratched almost like a wound in the glass, force a reevaluation of self. Her mother's reaction is instructive: "Oh my child! my child! cried she; the pride of my hope! Why was I not permitted to speak pardon and peace to thee! — Oh forgive thy cruel mother!" (L 500, 1398). Mrs. Harlowe's outcry circles upon itself. The parallel apostrophes seem almost equivalent: one cannot be thought without the other. Even the magic of love in the penultimate line evokes the too-lateness of the Harlowes' emotion. A soothing concord, sustained by mutual affection, was once possible; now, any effort of sympathy produces only discord and spasms of remorse. What makes the parallel between *Clarissa* and Donne possible is their participation in a particular lyric paradigm. Intimacy is constructed as a binary relation between a pure, immediate consensus and a mediated, even debased exchange founded on language, signs, and symbols. In both *Clarissa* and Donne, the speakers propose that a text can produce a particular kind of emotional intimacy, a union based on a confrontational aesthetic and predicated upon death, and both texts insist on emotional and physical boundaries of intimacy.

Given Clarissa's preoccupation with death, the structural parallels with one whom John Carey calls death's poet make sense. Belford's account of Clarissa's ordering her coffin, living within it, and even using it as a writing desk may remind us of Walton's account of the death of Donne:

> Dr. Donne sent for a Carver to make for him in wood the figure of an Urn, giving him direction for the compass and height of it; and to bring with it a board, of the just height of his body. "These being got, then without delay a choice Painter was got to be in readiness to draw his picture, which was taken as followeth. — Several charcoal fires being first made in his large study, he brought with him into that place his large winding-sheet in his hand, and having put off all his clothes, had this sheet put on him, and so tied with knots at his head and feet, and his hands so placed as dead bodies are usually fitted, to be shrowded and put into this coffin, or grave. Upon this Urn he thus stood, with his eyes shut, and with so much of the sheet turned aside as might shew his lean, pale, and death-like face. . . ." In this posture he was drawn at his just height; and when the picture was fully finished, he caused it to be set by his bed-side, where it continued and became his hourly object till his death.[58]

Donne's holy dying and his choice in funerary art were well known throughout the eighteenth century, reprinted as part of Walton's *Lives* but also printed with his poems and sermons. The constant presence of Clarissa's memento mori as she waits for death echoes Donne. Clarissa's funerary art finally surrounds her, like Donne's shroud; in it the emphasis on physical boundaries is absolute. As with "My Name, in the

Window," the power of the image is linked to that of the body: Clarissa's corpse, lying beneath the coffin's lid, is part of the motivating force behind the effect her self-elegy creates.

While in "My Name, in the Window" words are substitutes for the body, in others of Donne's self-elegies, body and symbol hold a different relationship, one whose contours help us more profitably understand Clarissa's own efforts.[59] It is here that emblems are important. In "The Relique" and "The Funerall" Donne fragments the speaker's experience, representing him both as the corpse on the verge of dissolution and as its sympathetic viewer. It is no wonder, then, that this image pushes Donne's imagination toward the thresholds of intimacy, the points where everything falls apart. In these poems, neither speech nor words is the chosen form of mediation between lover and mistress (as in "My Name, in the Window"). Neither is it solely speech that is expected to promote the illusion of consensus or shared emotion across the page. Donne relies on the manipulation of an emblem for this work in the first stanzas of "The Funerall" and "The Relique":

> Who ever comes to shroud me, do not harme
> > Nor question much
> That subtile wreathe of haire, which crowns my arme;
> The mystery, the signe you must not touch,
> > For 'tis my outward Soule,
> Viceroy to that, which then to heaven being gone,
> > Will leave this to controule,
> And keep these limbes, her Provinces, from dissolution.
>
> > > > > > > > > > > > > ("The Funerall")

> > When my grave is broke up againe
> > Some second ghest to entertaine,
> > (For graves have learn'd that woman-head
> > To be to more than one a Bed)
> > > And he that digs it, spies
> > A bracelet of bright haire about the bone,
> > > Will he not let'us alone,
> > And thinke that there a loving couple lies,
> > Who thought that this device might be some way
> > To make ther soules, at the last busie day,
> > Meet at the grave, and make a little stay?   ("The Relique")

Donne divides his speaker in two, imagining him as the corpse laid out for view — the body whose yearning is represented by voice and emblem—and as the consciousness that watches, aligned with ignorant parishioners past or future, and with us as readers. What binds these viewpoints together is the accretion of sensibility around a single image (for readers) or perception (within the poem's frame), that of an emblematic bracelet.[60] In the first poem, it is a sign of betrayal, a promise broken; in the second it is a sign of a promise not yet fulfilled. In either case, the power of the emblem comes not merely from its own qualities, its shape (the circle of eternity), its relationship to the giver (it is the product of her body and the fabrication of her hands), or the circumstances of its gift: the power of the emblem lies in the shock of its juxtaposition with the body. As is usual in emblem poetry of the seventeenth century, emblems here are infinitely personal, appropriated and deployed as markers of personal experience. We have here an emblem almost made flesh. The speaker's audacity is to wrap his body in a sign. The bracelet of hair appears with grotesque urgency, bright against the bone, as both emblem and "fact."[61]

When the symbolic meets the actual, things happen. Clarissa's tableau of emblems and verses, engraved within inches of her dead body, moves by this power, placing symbol so close to flesh that the two seem almost to meld.[62] As in the pair of Donne poems, Clarissa's emblems have been appropriated from a larger discourse; some have been given as questionable gifts, as well, by her betrayer:

> The principal device, neatly etched on a plate of white metal, is a crowned serpent, with its tail in its mouth, forming a ring, the emblem of eternity, and in the circle made by it is this inscription:
>
> CLARISSA HARLOWE
> APRIL X.
> [Then the year]
> AETAT. XIX.
>
> For ornaments: at top, an hour-glass winged. At bottom, an urn.
> Under the hour-glass, on another plate, this inscription:
> HERE the wicked cease from troubling: and HERE the weary be at rest.
> Job iii.17
>
> Over the urn, near the bottom:
> Turn against unto thy rest, Oh my soul! For the Lord hath rewarded thee. And why? Thou hast delivered my soul from death; mine eyes from tears; and my feet from falling.
> Ps. cxvi. 7, 8

Over this text is the head of a white lily snapped short off, and just
falling from the stalk; and this inscription over that, between the principal plate and the lily:
The days of man are but grass. For he flourisheth as a flower of the
field: for, as soon as the wind goeth over it, it is gone; and the place
thereof shall know it no more.
Ps. ciii. 15, 16.   (L 451, 1305–6)

The final emblem reflects the image Lovelace uses to describe Clarissa,
drugged and pleading, just before he rapes her: "And down on her
bosom, like a half-broken-stalked lily, top-heavy with the overcharging
dews of the morning, sunk her head with a sigh that went to my heart" (L
256, 881). Like the bracelet given in "The Funerall," this is an emblem
whose presence speaks betrayal. The brutality and deception of Lovelace, however, are rebuked and all but erased by the emblem's accompanying text. Clarissa may be as a flower in the field, but so is Lovelace,
and with Clarissa's passing, the marks of Lovelace's brutality disappear as
well.

The second emblem turns the body (whose earthly rewards Lovelace
seeks) into ashes, rejected in favor of heavenly treasure. The other emblem is also a reappropriation of ideas connected to Lovelace: "an hour-
glass winged" figures the speed with which time passes; this basic signification is available to two primary interpretations within the text. The
briefness of the human lifespan is a staple warning of conduct books and
sermons, reminding us, as does Wither in his *Collection of Emblemes,
Ancient and Moderne* (1635), "Live, ever mindfull of thy dying; / For,
Time is always from thee flying" (Emblem 77). However, images of
time's swift passage are also linked to the *carpe diem* tradition, to the woo-
ing lover whose desires speed him as fast as Marvell's winged chariot—to
Lovelace, even if he never makes the sort of offers of Marlowe's Shepherd or Mr. B. (and he is thus spared the replies of a Nymph or a
Pamela).[63] Clarissa's chosen text makes the address to Lovelace specific:
he is the wicked one who has troubled her most.

Through this use of emblems, Clarissa is working to create an image
of self around the dissonance of two discourses, one of her own, one of
her betrayer's. Herbert, too, uses dissonance between emblems to frame
his imagined self and to frame his particular lyric project.[64] He is not
menaced by a Lovelace; for him the danger of betrayal comes from
within. Herbert's well-known dialogic strategies often involve an allegorical figure whose presence enables him to voice divisions within his

soul. This is the structure of "Hope," where the poet stages a dialogue of emblems:

> I gave to Hope a watch of mine: but he
> > An anchor gave to me.
> Then an old prayer-book I did present:
> > And he an optick sent.
> With that I gave a viall full of tears:
> > But he a few green eares:
> Ah Loyterer! I'le no more, no more I'le bring:
> > I did expect a ring.

Barbara Lewalski renders the poem less cryptic, translating its emblems into their plainer meanings: "The speaker gives his watch (time), and receives in return an anchor (hope); he then gives an old prayer-book (his long-continued devotion) and receives an 'optick' glass (with which to see . . . heaven afar off). He responds with a 'viall full of tears' (his repentance), and is given a few 'green eares'" (203). Herbert is waiting for God, waiting for the assurance of grace, and, as Lewalski notes, the ring of the poem's last line is the symbol of a union constantly deferred. "Hope" reveals the other side of Herbert's construction of his speaker as child: weakness and impatience. The speaker's final retreat is subject to a lesson his limitations do not allow him to articulate: "The point, which the reader should infer by interpreting the emblems better than the speaker, is that the business of Hope is with expectation, not fruition: the speaker must patiently wait to receive his ring hereafter" (Lewalski, *Protestant Poetics*, 203).

The speaker's voice and desires (as represented by the emblems he chooses) and the emblematic offerings of Hope are two alternatives with which the poet feels equal dissatisfaction. The ideal (waiting) cannot satisfy, and the infantile (wanting) cannot be sustaining. This dissonance is instructive, and Herbert's decision to present emblems as images without explication, supported only by their dialogic relation, is key to the pattern of significance. The emblems appear almost as slides — or as individual woodcuts — and the gaps between them open up not only space for interpretation but also time for contemplation. Each emblematic reference slows down the poem, gives the reader (and Herbert) time to weigh each mode, each option. Herbert is spectator of his own internal struggle and emerges as spectator and poet simultaneously, in appearing as the consciousness that can understand the poem's "lesson" even if he doesn't get it — even if that lesson remains unprofitable. All of this happens between the poem's frames, in the time of "loitering," where and when Herbert gives the poem and himself over to interpretation.

Returning to *Clarissa*, we may find a similar structure. Each of her emblems is contested: a final meaning is reified, but not naturally so.[65] On one hand, there is the work necessary to interpret the tableau (Mrs. Hervey's tears keep her from even reading it);[66] on the other, the novel's story dramatizes the impossibility of earthly coexistence, or even supremacy, for either alternative the emblems offer. Even if one discourse (that of moral rectitude) is correct, it cannot withstand the temporal challenge offered by the other. Clarissa's goodness is effaced, as a flower in the field; Lovelace's wickedness ends in misery. If there is a place where this dissonance can be resolved, it is elsewhere — in the hereafter, or at the lyric moment, that of confrontation with the reader.

In "Hope," Herbert's emblems must wait for a resolution that occurs only in the imagination of the poet or the informed reader, outside the poem, outside its given figures and forms. If Herbert's poem is a lyric, if it is more than an accumulation of emblems (and not just because of meter or line length); if it rings with the voice of "another David," it does so because of the consciousness that is drawn around it — the poem achieves a lyric intensity when it realizes the presence of a mind that contains all the poem shows and more, the consciousness of the poet who gets the lesson the dialogue has to teach. Clarissa's set of emblems emerges as more than a conventional display for much the same reason. What makes it lyric has to do with how the self is positioned vis-à-vis the tension surrounding each symbol, with how and why the self is able to speak through. Part of the answer lies in the sense we have of circling a self, of drawing ever closer to an invisible core whose presence we feel but which is materially or denotatively absent. Clarissa's body is hidden beneath; her soul has flown away; the record of her consciousness sits, starkly posed between these alternatives.

In drawing this frame for the representation of her consciousness (and only a frame, because she is missing), Clarissa forever gives herself over to the necessity of interpretation and mediation. With her self-elegy, she has given up the illusion of perfect transparency. Her "principal device" is a demonstration. The emblem-inscription pair shows in miniature the structure of the entire elegy: just as her body is wrapped in words, her name is surrounded by the most recognizable of emblems, the snake swallowing its tail. Something is between her and the phenomenal world. She is subsumed in eternity both in figure and in truth. The typographical emphasis on HERE, on the landscape opened after the grass is gone, after death and the Lord have given their reward, works to underline the impossibility of true earthly mutuality.[67] To use Donne's terms again, love's unity-making magic can only, really, be God's.

I have argued in this chapter that *Clarissa*'s affective prose, its ability to create an emotional context that draws us in and invites our participation, relies on the strategies of biblical and seventeenth-century lyric poets. I have chosen moments in the text that carry extraordinary amounts of emotional weight, whose structural characteristics mimic those of the lyric; however, they are only exaggerations of what goes on throughout, as I will show in Chapter 5. The affinity between lyric and novel is one of convention: before realism became Realism, the strategy of the novel was not so much to defamiliarize (in a Shlovskian manner) as to create resonance. A moment of psychological intensity may be recognized as realistic not only because it jives with one's own experience but because it participates in a familiar and recognizable discourse: this is one meaning of authenticity. Clarissa's experience is readable, and thus provisionally shareable, because its language carries discursive authentication, an authentication given in part by contemporary daily religious life.

In exploring the resonance between Richardson's use of lyric and those of his precursors, I have been able to foreground some key features of one version of lyric. What makes Job's, Herbert's, or Clarissa's complaints poignant is the threat of the foreclosure of consensus as much as the record of suffering. At issue is an affective program, an attempt to frame sense and make it not just understandable but shareable, to offer up personal experience as more than individual — as participatory. In Herbert, Donne, *Clarissa*, and Job, we see the terrible isolation in suffering that drives each to speak, and each, to thoughts of death. With Donne, we see the outlines of the self-elegy, relentlessly pushing the poet to contemplation of mutuality and its loss, and of the figures that sustain it. Herbert, as in "Clasping of Hands," desires God to resolve the separation of savior and sinner in an ecstatic fullness, where there is "no Thine and Mine"; we also witness a search for alternatives, for modes of expression and kinds of exchange that join the individual in emotional union with the world beyond. In Job, we saw the desire to lie "in the quiet grave" (3:13), where, as in the verses quoted by Clarissa, "the wicked cease to trouble . . . and the weary are at rest" (3:17) — all part of the recognizable and poignant genre of the lament. These all come together in Clarissa's self-elegy — a testimony to the impossibility of true earthly mutuality, as well as a demonstration of the power of the lyric, if not to overcome the disjunction of human subjects, at least to make sensible the lack — or loss — of mutuality.

The final question here is this: what does Richardson do to the lyric in thus adapting it? Most obviously, the integrity of form is destroyed — the lyric is dilated and diffused, its conventions spread over many pages and a vast stretch of time. In its place is an integrity of the subject, a record of consciousness and its desire to reach outward. Subjectivity in these terms is an ideal construction that seeks the participation of others in imaginative intimacy (a search whose failures are as important as its successes). Response becomes as much a part of the lyric moment as the artifact or carefully worked object. For Donne, response is conjectural (the probable actions of the future viewers of the corpse, the possible infidelity of the mistress, the future lover such as he) and often vague (the lover will part far purer than he came); for Herbert, response is often absent (God's answering voice) or only present by proxy and for a fleeting moment (the final chime of "Denial"). The presence of response in *Clarissa*'s self-elegy signifies the beginnings of the paradigm of sensibility and the tableau of sympathetic exchange (which we reencounter in Wordsworth's first published poem, "On Seeing Miss Helen Maria Williams Weep at a Tale of Distress" [1787]). These alterations to the lyric are important, in part because they suggest that lyric is seen as adaptable, absorbable, and ultimately changeable; that it is flexible, not fixed; that its language and structures are available to be adopted by any and all properly disposed comers; and that generic boundaries are as open to imaginative crossing as the boundaries of personal experience.

Two

Modes of Absorption: Lyric and Letter
in Behn, Haywood, and Pope

By the time of *Clarissa*, there was a substantial history of inter-relation between letter and lyric. I begin tracing that history in romance, moving toward the generic mixtures popularized by Behn in her poetry and prose. My primary focus of attention rapidly becomes the heroical epistle, a verse form begun with Ovid where an abandoned woman by turns upbraids and beseeches her lover. This tradition was crucial to the early novel and is fundamental to the best-selling works of fiction on which I focus: Behn's *Love-Letters between a Nobleman and His Sister* (1684–87), *Les Lettres Portugaises* (1678), and Haywood's *Love in Excess* (1719).[1] The use of lyric conventions in these works makes a striking contrast to the approach to the lyric mode in Behn's poetry and in two emotionally charged epistles by Pope, "Eloisa to Abelard" (1717) and "Epistle to Dr. Arbuthnot" (1735). For Behn, Pope, and Haywood, lyric is often submerged; their responses to and uses of the mode characterize a larger scene in the early century. There are two strains here under consideration — the absorption of lyric into the novel and its frequent renunciation in poetry.

Most theories of the novel's development do not account for or even mention the presence of poetry in "prose" romance.[2] Wlad Godzich and Jeffrey Kittay remind us that prose is historically a latecomer; in almost every culture literature is first written in verse.[3] British and Continental traditions are no exception: romance begins as a metrical form, but as metrical romance dies, lyric remains as a ghost in the prose. The earliest English example of this comes with Gascoigne's *Adventures of Master F. J.* (1573),[4] but French practice predates this to around 1215 and Jean Renart's *Guillaume de Dole*:[5] on both sides of the channel, poetry exercised

charms over romance writers working largely in prose. R. S. White's
account of lyric insertions in Elizabethan and Arcadian romance suggests that a major function of the interpolated lyric was to provide a
formalized glimpse of interior life. F.J. in Gascoigne's *Adventures* is "constantly composing poems and sonnets . . . either as declarations of love to
be read by his mistress, or lovely reflections upon his own melancholy
circumstances."[6] Works like D'Urfé's highly influential *L'Astrée*, Sidney's *Arcadia*, or Wroth's *Urania* combine prose narratives with lyric
forms from madrigal to lament, epithalamium, or sonnet. Samuel Sheppard's 1650 *Loves of Amandus and Sophronia* includes odes, an elegy (complete with mourning border), and an epithalamium. In the *Arcadia*,
poems often reveal the hidden, as secrets and emotions, things with
which neither narrative nor dialogue is entrusted. Poems, as Sidney puts
it, are "the badges of . . . passions" in his romance, the formal external-
ization of what lies within.[7] But lyrics do not belong to pastoral romance
alone. Even their heroic counterparts contain songs that erstwhile lovers
seem unable to do without.[8] Whether these lyrics are "written as solitary
self-communication . . . as deliberate communication, [or] . . . unin-
tended revelation to others," White writes, they bring prose toward "the
sanctified status of poetry" ("Functions of Poems and Songs," 395). In
the grand tradition of Renaissance rhetoric, poems are virtuoso renderings of sensibility, both concentrating and displaying emotion.

The French tradition (as well as those of Italy and Spain) contains
earlier examples of this usage.[9] In Maureen Barry McCann Boulton's
study of lyric and French romance, among the six functions of the lyric
insertion that she identifies, half tend to make interior, private experience accessible to others, both within the narrative and outside it.[10] Over
the history of the practice, "the attribution of a song to a character for
the purpose of expressing or analyzing his (or occasionally her) sentiments . . . eventually became the most successful application of the
device" (*Song in the Story*, 20). In Sidney's case, this use of lyric would
seem second nature (the better, gilded nature that only poesy can offer);
he had been working on the representation of emotions in both *Certain
Sonnets* and *Astrophil and Stella*. Like the romance, the sonnet sequence
exploits context and interrelation, offering poems as part of a larger,
loosely narrative whole (even though each lyric may be extracted and
stand on its own).

Beyond explanations specific to a particular poet's practice, there are
literary-historical reasons for the use of lyrics in prose fiction to provide
expressions of interior states. There is the tradition represented ex-

plicitly by Dante connecting high or intense emotion to lyric utterance: "arms and love" were chief among the "lofty subjects [that] should be presented in the highest style, and cast in the most perfect form, the *canzone* or *chanson*" (Boulton, *Song in the Story*, 14). Of course, the mere mention of emotion (in the context of action, as well) is insufficient to indicate that the representation of interiority is at stake, but any perusal of Dante's *Vita Nuova* will suggest that the poet had this in mind. *La Vita Nuova*'s account of creativity, the dream life, and the construction of self relies on lyric; sonnet and meditation, lyric and internal conflict, are sewn close.

The literary history of courtly love also influences the use of lyrics in prose. As Boulton notes, even the monologue had close rhetorical ties to the *chanson d'amour* (*Song in the Story*, 24). While Stephen G. Nichols has recently challenged this argument, most scholars agree that troubadour lyrics are an important (though certainly not exclusive) source of romance psychology.[11] The connections between lyric and romance hold up at the other developmental end as well. Edith Rickert suggests that with the advent of print, the early romance took two paths, one in prose and one in the form of the popular ballad.[12] Later, literary ballads like "La Belle Dame Sans Merci" would carry on some of the tendencies of romance.[13]

§ If the inserted lyric in romance makes emotion visible, understandable, and affective, it is akin to the function of letters in epistolary narrative.[14] Boulton and White have noted that lyrics—typically love sonnets—are frequently used in romance as missive or letter. Given the material history of lyric and letter, this makes perfect sense: "In the Renaissance, lyric poems served as instruments of social intercourse: they could be passed personally to friends and family members, performed in social gatherings, sent as verse epistles or as accompaniments to prose letters."[15] This condition was suggestive to imaginative minds (if the frequent use or styling of lyric as letter in Wyatt, Sidney, or Surrey is any indication); the unimaginative could learn the connection from sixteenth-century letter manuals.[16] Donne's statement about intimacy and the personal letter is an excellent reminder. For him, the controlling metaphor for epistolary intimacy is also that of sexual and lyric intimacy in "The Extasie": "I make account that this writing of letters, when it is with any seriousness, is a kind of extasie, and a departure and secession and suspension of the soul, which doth then communicate it self to two bodies: and as I would every day provide for my soul's last convoy, though I know not when I shall die: so for the extasies in letters, I often times deliver myself over in writing."[17] The material resonance between lyric and letter became more pronounced as print took over: "The lyric . . . as the most occasional of the literary kinds (with the exception of the personal letter), was slower to make the transition from manuscript culture to print culture than such other forms as prose fiction, poetic romance or epic, or drama" (Marotti, "Manuscript, Print," 56).

Theorists of the novel have long argued for the importance of print in the development of the genre. As Hunter writes, "Print had, of course, been around for centuries by the time the novel began to emerge. . . . [But it] is the emerging novel that systematically begins to use a full range of print possibilities in developing and holding its relationships with readers."[18] The early period of development for novels roughly corresponds to the emergence of published correspondence; the relatively late appearance of poetry in print only slightly predates the fitful emergence of the novel genre. Hunter persuasively argues in *Before Novels* that the development of the novel was connected to an increasing public appetite for printed novelty in any shape. In the print age, the presence of epistle or poem in prose fiction may also be related to the cultural currency, the "newness" of epistle and poem as print objects.

§ As Hunter and McKeon maintain, the relation between novel and romance is not accurately described as developmental; instead, romance was one of many discourses and genres with which novels would engage. Moreover, the relationship between romance and novel involves more than questions of verisimilitude. At least one late romance writer or early novelist (variously understood) transformed the romance technique of lyric insertion, not by simply placing lyrics into her prose, but by a more thorough kind of absorption. Aphra Behn broke a new path by rendering traditional lyric forms in prose rhythms — and within the frame of the letter. Even given the tendency of Restoration narratives to pose difficulties for categorization, Behn's *Love-Letters between a Nobleman and His Sister* (1683–85) is a thorny case.[19] It begins as a series of epistles, yet ends with a mainly third-person narrative; it has the historical basis of the *roman à clef,* yet it shows formal and aesthetic concerns that go beyond the scope of *récit.* The nobleman of the title is Ford, Lord Grey. His scandalous elopement with his sister-in-law and his support of Charles II's bastard son Monmouth provided the public with news, scandal, and the kernel of Behn's Tory-minded tale. It is not useful here to identify *Nobleman* unequivocally with one genre. As McKeon, Hunter, and others have argued, these categories have a dialectical history; they emerge only as products of historical processes, as the outcome of interactions that are by no means complete at the moment a work like *Nobleman* attains its fame. *Nobleman* is intriguing precisely because it is both novelistic and romanesque, yet neither novel nor romance. We cannot say that it is a species of the form in transition without committing a teleological fallacy; we can say that it captures the changes and fluxion that are the history of prose fiction in the greater eighteenth century.[20]

§ Whereas Sidney's 1593 *Arcadia* interweaves eclogues and songs (there are seventy-eight poems altogether) with prose narrative, Behn's 1680s *Nobleman* includes in its letters passages best described as prose versions of these pastoral forms.[21] Philander begins a letter thus to Silvia:

> Say fond Love whither wilt thou lead me? thou has brought me from the noysey hurry's of the Town, to charming solitude; from Crowded Cabals, where mighty things are resolving to loanly Groves, to thy own abodes, where thou dwell'st, gay and pleas'd, amongst the Rural Swains in shady homely Cottages; thou hast brought me to a Grove of flowers, to the brink of Purling Streams, where thou hast laid me down to contemplate on *Silvia!* to think my tedious hours away, in the softest imagination a Soul inspir'd by Love can conceive; to increase my Passion by every thing I behold, for every Sound that meets the sense, is thy proper Musick, oh Love! and every thing inspires thy dictates; the Winds a round me blow soft, and mixing with the wanton Boughs, continually play and Kiss; while those like a coy Maid in Love resist and comply by turns.[22]

This passage is closely related to pastoral lyric, as perhaps one might expect from a poet whose "main mode" was precisely that.[23] The opening address to Love is typical of pastoral and other lyric subgenres, as is the layering of apostrophe or invocation and addressee; while Love is invoked and addressed, the letter is directed toward the absent lover, Sylvia.[24] As in the *Arcadia*, pastoral language is motivated by political context; here it is the anti-Royalist cabal of Monmouth; for Sidney's Musidorus, it was enforced rustication after his shipwreck.[25] We recognize the Rural Swains, the homely Cottages, the emphasis on contemplation, as stays of the pastoral tradition. Philander, like a good pastoral poet, also lingers lovingly over words, as in the near-rhyme and rhythm pair "to loanly Groves, to thy own abodes."

Like its romance precursors, this passage appears as a kind of caesura;

it is not that there is a great deal of action under way, but rather that interior events preclude other kinds of activity. Love is a bar to the civilizing business of humanity, taking away attention and energy from social tasks. Philander's attention is certainly drawn from the political fray, but his meditation and style are important in another way: Behn chooses the language traditionally associated with the amorous meditative pause in romance, specifically as it may be used as a highly formalized emotional offering, designed to create a rising, mirroring response in its lady reader.[26] Lyric is a site for creating emotional consensus. Behn frequently has recourse to such poetic language throughout the first-person, epistolary portions of the work, when evocative rather than merely illustrative accounts of emotion are necessary. The "necessity" of which I speak is as much aesthetic as it is expedient (for the purposes, e.g., of seduction or reproach) — it is part of a decorum linking emotion to proper poetic expression. Lyric is present in Behn where emotional response is crucial, and where that response must be mediated by artful, and not merely adequate, self-presentation.

When Philander has abandoned her, Sylvia has "recourse to pen and paper for a relief of that heart which no other way cou'd find it; and after, having wip'd the tears from her eyes she writ" a letter that I have divided, going by sound and sense, into "lines" (*Nobleman*, 143):

> Hast thóu forgót thy wóndrous Árt of lóving?
> Thy prétty cúnings, ánd thy sóft decéivings?
>   Hast thóu forgót 'em áll?
>   Or hást forgót indéed to lóve at áll?
> Has thý indústrious pássion gáther'd áll the swéets,
>   and léft the rífled flówer to háng its wíther'd héad,
>   and díe in shádes neglécted,
>   for whó will príze it nów,
> nów when áll its pérfumes fléd.   (144, scansion added)

It is to passages like this, perhaps, that Montague Summers refers when he calls *Nobleman* "romantic and sentimental, with now and again a pretty touch that is almost lyrical in its sweet cadence."[27] As in Philander's letter above, internal rhyme and an insistent though varying meter emphasize the strangeness, the unprosaic nature of this writing. The insistent stress encourages scansion, and when scanned it is strongly reminiscent of metrical patterns in Behn's Pindaric odes. If the above passage were in a poem, it would divide 5-5-3-5-6-6-3-3-4 and would have a clear rhyme scheme: aabbcdded.[28] Usually, Behn's lines are divided on the basis of the number of stresses, varying from the infrequent hexameter line to a general mixture of pentameter, trimeter, and tetrameter. Behn also tends to work with pairs of lines such that the stronger meter of the first clarifies and governs that of the second: all of these are characteristic of the above passage. In particular, this passage resembles the variations used in Behn's Pindaric "On Desire," the ode closest in theme to *Nobleman*, as Janet Todd has suggested.[29] It is also close to this passage in rhetorical strategy, both being dominated by questions and a tone of accusation; moreover, in "On Desire" stanzas usually begin with two pentameter lines and end in a single pentameter or tetrameter one.

The irregularity of Pindarics in the seventeenth and eighteenth centuries is important to changing poetics and suggests several reasons for the similarity between Behn's odes and the above passage. Cowley's experiments with the ode ignited extensive debate and imitation, largely because poets and critics were intrigued by his claims for the emotional potential of the form. The ode was supposed to be reserved for the greatest and highest of passions: this certainly encompassed the public passions of awe or reverence (see the public odes of Dryden or Behn herself) as well as, though less frequently at first, more private ones (as in "On Desire"). As the number of "Pindaric" odes increased, purists took the alarm. In 1706 Congreve cried out against them: "The character of these late Pindarics is a bundle of rambling incoherent thoughts, expressed in a like parcel of irregular stanzas, which also consist of such another complication of disproportioned, uncertain, and perplexed verses and rimes."[30] Congreve's attack on the Pindaric seems almost like a complaint that these poems contain nothing of the discipline and order, either by meter, rhyme, or stanzaic division, that usually distinguishes poetry from prose.[31] Behn's versification is by no means consistent, and scansion is often difficult; the irregularity of her odes, and of Pindarics in general, is meant to be an index of the level of passion that moves them. Although by 1728 Edward Young was insisting that the proper ode should be "more remote from prose than any other [kind of poetry], in sense, sound, expression, and conduct," the freedom given by the Pindaric, at least as practiced by Behn, lends itself to absorption in prose because of its multiform irregularity.[32]

Whatever the looseness of the Pindaric, Behn sticks to a kind of decorum in choosing the literary language most often associated with the emotion she portrays. As Todd points out, Sylvia's lack of self-control is variously cast; as the novel progresses, "it is expressed more in ungovernable rage than in sexual voraciousness, frequently conveyed in the repertoire of theatrical tragic language."[33] Indeed, Behn's dramatic training structures her prose, a connection more frequently considered than her lyric sensibilities.[34] This raises the question whether some of the tactics used in the "lyric" passages above are closer to aspects of Restoration drama and soliloquy than to lyric. There are two crucial distinctions both in the general use of soliloquies and in Behn's own. Soliloquies tend to two basic kinds: (usually rational) deliberations about action (or inaction, as in *Hamlet*) and commentary about emotion. They give information about motive that conversation could not plausibly reveal or that must remain secret for dramatic purposes.[35] Behn's soliloquies work in both these ways, and, syntactically, they show markings of orality that distance them from the more polished form of Sylvia's or Philander's letters.[36] Even when the language is not paratactic, Behn's soliloquies do not show the larger structure or development of a central metaphor that marks these letters.[37] There is, however, as with the use of apostrophe, potential for overlap in dramatic and lyric forms — understandable given the varied ground of Shakespeare's, Jonson's, or Behn's own plays. The mixed nature of Behn's language serves to underline the sort of generic flexibility that she (and later novelists) are able to command. Behn's choices in language are linked to associative factors: she draws on drama for hectic emotions and for weighted considerations, on lyric for loss, attenuated desire, and gentle lament.

The generic decorum of *Nobleman* extends to include principles of epistolary texts like *Les Lettres Portugaises*. This set of five epistles, now attributed to Guilleragues, was believed until the mid–twentieth century to be the authentic outpouring of Marianne Alcoforado, a Portuguese nun abandoned by a French cavalier. These letters have taken on an extraordinary significance in the history of British fiction since their 1678 translation by Sir Roger L'Estrange.[38] As a precursor to the epistolary novel, however, the text is surprisingly non-narrative. The letters externalize a struggle not of the immortal soul, as in Augustine, but of the amorous spirit; they attempt to communicate in the fullest sense of the word, to transmit not just words and their meanings but emotions, to create a kind of consensus.[39]

While tracing the language of *Les Lettres Portugaises* would prove interesting, French poetics is not my expertise. However, attention to the embellishments of L'Estrange suggests the influence of English poetic ideals on his translation. For the most part, L'Estrange tends toward poetic forms of compression: "il ne leur [les yeux] reste que des larmes et je ne les ai employés à aucun usage qu'à pleurer sans cesse" becomes "[my eyes] have Serv'd me but to weep withall" (note the perfect iambs).[40] Where L'Estrange is more wordy than the Nun, it is to introduce rhetorical balance: "Ah! j'en meurs de honte: mon désespoir n'est donc que dans mes lettres?" is rendered "Why do I not die of shame then, and shew you the despair of my Heart, as well as of my Letters?" (Guilleragues, *Lettres*, 72; Würzbach, *Novel in Letters*, 10). Generally, in seeking the correct idiom in which to render the Nun's passion, L'Estrange relies heavily on the language of English love poetry. In writing, "Am I then never to see those Eyes again, that have so often exchang'd Love with Mine, and Charm'd my very soul with Extacy, and Delight? Those eyes that were ten thousand worlds to mee, and all that I desir'd," he exchanges what should literally translate as "eyes in which I saw so much love" for the amorous reciprocity of a "metaphysical" like Donne; eyes that "made me know transports that overwhelmed me with joy" and that "were all things to me" become a poet's microcosm of delight (Würzbach, *Novel in Letters*, 5).[41] While the Nun tries to convince and convict her estranged lover by turns,[42] L'Estrange consistently makes poetic rather than forensic choices: statement is replaced by image, as the poetics of amorous debate require.

L'Estrange's choices are of a piece with the contemporary reception of the *Letters* in both French and English. On both sides of the channel, they were quickly rendered into verse. One of the English translators wrote: "And tho' the Original are in Prose, yet the Stile is so Poetical, that it Encourag'd the Author to put his Translation into Verse."[43] These verse renderings, both in France and in England, are second-rate, but the description of the letters as "poetical" is instructive. In addition to the rhetorical complexity of L'Estrange's translations and of the original, the absence of narrative and the emphasis on emotion linked them strongly to lyric forms.

Behn wrote another epistolary piece closely related to *The Portuguese Letters*, and revealing a similar lyric influence. *Love Letters to a Gentleman* is a series of eight epistles addressed to "Lycidas" (most probably Behn's lover, John Hoyle) and signed "Astrea." Like *The Portuguese Letters*, these are not a narrative sequence, but unlike their precursor, they do not chronicle a process of letting go. Behn's letters are a rhetorically charged set of fragments that, far from ending with dismissal, cease with the injunction, "I beg you will not fail to let me hear from you, today being Wednesday, and see you at night if you can."[44] *Gentleman* appeared in 1696 in *The Histories and Novels of the Late Ingenious Mrs Behn* and is more abstract than truly personal letters would be; however, it also seems autobiographically based.[45] No answers to the letters are known.

Gentleman shows traces of lyric influence in its descriptions of mental

processes. Particularly, Behn's use of metaphor owes a debt to poets like
Donne: "I do but (by this soft entertainment [writing]) look in my heart,
like a young gamester, to make it venture its last stake. This, I say, may be
the danger; I may come off unhurt, but cannot be a winner: why then
should I throw an uncertain cast, where I hazard all, and you nothing?
Your staunch prudence is proof against love, and all the banks on my
side. You are so unreasonable, you would have me pay, where I have
contracted no debt, you would have me give, and you, like a miser, would
distribute nothing. Greedy Lycidas!" (147–48). Behn here uses a traditional conceit of the contest of love; in characteristic Donnean fashion,
she first internalizes the conceit as drama (as in "Valediction: Forbidding Mourning"), then proceeds to use it as amorous argument ("The
Flea").[46] Behn/Astrea makes the conceit a new horizon of experience
and does not let it go until its usefulness is exhausted. The internaliza-
tion of metaphor underlines the difference between this language and
that of most drama — the conceit here is a site for meditation as much as
illustration.[47] The letter in which the passage appears is given further
"metaphysical" intonation. She moves quickly from the dicing conceit
to "Would my fever cure you? a curse on me, make you blessed? Say,
Lycidas, will it? I have heard, when two souls kindly meet, 'tis a vast
pleasure, as vast as the curse must be, when kindness is not equal" (148).
Donne's vocabulary of violently bruised yet tender sensibility, the vocabulary of poems like "The Dampe," is here.

The traces of poetic traditions in these prose heroic letters, as well as
the verse renderings of *The Portuguese Letters* (and even of *Nobleman* in
1735), may well be related to the parallel tradition of heroic verse epistles dating from Ovid's *Heroides*. These poems are elegiac and narrative,
but that distinction is somewhat fraught. Heroic epistles are written in
elegiac couplets, a meter used in both lyric and nonlyric subgenres. In
addition to a heavy narrative presence, heroic epistles are distinguished
from traditional lyrics in length and in verse form. However, heroic
epistles share with certain kinds of lyric a heavy emphasis on emotion. As
Anne Williams notes, based on a construction of lyric as a subjective
mode, "the heroic epistle . . . [although] not usually thought of as a lyric
genre . . . offer[s] obvious opportunities for lyricism — for a poem organized according to the motions of the letter-writer's consciousness."[48] In
accord with a more strict construction of lyric, there is evidence that
"Ovid, imitating Sappho, designed the *Heroides* to be sung" (Kauffman,
Discourses of Desire, 54), and James Wellington has argued for a broader
historical connection based on twin associations with music and emo-

tion: "It has been insufficiently remarked that a genre comparable to the heroic epistle in poetry enjoyed a distinguished parallel existence in music during the seventeenth and eighteenth centuries."[49] Like Ovid's poems, these works progress "according to sharply contrasted emotional segments. . . . The same principle of opposition has often been discussed as a significant characteristic of *Eloisa to Abelard* as well as of the heroides" (Wellington, *Eloisa to Abelard*, 31). For Dryden, heroides were important locations for the exploration of passionate experience, showing "the various movements of a soul combating betwixt two different passions."[50] Dryden connects such combat with drama, but whether or not heroic epistles are lyrics, in their representations of the emotional aspects of subjectivity, they explore territory that would become increasingly proper to the lyric over the next few centuries.

When Sylvia realizes that Philander has cast her off, she writes a heroide in the voice of reproach, and like Sappho, Œnone, or Ariadne, upbraids her lover for seducing and then abandoning her. Sylvia even sees herself as Ariadne (abandoned by Theseus), her predecessor in genre and dilemma (*Nobleman*, 144). Like Ovid's heroines, she makes much of the scene of her abandonment and the moment of writing; Behn, like Ovid, mixes genres.[51] Along with Ovidian elements is the language of reproach (of self and lover) common to Restoration heroic tragedy.[52] This heroic epistle also shows traces of lyric genres — it is in this letter that the passage "Hast thou forgot thy wondrous Art of loving," so close in form and style to Behn's odes, appears.

In a collection published by Tonson, Behn offers her own verse heroide, "A Paraphrase on Œnone to Paris" (1680). The poem is closer to imitation than paraphrase: Behn changes the tone of Ovid's epistle and makes several additions to the original scheme.[53] Among the latter are two verse paragraphs that stand out from their surroundings in ways suggestive of lyric influence. Both of these rely on pastoral imagery much more than either the rest of Behn's epistle or Ovid's original. As with the pastoral segments in *Nobleman*, these lines could easily figure as a lyric in something like the *Arcadia*:

> Now uncontroul'd we meet, uncheck't improve
> Each happier Minute in new Joys of Love!
> Soft were our hours! and Lavishly the Day
> We gave intirely up to Love, and Play.
> Oft to the cooling Groves, our Flocks we led,
> And seated on some shaded, flowry Bed;

Watch'd the united Wantons as they fed.
And all the Day my list'ning Soul I hung,
Upon the charming Music of thy Tongue,
And never thought the blessed hours too long.
No swain, no God like thee cou'd ever move,
Or had so soft an Art in whispering Love,
No wonder that thou wert Ally'd to *Jove*.
And when you pip'd, or sung, or danc'd or spoke,
The God appear'd in every Grace, and Look.
Pride of the Swains, and Glory of the Shades,
The Grief, and Joy of all the Love-sick Maids.
Thus whilst all hearts you rul'd without Controul,
I reign'd the absolute Monarch of your Soul.   ("Œnone," ll. 67–85)

The three sequential triplets create a unique situation in the poem and mark an intriguing artistic choice. The base pattern of "Œnone," as the genre requires, is the elegiac couplet; the set of triplets both interrupts this pattern and creates larger than usual internal groupings, the largest nonstanzaic rhyme division possible in elegiac verse. These units allow a greater cohesion and aural resonance than the couplet provides. Generally, the main formal distinction between elegiac and stanzaic verse has to do with the way sense units are constructed around rhyme: whether the poet uses a ballad stanza, terza rima, or octave and sestet, these patterns provide a different kind of formal complexity than the heroic or elegiac couplet can offer. Throughout "Œnone," triplets correspond to increased emotional intensity; the three triplets here suggest an emotional apogee as well as serving to encompass the temporal excess Œnone describes. Behn does not here build in stanzas pretty rooms — elegiac conventions disallow the spreading of sense or event from stanza to stanza. She does the next best thing. The couplet cannot (or at least does not) contain the emotion she here puts in play; a lyric stanza might suit better. Another of Behn's additions gives some confirmation to this suspicion:

Now like a Ghost I glide through ev'ry Grove,
Silent, and sad as Death, about I rove,
And visit all our Treasuries of Love!
This shade th'account of thousand Joys does hide,
As many more this murmuring Rivers side.
Where the dear Grass, as sacred, does retain
The print, where thee and I so oft have lain.

Upon this Oak thy Pipe, and Garland's plac'd,
That *Sycamore* is with thy Sheephook grac't.
Here feed thy Flocks, once lov'd though now thy scorn;
Like me forsaken, and like me forlorn!   ("Œnone," ll. 181–91)

Similar sentiments are found in the "Sapho to Phaon" heroide (a version by Pope is included in Tonson's collection), itself significant because of Sappho's identification as queen of lyric verse and mistress of emotional registers. More significant, however, is that when Behn retreads this ground, she does so in lyric verse. "On the First Discovery of Falseness in Amintas," a later lyric also heroical in tone, echoes the sense and style of the stanza from "Œnone":

There on a Bed of Moss and new-faln leaves,
    Which the Triumphant Trees once proudly bore,
Thô now thrown off by every wind that breaths,
    Despis'd by what they did adorn before,
And who, like useless me, regardless lye,
While springing beautys do the boughs supply.   (ll. 25–30)[54]

In reimagining the scene of abandonment and melancholy Behn gravitates toward lyric verse, not just in "Amintas" but also in "The Reflection." Behn seems to find the elegiac couplet inadequate to this kind of expression (and lyric verse more so); as we have seen, she also abstracts tonal and stylistic markers from lyric and places them in prose in her fiction.

The distinction I am here exploring between stanzaic and elegiac verse may seem specious, but considering the almost total ascendance of the heroic couplet soon to be accomplished in Augustan poetry, Behn's experiments with lyric nuances are particularly important. Emotional intensity is representable in any verse form, but the accumulated richness of the lyric repertoire offers a poet like Behn — a writer already invested in generic innovation — something not easily refused. If, by the end of the next century, forms like the sonnet or ode would become the chief loci of emotional expression in the poetic canon, these indications of dissatisfaction with couplets in treating subjects of emotional magnitude are significant.

Behn's prose offers specific corollaries to her lyric concerns. Let us return briefly to the prose "eclogue" from *Nobleman* with which this discussion began. However heavily marked that passage is by poetic cues, it is, of course, not a poem. If it were, it would not be amiss to call it a bad poem: in foregrounding lyric characteristics of the prose I am not undertaking the sort of claim for aesthetic value usually associated with "lyricality." This is an argument, rather, about diction, morphology, and address. But in saying this would be bad verse, if it were verse, I am also calling attention to Behn's insistence on interspersing recognizably poetic language with equally recognizable prosaic usage: "Say fond Love" and "the noysey hurry's of the Town" are followed by "Crowded Cabals, where mighty things are resolving."[55] Behn seems intent on grafting poetry onto prose, but it is a curious mixture. The presence of the pastoral is relatively easy to understand; its amorous language carries with it passion, artistic meditation, courtliness (manners of the Golden Age), and artificiality. It is not that the pastoral fails to be powerful and affecting; rather, that artificiality is what draws manipulative and faithless Philander to the form. The question then arises, why not use a straightforward lyric?

Given a certain type of motivation (the wounded lover, the apprehensive swain), pastoral language and imagery and even the cadence of poetic composition seem to Behn imaginatively appropriate; given her refusal to employ poems in these situations, however, we may conclude that she deems verse lyrics imaginatively — or functionally — *in*appropriate. Balancing lyric within prose allows Behn to fine-tune her field of representation. Critics like Judith Gardiner have found the sliding perspectives in *Nobleman* to be the essence of her narrative skill: "Moving between empathy and judgment, constantly adjusting the distance between readers and characters, Behn involves us in a comedy of sexual embarrassment, a tragedy of lost innocence, and a melodrama of erotic struggle, first through apparently unmediated letters, then through a third-person narrative. Drawing on old conventions, she helps create that new mixed genre, the novel" ("First English Novel," 210). Behn uses first- or third-person narrative strategies to control the distance of the reader from her work; she uses lyrically inflected prose to control the focus, to elevate or foreground emotions or ideas. Lyric prose gives texture to representation.

No contemporary would use a string of sonnets in such a context; each moment/poem requires too much intensity, a level of emotional concentration difficult to sustain. Likewise, the introduction of a complete lyric induces a disjunction, a sudden split in the pattern of representation, which the greater subtlety of lyric inflection may overcome. To take the connection to romance further, it is as if Behn dilates the experience of a Musidorus or Cleophila, widening it to fit the larger space of a letter. Emotions that would motivate the presence of a song in pastoral romance introduce the lyric mode in Behn, but as a variation within her prose. Behn explores the continuity of experience in the letter, and in doing so forbears the sudden jumps in register apparent in the *Arcadia* or its kin; she does not formally separate lyric on the page, she produces lyrically inflected prose.

The one moment in which Behn includes a verse lyric offers confirmation of this interpretation. Philander writes to Octavio an account of his first sight of Calista: resting on "the shady brink" of "a little Rivulet," he overhears her singing a lament, which he reproduces in full for his friend (*Nobleman*, 173). Lyric only appears as a separate kind in *Nobleman* when it represents the subjective experience of another, not the fictional writer. The focus, the grain of representation must radically shift to encompass it. Lyrics are interpolated in Behn when the experience is proper to the speaker; they are blended in with surrounding prose, as in the blazon following Calista's song: "But, Oh my Friend! how shall I present her to thee in that Angel form, she then appear'd to me? all young! all ravishing as new born light to lost benighted Travellers; her Face, the fairest in the World was adorn'd with Curls of shining jett ty'd up — I know not how, all carelessly with Scarlet Ribbon mixt with pearls; her Robe was gay and rich, such as young Royal Brides put on when they undress for joys! her Eyes were black, the softest heaven e're made" (174).

Behn's mixture of lyric and prose had an extended afterlife. Most immediately, literary experimentation in the early eighteenth century combined poetry with a range of forms. Lyrics appeared in narrative frameworks in manuscripts by women poets throughout the late Stuart period, as Carol Barash has shown.[56] In fact, she maintains, poetry was fundamental to the literary consciousness of most contemporary women writers: "virtually every woman who kept a diary or commonplace book wrote or copied verses now and then. And, judging from the poetry transcribed in commonplace books, many of these women read a great deal of it" (*English Women's Poetry*, 20).

§ The combination of tradition and example in romance, Behn, and the commonplace book or diary suggests a cultural context for the continued presence of lyric in prose fiction in the eighteenth century. One of the best-selling novels of the early century, Eliza Haywood's 1719 *Love in Excess; or, The Fatal Enquiry* (published the same year as *Robinson Crusoe* and equally popular), shows the same sense of generic flexibility visible in *Nobleman*. Haywood's partially epistolary story traces the intrigues of the ambitious Count D'Elmont as he goes from seducer to seduced and is eventually redeemed by faithfully loving Melliora. As Richard Savage wrote in a puff in the second volume of *Love in Excess*, Haywood possessed a genius for evocative description:

> Thy prose in sweeter harmony refines,
> Than numbers flowing thro' the Muse's lines;
> What beauty ne'er could melt, thy touches fire,
> And raise a music that can love inspire;
> Soul-thrilling accents all our senses wound,
> And strike with softness, whilst they charm with sound!
> When thy Count pleads, what fair his suit can flye?
> Or when thy nymph laments, what eyes are dry?
> Ev'n Nature's self in sympathy appears,
> Yields sigh for sigh, and melts in equal tears;
> For such descriptions thus at once can prove
> The force of language, and the sweets of love.[57]

Savage stops short of claiming poetic status for Haywood but insists on a lyric character in her prose — its musicality, sympathetic force, and linguistic virtuosity. Indeed, the passion and eroticism of Haywood's writing are partially the result of her adaptation of the language and sentiment of courtly lyric.

As in *Nobleman* or the *Portuguese Letters*, the amorous epistle carries lyric echoes. D'Elmont writes: "No, no fair, injured softness, return, and bless the eyes of every beholder! Shine out again in your native lustre, uneclipsed by grief. The star of beauty and the guide of love. — And, if my unlucky presence will be a damp to the brightness of your fires, I will for ever quit the place. — Tho' I could wish you'd give me leave sometimes to gaze upon you, and draw some hoped presages of future fortune from the benignity of your influence" (*Love in Excess*, 99). The flavor of courtly address from *Astrophil and Stella* or *Amoretti* waits behind these lines, even altered by the effects of epistolary intimacy. Without the constraints of form in sonnet or canzone, given the freedom of a letter, D'Elmont may change registers without comic effect or disrupting the emotional timbre of his words. The aptly named Frankville also uses this strategy (after lamenting the insufficiency of sympathy, a central problem in eighteenth-century lyric, as I will show) in his attempt to describe the birth of his passion for Camilla:

But if language is too poor to paint her charms, how shall I make you sensible of the effects of them on me! the surprize — the love — the adoration which this fatal view [his first of Camilla] involved me in, but by that which, you say, your self felt at the first sight of Melliora. I was, methought, all spirit, — I beheld her with raptures, such as we imagine souls enjoy when freed from earth, they meet each other in the realms of glory; 'twas heaven to gaze upon her. But Oh! the bliss was short, the envious trees obscured her lustre from me. — The moment I lost sight of her, I found my *passion* by my *pain*; the *joy* was vanished, but the *sting* remained. (196–97)

Although Frankville might wish that D'Elmont's experience of love would make description superfluous, it does not; the descriptive language he chooses, proving "the force of language and the sweets of love," in Savage's words (86), is both that of Platonic idealism and the poetry it inspires. The lyric of rapture (e.g., "The Extasie" or "Aire and Angels") aligns speaker and reader with ideals of love so that the language intimates the structure of delight, attempting to draw it within sight, if not within reach. Lyric speech in this case aims at affective description, aims to represent experience so that it approaches consensuality. The poetic character of this description, culminating in what is nearly a tetrameter couplet, provides its own set of pleasures, enhancing and balancing the pleasure of the emotions described. Here Frankville/Haywood also mixes poetic description with narrative in a way evocative of verse romance (Spenser, especially), allowing subjective registers of emotion to coexist with and not to impede narrative progression.

Haywood includes verse lyric twice in *Love in Excess*, both times in letters or other written communication. She uses lyric with the need to evoke as well as describe, as did Behn. D'Elmont's brother Brillian, in a fit of amorous despondency, scratches a couplet on a pedestal: "Hopeless, and silent, I must still adore, / Her heart's more hard than stone whom I'd implore" (76). His beloved Ansellina, happening along, responds with a couplet of her own: "You wrong your love, while you conceal your pain, / Stones will dissolve with constant drops of rain" (76). Like Romeo and Juliet, these two lovers join one another in completing a poem; here, as in the play, the mutual poetic endeavor implies a special kind of intimacy. They are brought together as the emotionally expansive voice of lyric.

Camilla, separated from Frankville, sends him a lyric in a letter: "The unfortunate Camilla's Complaint to the Moon, for the absence of her Dear Henricus Frankville." She prefaces this charmingly titled poem by setting the scene of its composition: "Gazing on the moon last night, her lustre brought fresh to my memory those transporting moments, when by that light, I saw you first a lover; and, I think inspired me, who am not usually fond of versifying to make her this complaint" (205–6). In figuring the scene of Frankville's declaration of love, the picture of Camilla's emotions is as important as (if not more than) the landscape. Still more crucial is Frankville's emotional alignment with both its poetic and erotic tones: "Pity the extravagance of a passion which only charms like thine could create, nor too severely chide this soft impertinence, which I could not refrain from sending you, when I can neither see you, nor hear from you, to write, gives some little respite to my pains, because I am sure of being in your thoughts" (207). Although she explicitly asks for "pity," her poem calls for a different response, stirring the memory of their first erotic encounter.

Haywood's use of verse underlines the ability of lyric to work for affective consensus (or the requirement that it do so): shared sensibility is its end (and occasional means). Lyric is most often subjective, but there is no reason that its subject must always speak for him- or herself; Milton's use of interpolated and impersonal sonnets in *Paradise Lost* testifies to this. From the invocations to the "Hail Wedded Love" epithalamium and multiple sonnetlike moments, *Paradise Lost* testifies to Milton's "explorations of the lyric possibilities within epic form."[58] Anna Nardo identifies the interpolated sonnets in *Paradise Lost* based on their "bipartite structure, particular imbalance of parts, and turn of thought so characteristic of the Italian sonnet" ("Submerged Sonnet," 23); even though these segments may be shorter or longer than fourteen lines, they retain the basic character of a lyric form. The resultant fragments range in theme from "God's fifteen-line laud of the warrior angel in book IV" to Eve's love-sonnet in Eden (4:639–56) and the poem's final thirteen lines ("Submerged Sonnet," 28). These embedded lyrics tend toward songs of praise, even in despair, and serve to forge emotional alliance between readers and our fallen parents. The power of the final lines of the epic involves a lyric effect: "Although these thirteen lines are narrative and no speaker comments, Milton here is not confined by the 'laws' of genre. This conclusion, a remarkable mingling of both decorums and genres, expresses the emotions appropriate to the single narrative scene of expulsion, the larger drama of the fall, and the epic vision of the total work. As the narrator refrains from comment, Adam, Eve, and the reader experience the tragedy of loss, the heroism of hope, and the ever-present possibility of lyric love simultaneously" (33). Stripping the sonnet of an overt "I," Milton uses lyric nonetheless to draw readers into accord with a subject-position, a framework of sensibility and emotion laid out in the beautiful compression of these last lines.

Haywood similarly makes use of depersonalized lyric, diffusing lyric sensibility throughout her prose. This is clear in the partner piece to Camilla's nocturne. Earlier in the novel, the "inconsiderate" Amena puts herself in a dangerous situation with D'Elmont (who is too attractive for anyone's good) (*Love in Excess*, 63). She steals from her father's house and enters the Tuileries in the dead of night. Amena places herself in circumstances where only one thing can happen. Haywood's eroticism often approaches the pornographic; here, however, she replaces the physical and emotional aspects of the scene with poetic landscape description:

> all nature seemed to favour his design, the pleasantness of the place, the silence of the night, the sweetness of the air, perfumed with a thousand various odours wafted by gentle breezes from adjacent gardens compleated the most delightful scene that ever was, to offer up a sacrifice to love; not a breath but flew winged with desire, and sent soft thrilling wishes to the soul; Cynthia her self, cold as she is reported, assisted in the inspiration and sometimes shone with all her brightness, as it were to feast their ravished eyes with gazing on each others beauty; then veiled her beams in clouds, to give the lover boldness, and hide the virgins blushes. (63)

Haywood draws on the language of Ovidian narratives and Renaissance epyllia, but more importantly, she makes the landscape an *alibi* for emotional and psychological events. This is more than the pathetic fallacy: it is not precisely that the landscape is in sympathy with (or mimics) Amena's emotional state but that poetic description with its use of tropes and figures gives access to Amena's emotions without giving us access to Amena herself. It is literally an alibi, an alternate site, for subjective experience. The landscape is not important so much because it mirrors Amena's experience (or vice versa) but because it allows readers to echo it, to come into alignment, understanding, consensus with it.[59]

When, immediately following this description, Haywood asks, "What now could poor Amena do, surrounded with so many powers, attacked by such a charming force without, betrayed by tenderness within?" the answer has already been given. Poetic description provides an evocative, almost parallel version of Amena's rising passion and waning discretion. The description of her passions, which would seem to answer the question, does not: "Vertue and pride, the guardians of her honor fled from her breast, and left her to her foe, only a modest bashfulness remained"

(63). This may define her state, but it does not call for the reader's emotional response, as did the earlier view of moon and winged breaths. The language of the passions is not entrusted with evoking affect; poetic language carries this burden.[60]

Haywood frequently thus extracts lyric sensibilities and language from their first-person home and uses them to suffuse an entire scene with emotional fervor, a sort of landscape erotics. Most frequently this draws on figures like those of Donne's "Extasie." Of Melliora and D'Elmont, she writes, "With these words she sunk wholly into his arms unable to speak more. Nor was he less dissolved in rapture, both their souls seemed to take wing together, and left their bodies motionless, as unworthy to bear a part in their more elevated bliss" (130).[61] More powerfully still, "The Extasie" appears in their final reunion (this particular lyric could be "their song"): "A while their lips were cemented! rivetted together with kisses, such kisses! as collecting every sence in one, exhale the very soul, and mingle spirits! Breathless with bliss, then would they pause and gaze, then joyn again" (265). "Cemented" seems to come from "The Extasie," where the lovers sit, their "hands . . . firmely cimented" (1.5), and Donne's ecstatic lovers gaze at each other so intently that their eyes were "thred . . . upon one double string" (ll. 7–8). Haywood's scene is more erotically explicit than Donne's (she writes of "straining gasps"), for her aims are different; she certainly, however, makes use of the vocabulary Donne and lyrics like his have given her.

The hypertrophic figures of emotion in *Love in Excess* would not remain in style. Haywood recognized them as excessive, if the title is any indication; nonetheless, she expected them to be affective. They are clearly influenced by Renaissance sensibilities, and there is often a dash of the Miltonic;[62] this flavor makes them seem retrogressive. Haywood's reliance on models of the previous century was crucial in a period when contemporary lyric was on the wane, crowded out, perhaps, by a new star in the sky.

§ Pope is no stranger to lyric or the personal; he stars, sometimes wickedly, in poems from Horatian ode to epistle and beyond, but while he feels the powerful attraction of Renaissance versions of lyric, he ultimately refuses them.[63] I am interested in the contours of Pope's refusal of these lyric genes and their relation to the epistle. Pope was led to explore the parameters — and consequences — of forbidden and hopeless passion in "Eloisa to Abelard" (1717) after encountering John Hughes's 1713 translation of the letters of Heloise and Abelard (letters embellished and fictionalized over the course of a few hundred years). As with all of the *Heroides'* heroines Eloisa has been abandoned; however, because of her lover's castration and her own life in a convent, she does not have the hopes for reunion her predecessors cherish. While Eloisa is torn between desire and the impossibility of fulfillment, Abelard does not suffer thus, for he is freed from the carnal: "the fates, severely kind, ordain / A cool suspense from pleasure and from pain" (ll. 250–51). Eloisa's body is both painfully present and made obsolete by the violence done to Abelard; her passion for him remains in every vein, but with no hope of satisfaction. There are perverse splits between desire and fulfillment, between interior and exterior realities, and within her own soul. This consciousness of division shapes the poem; its partner is a yearning for reciprocity and union.

When Eloisa and Abelard were lovers, their physical intimacy, if not a guarantee of their emotional union, offered a correspondence between emotional and physical experiences. Eloisa's bodily pleasure constantly verified her emotional place in the world. But, from the first lines of the poem, that comforting verification (or reification) of her interior experience is revoked. Her wonder at the difference between that anterior state of being and her current one motivates the question with which the poem begins: "In these deep solitudes and awful cells," what does passionate disturbance mean? Abandonment and the cloister emphasize for Eloisa the always-present separation of consciousness and its objects, a disjunction that, though here a source of pain, enables her to "hide" Abelard's name "within that close disguise" of her heart (l. 11).

Eloisa longs for an ecstasy of epistolary communication to replace what she has lost:

> Then share thy pain, allow that sad relief;
> Ah, more than share it! give me all thy grief.
> Heaven first taught letters for some wretch's aid,
> Some banished lover, or some captive maid;
> They live, they speak, they breathe what love inspires,
> Warm from the soul, and faithful to its fires,
> The virgin's wish without her fears impart,
> Excuse the blush, and pour out all the heart,
> Speed the soft intercourse from soul to soul,
> And waft a sigh from Indus to the Pole.   (ll. 49–58)

This passage echoes Donne's descriptions of letters as "a kind of extasie, and a departure and secession and suspension of the soul, which doth then communicate it self to two bodies," an ecstatic sharing linked to

that of "the dialogue of one" in "The Extasie."[64] The mutuality for
which Eloisa longs is as much lyric as it is epistolary. Quoting Eloisa's
desire for a "happy state! when souls each other draw, / When love is
liberty, and nature law: / All then is full, possessing and possessed" (ll.
91–93), Leo Damrosch suggests that "Pope imagines a pre-artificial
state in which, as in Donne's lyrics, mutual understanding might be
perfect and love might impose its own irresistible law."[65] Reuben Brower
has also sensed Donne's presence in the poem: "If Pope was not in fact
remembering Donne's poem, he was remembering [a certain kind of]
poetry of love."[66] Eloisa recalls and laments the passing of a world of
mutuality, which is also one of lyric; Pope himself is not far behind. In
the final verse paragraph, the poem's memory of Donne and lyric inten-
sifies. As Williams has noted, Eloisa finds relief in imagining a scene that
echoes "The Canonization" (25–26). She hopes the tomb she will share
with Abelard will be a place of pilgrimage for lovers in years to come:

> If ever chance two wandering lovers brings
> To Paraclete's white walls and silver springs,
> O'er the pale marble shall they join their heads,
> And drink the falling tears each other sheds;
> Then sadly say, with mutual pity moved,
> Oh may we never love as these have loved!   (ll. 347–52)

Just as in Donne's "We'll build in sonnets pretty rooms," poem as well as
stone is to be the lover's memorial: Eloisa imagines "some future bard"
who will sing of their fate (l. 359).

We should read the future bard's sentence to "image charms he must
behold no more" with double reference: the faded image is cast as Pope's
memory of a lover, but this vision of the lost past is also an image of lyric.
However, if Pope is remembering Donne's lyrics in this poem, he does
not imitate them. Allusions to lyric are as close as he will come, and he
does not make these in *propria persona*; like Eloisa's experience, the poem
is divided between (lyric) ideal and (stylistic) reality. In Behn's or Haywood's epistles, lyrics are absorbed into the surface of the prose, expanding the sensuous possibilities of speech. Here, lyric appears as a tangential presence, touching just beneath the surface but always passing on,
and passing away. Pope approaches amatory lyric in an oblique gesture
that is also one of renunciation, just as Eloisa's letter bids good-bye to a
fantasy of complete mutuality. Part of the pathos of this poem comes
with its echoes of a poetic past. For Eloisa the lyric moment (the ideal
"pre-artificial world" of lovers' communion) is fled, because sensual

communion is no longer possible; for Pope the lyric moment has passed because its idiom and structure have been buried in neoclassical Elysian fields (its heroes do not walk about).

Pope's elaborate approach to lyric in "Eloisa to Abelard" is exemplary; another of his epistles, "Epistle to Arbuthnot" (1735), makes an equally palpable gesture. Ostensibly, this poem is in the mode of his other satirical letters; however, "Arbuthnot" is at base a poet's complaint, a genre with strong lyric affiliations.[67] Complaints traditionally are songs lamenting and sometimes detailing abuse, pleas for sympathy that carry tones of outrage. Cowley's complaint of the 1660s (probably the most famous before "Arbuthnot") is just this, an ode that describes the neglected poet's vision of his Muse and his betrayer.[68]

Cowley uses multiple voices and personae in "The Complaint," beginning with an impersonal narrator, shifting to the voice of the Muse, and ending with what "The Melancholy *Cowley* said." The poem drips with pathos from the first lines:

> In a deep Vision's intellectual scene,
>   Beneath a Bow'r for sorrow made,
>   Th'uncomfortable shade,
>   Of the black Yew's unlucky green,
> Mixt with the mourning Willow's careful gray,
> Where Reverend *Cham* cuts out his Famous Way,
>   The Melancholy *Cowley* lay.

While most of the poem remains thus bordering on Cowley's consciousness (ostensibly exterior, but heavily overlaid with his woes), we eventually fall into his inner world:

> The Melancholy *Cowley* said:
> Ah wanton foe, dost thou upbraid
> The Ills which thou thy self hast made?
> When in the Cradle innocent I lay,
> Thou, wicked Spirit, stol'est me away,
>   And my abused Soul didst bear
> Into thy new-found Worlds, I know not where,
>   Thy Golden Indies in the Air.   (ll. 83–90)

Since the mid-eighteenth century (up to which time he was the most popular English poet) Cowley has lost much clout; however, this poem is surprisingly good, given Johnson's acerbic and dismissive assessment in *Lives of the Poets:* "he published his pretensions and his discontent in an

ode called *The Complaint*, in which he styles himself the *melancholy* Cowley. This met with the usual fortune of complaints, and seems to have
excited more contempt than pity."[69] Considering the space Johnson devotes to Cowley's other odes, this comment is truly contemptuous: more
lines are given to a parody of the poem than to "The Complaint" itself.
For a century that placed great value on pity, it may seem odd that a call
for it meets only (and seemingly for Johnson, justly) with contempt. It is
the hint of *interest,* or rather self-interest, that sours this poem for the
century's greatest critic. Perhaps lyric, focusing too much on the self, is
indecorous.[70]

Pope struggles in his "Bill of Complaint" against the same threat of
self-interest. As he writes in the poem's advertisement, self-defense is
"so Awkward a Task" that he almost never completed it, whatever his
provocations. Pope uses humor and a brittle wit (in addition to Arbuthnot's moral umbrella) to stave off charges of self-pity and interest.
But in order to access the bitterness he feels, he must do something. If a
poem such as Cowley's violates public decorum by using lyric unfairly—
to raise pity and move his patrons to action—Pope stretches poetic
decorum with his first lines: "Shut, shut the door, good *John!* fatigu'd I
said, / Tye up the knocker, say I'm sick, I'm dead." It takes a gesture
toward the stage, a dramatic opening of monologue and scene, for Pope
to speak of "this long Disease, my Life" (l. 132). Pope even ventures to
praise himself primarily in a string of negatives:

> Not Fortune's Worshipper, nor Fashion's Fool,
> Not Lucre's Madman, nor Ambition's Tool,
> Not proud, nor servile, . . .   (ll. 334–36)
>
> not in Fancy's Maze he wander'd long   (l. 340)
>
> Laugh'd at the loss of Friends he never had,
> The dull, the proud, the wicked, and the mad;
> The distant Threats of Vengeance on his head,
> The Blow unfelt, the Tear he never shed.   (ll. 346–49)

As in "Eloisa to Abelard," Pope will not speak of emotion or self with
comfort in an early modern (rather than classical) lyric voice. Especially
in his epistolary mode, self and writing for Pope press against one another, as in Epistle 1.i, where he offers to give up writing (though he of
course does not): it "keeps me from myself" (41).[71] There are modes
appropriate to self-revelation, but lyric is not one of them.

In the next chapter, I connect this difficulty to shifting ideals in moral aesthetics, but here I wish to point out the rapidly changing status of lyric and letter as partner forms in representing subjective experience. For Pope, amatory lyric is a temptation that must be refused, as in "Eloisa to Abelard." Lyric may pose a violation of decorum: a lyric call for pity or exposition of his wrongs would only open him up to further abuse. Thus, "Arbuthnot" is a refusal of one kind of lyric personality in favor of a mixture of genres and tones. Pope even presents himself as a subject of praise, a lyric subject (as in lauds or hymns), as a series of negations. A contrary motion is at work in the novelists I have discussed. Behn seeks out lyric and brings it transformed into her prose. Haywood also uses lyric inflections in her novels, expanding upon the usual use of lyric in letters as first-person form to suffuse entire scenes with sensual power. Chronologically, from Cowley to Pope or Behn to Haywood, there is a shift in the tone of personal speech and the attitude toward or use of lyric for this purpose. The change I have here sketched becomes increasingly evident in the poetry of the early and mid–eighteenth century, and the next chapter begins to assess tensions surrounding lyric in the works of some of the century's major poets.

Three

Lyric Tensions: Sympathy, Displacement, and Self into the Midcentury

Lyrics appeared in a variety of shapes in the first half of the eighteenth century, and in this chapter I sketch the contours of lyric expression in the context of challenges to it, tracing forces that governed the absorption of lyric into the novel genre.[1] Lyrics in the period belong largely in three nonexclusive categories. A contemporary critic would recognize lyric in hymns and psalms, odes, or certain kinds of light verse (mainly pastoral or amorous songs, but Anacreontic odes and ballads, too). All these are not equal. The most prevalent lyric kind is the hymn, present in its congregational form or used for more personal purposes, as with Elizabeth Singer Rowe, Mary Leapor, or Isaac Watts. The poet/singer, as a single voice or in company with others, laments, gives praise or thanks, or pleads for closeness with God. These lyrics are about emotional and spiritual community, either with other Christians or with the divine being.[2] Praise and emotional elevation (even excess) also characterize one of the grandest genres of the period, the greater ode. The Pindaric, inaugurated by Cowley in the mid–seventeenth century, became a (contested) model for sublime and patriotic expression from Dryden and Behn through the romantics. Horace, Alcaeus, Sappho, and others also lent voice to lyric verse.[3] Light verse can be broadly divided into two subcategories: the offspring of Cavalier poetry and province of poets like Matthew Prior, Joseph Addison, and John Gay, and the broadside ballad.[4] Most important, lyric in the period took on a strongly social character, constantly measuring itself by (or mocking) standards of decorum, audience, and authority.

Each of these kinds fits into a hierarchy based on propriety and manner of expression that ranged from encomia of gods and men, those kinds so well received by Plato, to subliterary doggerel verse (Maclean,

"Action to Image," 410). In line with the prevailing standards of moral criticism, erotic lyric ranked quite low: the moral questions surrounding eroticism (figured as libertinage or bucolic excess) influenced perceptions of the "lower" kind of lyric throughout the early century.[5] Shaftesbury felt that "there is this difference only between [the muses of lyric] and the more heroic dames: that they can more easily be perverted and take the vicious form. For what person of any genius or masterly command in the poetic art could think of bringing the epic or tragic muse to act the pander, or be subservient to effeminacy and cowardice?"[6] Lyric as category, then, was subject to fragmentary pressures: on one hand, it was liable to moral denigration, and on the other, it was elevated to almost unreachable heights with the greater ode. Margaret Doody partly attributes the unstable status of lyric to the perversions brought about by satire, and the taint left by Rochester and others, and Nigel Smith comments that a general resistance to lyric genres began with the discrediting of amorous lyric around the Civil Wars.[7] The greater ode and hymn were the beneficiaries of a new critical attention to the importance of emotion in composition and effect — the concern that helped marginalize erotic verse.[8] It is in this period that the shift to an emotional emphasis in verse would become codified in criticism (whatever the actual practice of the preceding years).[9]

Given the new critical attention (paid by John Dennis, Robert Lowth, Simon Patrick, and others) to the psychological and emotional characteristics of lyric verse, we may retrospectively, but not too anachronistically, expand an inquiry into the cultural and literary domain of the lyric to include poems like Watts's "Hurry of the Spirits, in a Fever and Nervous Disorders" (1734) and Finch's "Life's Progress" (1709) or "A Nocturnal Reverie" (1713), poems of personal importance whose mood is of moral meditation or instruction. Many of these poems do not use a rhyme or metrical scheme traditionally associated with lyric, but considering that lyric during this time increasingly tends toward the presence of an expansive emotional consciousness, these poems have lyric affinities. Such poems also participate in the kind of elevated emotion contemporary poets and critics associated with the sublimity of the Pindaric or the odal hymn. In effect, lyric in the early eighteenth century is unstable as a larger critical or creative category, and is also subtly expansive.

The mood of recent criticism has been toward a broadened conception of lyric based on an understanding of its instability in the period, teaching us that an accurate analysis of the lyric mode in the Augustan era requires a creative approach. It is imperative to look for lyric to appear in new places or in different ways: in the verse epistle, the Horatian imitation, or the satirical poems of Swift.[10] Another key form of lyric in the early decades of the century is the absorbed lyric: this includes the fragments woven into novels such as *Love in Excess*, but also the songs of *The Beggar's Opera* or lyric passages in a long *sui generis* poem like *The Seasons*. In this chapter I attempt to understand the context of lyric absorption, to isolate characteristics of the contemporary lyric that influenced its appearance in other forms.

My other concern here is to continue the revision of "preromantic" accounts of eighteenth-century lyric that focus largely on a handful of poets and a small canon of works: Thomson's *Seasons*, the odes of Collins, Gray, and the Wartons, Akenside's *Pleasures of the Imagination*, Winchilsea's "Nocturnal Reverie," Cowper's *Task*, the works of the Graveyard School, the sonnets of Bowles and Charlotte Smith, the ballad revival, and the sentimental verse of poets like Helen Maria Williams, among very few others.[11] These are, of course, poems the romantics themselves identify as important influences, and not all are strictly lyric; their presence in a reconstructed poetic tradition (all traditions are necessarily back formations—this is not a problem or a fault, as long as care for historical accuracy is taken) is the result of tracing particular conditions: the conception of nature in descriptive poetry; the development of the creative imagination; the history of the poetic self as a nexus of threads of observation and description; the treatment of mourning; the emergence of the poetry and culture of sensibility; patterns of satire and irony; and so forth. The novel intervenes at significant points in these developing literary trajectories; I reexamine the poetry that is part of these histories of transformation in the years leading up to the midcentury. The period under concern begins around 1720 and extends through the early 1750s, the time corresponding to the publication of the signal works of the early novel tradition, from *Robinson Crusoe* to *Sir Charles Grandison*. These poems are the first written with the novel as an active presence on the literary scene.

Eric Partridge made this connection in 1924. In *Eighteenth-Century English Romantic Poetry*, he traces three periods of major development before *Lyrical Ballads*: 1713–30, 1742–51, and 1771–98. The first of these includes the poetry of Winchilsea, Thomson, and Allen Ramsay. He argues that the second is fostered by "the great period of the eighteenth-century novel, from *Pamela to Humphry Clinker* . . . : while the novel flourished, so, to a lesser extent, did poetry."[12] While I do not agree that from 1753 to 1761 only "two notable novels, *Rasselas* and *Tristram Shandy*" appeared, I believe that novel and poetry have a symbiotic relation. Partridge argues that this relation involves the novel's innovations in character, scene, and emotion.[13] I here extend Partridge's beginning to include questions of the social validity of the personal.

The following pages offer some necessary background to question novelists' progressive redefinition of writing. What are the contours of personal experience in the poetry that, in the view of critics from W. J. Bate to Marshall Brown, had the greatest influence on the trajectory of the lyric in the years to come? What, in the history of lyric, do these poems contribute, and what do they leave unspoken, unheard, and unseen? In answering these questions, I focus primarily on *The Seasons*, Collins's "Ode to Evening," and Gray's "Elegy Written in a Country Churchyard" and "Ode on a Distant Prospect of Eton College," but the argument extends to a range of other poems (adumbrated throughout). Lyric in this chapter is a special kind of personal utterance, a view that may at once seem both too broad and too narrow. This approach is intended to be heuristic rather than definitive: I begin with a set of lyric subgenres — hymn, laud, ode, and nocturne — and proceed to explore the position of personal expression within them, looking to distinguish the parameters involved in expressing personal experience. Among poems that had significant influence in the development of lyric (in the case of *The Seasons*), I have chosen individual works or fragments where readers are placed in close contact with a speaking "I" — not because there are not other kinds of lyric but because my interest here is in personal utterance. What happens in midcentury poems where an "I" speaks of itself? Bodies disappear.

These poems place a peculiar set of features at the basis of self-representation. Theories of sympathy and the constraints of personal or sexual decorum offer significant challenges to lyric, culminating generally in a displacement of the lyric body and voice. My aim is to examine the instability prevalent in the poetry of the self-as-"I." I read these poems in terms broadly applicable to questions of genre and as parts of a literary landscape that had suddenly, drastically, expanded. This chapter highlights various aspects of what may best be described as a suspicion of personal speech in contemporary thought and poetics. Poets like Thomson, Winchilsea, Collins, and Gray consistently locate the possibilities of shared sensible experience in communal voices and shifting personifications, concealing bodies even as they attempt to represent bodily experience.

§ It might seem strange to begin an exploration of lyric utterance in eighteenth-century British poetry with Thomson's *Seasons* (1726–46).[14]

The poem has no scenic unity; unlike most lyrics, no dramatic situation calls it into being; with its myriad diction, it can be said to have no single clear voice, speaking now in the terms of a geologist, now as the narrator of a romance, now in a tone reminiscent of Virgil's *Georgics* or of *Paradise Lost*. Generically, the poem is remarkable: Johnson describes it as altogether "of a new kind."[15] Still, it is here that major twentieth-century constructions of preromanticism often start, for the poem absorbs lyric in interesting ways.[16] Thomson was arguably the most popular British poet from the death of Pope to the end of the century. His approach to the lyric, especially as a register of emotion, is important both as an index of contemporary stylistics and as a way of gauging the manner of his later influence. Thomson allows me to organize a set of facts about the uses of lyric in midcentury poetry that this book goes on to explore: the contours of lyric absorption, the importance of landscape, the question of sympathy, problems of meditation, and what I am calling the displacement of the lyric voice and, often, of the lyric body.[17]

In *The Daring Muse*, Doody argues for the primacy of the poet-as-speaker in Augustan verse: "the reader must feel with the poet, see things as he sees them, accept the mental connections and associations that his recorded experience brings into play. It is almost a rule of necessity that a *sui generis* poem must have a well-developed 'I' as a means of unifying the poem" (73). If the "I" of the speaker is intended as a means of unifying *The Seasons*, it does not do a very good job. Multiple kinds of speech and the ways of seeing or knowing they imply (Newtonian physics, Spenserian romance, Miltonic epic, the nascent science of geology) suggest not so much the vision of a single "I" as the accumulated knowledge of an entire society.[18] One man has brought these disparate images and kinds of knowledge together, but what filters perception and shapes representation in Thomson is system rather than self—the harmony of creation or the moral music of nature. As he describes his subject in the concluding "A Hymn on the Seasons,"

> These, as they change, Almighty Father! these
> Are but the varied God. The rolling year
> Is full of thee . . .   (ll. 1–3)

> Mysterious round! what skill, what force divine,
> Deep-felt in these appear! a simple train,
> Yet so delightful mixed, with such kind art,
> Such beauty and beneficence combined,
> Shade unperceived so softening into shade,

And all so forming an harmonious whole
That, as they still succeed, they ravish still.   (ll. 21–27)

All vision is subordinate to moral knowledge, to the understanding that
there is one mind (not the poet's) that governs nature. In view of this universal mind, no single self is adequate — the last lines of the "Hymn"
evoke this on a personal scale: "But I lose / Myself in him, in light ineffa-
ble! / Come then, expressive Silence, muse his praise." In this lyric the self
is a vanishing point; more important is the praise of many voices: "Nature, attend; join every living soul / Beneath the spacious temple of the
sky, / In adoration join; and ardent raise / One general song!" (ll. 37–40).

What may seem like poetic humility has other implications. The
poet's "I" is subordinate throughout the poem; most often it is hard to
place him in his landscape. As Patricia Meyer Spacks argues, much of the
earliest imagery in *The Seasons* is too allegorical to be attached to mimetic sight: "And see where surly Winter passes off / Far to the north,
and calls his ruffian blasts" (ll. 11–12) draws our attention to no visible
event.[19] This oblique visual frame denies perspective and suggests the
slipperiness of the poet-self:

Come gentle Spring, ethereal mildness, come;
And from the bosom of yon dropping cloud,
While music wakes around, veiled in a shower
Of shadowy roses, on our plains descend.   (ll. 1–4)

The deictic "yon dropping cloud" seems to invoke a particular place, but
the idea that this stretch of landscape is the home of a particular soul, the
speaker, is subordinated to the communal — "our plains." This is the
voice, ideally, of a we, and it sounds in a landscape where the individual is
often effaced. As John Barrell argues, Thomson's speaker "see[s] the
landscape, not as something in which he is involved, and which is all
around him, but as something detached from him, *over there.*"[20] A similar practice marks an earlier, generically important topographical poem,
Finch's "Nocturnal Reverie" (1713), which enacts an elaborate deferral
of the speaker's appearance until four lines from the end. The completion of the phrase with which the poem begins, "In such a night," is
finally achieved as an individual "me" only to fade immediately into a
communal and proprietary "our" at the poem's end: "In such a night let
me abroad remain, / Till morning breaks, and all's confused again: /
Our cares, our toils, our clamours are renewed, / Or pleasures, seldom
reached, again pursued."[21] For Winchilsea, it seems a kind of sexual

decorum — a woman alone in such a night makes so odd a figure that the less she is seen, the better. Yet, her male counterparts in topographical poems seem also subject to a decorum enforcing bodily disappearance, as in Pope's "Windsor Forest" (1713), Joseph Warton's *Enthusiast; or, The Lover of Nature* (1744–48), or Akenside's *Pleasures of Imagination* (1744); this seems characteristic of this meditative mood.[22]

The decorum to which bodily presence is subject is one of community identity and sympathetic possibilities. *The Seasons*, as Dustin Griffin points out, is concerned with a national sense of place; land is defined via "a series of patriotic topoi" (*Patriotism and Poetry*, 75). This pressure toward conceptions of the poetic subject as political and national is in line with the patriotic lyrics of Collins, Akenside, Gray, and others, as Griffin shows: these poems make personal emotion matter by making it national. There are other pressures outward: Thomson emphasizes multiplicity in the shape of shifts in voice (alterations in the identity of the speaker) or stories that require sympathetic involvement (shifts in the allegiance of reader and poet alike). As its eighteenth-century theorists claim, sympathy is an imaginative voyage outside the self, toward the other; and, in its moralist perfection, sympathy involved an approximate substitution of other for self — or rather, an effort to come as close to that ideal as possible.[23]

Thomson actively promotes sympathetic substitution. A passage of fewer than one hundred lines in *Summer* encourages sympathetic involvement with the inhabitants of a bed of roses, battered by the heat; a flock of birds retreating from the glare; two dogs; various insects trapped by "the villain spider . . . cunning and fierce"; a "drowsy shepherd"; and a nameless he "who muses through the woods at noon" — one of many periphrastic Thomson surrogates (ll. 199–286). In each encounter, Thomson offers his readers an imaginary sensual grasp of the experience of each of the wood's inhabitants.[24] These frequent shifts of consciousness are partnered with shifts in the landscape; the cumulative effect is often disorienting. In *Summer* we pass from "brightening fields of ether" (between earth and sun) to the dangerous depths of a "world of slaves" — Black Africa (ll. 1, 885). We view the whole of Scotland in *Autumn*, but on the way, stop by "Asian Taurus," "The Dolpine Hills," "Abyssinia's cloud-compelling cliffs," and "the dire Andes" (ll. 783–806). In moving rapidly from place to place, Thomson seems to emphasize that any hold on the landscape is ultimately illusory; this is part of the effects of empire, reaching out toward a world largely invisible to individual Britons.[25] The instability here is also linked to questions about lyric, as is clear in the long parable of the Flood in *Spring*; Thomson laments the Golden Age of pastoral poetry when "music held the whole in perfect peace" (l. 267):

> The first fresh dawn then waked the gladdened race
> Of uncorrupted man . . .   (ll. 242–43)

> And up they rose, as vigorous as the sun,
> Or to the culture of the willing glebe,
> Or to the cheerful tendance of the flock.
> Meantime the song went round . . .   (ll. 246–49)

After showing Nature's bounty and that of the accompanying lyric, Thomson proceeds to suggest that it is denied to later days:

> But now those white unblemished minutes, whence
> The fabling poets took their golden age,
> Are found no more amid these iron times,
> These days of Life! Now the distempered mind
> Has lost that concord of harmonious powers
> Which forms the soul of happiness; and all
> Is off the poise within.   (ll. 275–81)

We are barred both from the enjoyment of the land and from this enjoyment represented and shared—"the song went round"—in lyric. In Thomson's theodicy, it is the "extinct[ion of] each social feeling" that brings on the Flood (l. 305), and "The Seasons since have, with severer sway, / Oppressed a broken world" (ll. 317–18). The inhospitableness of the landscape goes hand-in-hand with the absence of the pastoral communal song; both are the result of a moral failure.

The Seasons makes two basic suggestions for easing this moral malaise: lose the self in Nature and temper the sense of self by sympathetic interaction with others. Because there are facts of the landscape that (usually) cannot be altered—the brutality of seasonal change, the presence of a torrent or precipice—we must attempt instead to find the unifying principle behind them.[26] This transcendence of smallness and singleness of vision is parallel to the course of the sympathetic voyages undertaken by readers from spider to fly, from the joys of lovers to the pains of death. However, these twin moral practices, one of imaginative involvement in the world, one of imaginative involvement with others, are only approximations of true unity between self and the totality beyond it: no matter how hard we try, we are still single souls in single bodies. The connection between this kind of unity and lyric (especially the potential for shared emotion it entails) is highly evocative. Thomson links lyric and social virtues by recalling the perfection of the lost "round[s]" of pastoral song; this perfection is compared to the emotional importance carried by the sympathetic demands of the text and to the merging of self with other figured by the poem's closing hymn.

Thomson's emphasis on sympathetic involvement of course redounds to an eighteenth-century concern with subjective isolation. In the empiricist view, the radical disjunction between world and self resolved by Descartes through the presence of God is no longer thus dismissable. For Locke's followers, epistemology becomes a question of sense impressions, beyond which the world is unverifiable and unknowable. The self is placed at the center of the perceived universe, a universe constantly expanding for eighteenth-century Britons, but it is alone there; because sense data are limited to a single perceiver, individual perceptions have only personal significance. To take a phrase from a poem by Watts, we "dwell inclosed in solid orbs of skull," entrapped by our own subjectivity. In the wake of the Civil Wars and in the time surrounding the Act of Union, such isolation became a crucially pressing concern.[27] Eighteenth-century moral humanists approached the greater problems of isolation in part through questions of sympathy: if the singularity and limitations of sensible experience are primary indices of subjective isolation, any indication that these limits can be transcended offers salvation. For thinkers like Shaftesbury (the author most often linked to Thomson), social emotion approximates communal experience; it saves the self from isolation and simultaneously gives significance to personal experience.[28] If the significance of personal experience is in question, descriptions of one's experience or attempts at communicating it are under suspicion as well. Shaftesbury encapsulates this uneasiness in 1710:

> An author who writes in his own person has the advantage of being who or what he pleases. He is no certain man, nor has any certain or genuine character; but suits himself on every occasion to the fancy of his reader, whom, as the fashion is nowadays, he constantly caresses and cajoles. All turns upon their two persons. And as in an amour or commerce of love-letters, so here the author has the privilege of talking eternally of himself, dressing and sprucing himself up, whilst he is making diligent court, and working upon the humour of the party to whom he addresses.[29]

Even given the importance of emotion for Shaftesbury, the expression of emotion is a problem: sensible experience is a risky subject because it is unverifiable beyond the bounds of skull and skin. Emotional communications may be deceptive (the concern of moralists like Shaftesbury) or merely inconsequential (the extreme conclusion that may be drawn from empiricist epistemology).[30] Sympathy validates expression as well as experience.

The chameleon possibilities of sympathy are useful to Thomson, but they carry their own risks; nowhere is this more important than at the juncture of personal expression with lyric convention.[31] Far from being a poem about the self, *The Seasons* concerns the natural world, a world that is beyond any single being, even as it includes each of us. When Thomson emphasizes the speaker's position in his landscape, it is because self-representation has communal (often patriotic) significance. Personal experience in Thomson is most important when it is shared, when it is the product of sympathy and human community.[32] Accordingly, the kind of lyric most common in *The Seasons* is not that which emphasizes the "I." The laud or hymn provides Thomson with a model for emotional utterance because it mixes the self with what is beyond it. Songs of praise tend to present the poet/singer as subordinate to his or her subject and simultaneously glorified by his/her ability to become lost in the stream of praise; the poet merges with the object in singing of it.

What truly counts as lyric in *The Seasons* is communal song.[33] In singing his part, the poet has two choices:

> To me be Nature's volume broad displayed;
> And to peruse its all-instructing page,
> Or, haply catching inspiration thence,
> Some easy passage, raptured, to translate,
> My sole delight, as through the falling glooms
> Pensive I stray, or with the rising dawn
> On fancy's eagle-wing excursive soar.   (*Summer*, ll. 192–98)

The poet may stray, pensive, and think of the natural world; this results in description of the world beyond the self. Or, he may imaginatively leave his body behind and "excursive soar" where the constraints of body, climate, and place could never lead him. The "I" of *Summer* eventually fades away with the heat that torments it and ultimately disappears in vastness.

In accord with this pattern, lyric subgenres in *The Seasons* are most often those where the "you" dominates, as in the first "Amanda" section

in *Spring* (Amanda is Elizabeth Young, whom Thomson wooed unsuc-
cessfully in the early 1740s):

> Come then, ye virgins and ye youths, whose hearts
> Have felt the raptures of refining love;
> And thou, Amanda, come, pride of my song!
> Formed by the Graces, loveliness itself!
> Come with those downcast eyes, sedate and sweet,
> Those looks demure that deeply pierce the soul,
> Where, with the light of thoughtful reason mixed,
> Shines lively fancy and the feeling heart:
> Oh, come! and, while the rosy-footed May
> Steals blushing on, together let us tread
> The morning dews, and gather in their prime
> Fresh-blooming flowers to grace thy braided hair
> And thy loved bosom, that improves their sweets.   (ll. 481–93)

The invitation continues, shifting from a personal appeal to a description of a more abstract "hurried eye" throughout the next twenty or so
lines (l. 518 ff.). This passage, like the similar pastoral to "Melinda" in
Autumn (ll. 610–24), borrows from a lyric repertoire: the apostrophes
and invitations, the twist on the *carpe diem* topos, the courtly description
of the beloved. The joyous presence of personal emotion is grounded by
another human being, by something exterior made present by the force
of desire and imagination. The self is most present when its experience
can be fixed, marked, and even represented by invocation of another.

In *The Epistolary Moment* Dowling argues that the distaste or uncertainty with which the lone voice is met throughout the era is crucial to
the popularity of the letter in eighteenth-century literature — novel,
verse, essay, or wherever it might be found. The fiction of correspondence links author to audience, no matter how isolated each may be. It is
thus that "the eighteenth-century verse epistle will move to engage the
new terror of a post-Cartesian or post-Lockean solipsism, but it is more
immediately the means through which the epistle lays bare a problem of
audience always repressed or hidden in the lyric situation" (10). This
concern with audience is indispensable to Augustan lyricism.[34] Subgenres that rely on a logic of external relation, like invitation, then, are
key for poets seeking ways to speak of the self in lyric terms — especially
for poets who, because of gender or class, are constrained to justify their
poetic ambition. Mary Masters and Leapor, for example, use invitations
(along with hymns) as mainstays of their lyric repertoires.[35]

This logic of the exterior extends from the "you" emphasis of the invitation to practices of imitation, where respected models for both speech and personality like Virgil, Horace, or Milton are key.[36] The laud of the sun in *Spring* works thus, using a Miltonic model of personal speech:

> Hail, Source of Being! Universal Soul
> Of heaven and earth! Essential Presence, hail!
> To thee I bend the knee; to thee my thoughts
> Continual climb, who with a master-hand
> Has the great whole into perfection touched.   (ll. 556–60)

Each season flaunts such passages.[37] *Autumn* holds the famous appeal (*Penseroso*-like) to "Philosophic Melancholy" (ll. 1004–36), as well as the effusive closing address to "Nature! all-sufficient!" Following Thomson's plea for respite from the heat in *Summer* is another short hymn where the weight of apostrophe, "Welcome, ye shades! ye bowery thickets, hail!" is balanced not by references to the self but by a sympathetic involvement with a "hunted hart" who seeks the cool darkness (ll. 469–81).[38] Thomson emphasizes the transcendent powers of praise; the experience of the individual subject becomes significant, and therefore speakable or singable, within the possibilities of epideixis. These embedded lyrics give significance to personal experience by linkage to an outside stabilizing presence: it may be the validation of the personal voice that comes in employing it, as did Milton, in the praise of God; it may more simply be the imaginative stabilization of self that comes with focus on an external object. Whether or not these are philosophically adequate supports of subjective experience, they are poetically adequate, partially because of the weight of tradition. An established occasion of speech — invitation to the beloved, praise of the Father — makes private experience utterable.

§ The hymn was, of course, the most common lyric genre during the eighteenth century. The congregational hymns of Watts or the Wesleys offered a framework for the socially sanctioned experience of emotion, and metrical translations of the Psalms gave the highest sanction to emotional effusions for the devout, as the authority of Plato did for others.[39] Thomson's hymns, either as self-sufficient poems or as parts of *The Seasons*, offer an emotional experience whose utterance need never excite shame, fear, or loneliness.[40] The "I" or "we" of the hymn is an emotional form (to alter slightly Benveniste's formulation) open for all believers to fill. Unlike the speaker of a secular lyric, the singer of a hymn is never alone, and company may have interesting effects.

A hymn on creation is the centerpiece of one of the major influences on *The Seasons*, Shaftesbury's *Moralists* (1705). The rhapsodic praise of Theocles, Shaftesbury's *altera vox*, is cast as a "celestial hymn" in terms Thomson may have adopted (*Characteristics*, 2:97).[41] The same disembodied eye sweeps each piece: Philocles requires "wings of fancy. How else shall I fly with you through different climates, from pole to pole, and from the frigid to the torrid zone?" (2:119). Freed from bodily constraints, the mind can travel in ecstatic exploration of the greater world. As with *The Seasons*, landscape blends with the sublime to produce ongoing human drama; that landscape is always moral, and the experience of the group is indelibly marked on the ground it inhabits, just as the group's accumulation of knowledge is marked in the voice that guides our imaginations. This admixture of social and personal is figured in *The Moralists*, as in *The Seasons*, using adaptations of the hymn. Theocles' speech is quite self-consciously poetic (written in "loose numbers" [2:98]) and explicitly competes with pastoral lyric tradition.[42] Hymnal language coexists with a clear concern about the viability and status of personal speech, as in Thomson: Theocles cries to Nature, "To thee this solitude, this place, these rural meditations are sacred; whilst thus inspired with harmony of thought, though unconfined by words, and in loose numbers, I sing of Nature's order in created beings, and celebrate the beauties which resolve in thee, the source and principle of all beauty and perfection" (2:98).

Although he invokes solitude, Theocles is not alone: his voice appears through the intervention of another, reported by Philocles in a letter to his friend Palemon. Shaftesbury wishes to emphasize the communicability of passion while also obscuring or complicating its source: "Again and again I bid you beware; 'you knew not the danger of this philosophical passion, nor considered what you might possibly draw upon yourself, and make me the author of. I was far enough engaged already, and you were pushing me further, at your own hazard'" (2:25). The representation of Theocles' passion carries the potential of infection, but the presence of Philocles as scribe cuts us off from its originating body; Shaftesbury maintains intimacy of communication through the letter but frees us from the dangers of being too close, chief among them interest and personal display. The elaborate relay addresses the problem of Theocles' self-interest; he is not publishing his own meditations (a practice called "indecent" in "Advice to an Author" [1:109]).

Individual rhapsodic excess is filtered by social activity and social con-
sent; the letter provides a comfortable context for lyric.[43] The impassioned body and soul do not reveal themselves.

Two people are present at the moment of the rhapsody and another
waits offstage: this redoubling is crucial for Shaftesbury, for whom even
the self is dual.[44] All thought, passion, deliberation, and choice should be
subject to an inward colloquy: "This was, among the ancients, that celebrated Delphic inscription, *Recognize yourself*, which was as much as to
say, divide yourself, or be two" ("Advice," 1:113). We are, ideally, to
import the social into the self, thus guaranteeing the moral value of our
thoughts. Somewhat paradoxically, this practice should help to stabilize a
self constantly threatened by dissolution (cf. Marshall, *Figure of the Theater*, 40–45); it is designed to produce a continuity of self over time: "Let
me observe, therefore, with diligence, what passes here . . . ; 'whether,
according to my present ideas, that which I approve this hour, I am like to
approve as well the next; and in case it be otherwise with me, how or after
what manner I shall relieve myself, how ascertain my ideas, and keep my
opinion, liking, and esteem of things the same' " (1:194; single quotation
marks indicate self-address). The soliloquy is also designed to produce
literary work, although the musings it involves should themselves never
be published.

The Moralists in this context carries a fundamental sense not just of
a doubled but of a displaced self. In his "proof" of God's existence,
Shaftesbury argues that every living thing has some "genius" that makes
it cohere, makes it (like Leibnitz's monad) itself and no other (2:100).
This is especially true of human beings: "Truly . . . as accidental as my
life may be, or as random that humour is which governs it, I know
nothing, after all, so real and substantial as myself. Therefore if there be
that thing you call a substance, I take for granted I am one" (2:103).
Shaftesbury extrapolates this argument to cover all of nature: "Is not this
Nature still a self? Or tell me, I beseech you, how are you one? By what
token? Or by virtue of what? 'By a principle which joins certain parts,
and which thinks and acts consonantly for the use and purpose of those
parts.' Say, therefore, what is your whole system a part of? Or is it,
indeed, no part, but a whole, by itself, absolute, independent, and unre-
lated to anything besides?" (2:104).

Shaftesbury balks at any real analysis of selfhood, relying on it instead as a lowest threshold of the single mind of God or Nature: the
human self exists as a part whose contingency (on weather, illness, each
other), coupled with its self-awareness, serves to indicate the larger unity

of the whole.[45] The question of selfhood becomes lost in the question of God; if we have trouble believing in our own unity (thinkers from Locke to Hume certainly did), our questions are put aside by sleight of hand: "For be the difficulty ever so great, it stands the same, you may perceive, against your own being as against that [of God]" (2:103). For the (willing) skeptic, the shadow cast by the idea of the self is the greatest indication of any greater being or purpose, but self is more important as the maker of a shadow than as substance. The self is the gnomon, God the sun.[46] Shaftesbury's view of the self in nature ends with the dissolution of particularity in "a universal union, coherence, or sympathising of things" (2:107).[47] His meditation concludes with his being "struck with the sense of this so narrow being"; this narrowness must be escaped, and so he turns to the boundlessness of nature and God: "I venture thus to tread the labyrinth of wide Nature and endeavour to trace thee in thy works" — not, significantly, to trace *me* in them, to situate the self in response to them (2:98–99). Shaftesbury refuses to stop, even for a little while, within the bounds of human embodiment.

The peculiarities of Theocles' hymn now become more clear: the elaborate tergiversations performed by the speaker; the complexities of solitude in the presence of others; the insistence on reported speech rather than direct manifestation of emotion.[48] It is here as well that Shaftesbury allows fuller access to Thomson and his meditative poetry.[49] In both authors the process by which the speaking subject — and the lyric subject — are placed in relation to the larger world as landscape or as society leads to *dis*placement: the slipperiness of the poet-"I" in Thomson and his reliance on the outside to give meaning to the internal; Shaftesbury's refusal to write of the self as anything but a shadow whose origin, whose sun, is God. There is a close connection between the position of the self, the decorum of personal speech, and the use of lyric. Contemporary discourses of interest, sympathy, and social sentiment render personal utterance suspect; lyric is shaped accordingly.

Both Thomson and Shaftesbury imagine poetry as a way of formally imitating the dimensions of human emotional connection. Because lyric, especially when situated with other modes or genres focusing on connection (like the epistle or invitation), may model community, it also models community's flaws. Lyric, conceived socially in this way, places the self in awkward but necessary relationship to the world surrounding it. This conception of lyric is at the base of the adaptation of lyric in novels and of the absorption of lyric in the georgic, pastoral, or meditative poetry of the period, from Winchilsea or Thomson to Akenside or the Wartons. It is also at the root of the revival of the ode by Collins and Gray: their poetry refines the constrained position of the self of Thomson, Winchilsea, and Shaftesbury. However, for Collins and Gray, the georgic, pastoral, meditative, and descriptive impulses (diversely described) become more immediately and closely balanced against the voice of a particular meditative speaker, and in their odes, the tensions between the personal and the poetic become more marked and disruptive.

§ Although Spacks and other critics have encouraged a reevaluation of the problem, Collins is often identified as a failed poet—one whose promise was great but whose works rarely fulfilled it. The "Ode to Evening" is a particularly potent—or impotent—example. The final movement of the poem is usually seen as unsatisfactory, the overall structure is daunting, and it is easy to get lost within the vagaries of syntax and imagery.[50] I wish to recast these concerns in terms of the relationship between the speaker's body and the expression or identification of pleasure, for here is one key to the generic particularities of the poem.

From the beginning, the speaker's relationship to Eve is explicitly sensual, based on language and sound: "If ought of Oaten Stop, or Pastoral Song, / May hope, chaste *Eve*, to sooth thy modest ear" (ll. 1–2). The pictorial aspects of personification, those most closely associated with the device, are explicitly subordinate to an approach that emphasizes other senses.[51] It then becomes significant that the weight of this sensual experience falls on Eve's "body," not the speaker's own. Any instability, oddity, or confusion in the poem may be attributed to the emphasis placed on an imaginary body, to a tension between description and allegory. The poem's fiction relies on one's willingness to imagine a body for Evening, however "ethereal" (l. 7). In comparison to Eve's sensual presence, the poet's body is obscured:

> Now Air is hush'd, save where the weak-ey'd Bat,
> With short shrill Shriek flits by on leathern Wing,
>   Or where the Beetle winds
>   His Small but sullen Horn,
> As oft he rises midst the twilight Path,
> Against the Pilgrim born in heedless Hum.   (ll. 9–14)

The deictic "now," indicating a present time, might also suggest the poet's presence, but he first appears not as an "I" but as the Pilgrim assaulted by the surrounding world. The Pilgrim is present only as he is confronted and impeded by a world so separate it does not even notice him. He and the Beetle are reciprocally brought into physical being ("born") by their confrontation, yet he is tangential, almost metonymically present (through contiguity with that which assaults him). The Beetle is also a logical impediment, a disruption, coming between the echoing "Now air is hush'd" and "Now teach me . . . / To breathe some soften'd Strain, / Whose Numbers stealing thro' thy darkning Vale, / May not unseemly with its stillness suit" (ll. 15–18). The speaker wishes for a delicate absorption into stillness, to be diffused, and decorously to abide, even when he cannot do so (if the Beetle's sudden assault in the quiet is any indication).

As Evening slowly approaches, the poet begins a disappearing act in earnest, retreating to a pastoral hut that

> Views Wilds, and swelling Floods,
> And Hamlets brown, and dim-discover'd Spires,
> And hears their simple Bell, and marks o'er all
>> Thy Dewy Finger draw
>> The gradual dusky Veil.   (ll. 36–40)

The speaker, driven inside by the cold (ll. 33–34), is subject to another metonymic replacement by the Hut, which views, hears, and marks. This process of crumbling and erasure "is the most revealing instance of the ode's practice of eroding the outlines of discrete localized entities" and becomes devastatingly quick in the series of personifications at the poem's climax.[52]

Evening is a figure of unattainable desire — *chaste* Eve. "Ode to Fear" is propelled by the need to feel; "Ode to Evening" is guided by a frustrated desire to enjoy as fully as possible (the poem begins with a plea for pleasure). The speaker, inside the Hut, creates a series of pictures representing an ideal union between himself and Eve:

> While *Spring* shall pour his Show'rs, as oft he wont,
> And bathe thy breathing Tresses, meekest *Eve!*
>> While *Summer* loves to sport,
>> Beneath thy ling'ring Light:
> While sallow *Autumn* fills thy Lap with Leaves,
> Or *Winter* yelling thro' the troublous Air,
>> Affrights thy shrinking Train,
> And rudely rends thy Robes.   (ll. 41–48)

These personifications instantiate a series of doubled or reciprocal relations between the poet and his subject.[53] The seasons' joyous activity in Evening's shade is the focus of the speaker's envy. If the poet were in the ideal landscape he pictures, he, like Eve, would receive the ministrations of the season; within her, he would be united with her as well. So, when Spring's showers bathe Eve's tresses (the trees, grasses, flowers), the poem provides two possibilities for positioning the speaker. He may imagine himself, like Spring, in close relation with Eve's body, delighting in Spring's touch on her hair; equally, he may picture himself outside the Hut, *inside* Evening, where he, like she, would be washed clean. The speaker's body, outside in the broad air, would converge with Eve's own. This pattern is repeated in each of the scenes. Summer's gaiety in evening is pictured with longing: the poet too would like to play beneath her lingering light, and if he were outside, Summer's sport (warmth, buzzing crickets) would please him as well. Autumn, dropping leaves in Eve's lap, would do the same to any pilgrim seated within her robes. The potential for shared pleasure brings poet and Evening together.

With the arrival of Winter, however, these fantasies of enjoyment cease. Up to this point, Collins could imagine himself outside, within Evening, sharing in her pleasure, his body mapped onto hers. Here, however, Winter not only prevents the speaker's union with Eve, his being outside in full enjoyment or possession of the twilight, but Winter also "rudely rends" Eve's robes, shortening her reign as Earth tilts at the poles. Eve and the speaker are both threatened by Winter: as with the other seasons, Winter's actions bring Eve and the speaker together in an analogic relation, but not this time into imaginative proximity. The two are sundered at the last moment. These lines divide the speaker's imagined body, pushed one way be desire (outside, into Evening), another by necessity (inside, from the cold).[54]

Sherwin argues, "While twilight functions as a sustaining perpetual ground that fosters the coalescence of subject and object, Evening's role is to solidify that ground by rendering the scene imagination's landscape" (*Precious Bane*, 119). The problem in the poem, however, is that any solidification of the union between Evening and Collins is endangered by the physical: the closer we get to physical representation of the speaker and that of his pleasure (his body and Evening's), both rent by Winter's sharpness, the more unstable everything becomes. This is not merely the result of Collins's confused use of imagery (Gray's accusation), nor is it born merely of problems of personification, tension between allegory and description, or the disjunction between the imaginary and the real. As much as these contribute to the confusing multiplication of positions in which the speaker's body appears, there is also an overall unease in the poem with the speaker's physical being.[55]

This is part of Collins's concern with self-representation. Spacks maintains, "The boundaries of justifiable entitlement presented both a personal and a poetic dilemma. . . . What can I write about? How do my public obligations as poet relate to my private impulses? Do my feelings impede or energize my verse?"[56] The speaker in "Evening" is barred from complete pleasure in the landscape; when he tries to achieve union and pleasure — and to sing of it — he is divided, fractured, and displaced. Thus, at the end of "Ode to Evening," the poetic function is given over to social and personal abstractions. While the Seasons make their rounds,

> So long sure-footed beneath the Sylvan shed,
> Shall *Fancy, Friendship, Science*, rose-lip'd *Health*,
>> Thy gentlest Influence own,
>> And hymn thy fav'rite Name!   (ll. 49–52)

Cut off from pleasure, the poet cannot himself speak it, and the problem of the body still remains: the happy possibility of rose-lip'd Health is substituted for the broken body of the poet.[57]

"Ode to Evening" makes the most dramatic case for the problem of emotional and bodily experience in Collins's poems; there are others. In odes like "Simplicity" or "The Passions," the "I" is a placekeeper or storyteller, a convenient hook on which to hang a sight or sound, while in others, it doesn't appear at all. In "A Song from Shakespear's Cymbeline," lyric and dramatic weight come from a speaker who is excluded from the scene he describes and from its community. The speaker, on the outside of events and enacted emotions, establishes himself as an invisible social voice.[58] Similar bodily quandaries operate in the "Ode Occasioned by the Death of Mr. Thomson."[59] In "Fear," the poet-speaker longs for emotional experience, and with it, the ability to craft evocative images. As in "Evening," in "Fear" Collins longs to be one with the object of desire "Like Thee I start, like Thee disorder'd fly" (l. 8), but he cannot. The speaker's "throbbing Heart" (l. 42) signals the presence of Fear, but its power, in his view, escapes him.[60] The speaker's body is there, but the core of emotional experience is beyond it. Sign or symptom (quickened heartbeat, etc.) and representation are split: the body is the site of the sign; art lies elsewhere. This subgenre, the poem as plea for feeling, is another significant category of lyric in the midcentury; poems like Joseph Warton's "Ode to Fancy" (1746), Leapor's "Request to the Divine Being" (1748), or Frances Greville's "Prayer for Indifference" (1759) exhibit a similar paradigm of longing and self-effacement.

§ Gray's lyrics display a variation on these tensions between personal experience and representation. The problem of the speaker's presence over the course of "Elegy Written in a Country Churchyard" (1750) has become a familiar element of criticism. The speaker's voice fades away (as it does in its precursor, Parnell's "Night-Piece on Death" [1721]), and in the final lines, the poet seems to address himself as "thee" (l. 93), some hoary-headed swain relates the history of the poet, and the poem closes with an epitaph of uncertain "authorship." I do not wish to reopen this issue beyond a basic statement: the *Elegy* ends in a chorus of voices among which that of the erstwhile speaker is silent. The gradual elision of the speaker's voice is characteristic of a complex of issues surrounding personal experience; these problems coalesce around the issue of sympathy and are fundamentally linked to Gray's idea of lyric. From the opening stanza, the lines of life are drawn away from the speaker; the landscape is emptied, leaving "the world to darkness and to me."[61] He may be left with "the world," but with the absence of people, animals, and light, what does that mean? He has the barest framework of human experience — death on one hand, and potentiality on the other. When we are finally given a glimpse of the surrounding world, it is the home less of the speaker than of the dead:

> Beneath those rugged elms, that yew-tree's shade,
>   Where heaves the turf in many a mould'ring heap,
> Each in his narrow cell for ever laid,
>   The rude Forefathers of the hamlet sleep.   (ll. 13–16)

The trajectory of physical description, the pattern of deixis, points to their enclosure, not his.[62]

Readers are moved continually closer to the lost villagers, asked to envision their plight. However, the negations sown throughout the poem — darkness, silence, the absence of community, and so on — function as blocks to imagination. Gray presents his readers with things difficult or impossible to see in reality: bodies within the earth, gems in the ocean's caves, mute Miltons or a guiltless Cromwell. A central concern here may be to stretch the imagination, but the process by which this is accomplished is one that denies or forecloses sight, moving farther into darkness and the unseen, closer to oxymoron and paradox. The challenge to the reader's imagination is a challenge to the limits of sympathy, for the failure to imagine the villagers' lot would ultimately be a failure of sympathetic involvement. Adam Smith gives almost a rough sketch of the poem a few years later in *The Theory of Moral Sentiments* (1759):

> We sympathize even with the dead, and overlooking what is of real
> importance in their situation, that awful futurity which awaits them,

we are chiefly affected by those circumstances which strike our sense, but can have no influence upon their happiness. It is miserable, we think, to be deprived of the light of the sun; to be shut out from life and conversation . . . ; to be no more thought of in this world, but to be obliterated, in a little time, from the affections, and almost from the memory, of their dearest friends and relations. . . . The tribute of our fellow-feeling seems doubly due to . . . [the dead] now, when they are in danger of being forgot by everybody. . . . That our sympathy can afford them no consolation seems to be an addition to their calamity.[63]

This is the imaginative drive of Gray's poem (and is also evocative of the "Sonnet on the Death of Richard West" [1742]): a consideration of how far the imagination may bring us in feeling for (no longer with) people whose deaths confirmed the limitations of their lives. As in Smith's description, however, in Gray any efforts at sympathy are forestalled by isolation.

The emotional ends associated with lyric by predecessors like Thomson or Dryden — community of feeling or consensus — seem quite close to those of sympathy; Thomson and Shaftesbury sew them together, and eighty years later, sympathetic involvement will be fundamental to Keatsian creativity. There is a difference, however, between an artist's ability to efface his own character and step into that of another and a cultural requirement that instructs us all to do so for the sake of our souls and the proper functioning of society.[64] If moral worth is constantly measured by the ability to step outside the self, an author representing "his own" experience faces a daunting task. How can one's own emotions be the ground or center of representation when moral aesthetics calls for decentering or displacing the self?[65]

The disappearance of the "I" as speaker over the course of the "Elegy" thus corresponds to Gray's concern with the properly sympathetic. Through entering into the plight of the villagers, the poet is partially wiped away, moving into the darkness of night and the world of the dead.[66] For theorists like Smith, sympathy is an escape from isolation: a sufferer "longs for that relief which nothing can afford him but the active concord of the affections of the spectator with his own" (Smith, *Moral Sentiments*, 22). The "I" as the lyric subject in this case is tricky: to achieve the effects of sympathy, the poet has to be presented as object, not subject.[67] The offering of sympathy for the poet is imagined in the form of the closing epitaph, but it is not claimed as a "right" (contra Lonsdale, "Poetry of Gray," 32). In contemporary theory, sympathy is a natural human response and part of our ethical duty, but it is never a *right* that can be claimed for the self; it can only be achieved through painstaking self-positioning and representation. This is clear in Smith's description of the expression of grief: "We are disgusted with that clamorous grief, which, without any delicacy, calls on our compassion with sighs and tears, and importunate lamentations. But we reverence that reserved, that silent and majestic sorrow, which discovers itself only in the swelling of the eyes, in the quivering of the lips and cheeks, and in the distant, but affecting coldness of the whole behaviour" (24). This course of behavior gains aesthetic superiority indirectly. Expressive restraint is necessary because human sympathy is incomplete: "The emotions of the spectator will . . . be very apt to fall short of the violence of what is felt by the sufferer" (21), and knowing one's audience, it is important to "lower . . . passion to that pitch, in which the spectators are capable of going along with it" (22). In effect, we must be spectators to our own grief to avoid vulgarity and garner sympathy.

When and how might personal lyric then be possible? There is a lyric model in Smith's poetics of grief, the death song of American "savages":

> Every savage . . . composes . . . what they call the song of death, a song, which he is to sing when he has fallen into the hands of his enemies, and is expiring under the tortures which they inflict upon him. It consists of insults upon his tormentors, and expresses the highest contempt of death and pain. He sings this song upon all extraordinary occasions, when he goes out to war, when he meets his enemies in the field, or whenever he has a mind to show that he has familiarised his imagination to the most dreadful misfortunes, and that no human event can daunt his resolution, or alter his purpose. (206)

The warrior's song bids defiance to the experience of pain: it is accusation, not effusion, and is in all these ways acceptable. Joseph Warton's "Dying Indian" (1755) is the British poetic equivalent of Smith's exemplum (the story is common in travel narratives). Like the poems of Ossian, "The Dying Indian" may not displace the body of the speaker in its world, but it does distance that body from the poet and an eighteenth-century English reader, removing it temporally or (more importantly) culturally and racially. We have a noble savage to deal with, not a pale Cantabridgian with antiquarian tendencies. In the processes of empire, lyric is placed at the margins or beyond.[68] Alone in the English countryside, figures like Gray must enter into a sort of endless self-displacement, constantly putting themselves in the position of others at even the most painful (and hence often private) moments: "As to love our neighbour as we love ourselves is the great law of Christianity, so it is the great precept of nature to love ourselves only as we love our neighbor, or, what comes to the same thing, as our neighbour is capable of loving us" (Smith, *Moral Sentiments*, 25). As with Shaftesbury, we must divide ourselves: Gray's self-address as "thee" in the poem's final movement indicates a similar understanding of the problems of self-representation.

An aesthetic of restraint also operates in Gray's "Sonnet on the Death of Richard West," where the poet is irrevocably isolated from sympathetic possibility. In his mixed praise of the sonnet in the Preface to *Lyrical Ballads*, Wordsworth focuses on the crux of the poem:

> A different object do these eyes require;
> My lonely anguish melts no heart but mine;
> And in my breast the imperfect joys expire;   (ll. 6–8)
>
> I fruitless mourn to him that cannot hear,
> And weep the more because I weep in vain.   (ll. 13–14)

Wordsworth is arguing for simplicity of diction, and in the process focuses on lines that emphasize isolation.[69] There is a romantic preference for the experience of the sole self here; however, what is interesting is also the tension between sympathy and lyric. At the level of description, it is the failure of sympathy that brings forth the most powerfully emotive lines in the poem; at the same time, we may detect allegiance to rules of moral sensibility.

With the sonnet, Gray chooses a form that demands discipline and restraint, and he presents his own emotions in the lines above using language quite plain in comparison to that which surrounds it.[70] The power of this poem comes partly by virtue of the tension between constraint and excess. There are tears, but they are those of silence and acknowledged sterility: Smith's praise of quiet dignity as the appropriate dress of grief would not ill-fit this sonnet, a poem never (appropriately enough) published in Gray's lifetime.[71] Gray's constant attention to the limits of sympathy and of personal emotion, as well as his concern over the degree to which a single voice is adequate in portraying it, could be why Smith gave him such high praise: "Gray . . . who joins to the sublimity of Milton the elegance and harmony of Pope, and to whom nothing is wanting to render him, perhaps, the first poet in the English language, but to have written more" (*Moral Sentiments*, 123–24).

The conflict between sympathy, self, and lyric is among the motivating concerns of the "Ode on a Distant Prospect of Eton College" — a poem offering an intriguing solution to the problem of self-interest. The poem's speaker longs for the past, when he purportedly "once . . . stray'd / a stranger yet to pain" (ll. 13–14).[72] Images of infantile bliss are tinged by the speaker's knowledge of the pain to come, but when it is time to represent that pain, pain the speaker shares, the poem shifts to personifications and to moral abstractions. If language is the dress of thought, images of experience not properly the speaker's own — the emotions of small children, the action of "The Ministers of human fate" (l. 56), or the platitudes of conventional wisdom — are the acceptable dress of emotion. This approach is usually understood as one of distance, in line with the poem's title. What I wish to emphasize is exactly what is distanced. Vision and the physical have an uneasy relationship to personal emotion, and radical shifts in imagination correspond to the requirements of emotional representation.

There are four shifts of subject and imagery or voice in the ode. The first stanza describes what might be visible from a distant prospect: "distant spires," "antique towers," "grove," "lawn," and "hoary Thames." Lines of direct sight correspond to appropriated emotion in the second stanza. The "happy hills" lend "momentary bliss," something delightful but quite foreign: they only "seem to sooth" (given Gray's experience of bullying at Eton, even that is whitewashed). The next three stanzas describe what might be seen by the poet but is not. The speaker is too far away to see the details Father Thames is asked to describe:

Who foremost now delight to cleave
With pliant arm thy glassy wave?
The captive linnet which enthrall?
What idle progeny succeed
To chase the rolling circle's speed,
Or urge the flying ball? (ll. 25–30)

The boys' "rosy hue" is too much in the distance to be visible (l. 45). Corresponding to these images, which might be seen but are not, we find emotion imagined, desired, but not attainable or even pure: "Still as they run they look behind, / They hear a voice in every wind, / And snatch a fearful joy" (ll. 38–40).

The final movement includes the pageant of horrors. These personifications are the province of imagination, unseen and unseeable, but they correspond to emotions the poet indirectly claims as his own. In his *Lectures on Rhetoric and Belles Lettres* (1783), Hugh Blair states: "If one has been long accustomed to a certain set of objects, which have made a strong impression on his imagination; as to a house, where he has passed many agreeable years ... when he is obliged to part with them, especially if he has no prospect of ever seeing them again, he can scarce avoid having somewhat of the same feeling as when he is leaving old friends."[73] In cases of what we now call nostalgia, and "innumerable" others, personification "is the very language of imagination and passion" (1:326). Eighteenth-century personification was far from a practice of "distancing" insofar as it made what passes within the subject graphically apparent. It did not disavow or estrange emotions so much as make them accessible.[74] More than any other signal, then, Gray's use of personification might well have alerted an eighteenth-century reader to the force with which the speaker feels the emotions portrayed. However, the strong pictorialism associated with the tradition allowed readers to encounter the poet as object and subject at once, subject to the emotions or fears that produce the image, and object of their horror and gruesome deeds. In effect, personification substitutes one body for another. Our attention is drawn to these *imagined* bodies — the "grisely troop" of Poverty, Age, and Death — and to a completely allegorical landscape — "the vale of years" (ll. 81–90). Thus, the speaker's body and his own landscape (that first offered to our sight) are now well hidden, marked over by the images he puts in their place.[75]

Physical representations and mimetic sight are linked to borrowed emotion (stanzas 1–2); imagined vistas are united to unattainable sensation (stanzas 3–4); only with allegorical bodies, physical substitutes, is emotion closest to the speaker (stanzas 5–8). The farther we are from the speaker's body, the closer we may come to his emotional experience, overwritten and replaced.[76] In the final stanza, the shift away from the physical is fully accomplished in terms of moral sympathy:

> To each his suffering: all are men,
> Condemn'd alike to groan,
> The tender for another's pain;
> Th'unfeeling for his own.
> Yet ah! why should they know their fate?
> Since sorrow never comes too late,
> And happiness too swiftly flies.
> Thought would destroy their paradise.
> No more; where ignorance is bliss,
> 'Tis folly to be wise.

This stanza eschews the visible for the spoken: proverb or motto is exchanged for emblem. If consensus is a preferred lyric outcome, this is one way of achieving it. The moralist language of the final stanza is a site of approximation — both poet and reader can move toward the same more or less neutral space. For Gray, sympathy and lyric are both mediated by a structure that refuses physical instantiations of selfhood.

While sympathy and lyric may strive toward shared experience, they conflict in practice. The tender boy who feels for another's pain may be alienated from his own, challenged with the threat of "unfeelingness" if he tries to represent or express it. The poem presents two alternatives; one replaces or displaces the other. The logic of sympathy as we see it in Smith requires us constantly to seek another's heart and another's view of our own; the logic of vision that drives Gray's poem shows one result of this practice — the flight from the self as palpable presence. The moral proverb, the statement stripped of personality, rendered as (ironic) truth and disembodied voice, allows for sympathy or shared experience without the disruption caused by the flesh.[77] Physicality is stripped away because it is the most pressing representative or reminder of self, self-interest, and self-focus.[78]

§ I have tried to demonstrate that concerns about community and representing the self, especially the physical self, as source of passion underlies lyric moments in Thomson, Shaftesbury, Collins, and Gray. Across class, gender, and generic divisions, other important contemporary poems reveal a similar approach to lyric. Leapor fears that her lyrics fail, her ambitions thwarted by (an erotic, classical) past and by class, ending her "Hymn to the Morning":

> Thus sang Mira to her lyre,
> Till the idle Numbers tire:
> Ah! *Sappho* sweeter sings, I cry,
> And the spiteful Rocks reply
> (Responsive to the jarring Strings)
> Sweeter — *Sappho* sweeter sings.[79]

Finch's speaker in "A Nocturnal Reverie" delays her appearance as an agent of desire as long as possible, finally appearing only to move immediately into the safety of a "we." "The Request," an anonymous poem in the 1739 miscellany *The Flowers of Parnassus*, seeks the pleasures of retreat, but only when the virtues of a conversational circle can be maintained, and retreat does not mean a lone body and voice in a pastoral landscape:

In such a State, secure from Noise and Strife,
In peaceful Solitude I'd pass my Life:
Blest with the Converse of a Female Friend,
With whom the Evenings of my Days I'd spend:
May mutual passions glow in either Breast,
As I in her, so she in me be blest.   (9)

Duck's antipastoral verse emerges in the voice alternatively of the Muse of Poverty and of a community of laborers. When they speak, their bodies register an alienation so intense that even whiteness, placed as marker of British subjectivity, is all but taken away:

When sooty Pease we thresh, you scarce can know
Our native Colour, as from Work we go;
The Sweat, and Dust, and suffocating Smoke,
Make us so much like *Ethiopians* look.
We scare our Wives, when Evening brings us home;
And frighted Infants think the Bug-bear come.[80]

Amidst this communal voice, the poet-speaker appears as "I," not when undertaking bodily labor, but only with the poetic labor of the extended simile (e.g., ll. 127–34); alone, the poet calls no body his own.[81] Doody notes that sensuousness in much women's poetry of the midcentury involves depicting the bodies of animals, fairies, or elves as substitutes for the bodies of female speakers, providing "a reflecting screen where sensation and reflection can be played with, away from the world of man-made regulations and cultural pressures."[82] Leapor often employs dream visions, leaving her body behind so that poetry may reign.[83] Anacreontics of the era function similarly, tending to conceal the subject as speaker so that "passion is manifest only under erasure."[84] The light verse of Matthew Prior shows another version of this concern:

What I speak, my fair Cloe, and what I write, shows
    The diff'rence there is betwixt nature and art:
I court others in verse, but I love thee in prose:
    And they have my whimsies, but thou hast my heart.[85]

Sincerity is pictured here as incompatible with the urbanity of lyric; the self appears to be falsified by display, too composed, designed, and artful. In other light lyrics, like those of Shenstone, the individual body or voice is often the object of ridicule or the mouthpiece of self-deprecating gaiety. In serious verse, the self appears most freely and physically when superseded by the divine presence, as in the hymn tradition, or when the body is so abused and decayed it is on the verge of dissolution, as in the fever poems of Watts or Smart, or many of the poems of Mary Chandler.[86] Collier, in "The Woman's Labour" (1739), like Duck, gives an account of toil in a communal voice; unlike Duck, Collier also writes of her experience of labor in the first person. As in fever poetry, pain brings Collier's body into view: "as on my Bed I lay, / Eas'd from the tiresome Labours of the Day."[87] The odes of the Wartons or Akenside generally figure the speaker as a guide in the world of ideas, a communal bard, or as invoker of the muses, and rarely as a physical presence.[88] John Sitter argues that the typical midcentury poet-speaker is isolated in nature, cut off from the madding crowd; I argue rather that the poet-speaker is often, even in company, cut off from his or her own body.[89]

Bodily absence as such is not new: while the erotic verse of the seventeenth century often focused on the speaker's physical presence, it is less often that we find the body of the speaker or a carefully defined set of surroundings in, let's say, Herbert.[90] The significance of the fractured or displaced body in midcentury poetry appears in the concentration of lyric and moral anxieties at this single, physical point of experience. At times this makes the speaker in this period a fugitive, as in the "Ode to Evening," the "Elegy Written in a Country Churchyard," or the "Ode on a Distant Prospect of Eton College." Also at times, the forces of sympathy — the need for sympathetic substitution of self for other (and vice versa) — make reading a vertiginous experience, as in *The Seasons*, and pull against lyric. There are exceptions to this pattern, like the "Sonnet on the Death of West" — unpublished, significantly, by the poet. "Grongar Hill," in its 150-odd lines, carries more of the speaker's physical presence than most other topographical poems, even if Dyer, like Denham in "Cooper's Hill," Thomson in *The Seasons*, Gray in "Ode on a Distant Prospect," or Collins in "Ode to Evening," also submerges the speaker in a moralized landscape of significant others that completes and concludes the poem.[91] Aaron Hill's "Alone in an Inn at Southampton, April the 25th, 1737" (1753), is a powerful personal statement of loss, as is Thomas Edwards's "Sonnet on a Family-Picture" (1753). An excursion into the weeklies, miscellanies, and single-poet volumes turns up a few more. In Akenside's "Ode on Lyric Poetry" (1745) the speaker joins the "Thespian choir" of Pindar and listens happily to Sappho, Alcaeus, and Anacreon; he asks the muse to grant Britain vibrant lyric verse without the "impious revels" Greece endured (l. 64). Like Shaftesbury before him, Akenside feels that lyric has its dangers and must be purified. Such a pure lyric is social, appropriate when "friendship and . . . letter'd mirth" gather together (l. 101). Other poems are comfortable with personal lyric, like Akenside's "Ode on Leaving Holland," Catherine Cockburn's "Platonic," Masters's "Returned in Answer to a Poetical Complaint," or Leapor's "Fields of Melancholy and Cheerfulness."[92] There are, however, very few canonical poems that can be placed beside these; the majority of poems prominent in the lyric tradition up to the 1760s or 1770s participate in the complex of moral, communal speech and physical disappearance I have laid out, and it is the construction of this tradition that concerns me here. Poets seem uneasy about the relationship of the body and its world to speech and the voice of individual emotional experience. The traditional line of the lyric passes from Renaissance to romantic through a group of poems with extreme bodily anxieties.

Four

Rhetorical Realisms: Chiasmus, Convention, and Lyric

No first-person form fares as well in the century as first-person fiction. In 1738, one of Newton's editors quotes "Fénelon: 'To make a work truely excellent it is necessary, that the author should so forget himself that the reader may forget him likewise, and have his attention engaged only on the subject.'"[1] First-person fiction challenges this principle; while Richardson may perhaps forget himself in Pamela, the character herself has no such option. Nonetheless, first-person narrative, in letters, diaries, or memoirs, accounts for around 40 percent of eighteenth-century fiction.[2] Wandering out in the night, in a graveyard, or by a river, people — or rather, lyric poets — seem to get lost: bodies disappear, voices fade away. By contrast, in novels, heroines speak from beyond the grave; bodies are so tightly controlled (often imprisoned) that it is impossible not to know where to find them. I am concerned here to explore what generic principles help shape this picture and how lyric and novel may work together.

The popularity of first-person fiction is not strictly mimetic. While real memoirs were (sometimes) well received and in some demand, their number was small. Most diaries written in the eighteenth century were not published then: fewer than twenty were both written and published between 1700 and 1750; the number goes up slightly to twenty-three in the last half of the century. Felicity Nussbaum points out that "diaries that *were* published in the eighteenth century are not introspective or personal but are most often travel- or military-oriented sea diaries or daily accounts of battles."[3] Similar personal accounts of events frequently appeared on a smaller scale in periodicals. The facts about memoirs are much the same.[4] Colley Cibber's were a scandal, as were those of his protégée, Laetitia Pilkington; in fact, most women's memoirs were published posthumously, and of those few, the majority were scandal-memoirs, written from an already compromised position (Nussbaum, *Autobiographical Subject*, 136). Even spiritual autobiography, beginning as a published form with Bunyan's 1666 *Grace Abounding*, would not really come into print vogue until the latter part of the following century, as Nussbaum notes. By contrast, in the 1760s alone, thirty-eight new works of first-person fiction, not including epistolary compositions, were published, suggesting that when it came to first-person descriptions of personal experience, fiction predominated.[5]

Nussbaum quotes Johnson on publishing autobiography: "He that sits down calmly and voluntarily to review his life, for the admonition of posterity, or to amuse himself, and leaves this account unpublished, may be presumed to tell truth, since falsehood cannot appease his own mind, and fame will not be heard beneath the tomb" (1). Johnson may not here live up to his usual psychological acuity, but we can see that publication of one's own experience is suspect; the fact of publication brings first-person narrative almost into the range of the fictional. Novel and autobiography, according to Spacks, share a significant response to crises over embodiment and individual expression (problems discussed in the last chapter): "Both save individual identity from pure subjectivity by converting human beings into objects: quite literally: pages with words on them: illusions of consistent substantiality. . . . To offer the self as an object of contemplation rather than a subjective consciousness and to convert one's awareness of self and others into a new image of personality—such acts of creation assert the possibility of making and present the world as something made."[6]

This is correct to a point, but it is not entirely satisfactory as an account of successful first-person writing (in an age wary of solipsism) when the lyric is also under scrutiny. The supposition that novels or autobiographies effect a shift from "pure subjectivity" would perhaps dovetail with the relative absence of lyric poetry in the period; however, the objectification Spacks describes is possible in any print form. The popularity of first-person narration is generally linked to a set of social processes with uncertain relations to genre: the strong positive sanction given to interest in the personal from religion (Protestant introspection), philosophy (empiricist epistemology), and economics (consumption, commodification, and the emerging conception of groups of people as markets for goods or services); new technologies (newspapers, chapbooks, and advice columns); and increasing (or at least steadily substantial) literacy rates, as well as diverse literary desires.[7] My first points of concern, then, are two: first, to inquire how and why an interest in the personal is satisfied in literary terms—why in one genre and not another; second, to determine what matter is considered both personal and interesting in a particular literary context.

When it comes to structuring representations of personal experience, contemporary poetry offers an intriguing case. Johnson's famous comment on *The Seasons* suggests a larger question: "The great defect of *The Seasons* is want of method; but for this I know not that there was any remedy. Of many appearances subsisting all at once, no rule can be given why one should be mentioned before another; yet the memory wants the help of order, and the curiosity is not excited by suspense or expectation."[8] The natural world for Johnson seems to offer no structural principles that could receive poetic translation; the emotional world fared little better. The revival of the ode offered interesting possibilities for giving order and shape to emotional experience, but many practitioners of the Pindaric became mired in the disorder or freedom (whichever you choose) that had originally ranked high among its attractions. Collins's odes are excellent examples. "Pity," "Fear," "Mercy," and "The Passions" experiment with odal structures: "Pity" is Horatian, disciplined, stately, measured; its Aristotelian partner, "Fear," is Pindaric, urgent, heightened, impassioned. What contains or orders emotions in these poems, however, is not the pattern of turn-counterturn-stand or a particular sequence of stanzas (regular or otherwise). The structure of passionate experience is determined by personifications like "*Danger,* whose limbs of Giant Mold / What mortal Eye can fix'd behold?" ("Fear," ll. 10–11), Vengeance, who "in the lurid Air, / Lifts her red Arm, expos'd and bare" ("Fear," ll. 20–21), or Pity, clad in "sky-worn Robes of tend'rest Blue / And Eyes of dewy Light!" ("Pity," ll. 11–12). The passions are figured as discrete objects—like Pity in her damp glory—which we, with "the Nations," publicly view ("Pity," l. 10).

These statuesque bodies replace fleshly or human ones; emotional experience is spread over several (relatively) discrete locations. The personifications in "Fear" or "The Passions" are Collins's way of giving form to emotion, but they create a pattern that relies heavily on fragmentation—not just from one body (Vengeance) to another (Danger), but, as in "Ode to Evening," the speaker's body itself may be fragmented by multiple visual and emotional impressions. Elsewhere, as in Gray's "Eton College," personal experience can be deliberately replaced by representations painfully other, painfully separate from the speaker. The speaker's experience is one fragment in a longer sequence. This is not entirely distant from the fragmentation of experience many feel from day to day, mood to mood, the self-difference so attractive and annoying to Locke or Hume; but what Collins or Gray presents is also an experience so disjointed that any sustained relationship between an emotion and a particular individual becomes extraordinarily difficult to imagine, being carefully concealed, destroyed, or hopelessly complicated.[9]

In eighteenth-century novels, personal experience characteristically looks different from this lyric model. Defining eighteenth-century subjectivity (or its dependent and partial cognate, interiority) has been difficult for scholars who have attempted it, in part because there is not one subjectivity but many; a careful examination of the mimesis of subjectivity would be a daunting undertaking as well. Fortunately, my object here is neither subjectivity or interiority per se, nor exactly its novelistic imitation. I am in fact arguing against the idea of strict mimesis of self, what Deirdre Lynch characterizes in Watt as the mistaken assumption that the development of the novel is a process by which "characters . . . came to be more like the real individuals who read them."[10] The important question here is how intense personal experience is represented in the novel. What are the strategies by which illusions of self become imaginatively accessible? Lynch offers a valuable corrective to theories that associate character inextricably with individualism and uniqueness. She argues that the concept of psychological depth as an attribute of literary character developed primarily in "romantic era" novels — those from the 1770s to the early 1800s. Character before the 1770s was largely "not . . . about individualities or inner lives."[11] Focusing on period literary criticism, she argues that "talk about character . . . was talk about the systems of semiotic and fiduciary exchange" (6), while social processes of Georgian and Regency England made reading character into the exercise in depth perception we know today. In tracing "character" as critical category, Lynch separates it from inner life; an important and accurate division. However, as my analysis of Haywood, Behn, and Richardson should show, the earlier part of the century reveals a concept of the inner world that is not limited in the way *Economy of Character* argues. One of Lynch's persistent suggestions is that an emphasis on the personal "detach[es character] . . . from the social text" (118). The personalization I research, by contrast, is about rooting inner life in a larger social world; indeed, this is a primary way that inner life emerges as a literary construct. The strategies of early novels seem concerned not just to produce such constructs but also to facilitate readers' involvement with them.

McKeon argues that the success of the novel is linked to its ability to mediate central epistemological and formal questions about knowing and representing truth and virtue. His innovation is to detail the discursive set of novels; he unravels the threads connecting novels to contests of culture. When McKeon approaches formal features (like claims to historicity), he takes them as indications not just of aesthetic ideology but also of this discursive set outward from the text. His formal argument, however, relies to a great extent on Watt. For Watt, novels approach interiority in terms of the processing of information through a series of fixed points, the filtering of thought and perception through positions defined by domestic circumstance, particularities of time (including questions of memory) and space, as well as social constraints and context.[12] Novels also tend toward other kinds of contextualization, strategies for giving context to reportage, from editorship to found documentation and eyewitness testimony. All of these are ways of defining the rules that give perception meaning, the ways experience enters into a generically — and discursively — defined space of significance.

The problem has been, however, that some prose fiction in the period seems to eschew many of the techniques central to Watt — especially early novels of amorous adventure. In reapproaching the question of novel form, I propose to pursue the discursive approach McKeon advances, but in rhetorical terms. One effect of my approach is that amatory fiction has a fundamental place. The first part of this chapter will map novelistic conventions as features that may indicate substance (mimesis of the real) but that more fundamentally provide tools for translating representation (the signs on the map) into objects (the places readers imagine). Novels, as Lennard Davis points out, "reduc[e] the cognitive space between reader and text":[13] I focus the discussion of "formal" realism not on mimesis, as a relationship between the text and the world, but on rhetoric, as a way of approaching relationships between text and reader and text and discourse.

§ I begin with a case familiar to students of the novel form. Recent criticism has revealed connections between *Pamela* and its amatory precursors, connections that discussions of formal realism tend to obscure. In terms of formal realism representation looks different in *Pamela* than it does in *Love in Excess*, and many commentators (like Lynch and Hammond) connect this to differing approaches to interiority. The content of character in these novels is different, but many of their rhetorical strategies look similar when we shift our method of inquiry. The celebrated intensity of self-revelation — that sense of an inner life contemporary readers found in *Pamela*—is broad and formless in traditional terms.[14] *Pamela* may shift from recounting a fable to an exceptionally personal and moving application of it (108–9) or from reporting a conversation to a minute account of her terror in overhearing it. Even in something so subjective as the tale of her suicide attempt, she moves from rapidly listing her clothing, the contents of her pockets, and her physical actions (210) to a description of her pain from a fall and her fantasies of her own death (212).[15] As a determining principle of representation, *Pamela's* consciousness is a rather gross filter; all sorts of things pass through it. The perceptions and thoughts she reports are the data that create consciousness—these data are formless in a traditional sense, lacking the prioritization or kind of shaping that genre constraints (in sermon, will, sonnet, or soliloquy) usually provide.[16] The genre constraints of the first-person novel are different, reflecting the situation of the perceiver rather than focusing on the regulation of data itself (the generic decorum of pastoral elegy or Petrarchan sonnet, for example, largely regulates what may be shown or felt, even as it forms the base of creative representation). *Subject matter* changes meaning, and so does the role of convention. This is the stuff of mimesis simply to the extent that it focuses the matter of representation.

Mimesis is not the only story, however, and interiority can be a bit of a red herring. *Pamela* is marked off from earlier texts, not just by concerns for the contextualization of experience that translate into location, date, or naming, but by concerns for the contextualization of speech— Watt's realism of presentation. Part of the stabilization of personal speech and experience in novels, first-person or not, is their invocation of a community against which (self-)representation makes sense, whether it is Pamela's parents as addressees of her letters, the interpretative recipients of letters in Behn's *Nobleman* or *Love in Excess*, or Fielding's "reader" as the addressee of his narrator (something exceeding realism of presentation). The conventions of "found" letters, editors, didactic narrators, or eyewitness accounts make these texts hospitable to the real, even while simultaneously emphasizing the constructedness, and hence the fictionality, of the representation.[17] These are questions of rhetoric, not just of mimesis, pointing toward how representations come into frames of knowledge.

In early novels, a central part of the artful contextualization of action and narration, their coming into knowledge, involves domesticity and domestic passions. That the novel as a genre takes hold of the domestic in a significantly new way is a critical assumption carried from Auerbach's *Mimesis* or Frye's *Anatomy of Criticism* through Watt, Armstrong, and Christopher Flint.[18] Of course, domesticity, broadly construed, has never been absent from literary representation, from the bible to Shakespeare, Sophocles to Etheredge, or ballads to the country-house poem, but in the novel, domesticity achieves new status as a sign for and a primary means of access to intimacy.[19] In weighing mimesis as matter against rhetoric as form, we find that questions of genre are most apparent when we inquire what about the role of the domestic is proper to early novels. The significance of novelistic domesticity does not lie in the realm, primarily, of mimesis — and neither do the components of Watt's formal realism: it is not the topos of domesticity, the domestic as an object or space of representation, that matters most. In the next few pages, I use the example of the domestic to rethink formal realism as rhetorical realism, part of what I am calling "chiastic" contact between real and fictional worlds. Chiastic sites are those places in the text where readers are asked to map experience of the world of dates, times, places, letters, and so forth onto the world of the fictional. By arguing in terms of chiasmus, I mean to offer an alternative to the idea of mimesis, to argue that novelistic conventions work not primarily by imitating reality but by showing us ways to move from the real as the space of reading to fictional worlds as spaces of imagining, and as locations where individual and cultural conflict can be mediated.[20]

The domestic in the novel increasingly becomes a privileged site for getting at the "truth" (to employ McKeon's term) of stories, representations, and characters. Bruce Robbins argues that building, perhaps, on the traditional dramatic use of servants as the point of contact between authorial intention and audience awareness, novels often use servants as windows on domestic life. In eighteenth-century drama, servants are a means (through asides and other devices) of crossing the divide between stage and audience: "whenever reference to the extradramatic world, the creator's intentions, or the audience's reception touches the limits of the aesthetic experience, there we find . . . servants . . . who enjoy a disproportionately intimate relation with the public."[21] In violating illusions of independence and transparency surrounding what happens on the stage, servants create a winking complicity between author and audience. Servants similarly offer readers access to the workings of fictional representation in novels, appearing first in amatory fiction as agents of plot (Brilliard in Behn's *Nobleman*, Amy in Defoe's *Roxana*) and later as narrators (Pamela). Servants often provide the rationale for access to the story — to houses, families, plots — and, as such, are indications of artifice, indications that the world we read is constructed for our benefit. As indications of narrative artifice and representations of domesticity, servants act chiastically to bring the world of the novel and that of the real into contact. They do not so much enact mimesis as offer novelists and readers sites for moving from reality as we construct it to a fiction of analogues and fantasies: "X" marks the spot. Chiastic sites also include specific times, names, and places, editors and correspondents, which, along with domestic servants, mediate fiction and reality; these are the places where authors move us back and forth between the fictional and the real.[22] These figures help create the novelistic ideal of the "fictional" as a category distinct from truth or lie, a category closely tied to the emergence of the novel as a cultural force.

Gallagher argues that the idea of fictionality grows in part out of moments in drama when boundaries between the world of the play and the world of its audience are crossed: most significant for her are dramatic prologues.[23] Behn's prologues present her authorial persona to the audience in the guise of the literary prostitute, another sort of domestic servant; the print prefaces are designed to perform authorial introduction more effectively. While actors, the machinery of the stage, and the presence of an (often raucous) audience interfere for Behn with direct communication between dramatist and the individual playgoer, print, with its relative privacy, brings the author's voice more clearly to the reader's mind (58). The voice of the printed preface refines the intimacy the prostitute-author figure (in the mouth of actor or actress) offers in the spoken prologue, signaling authorial intent and the constructedness of scenes to come. Behn's move to print was, in Gallagher's estimation, fundamental to her transition from drama to amatory novels. In novels, of course, an insistent attentiveness to the relationship between the fictional and the real, analogous to that of prologues and prefaces, surfaces in the form of "editors," "autobiographers," "correspondents," and highly audible narrators. With novels, as opposed to the performance of plays, this machinery of representation is what gives uninhibited access to authorial skill ("editors" help, actors hinder) and to the world born of the author's imagination.

As strategies of verisimilitude become novelistic convention, "truth" claims come to function as signals of the fictional and to engage discursive concerns over representation; they also serve as chiastic contacts between two worlds. This insistence on the boundaries between the worlds of fiction and reading often comes to rest on tropes and trappings of domesticity: through the figure of servants as narrators or agents of plot, through the role the family plays as the "author" of character, through the didactic connection between novelistic family life and appropriate readerly conduct, and even through the architecture of the home as a means of guiding and effecting plot (to misquote slightly Watt, *Rise of the Novel*, 175), the house and our means of penetrating it go together to open up consciousness as meaningful, accessible "space."[24] The domestic enables novelistic vision, and it does so through chiasmus.[25]

We may now return to questions of interiority. Strategies of chiasmus mediate the threats of solipsism that shape personal expression across genres (the problems of self-interest plaguing autobiography and the disembodiment of contemporary lyric).[26] As Gallagher argues, novels differ from poems, autobiographies, and plays as performed: readers make Pamela and Clarissa in our minds' eyes but are not at liberty to do the same (or to the same degree) for Pope or Gray, for Susannah Cibber or her father. The "fictionality" of novels is an invitation to imagine differently. Readers of autobiography (or Augustan personal poetry, as we recall from Johnson's scathing comments on Cowley) tend to question the very validity of the representation, its truthfulness, its accuracy, its pretenses to faithfulness (cf. Pope's concerns with self-fashioning or the problematics of Cibber's autobiography): all of these are questions of mimesis. Discourses of the real, like that of imitation, participate in the questions we ask of fiction, but the results of criticism may be wider: *Pamela* is an invitation to *Shamela*; fiction begets itself.

Gallagher argues that the extensive detail of novelistic realism served to ensure that objects of description were fictional, not real. Novelistic codes offer up fictional "Nobodies" who are individual and particular, and hence offer new possibilities for sympathetic involvement.[27] From a Humean perspective, some kind of similarity is required for sympathy (familial closeness is best). Without such likeness, an experience may be marked as belonging, emphatically, to someone else; it may seem too alien for sympathy to be possible. Fictional characters and their emotions have no strict referents, they belong to no one, and according to Gallagher they may bypass the problem of alterity, allowing a more complete form of sympathy than real life ever offers.[28]

Gallagher is correct that fictionality is not sufficient; the prosopopeia and personifications of midcentury poets also offer fictional bodies for emotion to inhabit, but there sympathy produces a fragmentary logic. Particularity (a question of mimesis and its degree of precision) is also at stake, but something else remains. The spaces of memory, projection, and personification are the imaginative and hence sympathetic spaces of

the midcentury lyric; however, they form a topos within the poem distinct from that of the speaker's present, dividing experience into the
exclusive parts visible in Collins and Gray. The mixture of real and
allegorical bodies produces disruption and instability: as Steven Knapp
argues, "Fictionality within a poem . . . depends upon the isolation of the
fictional agent [a personification] from those other agents, including the
poetic speaker, with which its fictionality is implicitly contrasted."[29]
Even though the real perforates the fictional in midcentury odes, as the
poet-speaker interacts with his creations one deflates the other. There is
no chiasmus or movement between; the landscapes of the imagination —
childhood (Gray's "Eton") or poetry (Collins's "Fear") — are forcefully
denied to the one figure who wishes to cross into them, the one figure
who even seems to stand at their origin.

In such cases, both the time of reading and the time of writing are
emphatically and intentionally *not* the same as the realm of emotional
involvement: Gray's speaker is alienated from almost every emotional
experience he imagines, either through the force of time or through the
exigencies of representation. The space of the poem is fractured, and the
poet's disappearing body signals that fracturing, marking the distinction
between the topoi of speech and feeling. Whether it is the reader or the
speaker, whoever does the looking sits on the outside, looking in. Remarkably, the physical components of representation are similar across
genres: from *The Seasons* to the "Eton College" ode, feeling is placed
within a world of landscape description, a world where mimesis seems
fundamentally at stake.[30] But mimesis itself is not enough.

The Nobodies of novels provide easier routes to sympathetic involvement because in addition to their fictionality and particularity, the
boundaries between their worlds and ours are drawn in hospitable ways.
Questions of fragmentation are key across genres: the fragmentation of
landscape and experience in *The Seasons* is linked to problems of nation,
economy, and empire, but also to problems of the self at home and
abroad, as I have suggested. McKeon argues that novels are successful
because they approach problems of fragmentation and instability (like
social and personal mobility) through a focus on "social historical condition[s]" and by particularity in specifying circumstances that serve explanatory functions (*Origins of the English Novel*, 215). If contemporary
poets encounter problems in arranging personal experience and in their
methods of moving in and out of the spaces perception defines, personal
experience in novels is given its form through being given both a frame
of circumstances *and* a mode of access to them. It is not just what is there

but how, and it is here that novelistic realisms become rhetorical. Concepts of history matter as explanatory tools, as McKeon argues; they provide a framework corresponding systems of social and political ordering with the personal and fictional. At the level of utterance, similar work is carried out by figures like the correspondent-autobiographer (who, like the editor-narrator, grounds speech in the machinery or personae of the real but also exists in closer contact to the story). These figures make the space of sympathetic, imaginative involvement identical with the imaginative enterprise of the text: speech and feeling coexist.[31] Novelists constantly call attention to the permeable divide between readers and characters/authors through evocations of developing systematic knowledge and through genre-specific machinery like the editor-narrator-correspondent who is the figure of permeability, of the capacity to cross back and forth between the imaginary and the real, private and public, and self and other.[32] Such chiasmus draws readers into the processes that enable representation, giving the points of contact through which fiction emerges into the world of experience.

With these chiastic sites, readers may cross the boundaries that "enclose" the inner lives of fictional characters. In creating the *outlines* of fictional beings in our imaginations, readers create their *content* as well: drawing a line around nothing defines something. The boundaries or borders of the self come into being through the conventions of novelistic representation — of so-called formal realism, in part — and become coextensive with the novel's machinery. The seams of the imagination, the boundaries of the self and its emotions, are reconstructed in the novelistic version of description and narration. It is this structure that underlies the most famous eighteenth-century representation of affective writing and its effects in reading: Mr. B. reading Pamela's letters, the turning point of the love plot. He takes her packet and walks by the pond that had been the scene of her near-suicide: "When he came, as I suppose, to the place where I mentioned the bricks falling upon me, he got up, and walked to the door, and looked upon the broken part of the wall; for it had not been mended; and reading on to himself, came towards me; and took my hand, and put it under his arm" (275). Reading and walking, Mr. B. maps the world of reading — the world of Pamela's inner life — onto the world of his own experience, and in this series of chiastic steps (checking his pond or the broken wall against those of the narrative) the world of representation receives it fullest instantiation in his own heart and body (a key contribution, as I will show, of amatory fiction).

For those outside the fiction, the figures of chiasmus signify points of contact between reality and fictionality. We have no pond against which to check the text, but we are provided substitutes in chiastic sites from correspondent to editor. These figures are double-faced, mediating experience of the fictional: the Richardsonian "editor," like us, "found" these papers and read them; the autobiographical narrator (as in Defoe) seeks to give us a guide for our own lives in recounting his or hers; the correspondent has an inevitable double address to readers in the text and outside it; the didactic narrator (as with Fielding) constructs the ethical conditions of reading. The other parts of the machinery of Watt's formal realism, like the proliferation of detail and the construction of domesticity within it, then may function as a call to imaginative involvement in the world with which readers have made contact, asking for a voluntary commitment on the reader's part to the ideal of "faithful" representation (verisimilitude rather than *vérité*), a kind of formal-ethical contact in which participation gives "rights" to enjoyment of the fictional worlds we create.[33] Formal — now rhetorical — realism here is a kind of proximation that constructs the fictional through moments of contact with the real, not through mimesis so much as through chiasmus. This is why at the moment when novelistic conventions become identifiable with claims to "truth," novels appear that are all but unconcerned with elegant mimesis: *Gulliver's Travels* or *Tristram Shandy*. In such works, chiasmus becomes so significant that mimesis is turned on its head; because chiasmus is so much at the heart of novel representation, these works are the products of a sensitivity to the terms and projects of the new genre.

Novels of amorous intrigue are key to the development of this rhetorical concern. The very success of formula fiction is rooted in a strategy that privileges chiasmus over mimesis. Warner argues in *Licensing Entertainment* that "the popularity of these novels seems to depend upon turning the empty ego of the central protagonist into a reader's seat from which readers can follow a blatantly self-interested quest for victory on the field of amorous conquest" (92). The mode of entry into these worlds of fiction is usually achieved or cemented by representing the effects of reading within the novel itself. Characters in the world of works like *Love in Excess* are overcome by the power of reading — usually reading recognizable books like *The New Atlantis* or Ovid's *Art of Love* (often, as Warner points out, referred to as a novel). The presence of books as objects of real-world reference initiates chiasmus both by mapping fiction onto the world of readers and of books we know and by suggesting the *mode* — affective — of the chiastic encounter with the text.

In Manley's *Adventures of Rivella* (1714), a fictionalized "auto"-biography rendered in the third person, her *New Atlantis* is reduced by an admirer "to a series of narrative high points in which a succession of aroused bodies are waked and available for 'possessing' both by seducers within the narratives and . . . by the readers' bodies, warmed and absorbed by Manley's 'enchanting descriptions'" (*Licensing Entertainment*, 111).[34] The logic of chiasmus as affective relationship is that of early formula fiction, drawing us into the fictional world by emphasizing the book itself as the site of crossing over. This concern with modes of reading is crucial to the discursive battles over representation that shape novels and to the ways fragmented experience can be made subject to both particular readers and broader discursive formulations. Indeed, the successful methods employed in amatory fiction to guide chiasmus onto bodies are disciplined by later novelists to form the conventions we now call formal realism (cf. *Licensing Entertainment*), organizing a different manner of making bodies and texts coincide.

§ Understanding novelistic representation through chiasmus allows us to understand the implications of using lyrics as parts of the narrative and descriptive machinery of novels: lyrics as literary objects provide a code of contact between discursive systems, as I will show. In combining lyric conventions with strategies of narrative (now) associated with formal realism, novelists achieved a solution to the impasse lyric had reached, the problem of the cohesive representation of the personal and the perceptual. However, given Watt's declaration that novelistic realisms are incompatible with "attention to any pre-established formal conventions" (*Rise of the Novel*, 13), it is important to consider how lyric might work within the pattern of chiasmus I have described, and how lyric may help map the worlds of fiction.

Lyric helps to assimilate the details of the novel's scene; formal sequences taken from lyric function within the framing system of novelistic experience. The "contents" of consciousness may be shaped and focused by applying techniques of and patterns from lyric. Lyric can be used to focus changes from inside to outside, from the surface of words to the emotions behind them: lyric can work with novelistic chiasmus. If odes like those of Collins or Gray fragment in organizing and representing assorted matter of personal experience, the novelistic approach to lyric is different. Novels themselves work around the assemblage of disparate generic parts, and lyrics as fragments within novels have specific functions. As with Clarissa's coffin lyric, absorbed lyric functions to create a substitute for fragmented experience, a surrogate community or consensus. In fact, lyric prose in novels often mediates, chiastically, between two viewpoints or experiences, describing and determining the relationship between them.

Lyric is used in novels in accord with a chiastic principle of contact between fictional and real. Lyric conventions are marks of artifice, like the convention of "discovery" in novels, and they give intimate access to the constructedness of representation. Like the rhetorical markers of novel fiction, lyric conventions may signal our mode of entrance into a fictional world designed to affect us strongly. What I am here describing is not an essential characteristic of lyric but a possible functional aspect as novels reveal it. The remainder of this chapter explores lyric in the novel as a tool of perceptual organization used in service of a rhetorical concept of realism. I will focus on the epithalamium, a lyric kind of extraordinary formal complexity that appears in the work of novelists on both sides of the traditional formal-moral divide — in both Richardson and Fielding, that is (though Fielding will not appear for awhile).

If elegy is important to Richardson's tragedy, epithalamium is key in his comedies (the latter precedent set in Aristophanes' *Peace* and *The Birds*). Richardson employs epithalamic structure and conventions in *Pamela* and *Sir Charles Grandison* to help shape emotional experience for public consumption. Weddings, like other rituals, have prescribed formulae essential to their proper performance. But in an account of nuptial events, not all of these activities need be represented; to the basic cultural formulae we may add artistic conventions, and from a religious or social tradition create a poetic one. Epithalamia, or wedding songs, are highly coded poems belonging to two basic kinds: the epic epithalamium includes a mythological account of the lovers' union featuring gods and goddesses as actors, while the lyric model gives a chronological account of all or part of the wedding day. Both types participate in elaborate conventional staging but are intriguing because they are a mixture of the real and the fantastic — two kinds of or orientations for convention.[35]

Spenser's *Epithalamion* is the British-Irish archetype for the lyric version of the genre; it is organized in part around a series of visual and verbal events, many of which are (understandably) more common in epithalamia than in actual nuptials: a refrain that slowly changes over time, a call at dawn to bride and groom to awake, the attendance of the bride by nymphs, the dressing of the bride by her attendants, praise of her modesty, praise of her beauty (inside and out), a detailed picture of the bride's progress to the altar (with careful attention to the church porch and door), an account of the ceremony, a description of the feast and attendant revelry, an invitation to darkness to speed on, a litany against ill fortune, a benediction for happiness and prosperity, and a sketch of the joys of the wedding night.

Richardson's descriptions of weddings in *Grandison* and *Pamela* are influenced by epithalamia like Spenser's in four ways: first, Richardson quotes from the tradition; second, in minutely chronological accounts, he draws attention to conventional moments encountered in wedding poetry, either by repetition or through inversion; third, he appropriates their conventions of narrative patterning; fourth, he recasts notes of disruption found in the poetic tradition to represent the difficulties and estrangements involved in his climactic unions. It is this last that is most important, for reading the descriptions of Harriet's or Pamela's nuptials against conventional epithalamia (here I primarily cite Spenser, Herrick, and Catullus) allows us to account for discordant notes that are deeply puzzling on their own. Lyric is used in these novels to create a kind of social vision.

In *Grandison*, the letters describing Harriet's wedding day begin in the epithalamic mode. The bride appears, trembling, at the break of day and is greeted (as is every member of the wedding party) with a stanza from an epithalamium ("whose," with Lady G., "I know not," but I suspect one of Richardson's circle, if not himself):

> *The day is come, you wish'd so long:*
> *Love pick'd it out amidst the throng:*
> *He destines to himself this Sun,*
> *And takes the reins, and drives it on.*

> It is indeed a fine day. The sun seems to reproach some of us; but Harriet slept not a wink. No wonder.

> I hastened up to salute her. She was ready dressed.[36]

The poetic gesture toward the bride's awakening is almost parodied in the prose that follows, suggesting a relationship of revision between novel and epithalamium. While the moments of awakening and of dressing the bride are key to the poetic tradition, Richardson uses that tradition only to deflate it: the bride is already up and, even without nymphs to attend her, she is dressed as well.

This humorous manipulation of convention (from Charlotte's pen) is an early indication of the mixed tone of the wedding letters in general. Charlotte and Lucy together record the nuptial events: as Charlotte writes, "For the humour's sake, as well as to forward each other, on the joyful occasion, we shall write by turns" (3:218). While this arrangement allows Lucy and her friend to participate as guests without missing a recorded beat, it also evokes the singing contests that often structure epithalamia. The narration is interrupted by competing voices, each woman wishing to have the job of praise (3:225). Charlotte's flippancy, however, provides a note of discord: her caustically pretty banter on marriage reminds us of the flaws marking her own union, flaws that are significant in the second half of the novel. Such a hint of disturbance is deeply conventional in the tradition of wedding poetry.

As Heather Dubrow, Virginia Tufte, and others point out, the genre typically attempts to domesticate discord, to delve into threats to marital bliss and subsume those threats in an ideal union.[37] Rarely is an epithalamium a song of unmixed joy. The nocturnal fears expressed in stanza 19 of Spenser's *Epithalamion* may seem idiosyncratic and outrageous but are generically appropriate:

> Let no lamenting cryes, nor dolefull teares,
> Be heard all night within nor yet without.
> Ne let false whispers, breeding hidden feares,
> Breake gentle sleepe with misconceived dout.
> Let no deluding dreames, nor dreadful sights
> Make sudden sad affrights;
> Ne let housefryes, nor ligtnings helplesse harmes,
> Ne let the Pouke, nor other evill sprights,
> Ne let mischivous witches with theyr charmes,
> Ne let hob Goblins, names whose sence we see not,
> Fray us with things that be not.

Spenser seeks to ward off the threats of darkness. While nothing supernatural threatens Harriet's wedding, Lady G.'s dissatisfaction is a most insistent sign of disquiet, often appearing as a kind of gnomic wisdom about women and love:[38] "What, then, is the stuff, the nonsense, that romantic girls, their romancing part of life not wholly elapsed, prate about, and din one's ears with, of *first* Love, *first* Flame, but *first* Folly? Do not most of such give indication of gunpowder constitutions, that want but the match to be applied, to set them into a blaze? Souls of tinder, discretions of flimsy gauze, that conceal not their folly?" (3:228). At another point, Charlotte writes bitingly of wedding ceremonies in general: "After all, Lady L., we women, dressed out in ribbands, and gaudy trappings, and in Virgin-white, on our wedding days, seem but like milk-white heifers led to sacrifice. We ought to be indulged, if we are not shameless things, and very wrong indeed, in our choice of the man we *can* love" (3:236). Lady L.'s classical reference to milk-white heifers underlines her poetic antecedents. Compare the proverbial warnings of Herrick in "Connubii Flores" (1648):

> 'Tis haste
> Makes waste;
>   Extreames have still their fault;
> *The softest Fire makes the sweetest Mault.*
> *Who grips too hard the dry and slip'rie sand.*
> *Holds none at all, or little in his hand.*   (ll. 48–53)

Charlotte makes a good partner for Herrick's speaker; equally flippant, she is also equally fierce. Charlotte understands the hesitance of her sacrificial victims, but Herrick advocates the end of maiden scruples at the beginning of wedded life, accusing women of insincerity in the same fears Charlotte condones: "Coynesse takes us to a measure; / But o'racted deads the pleasure" ("The Delaying Bride" [1648], ll. 5–6). The play of proverb and bitterness within the celebration — an aspect of Richardson's account that seems the most prosaic — is in fact deeply rooted in poetic conventions, an example of the mixed pleasures of the epithalamium as genre.

The bitter and discordant in *Grandison* weighs against the harmonic and the sweet; the letters begin with an exact account of how the couple's friends join to create the bridal procession, with bridesmen and -maids in their proper order (3:220). In calling attention to the composition of the bridal party, Richardson participates in the powerful concern for order, which lies at the heart of the epithalamium. As Dubrow notes, "The fundamental mode of these poems involves lines, lists, and sequences. . . . The invitation to guests and the description of the procession act out a fantasy of unification: separate and potentially even antagonistic participants — gods and goddesses, young and old, men and women — all join together in celebrating the marriage" (*Happier Eden*, 58). This urge to document the joining of families, fortunes, and social orders works against the threats to harmony that inevitably accompany these groupings of strangers (titled wealth with respectable gentility, in Harriet's case).[39] The dissonance of the account of Harriet's wedding day has its usual generic resolution: although Harriet's epithalamium does not close with prayers for future happiness, the bride's appearance does. We leave her, "eyes lifted up, surcharged, as I may say, with tears of joy, as in thankfulness" (3:237). Charlotte, the good epithalamic poet, gives the bride her blessing (3:237), but in line with her whimsical character, she can only close with jests. Like the competing shepherds of the third eclogue in Sidney's *Arcadia*, not all the singers at the marriage feast believe in conjugal bliss.

When Pamela describes her wedding day, she also employs lyric conventions to establish her structure of vision, and there are similar notes of disturbance intermixed with her joy. Pamela's account of her wedding seems at first as unusual as the nuptials themselves. In a scope unique in the novel, the letter she writes to her parents on her wedding day chronicles events from some time just before daybreak to her moments alone in the evening, just before going to bed; no other letter is as detailed in its account of a single day. There is no public ceremony, no large group of attendants; the wedding is held in secret, between servant and master, without proper celebration. Given the oddity of the proceedings, it is striking that several conventional features of the lyric epithalamium lie within Pamela's tale. Her epistle is divided into four parts, which follow emotional and rhetorical plot lines and close with a moment of emotional resolution (the two first) or an inherited structural device (the two last). It includes details of events (some of them strange, like the appearance of the three rakes) that, as I will show, correspond to literary tradition, and it is marked by tonal uncertainties that at first sound odd but take on importance when read against conventional epithalamia. In fact, Richardson seems to be remembering significant components of the poetry of marriage in *Pamela*, just as in the later *Grandison*. He borrows points of attention — moments, symbols, or events — that are conventions of the genre; these points function to focus readers on the emotionally significant, to indicate symbolic weight, and, as in *Grandison*, to represent conflict or confusion and to gesture toward resolution.

The wedding letter opens with Pamela's attendance by the antinymph, Mrs. Jewkes, as dawn approaches. Although Pamela has been awake most of the night, Richardson draws attention to daybreak and gives the traditional nod to parallel behavior between bride and groom: "I fancy my master has not slept much neither; for I heard him up, and walking about his chamber, ever since the break of day" (51). Although Richardson does not replicate the poetic convention of the call for awakening, he draws attention to the moment the convention usually marks, as he does in the account of Harriet's wedding.[40]

In line with epithalamic convention, the hopeful beginnings of the day and its celebration are mixed with less joyous notes. While Pamela's tremblings and expressions of doubt figure her distress, the misplaced revelry of Mr. B.'s brother rakes is a concrete expression of discord in harmony. These three rakes are an oddity in the novel; they have never before appeared, and will not again. Their presence seems unmotivated except by the convention, inherited from the Roman tradition of wedding poetry, that the groom's former partners in crime mock his loss of freedom (see Catullus's "Carmen LXI"). No actual Fescennine jocularity is represented in *Pamela;* such raw disturbance is instead displaced onto the three men who appear, uninvited, to take Mr. B. away from his bride. He may be unwilling, but he goes nonetheless — tradition (or secrecy and hospitality, as Mr. B. accounts for it) cannot be neglected. The appearance of the three rakes as revelry displaced rather than revelry made central signals that all threats will eventually be disciplined in the comedy's denouement.

The marriage of Pamela and Mr. B. is a violation of class allegiance, as his sister reminds us; as a novel concerned with class mobility and transgression, *Pamela*'s account of the wedding is highly concerned with marking off limits. Pamela's letter maintains the peculiar significance of the threshold in the epithalamium, with three such references throughout. As she recounts her procession toward the chapel (accompanied by her antinymph, Mrs. Jewkes), Pamela notes like Spenser the moments at the chapel door; Nan sits guard at the chapel threshold, drawing attention to a well-worn trope, even if its contours are not perfectly maintained (374). Thresholds also appear as closing devices in two of the letter's four parts. The nuptial letter ends when Mr. B. leaves Pamela at her chamber door (380), but more interesting, however, is the closure of the third segment. The reunion of the lovers after the rakes' departure takes place in open air; Mr. B. and Pamela exchange tender words, and the section ends by literalizing their new relation: "He kissed me very tenderly: and by this time coming to the house, we entered it together" (379); here the narrative comes to a pause.

The parallel moment in the marriage song has been well glossed by Dubrow: "Stuart epithalamia concern themselves with what is shut inside the house as much as with what is shut out. In going within the house the bride and groom are becoming stable, secure. . . . Allusions to thresholds imply the source of this stability. When they enter the house, the bride and groom are entering the society it represents: the architectural construction represents the cultural constructs they are accepting and gracing" (*Happier Eden*, 74). Both the perceptual and the symbolic content of the epithalamium permeate Richardson's prose; when Pamela and Mr. B. kiss and enter their house together, it signals the start of a new dispensation. Even without the fanfare of the public ceremony befitting the marriage of social equals, Pamela gets the literary and symbolic treatment of a highly valued bride.

Dubrow contends that the "structure and plot of the lyric epithalamium . . . respond to the tensions attending marriage in Stuart England," tensions around property, sexuality, and divisive national politics (47). In these poems of marriage, "what we most frequently encounter is a vision of Edenic serenity and order — a paradisaical vision evoked by poets who dwell, and know they dwell, in a garden infested with snakes" (49). The problems of the Stuart epithalamium — of inheritance, class, and runaway sexuality — are also those of *Pamela* and the heroine's wedding-day meditations and conversations. She doesn't fear the Pouke, but she does apprehend "the ridicule and rude jests of [Mr. B.'s] equals, and companions too, . . . and the disdain of his relations, and indignation of Lady Davers, his lofty sister!" (371). The wedding is the emotional linchpin of the novel, but it is so not just because of the power of fulfilled romance; it is the moment when the larger issues marriage is expected to resolve become most urgent and irrevocable.

In Spenser's *Epithalamion* a finely checkered *concordia discors* is present from the beginning (as it is in Pamela's letter). The first few stanzas insist that all be perfect for the bride — her nymphs are instructed to wash carefully, so "That when you come whereas my love doth lie, / No blemish she may spie" (65–66). She needs protection, like the deer, from "the wylde wolves which seek them to devoure" (69). These threats must somehow be damped: the litany against misfortune, which closes the poem, signifies the danger and attempts to ward it off, as in the supplications to Cynthia for fertility and easy childbirth (Pamela's letter also ends in prayer: "I went to my closet; and besought the Divine assistance in the conduct of my future life") (380). The discord surrounding marriage is usually never fully resolved in epithalamia, which most often conclude with hopes for, rather than guarantees of, fruition. Pamela's difficulties are not easily solved, either; her problems of virtue have a sequel. The lyric, however, allows access to a moment both troubling and glorious, an acceptable and familiar frame for representation, for aesthetic and emotional response.

Richardson's prose epithalamia are not unprecedented. Ancient rhetoricians like Himerius and Dionysius of Halicarnassus argued that lyric had an important place in prose compositions: "the poet should make use of all the flowers of poetry at his command, Himerius advising that a poetic style should be used even in the prose epithalamium. Dionysius, although he recommends a moderate prose style . . . suggests that at all times the diction should be elevated and poetic, and like his fellow rhetoricians, encourages imitation of Sappho and Homer" (Tufte, *Poetry of Marriage*, 132). Pastoral romances also include epithalamia as lyric insertions: Sidney's *Arcadia* and Sheppard's *Loves of Amandus and Sophronia* contain such moments. In bringing lyric into his prose, Richardson expands upon tradition wherein the poetic signifies emotional exuberance and stylistic refinement.[41]

Lyric contributes three strikingly different things to *Pamela*: emotional frame, visual and narrative content, and a pattern for representing confusion. Epithalamic conventions help to guide Pamela's letter; facts of perception as well as speech are given in line with poetic structures. Lyric provides an order for emotional experience familiar to the culturally literate; it creates an open frame for sharing the affective. Its conventions, like the components of formal realism, point outside the novel's world to one where rules regulate experience — rules of the world of bodies, names, places, or poetic vision. The novel's system of chiasmus enables, and even requires, that other modes of regulating and ordering experience become part of its repertoire of signification. The structure of epithalamia, like those of elegy, amorous lyric, or hymn, provides the novel with discursive leverage in creating chiastic moments that move readers into the text, especially the text as emotional construction.

The uses of epithalamia in *Pamela* and *Grandison* emphasize several important factors: as with Haywood's use of Donne, the ability of lyric to give access to emotions need not always be confined to the first person. The lyric in these circumstances mediates between two (or more) sets of emotions and experiences by aligning events with a particular pattern (as the epithalamium does so well) and, frequently, by connecting a set of perceptions to a structure that makes sense of them (moving from conflict to rapprochement, for example). These structural uses of lyric emphasize the concern with framing we find in novelistic accounts of emotion.

It is well to ask again how Richardson's adaptations of lyric perform alterations upon them — to inquire how lyric may work with and against a novel's realism. Part of the question involves the difference between a lyric epithalamium or elegy and the prose versions of them I have discussed. If Richardson's accounts of weddings include many conventions from verse epithalamia, they exclude others, as well as add things no previous poet would have considered appropriate. Some of these are plot-related, as in *Pamela:* the misleading statements Pamela makes to conceal her impending nuptials (374), the attention she pays to the activities and presence of her (formerly fellow) servants (373–74), the minute renderings of dialogue, the colloquial references to her own writing, and so on. What is particularly interesting, however, is that the epithalamium is usually not a genre that can be accused of ignoring details, down to time of day, the number of guests at a feast, or the quality and type of a wedding gown. Pamela's minuteness would seem, oddly, to fit right in; the difference lies in the kind of details that appear and how they are used. Richardson's adaptation of the lyric involves a simultaneity at the level of structure; the chain of events goes on, overlaid by a pattern of expression and attention that causes some moments to shine through, even while others may be suppressed. At least two modes of representation are under way, implying the kind of synchronicity shared by a person's two eyes, the blending of sight between one point of focus and another.

It is not entirely an oversimplification to say that what are blended are the mundane and the extraordinary. The two categories become recombined in a number of ways: everyday life with the significance that life is given by a unique individual consciousness; the contact of servant virtue with the splendor of the gentry; individual experience expanded by the clarity, dignity, and consequence of generic convention (itself a kind of ritual). Lyric enables novels to bring experience to knowledge. In *Pamela,* formal integrity is replaced by perceptual and subjective integrity (as in Clarissa's self-elegy); in *Grandison,* formal integrity is subject to revisions of character and questions of plot. Both of these developments reappear in later lyrics, the first resurfacing in the perceptually organized lyrics of the romantics — poems that often took on new forms, like the Greater Romantic Lyric; the second returns in the dramatic monologues of the next generation. The mixed field that belongs to the novel and the changing domain of the lyric also interact chiastically, especially at first through the possibilities of satire: dressing pins, hats, and broken shins (Pope and/or *Pamela*) eventually meet up with filling stations, dirty doilies, refrigerators, and wheelbarrows.

This expansiveness has a significant immediate ramification, as we have seen: the linkage of the domestic with the subjective as a complex site of novelistic representation. The epithalamium begins with a domestic institution (or rather, surrounds the moments of its beginning), but *Pamela* opens the epithalamium up to the home — to parlors and breakfast rooms, in addition to bedchambers — and its operations: servants and patronage, secrets and matters of display. One of three verse lyrics included in *Pamela* is a suggestion of the possibilities involved. On leaving Bedfordshire, Pamela composes "Verses *on my going away*," which begin:

> Attend, my fellow-servants dear,
> A grateful song demands your ear;
> The dictates of a heart sincere,
>> Presented you by Pamela.

> I long have had a blissful fate;
> Exalted by the good and great,
> Yet to her former humble state
>> Content returns your Pamela. (121)

The poem continues for ten stanzas, exhorting the other servants to piety, virtue, and honor in poverty: it forms a counter to the claims to class/literary value, which epithalamium and amatory fiction have established (placing Pamela in the company of poets like Mary Leapor). Pamela's verses may be insipid, but one other thing is certainly true — they form, purely and completely, a domestic lyric. As I have argued, domesticity in the novel and the lyrics that follow it is a path to, sign of, or even substitute for, intimacy. Domesticity becomes the testing ground of convention and the proving ground of emotional representation. While it may be a space amenable to satire in disrupting hierarchies of significance (for Fielding or for Swift or Pope), it is also a space where the proximity and familiarity that satire brings may invigorate old conventions and form new ones.

To state it boldly, the potential for lyric structures to organize the perceptual is more central to novelists in the midcentury than to poets, in part because of the generic structure of chiasmus that novels employ. Poetic structures are used in novels to lay out the shape of experience, and in them it becomes possible to reinsert the body within a perceptual frame, a move whose significance may be most apparent in the problems displayed in midcentury odes. Lyrics offer a set of conventions that, along with the rhetoric of realism, allow readers to enter a fictional world bound by rules. We have seen that narrators, correspondents, and autobiographers, specific names, times, and places, and affective visions of reading act as chiastic contacts between our worlds and the worlds of fiction; they are the sites through which fiction emerges. Lyric conventions also shape the emergence of the fictional into the reader's worlds of life and imagination. They announce the constructedness of the worlds we read and of the experiences they represent, so that we may reconstruct these worlds for ourselves and submit them to the political and social critiques of novelistic discourse.

In line with this need to provide contacts between two worlds, the use of lyric in the novel often involves doubling, as with the dual perspective associated with the epithalamium in Richardson or, as I will show in the next chapter, with the consensus (or approximation of two people or kinds of emotion) produced in *Pamela* by reading (Mr. B. reading the Psalms) and writing lyric (Pamela imitating them). The generic structure of the novel employs lyrics as part of its chiastic strategies. Chiasmus, however, can involve conflict; the adaptation of lyric convention invokes literary pressures that the use of epistolary conventions does not. The superstructure of genre may influence the kind of interaction produced in chiastic citation. The paradox of Pamela's verses on her own humility is one example of these problems, but at their root is the disjunction hinted by my reference to Pope — Pamela's scraped shins and Belinda's raped lock both function in literary terms as violations of decorum that produce satirical potential. The problems of the relationship of lyric to novel, following upon questions of decorum and scope, are the subject of the following chapter.

Five

The Limits of Lyric and the Space
of the Novel

Movement between one genre and another is not always felicitous or straightforward. A language so highly coded as that of lyric may sit strangely when its context shifts; Fielding's sometimes mocking use of poetic convention suggests the complications at the base of generic appropriation. If lyric offers novelists a rich language of emotional description, it is a language with limits. I begin here with Fielding's burlesque as a way of approaching the problem of generic crossover. Lyric, as a set of conventions linked to literary and social practices, provides a site where the challenges of genre and rhetoric may be negotiated. Questions of generic interaction become questions of development; novelists' approach to the limits of lyric helps to push beyond them. Works by Fielding, Richardson, Frances Brooke, Charlotte Smith, and others demonstrate the ways in which novelists, using lyric in combination with strategies from *ekphrasis* to free indirect discourse, create fictions of consciousness that enable readers' movements from the world of reading to the worlds of novels. The study of literary consciousness has been masterfully accomplished by many critics (Dorrit Cohn in particular); my goal here is to set forth ways in which eighteenth-century novels work out consciousness in relation to lyric.

Lyric often represents a kind of ideal — of beauty, decorum, communication between hearts — but it is an ideal that calls as loudly for violation as for worship. The transition of any ideal from one context to another exerts pressure upon it, defining as well as changing it. While Fielding speaks of humanly perfection wearing a fool's cap, Richardson cherishes ideals of virtue closer to his heart; Richardson uses lyric to think through the ideal and our constant falling away from it, while

Fielding employs lyric to spark laughter at our inadequacies. Lyric often appears in novels as a modification of the ideal by the satirical or real; the significance of these changes depends in part upon the kind of lyric involved and its relation to social and personal processes.

Fielding's insistent refusal of Richardsonian first-person expression brings forth a set of stylistic challenges. For Fielding, mock-lyric exists, too. In seeking the right languages to describe Sophia's beauty, Fielding resolves on those of epithalamium and ode. As with most of his recyclings of form, Fielding's use of lyric is partially tongue-in-cheek, aiming for "an elevation of stile, and all other circumstances proper to raise the veneration of our reader."[1] True to such intent, he begins his solemn scene with a burlesque of high Roman pastoral:

> Hushed be every ruder breath. May the heathen ruler of the winds confine in iron chains the boisterous limbs of noisy Boreas, and the sharp-pointed nose of bitter biting Eurus. Do thou, sweet Zephyrus, rising from thy fragrant bed, mount the western sky, and lead on those delicious gales, the charms of which call forth the lovely Flora from her chamber, perfumed with pearly dews, when on the first of June, her birthday, the blooming maid, in loose attire, gently trips it over the verdant mead, where every flower rises to do her homage, 'till the whole field becomes enamelled, and colours contend with sweets which shall ravish her most. (121–22)

This is a typical odal beginning (as well as echoing Chaucer); Fielding proceeds to invoke aid from the natural world to hymn Sophia's approaching beauty:

> So charming may she now appear; and you the feather'd choristers of nature, whose sweetest notes not even Handel can excel, tune your melodious throats, to celebrate her appearance. From love proceeds your music, and to love it returns. Awaken therefore that gentle passion in every swain: for lo! Adorned with all the charms in which nature can array her; bedecked with beauty, youth, sprightliness, innocence, modesty, and tenderness, breathing sweetness from her rosy lips, and darting brightness from her sparkling eyes, the lovely Sophia comes. (122)

This language emphasizes the conventional emotional connotations of a particular mode of lyric (the Horatian ode); while the lyric voice here calls youth inexorably to love, lyric itself is a response to love's call. Such language establishes the ground of description; Fielding then represents

Sophia through ekphrastic descriptions of her charms, comparing her to the most beauteous women known and supplying a blazon of her brilliance that culminates in a quotation from Suckling's "Ballade. Upon a Wedding" (1646).[2] Suckling's epithalamium, in line with Fielding's humor, hymns the wedding of a couple living at Charing Cross in "a house with stairs"—belonging to the merchant class, we may assume—in the voice of a poet-farmer whose grammar and sense of decorum are meant to amuse. However marked by class strata and the humor Suckling uses to describe them, the beauty of the bride and the emotional truthfulness of the representation transcend the fun at her expense; so it is with Fielding's treatment of Sophia.[3] Fielding's manipulations of literary tradition of course hold it at a distance of irony and humor; at the same time, the evident pleasure he takes (and gives) in the process draws us closer to the objects he represents. Fielding manipulates poetic language to lift objects carefully into view; while they may seem the results of curmudgeonly charm or idiosyncrasy, the tensions he creates between matter and form are endemic to the novel as it develops in the century.

The epithalamium, like the elegy, is closely related to a particular social event and is at home in the novel's social world, bringing its own model for anxiety and disruption. Hymn and psalm are similarly social kinds of lyric; they have close relations to activities with ritual forms like prayer and lamentation, but they have a typical literary shape, too. The hymnal model exhibits parts of the relationship between pure or ideal forms and the novel's concern with impure matter. The fundamental model behind the hymn—the most popular lyric kind in the eighteenth century—is the presentation of an "I" or a "we" whose experience is available for adoption by an individual or a congregation. In singing a hymn, the celebrant often seeks to conform herself to an ideal position of peace and tranquillity, a place of absolute correspondence between her will or emotions and the will of God. Richardson's heroines often seek such subjective and linguistic conformity, and in *Pamela*, while the epithalamium helps to regulate perception of external events, the lament or hymn indicates a possibility for regulating things internal, the perceptions of one's soul and the disturbances within it.

Richardson's reliance on this model is apparent in his adaptations of verse lyric. Trapped in Lincolnshire, Pamela adapts and sings a psalm that later becomes a major means of rapprochement between her and Mr. B. After their engagement, Mr. B. flaunts Pamela's skill before his friends as testimony to her moral "excellencies" (348–53). While he fares ill in her poem, appearing as the persecutor of innocence, he overcomes his own indignation and enters into Pamela's sorrows and triumphs. Pamela seeks both regulation and expression of her emotion through a lyric genre, a characteristic instance of eighteenth-century imitation; Mr. B. is also able thus to enter into her emotions, so that a double rapprochement (between Pamela and the ideal, and Pamela and Mr. B.) is effected around a lyric.

Two other poems appear in *Pamela*, each indicating a particular relationship between the world of the novel and lyric ideals. At the end of their story, Pamela and Mr. B. each present the other with a poem: Pamela's is again a lyric emphasizing the proper position of her heart and mind relative to her experience; Mr. B.'s is an amorous lyric in praise of Pamela. He limns the conventional organic relation between the beloved and harmonious nature, a linkage of the sensuous to a stable ordering of the world:

> The purple violet, damask rose,
> Each, to delight your sense, blows.
> The lilies ope', as you appear;
> And all the beauties of the year
>   Diffuse their odours at your feet,
>   Who give to ev'ry flow'r its sweet.

Poetry here may not order perception, as was the case with epithalamia, but it testifies to and exemplifies such regulation. The same sentiments are mirrored from prose to poetry: " 'Don't you with pleasure, my dear,' said he, 'take in the delightful fragrance, that this sweet shower has given to these banks of flowers? Your company is so enlivening to me, that I could almost fancy, that what we owe to the *shower* is owing to your presence. All nature, methinks, blooms around me, when I have my Pamela by my side' " (512). Pamela receives the lyric as emotional recompense; her husband has just described the arrangements he has made for her against his death and asked that for his good credit and hers, she never marry Mr. Williams:[4] "Thus sweetly did he palliate the grief, which the generosity of his actions, mixed with the seriousness of the occasion, and the strange request he had vouchsafed to make me, had occasioned" (513). The lyric again effects rapprochement or consensus, as well as situating Pamela within a class and literary hierarchy for which, as Richardson sees it, she is suited by her virtue.[5]

There is a problem, however. Mr. B. is aware that the poem functions through convention, not fact; lyric allows a seeming regulation and concord, the imagined equivalence of human and natural systems, as well as the proximation of aesthetic and physical experience (the same tense connection is manifest in Pamela's bizarre poem in praise of her own humility). The insistent mapping of literary convention onto "reality" aligns this use of lyric with rhetorical characteristics of novelistic realism and the paradigm of chiasmus, discussed in the last chapter. Here, the relationship of verse to prose is in part that of summary to lyric, but only in part. The verse as verse can function as a gift, a polished, aesthetically complete token of emotional exchange. But it also appears almost in quotation marks, an "as if" or symbol of a kind of expression held at a distance, subject to a suspension of disbelief. This distancing is not that of satire but of desire, self-knowledge, and even impossibility. The conventions Mr. B. employs he acknowledges to be false (in the manner of the pathetic fallacy); in essence, lyric conventions expand the possibilities of expression and comprehension but limit them as well. Whatever uses lyric conventions may serve in eighteenth-century novels, however they may be integrated within the novel's frame, they remain the focus of tension and struggle, whether it involves Mr. B.'s self-conscious tribute to Pamela's power, Pamela's odd self-tribute to humility, or the adoption of the dissonance common to epithalamia.

The ideals that lyric represents may shift, and each has another side. If the question is the possibility of representing absolute beauty, the answer may be the double voice of burlesque and convention; if it is the conformity of the soul to a religious ideal in the Psalms, the recognition of virtue and its tribute of love should, and eventually do, follow; if it is the perfection of pastoral bliss that is in question, the inevitable heaviness of the daily world may intervene. The religious ideal as doctrine and literary convention is brought into line with challenges to it, in *Pamela* (if not *Clarissa*). However, the challenge to pastoral lyric and the amorous ideal in *Pamela* or *Tom Jones* is different. It is at base a concern with the shape of language as it is put to its multiple uses, and it involves to some degree a question of generic discipline — of excess or even wishful thinking — and the competing constructions of the novel by Richardson or Fielding, of the romance, and of amatory fiction. By the mid–eighteenth century, the form of this disciplinary question had become predictable: the appearance of certain kinds of poetic language in novels was now so conventional as to become the subject of artistic concern and even parody — the path most strongly suggested by Fielding and one that lurks behind Richardson's own work.

As with Sophia, descriptions of a heroine's beauty in novels often rely on rhetorical traditions of literary pictorialism (some lyric in origin, some not). These *ekphraseis* suggest the contours of the relationship between mode, genre, and citation in the novel and offer a way of reading beyond parody or idealism. Although scholars may connect the parodic use of poetic language to mock-epic or -heroic styles and to practitioners like Fielding, as early as Congreve's *Incognita* (1691) poetic language had a questionable status when it appeared in prose: "But *Aurelian* . . . fancy'd he saw a little Nest of Cupids break from the Tresses of her Hair, and every one officiously betake himself to his task. Some fann'd with their downy Wings, her glowing cheeks; while others brush'd the balmy Dew from off her Face, leaving alone a heavenly Moisture blubbing on her Lips, or which they drank and revell'd for their pains; Nay, so particular were their allotments in her service, that *Aurelian* was very positive a young Cupid who was but just Pen-fether'd imploy'd his naked Quills to pick her Teeth."[6]

Two things are important. First, the elaborate descriptive idiom — that of lyric and of painting — is linked to a purely subjective perception that is defined by an emotional commitment (Aurelian *fancied* he saw). Second, the potential for parody in such lines (elaborated at different times by Shakespeare or Pope) points out the difficulties surrounding generic boundaries, ranging from those of the novel and romance to those of the sister arts of painting and poetry. The preface to Congreve's *Incognita*, a foundational comparative treatment of novel and romance, identifies romance with "lofty language" while asserting, "Novels are of a more familiar nature; come near us, and represent to us Intrigues in practice, delight us with Accidents and odd events, but not such as are wholly unusual or unpresidented, such which not being so distant from our Belief bring also the pleasure nearer us" (111). If *Incognita* is supposed to be a novel, it does not eschew lofty speech. Part of the problem is that it is hard to identify an emotional language of description in the early modern period that is not rhetorically complex.

The pictorialism of blazons or of Congreve's cherubs is that of *enargeia* or ekphrasis, terms from classical rhetoric that indicate careful visual descriptions (often but not exclusively of works of art) and evoke strategies of pictorial composition. Ekphrasis or enargeia may properly appear in different forms, in discourses as distinct as lyric and law. As Jean Hagstrum points out, ekphrasis most probably entered modern poetry from Greek romance and has at no point been confinable to a single genre, appearing in "epic, drama, epigrams, lyric, romance, and allegory" with equal ease.[7] Rhetoric is the hinge on which genres, as well as loose formal configurations like poetry and prose, are brought together.

They meet through questions of affect, through the relationship each constructs with its readers.

In the Renaissance, as Brian Vickers notes, there is an "almost . . . universal acceptance of the classical-medieval identification of rhetoric and poetic."[8] The emotional power of poetry, in particular, is linked to its use of rhetoric as both trope and figure, from Aristotle to Puttenham, but also to Dennis, Kames, and beyond. For critics like these, language, in prose or poetry, achieves emotional weight through a careful manipulation of rhetorical tools; it is also through rhetoric that prose and poetry may come together.[9] Poetry and prose are "seldom or never distinguish[ed] . . . in their rhetorical or expressive functions," so that Dryden will even speak of " 'the other harmony of prose' " (Vickers, *Classical Rhetoric*, 37). The novel's historically determined turn to rhetoric as a means of representing and evoking emotion, then, can barely escape being a turn, at times, to poetry: the two are thoroughly, mutually involved.

Ekphrasis, like other rhetorical figures, is impossible to restrain from generic crossover; it belongs more properly to language itself than to any particular literary kind. However, ekphrasis, like any other aspect of rhetorical embellishment, sometimes seems misplaced: the attempted reformation of the English language as public and scientific speech by thinkers associated with the Royal Society is indicative of such a changing sense of disciplinary or generic decorum. In the view of Thomas Sprat, historian of the Royal Society, eloquence is suspect because it influences belief without regard for truth: "Who can behold, without indignation, how many mists and uncertainties, these specious *Tropes* and *Figures* have brought on our Knowledg [*sic*]?"[10] The Royal Society sought to purify the English language for scientific purposes, in part, to remove from the language of empirical proof the kind of subjective quality associated with Aurelian's fancy. The attempt was not entirely successful.[11] Although its significance has at times been overestimated, the Royal Society's "plain speech" was part of a larger cultural phenomenon (in part nonconformist and Anglican) connected with early novels.[12] Rhetoric, with its claims to direct emotional power, moves in and out of genres. My adaptation of a term from rhetoric, chiasmus, rather than the more conventional term from aesthetics, mimesis, to address the novel's relationship to readers and the world of those readers is indicative of my belief that rhetoric is a primary tool for giving substance to generic shape. Rhetoric also brings with it confusion and contentions over power.

Whatever the generic expectation, ekphrastic moments like Aurelian's vision in Congreve persisted in novels as descriptive moments imbued with emotional import. Although ekphrasis has no original or simple generic affinities, certain kinds of ekphrastic description have become associated with particular styles and genres — the blazon and the lyric, for example. The elaborate diction connected with such ekphraseis would become increasingly associated with fiction as distinct from fact, and poetry as distinct from prose, in the years following Sprat and Congreve. In fact, Congreve's romance-novel distinction, however dialectically complex, and even wishful, accrues its own poetry-prose dimension with the romantics, but none of these distinctions is exact or complete. What is at stake in the use of poetically cast ekphraseis (blazons brought from lyric emphasizing subjection to beauty, emblematic patterns from the "metaphysicals," landscape descriptions from Restoration poets, etc.) is first, whether descriptive and rhetorical traditions are translatable from one genre to another, and second, whether the highly coded nature of some of these traditions assists or impairs — even corrupts — the genres into which they are translated.[13] Questions of style become questions of the rhetorical sensibilities of genres.

This was a central concern for writers of both poetry and prose and goes beyond the use of any single rhetorical figure. Gray — to the disdain of Wordsworth — felt there to be a clear divide between the language of prose and that of poetry, as he writes in a letter to West: "As to the matter of stile, I have this to say: the language of the age is never the language of poetry. . . . Our poetry has a language peculiar to itself: to which almost everyone, that has written, has added something by enriching it with foreign idioms and derivatives: Nay, sometimes words of their own composition or invention."[14] Gray's position is difficult to maintain, and critics from Dennis to Kames and Blair often did not. Gray's insistence on a purely poetic language buckles in the "Elegy Written in a Country Churchyard": "In 1765 he remarked . . . 'that the *Elegy* owed its popularity entirely to its subject, and that the public would have received it as well if it had been written in prose" (Guillory, *Cultural Capital*, 120). John Guillory argues that Gray's tendency to filter earlier poetic traditions (native and classical) results in a language very close to prose in the elegy:[15] "to say the poem was misread as though it were prose is to admit the degree to which the language of the poem is already the language of vernacular prose; it is to recognize the degree to which the poem normalizes its classical and Renaissance sources" (121). This is something like the "chaste" diction that Davie identifies in *Purity of Diction in En-*

glish Verse as the peculiar strength of many eighteenth-century British poets: the refusal to coin words, the limitation of poetic language to a naturalized range of speech, and the tendency (especially in Johnson, Goldsmith, or Crabbe) to give dead metaphors new life.[16] The relatively chaste diction of the "Elegy" is a perfect example for Guillory of the cumulative effects of vernacular prose forms on literary language.

Davie finds vernacular prose at the heart of poetic taste in the century, most notably in the letter and letter-as-art (25–26). In the move to purify the language that chaste diction implies and represents, the body of language becomes curiously mixed: "But not only the language of previous poetry can provide dead metaphors [to be revived by the poet]: they appear no less in conversation and in prose. Hence, pure diction can be found where a poet has tried to revivify the dead metaphors of studied conversation or artless prose. Indeed, who that has read the letters of Mrs. Boscawen or Mrs. Thrale could affirm that Johnson's personification, or Cowper's do not derive from letters or conversation?" (32). There is a constant interchange between verse and prose, and it is a commerce motivated by tensions over literary property. It is true that "eighteenth-century prose defined itself against . . . strategies" like "neologism, archaism, complex figuration and foreign borrowing," characteristics of Renaissance poetry and prose (Guillory, *Cultural Capital*, 121)—just as Watt argues for the novel's self-defined plainness against romance complexity—but the process of "normalization" is complex. Borrowings from poetry in novels are distinguished by functional determinations, most notably by the decision to abstract mode as a component of representation, allowing it to exist alongside character, plot, and ethical concerns in a larger text, often in studied incoherence or incohesion. The novel absorbs other discourses as a way of referring beyond itself to a world regulated by decorum, law, or history.

The potential for disruption involved in the use of poetry in prose becomes artistically important in eighteenth-century novels; if the smooth prosification of poetic sources marks Gray's "Elegy," the disjointed cast of its opposite marks *Incognita*. The highly coded ekphrasis of Congreve's blazon evokes older lyric and, wittingly or not, is subject to the possibility of parody based on its conventionality. Genres (amorous lyric, novel, and romance), mode (lyric and narrative), and rhetoric meet at this intriguing moment, and the conjunction reveals the novel's flexibility, its capacity to make linguistic relations significant.

If satire or burlesque is not the outcome of such interaction, other forms of disillusion or distrust may be: the self-described dangerous vanity of the heroine in Charlotte Lennox's *Life of Harriot Stuart, Written by Herself* (1750) is illustrative of the patterns at midcentury (a point at which the novel had gained sufficient self-consciousness to register a broad range of generic difficulties and solutions). Harriot writes a letter to a friend describing a romantic adventure: "As soon as [her lover] had taken his leave, I wrote to my female friend, whom I called Sylvia; and, in a truly romantic style, related the whole adventure. But when I came to describe the person, an involuntary impulse made me throw my thoughts into verse; and this first attempt in poetry was thought so tender and so passionate, that it procured me the name of Sappho, a distinction which agreeably soothed my vanity" (66). This self-love leads Harriot into danger—her skill at writing poems about the passions inspires men with the belief that she is as warm and inviting as her verse; she is abducted several times and stabs a man to prevent his raping her. Harriot attributes her woes directly to her truck with the muses: "I had reason . . . to repent the employing of my pen so much on the subject of love: my style was rather too warm and passionate for one of my years; and the following poem ["A Hymn to Venus"] was, perhaps, the first cause of one the most cruel adventures of my life" (147–48). Subsequently, a set of verses become the "first cause of the perplexing adventures in which I was afterwards engaged" (242): lyric is dangerous, and its use in this novel is linked to a language of critique involving gender, character, genre, and rhetoric (as style and persuasion gone awry).[17]

Harriot's perplexing adventures, born of her verse, are of the sort—rape, abduction, near-shipwreck, imprisonment in a convent—that Lennox later denounces as quixotically romantic. In *The Female Quixote* (1752), Arabella must learn (like Austen's later Catherine Morland) that neither realism nor modern-day England allows for the villainy or virtues of old romance. The false distinction between romance and novel based on verisimilitude and wild adventures, of course, does not hold up in eighteenth-century prose fiction, especially as novelists move toward the Gothic. Nor, however, does a distinction based on diction and figurative language. The high-flown language of romance, which Congreve decries, the language of love so closely linked to lyric in something like the *Arcadia*, bleeds into novels, and its normalization is part of the dialectical relationship constructed around verisimilitude, which characterizes the history of "novel" versus "romance," and which also shapes that of prose fiction versus poetry (cf. McKeon, *Origins of the English Novel*). Congreve cannot forbear occasionally using the languages of lyric and of romance, and neither can Lennox, Haywood, or Richardson. Prose may sometimes regularize poetic usage through cliché and (sometimes hackneyed) metaphor, but prose fiction — the artistic manipulation of the linguistic and loosely formal base constituted by "prose" — behaves in a more complex fashion. The use of tropes and figures as attendant upon the manipulation of lyric convention is contingent on proximal and distant history: what ekphrasis means depends on what it has meant, just as Harriot's lyrics (dangerously) implicate her in an erotic literary history. These literary histories are not prescriptive or stable; they introduce uncertainties that can create new significance.

In addition to overt claims to moral instructiveness, part of the novel's claim to membership in the belles lettres comes with its free and capable manipulation of rhetoric as a tool in just representation. The manipulation of style and rhetoric and the amalgamation of prose and poetry in novels is complex: lyric is not the only poetic language to have a significant place in the novel's just representations. Lyric genres can be identified by particular tropes and language, but other kinds of poetry, epic, moral, or didactic, leave their mark. In Frances Brooke's *Lady Julia Mandeville* (1763), an important midcentury novel now too much neglected, letters from the hero's father resemble moral verse epistles or Thomson's didactic poetry, with exaggerated encomia of virtuous men and of the excellent management of their estates: "Plenty, the child of industry, smiles on their humble abodes; and, if any unforeseen misfortune nips the blossoms of their prosperity, his bounty, descending silent and refreshing as the dews of Heaven, renews their blooming state, and restores joy to their happy dwellings."[18] Doody has pointed out the similarity of novels to the loose, long didactic poem, focusing on length and breadth of representation in both forms;[19] the similarity of these two Augustan kinds suggests the role of mixed styles and of stylistic decorum in both of them. Like epic or the novel, these long poems draw upon several modes — if epithalamium and sonnet exist in *Paradise Lost*, hymns and complaints are carefully woven into *Night Thoughts*. They provide a scope for experimentation and a way of approaching completion (or extreme and satisfying variety) at the level of subject and style. From the other direction, the mixed language of these works offers readers (some of whom are writers, too) training in the proper use of varying kinds of poetic speech, and from novel to poem and back the influence is evident. Such experimental works contribute progressively to a decorum of generic appropriation, showing how, when, and why what language is appropriate. Prose absorbs poetry, and poetry may take on a prosaic cast, disciplined by decorum but also by ethics.[20]

These polyphonic compositions generally serve to emphasize the role played by each voice in the greater whole. The novel approaches such polyphony — or heteroglossia — as both signification and evocation. The instability of rhetorical usage or of citation becomes linked to the status of an utterance, and with it, the status of a speaker: the language of lyric becomes doubly the language of self in novels because it is the language of a *particular* person, of subject and individual. The novel's adaptation of lyric conventions often becomes an adaptation of rhetorical trope (or, more rarely, figure), and the linkage of lyric to rhetoric becomes a linkage to speech and to persons. Lyric speech evolves as an ethical signifier of character in a way crucial to novelistic ideas of subjectivity and to developing ideas of lyric voice.

§ Novelistic prose adapts lyric language as a limiting factor in its practices of description: lyric shapes perception, formalizes reportage, and provides a framework enabling emotional experience to be shared from writer (within the text and behind it) to reader. But novels often intensify formal moves by replicating linguistic structures in ethical ones. In line with the novel's generic formulae, its use of lyric often appears as part of a question of the ethics of individual taste.[21] Brooke's novels allow us to understand this process, emphasizing the limits of lyric modes of expression through a relation of language to character. Brooke wrote several delightful novels from the 1760s onward, as well as plays, operettas, and lyrics; this familiarity with multiple genres served her well.[22] The epistolary *Lady Julia* chronicles the tragic love between two cousins, Henry and Julia; their doomed romance runs parallel to the romantic reformation of their friend Lady Anne, whose resolve to be a witty widow finally gives way to sincerity and love. The novel offers a linguistic model of romantic purity: the hero, Henry, frequently employs lyric prose to define his romantic vision:

> Oh! Mordaunt! when I behold her, read the soft language of these speaking eyes, hear those harmonious sounds — who that has a soul can be insensible! — yet there are men dead to all sense of perfection, who can regard that angel form without rapture, can hear the music of that voice without emotion! I have myself with astonishment seen them, inanimate as the trees around them, listen coldly to those melting accents — There is a sweetness in her voice, Mordaunt, a melodious softness, which fancy cannot paint: the enchantment of her conversation is inexpressible. (117)

This description presents, as does Haywood's *Love in Excess*, tropes and figures whose cultural associations lie with lyric. Henry's linguistic choices reflect his self-vision: he regards himself as an updated courtly lover whose honor contends for primacy with his love, and his sincerity is marked linguistically by his straightforward use of poetic tradition. Lady Anne, on the other hand, is a wit and uses poetic allusion with a satiric flair:

> We have been dining *al fresco* in a rustic temple, in a wood near the house: romanesque, simple; the pillars trunks of ancient oaks, the roof the bark of trees, the pavement pebbles, the seats moss; the wild melody of nature our music; the distant sound of the cascade just breaks on the ear, which joined by the chant of the birds, the cooing of the doves, the lowing of the herds, and the gently-breathing Western breeze, forms a concert most divinely harmonious.
>
> Really this place would be charming, if it was a little more replete with human beings. (68)

This descriptive catalogue is resonant with the work of another Lady Anne: Finch's "Nocturnal Reverie" (1713) lists similar bucolic delights (Zephyr's wings, "When darkened groves their softest shadows wear, / And falling waters we distinctly hear," and "unmolested kine," etc. [ll. 3, 23–24, 34]) and closes with a plea to remain abroad, alone, "in such a night." Brooke's Lady Anne imitates — and then rejects — Finch's bucolic vista. She sees the same scene and only wants some decent company. For her, lyric is a habit to be donned or removed, to be used for playing dress-up — at least at first. Eventually Anne herself is overcome, much like Henry, and wit gives way to poetic tradition; an available language for describing emotional intricacies is highly important after her friend Julia's death, and the use of poetic convention becomes an indication of Anne's moral worth:

> I gaze on the once matchless form, and all vanity dies within me: who was ever lovely like her? yet she lies before me a clod of senseless clay. Those eyes, which once gave love to every beholder, are now robbed of their living lustre; that beauteous bosom is cold as the marble on the silent tomb; the roses of those cheeks are faded; those vermilion lips, from whence truth and virtue ever proceeded. . . . Look here, ye proud, and be humble! which of you all can vie with her? youth, health, beauty, birth, riches, all that men call good, were hers: all are now of no avail; virtue alone bids defiance to the grave. (206)

What force has the imagination over the senses! how different is the whole face of nature in my eyes! the once smiling scene has a melan-

choly gloom, which strikes a damp through my inmost soul: I look in
vain for those vivid beauties which once charmed me; all beauty died
with Lady Julia! (209)

In the first excerpt, the moralist language is common enough, but the
description of Julia's body is conventionally elegiac in the vein of Milton's "Lycidas" or Donne's "First Anniversarie." Julia's death is the cata-
lyst in Anne's decision to marry a longtime friend. Anne's conversion to
elegy then aligns style with substance: she is a convert to love and poetry
at once, even if the two occasionally use different idioms. In *Lady Julia*,
lyric becomes a window not merely on emotion but also on character; its
proper use indicates moral worth and social commitment: Anne's willingness to enter marriage, with its gendered political, moral, social, and
emotional constraints, is related to her final linguistic allegiance. There
is an ethics of public and private speech.

Lyric becomes linked to the wider discursive fields that underpin
novelistic didacticism. Novels, like other realist fictions, may create a
web of literary cross-references that bring the fictional world into relationship with the real one — while heroines of romance don't read of
their counterparts, heroines of novels do so all the time. This wry kind of
self-reference both points out fictionality and supports claims to verisimilitude in typical chiastic fashion. The same rhetorical system is at
work in the use of poetic convention as of names and dates — poems and
poets are objects in the real world, and references to them buttress
novelistic substantiality.

The root processes here are partly related to the relative valuation in
the period of various kinds of lyric. As I argued in Chapter 3, some lyrics
(Anacreontics, Cavalier poetry, etc.) were suspect, while others had religious or social validation and support. Richardson, a careful practi-
tioner of lyric adaptation, enforces the violence and rakishness of Lovelace's temper through a lyric paradigm. Clarissa works within a model of
religious poetry, putting herself close to a divine like Dr. Donne (especially in her death preparations); Lovelace is closer kin to the Jack Donne
of *Songs and Sonets*, to Rochester or Cavalier poets.[23] The violence of
Lovelace's passion in the fire scene (after his failure to rape or seduce
Clarissa) brings him close to the style of the bereaved Donne or King:

> I have been traversing her room, meditating, or taking up everything
> she but touched or used: the glass she dressed at I was ready to break,
> for not giving me the personal image it was wont to reflect, of *her*,
> whose idea is for ever present with me. I call for her, now in the tender-

est, now in the most reproachful terms, as if within my hearing: wanting *her*; I want my own soul, at least everything dear to it. What a void in
my heart! What a chilliness in my blood, as if its circulation were ar-
rested! From her room to my own; in the dining-room, and in and out
of every place where I have seen the beloved of my heart, do I hurry; in
none can I tarry; her lovely image in every one, in some lively attitude,
rushing cruelly upon me, in differently remembered conversations.

But when in my first fury, at my return, I went up two pair of stairs,
resolved to find the locked-up Dorcas, and beheld the vainly-burnt
window-board, and recollected my baffled contrivances, baffled by my
own weak folly, I thought my distraction completed, and down I ran as
one frighted at a spectre, ready to howl for vexation; my head and my
temples shooting with a violence I had never felt before; and my back
aching as if the vertebrae were disjointed, and falling in pieces. (L 228,
740)

The language here is poetically rich: the rhythm is strong (and not the
blank verse of drama) and is occasionally enforced by near rhyme (as at
the end of the first paragraph — hurry/tarry, none/one, upon/conversa-
tions) and assonance (lovely, lively, cruelly); the first paragraph is conventionally elegiac in mood, with the lingering on place striking a note
often found in the pastoral tradition (compare Spenser's "Lacking My
Love"),[24] the violent apprehension of the speaker's body as breaking and
subject to despair echoes the physical self-consciousness of Donne ("A
Valediction: of My Name, in the Window," or "The Dampe," for example; we also see such physical awareness in Petrarchan elegy and King's
powerful "Exequy"). Rooting his despair in his bodily pain and focusing
his desire on the beloved's missing reflection (the absence of the image
mirroring the Platonic departure of his soul), Lovelace treads the path
of many Renaissance poets, aligning himself with wasteful, powerful
passion.

The letter from which this passage is taken varies in tone and mode,
moving from narration of Clarissa's escape to description of Lovelace's
pain; it is in expressing his anxiety that Lovelace returns again and again
to language that foregrounds his conceit of virtuosity: "But nobody ever
loved as I love! — It is even increased by her unworthy flight, and my
disappointment. Ungrateful creature, to fly from a passion thus ardently
flaming! which, like the palm, rises the more for being depressed and
slighted!" (742). This reference to the palm tree is biblical and lyric,
evoking the passionate union of the Song of Songs:[25]

> This thy stature is like to a palme tree,
> And thy breasts to clusters of grapes.
> I said, I will goe up to the palme tree,
> I will take hold of the boughes thereof.   (7:7–8)

The image of the lover climbing up the palm tree, straining down its fronds as he imagines consummation, resonates with Lovelace's vision of his passion. The connection is made more striking by the echo of the Song of Songs ("My beloved is mine, and I am his") in the long passage quoted above. Lovelace describes his fevered, pointless search for Clarissa ("From room to room," etc.) in language like that of biblical epithalamium:

> By night on my bed I sought him whome my soule loveth.
> I sought him, but I found him not.
> I will rise now, and goe about the citie
> In the streets, and in the broad wayes
> I will seeke him whom my soule loveth:
> I sought him, but I found him not.   (3:1–3)

> My soule failed when hee spake:
> I sought him, but I could not find him:
> I called him, but he gave me no answere.   (5:6)

> I charge you, O daughters of Ierusalem, if ye find my beloved,
> That yee tell him, that I am sicke of love.   (5:8)

The trope of an almost endless, painful search for the beloved is developed in pastoral lyric (e.g., Spenser's "Lacking my love"), but its epithalamic roots in the Song of Songs are, for someone like Richardson, equally strong (and more "true"). In *Clarissa* the mixture of wedding poem and elegy is highly suggestive, for while the novel moves inexorably toward tragedy and elegy, Lovelace is constantly preparing for comedy and marriage.[26] As always, he misuses the language he borrows: he misreads Clarissa, he places epithalamium with elegy; he sends whores instead of Jerusalem's daughters; he violates linguistic and bodily purity.[27]

Lovelace's rakishness is poetically coded: his accounts of lustfully watching Clarissa faint, as she cries with a covered face or sighs in repose, are quite close to the scene described by Sidney in "Have I caught my heavenly jewel," from *Astrophil and Stella*, as is Lovelace's self-chastisement at having stolen only a kiss and a grope and, to borrow Sidney's words, "no more taking."[28] Lovelace's are the morals of a courtier-rake poet, as much as of a villain from *Venice Preserv'd*. As Doody argues, Clarissa is less committed to drama than is Lovelace: "she is not 'play-acting' " and responds in dramatic style only after Lovelace, in his adaptation of drama, forces "the role of victim . . . upon her" (*A Natural Passion*, 118). Clarissa's ethical identity and her moments of transcendence are expressed through a socially valid lyric model;[29] Lovelace's dramatic identity as a tragic villain exists side-by-side with his use of a morally suspect lyric tradition and his perversion of a true (biblical) lyric voice. Placing lyric thus next to drama reveals both the flexibility of lyric when it is constructed as a mode and the porosity of the novel's prose. Novelistic structures of appropriation are shaped by principles ranging from the ethical or perceptual to the demands of plot — the position of the lyric within these patterns refines readers' awareness of the complexities of inner experience, encourages us to share in it, helps us to identify it, and even judge it.

The union between mode and ethics is elaborated in another popular midcentury novel, Elizabeth Griffith's *Delicate Distress* (1769). Griffith's novel provides the opportunity to examine both terms in the novel's ethics of form, to look at character as well as closure and coherence. The absorption and modification of lyric always takes place within the framework of a novel's commitments, be they political, moral-didactic, or formal (not exclusive categories). Griffith uses lyric to define aspects of taste, in line with emerging ideals of the age of sensibility and proper female behavior. Lady Straffon, another witty matron, mocks pastoral lyric conventions, and with them, those of romance:

> half the simple girls who are now pining for love, by murmuring rivulets, or in shady groves, would forget the dear objects of their passion, if they had not a female confidante, as silly as themselves, to whom they daily recount the fancied charms of their Adonis, and utter vows of everlasting constancy. (140)

> Does Fanny Weston still sigh in concert with the Æolian lyre? or have the equinoctial blasts so chilled her flame, that she prefers a warm room, and chearful company, to lonely meditation, and soft sounds? (141)

On the other hand, Lady Woodville uses poetic language without a blush:

> The trees have lost their verdure, and the birds cease to sing. But though the autumnal season, may have produced these effects, I begin

to fear there is a greater change in me, than in any of the objects that surround me.

Yet am I in the spring of life, not ripened even to summer; while like a blasted flower, I shrink, and fade. Say, Fanny, why is this? the animal, and vegetable world bloom in their proper season, youth — while amongst those whom we call rational, grief steals the rose, from the downy cheek, and flowing tears oft dim the brilliant eye. Lord Seymour is unhappy; Thornton sighs; and my loved lady, seems wretched; — need I go on, and close the climax, with my breaking heart! (141)

Lyric is part of novelistic dialogism — a possible voice whose assumption has meaning in terms of plot as well as of ethical values. If romance — associated with pastoral lyric — is silly and suspect, the ethics of style is an ethics of genre. What comes to rule the roost when styles are absorbed, reworked, elevated, or condemned?

One way of answering this question is to examine closure.[30] Although passages like those above do not have the tightness of similar lyrics (by Bradstreet or Spenser, let's say), they have their own formal integrity within the novel, constituting segments that, against the background of the surrounding speech, stand out in a coherent way.[31] This coherence deserves comment: Lady Woodville's letter achieves closure in accord with epistolary (rather than lyric) conventions — "I am not able to write more, at present, but will answer all your queries, by next post — Till then, adieu" (142).[32] Emotional closure can only come with the resolution of the plot — any emotional episode only offers a provisional ending in constant expectation of the denouement. The significance, then, of absorption of, or abstraction from, lyric is the abstraction itself; lyric is stripped of some elements of form to leave an emotional and imagistic or linguistic core. Bared to this degree, lyric serves to illuminate objects, people, and positions within a larger scheme.[33] The absence of lyric conventions of closure and resolution furthers this use; completion is deferred, so that lyric, as a way of focusing emotion, appears episodic. Lyric nestles within a novelistic whole, submitted to rules beyond those of the mode itself or of any genre (pastoral elegy, sonnet, etc.) that lies at its historical heart. But what gives lyric coherence and identity in this context is its subjection to rules that lie beyond it.

This is why the comic community of Smollett's *Peregrine Pickle* (1751) is established early in the novel through the use of Anacreontic. Peregrine's father, Gamaliel, has taken refuge in a public house shortly after his retirement to the country. After the landlord has described

Gamaliel's new neighbors, one of the strangest of these, Captain Trunnion, appears, cursing and storytelling. Gamaliel sits on the edges of this strange new group until the boatswain starts playing his pipe:

> The commodore, the lieutenant and landlord joined in the chorus, repeating this elegant stanza,
>> Bustle, bustle, brave boys!
>> Let us sing, let us toil,
>> And drink all the while,
>> Since labour's the price of our joys.
>
> The third line was no sooner pronounced, than the cann was lifted to every man's mouth with admirable uniformity; and the next word taken up at the end of their draught with a twang equally expressive and harmonious. In short, the company began to understand one another.[34]

Mr. Pickle, the landlord, and the company have come to an "understanding," and it is lyric (with a little help from booze — but that's what Anacreontics are about) that achieves what conversation and storytelling cannot. Gamaliel's taciturn nature gives way to community only under the force of drunken song. Again, lyric functions within a set of social and generic rules that suit a range of novelistic styles, and it functions to fuse individual consciousness with the community around it.

I have indicated a variety of ways in which lyric language may mark the boundaries of interior experience, contributing to the makeup of a particular fictional world and to the way that world becomes recursively defined against and implicated by considerations of genre and rhetoric. The limits of the use of lyric in the novel, whether the result of generic incongruities or not, form an important intersection with the limits of novelistic self-expression. Their disjunction provokes irony; their union is often harmonic. It is time to inquire what, in representing personal experience, the novel does beyond the borders of lyric. The language of lyric and that of novelistic subjectivity have much in common; what they do not have, at this moment in their histories, is equally interesting. It is here, in addition to the kind of direct revisions of lyric I have described, that the possibilities and conceptions of the personal expand dramatically, and it is also here, looking ahead, that the lyric also expands.

§ In the last chapter I discussed chiasmus as a broad structural principle surrounding novel constructions of literary consciousness. That discussion included an analysis of the way sympathy is built and extended through narration and perception; in the remainder of this chapter I approach techniques of narration and description as means for marking out the space of consciousness and moving readers into it. Internal events are offered to view so that selection and discrimination are frequently subordinate to a fiction of completeness; more emphasis is often placed on an emotion than on a character; and traditional decorum is subordinate to a new supremacy of the knowledge of world and of self. The novel's conventions for representing the self redefine what generic conventions may be, what meaning they create and lift into prominence. There is a developmental story to be told about literary technique, but that is not most important for the purposes at hand. I examine here a set of examples from major texts in the history of the novel (*Roxana*, *Fanny Hill*, *Miss Betsy Thoughtless*, *Cecelia*) that enable us to understand the techniques that make fictional "subjectivity" available to readers. I have chosen these examples not with an aim to completion but rather to identify within a very large field texts that can push forward a discussion about the generic aspirations of novel writing.

In early novels, consistent and even coherent character is not as important as constructing episodes of passion.[35] Whatever the "flatness" of a character in *Love in Excess*, for example, Haywood has an investment in drawing isolated moments of pure passion (e.g., Melliora in the throes of love, the jealousy of Alovisa). Defoe in the same period is also concerned with representing moments of transformation. The texture of his novels is one of thick and even confusing personality, from *Robinson Crusoe* (1719) or *Captain Singleton* (1720) to *Moll Flanders* (1722) and *Roxana* (1724); in each of these a set of pivotal emotional experiences is rendered in great detail (Moll's realization of incest, Captain Bob's experience of the sublime in a sea of ivory, Crusoe in terror on the beach, etc.). With *Roxana*, Defoe exhibits a descriptive agility that reveals that the representation of intensity is among his primary concerns. When the heroine, incognita, first encounters her daughter after a separation of twenty years, she is overcome, and as much as readers might feel Roxana's desires, we may also feel Defoe's urgent need to paint them:

> I cannot but take Notice here, that notwithstanding there was a secret Horror upon my Mind, and I was ready to sink when I came close to her, to salute her; yet it was a secret inconceivable Pleasure to me when I kiss'd her, to know that I kiss'd my own Child; my own Flesh and Blood, born of my Body; and who I had never kiss'd since I took the fatal Farewel of them all, with a Million of Tears, and a Heart almost

dead with Grief, when *Amy* and the Good Woman took them all away, and went with them to *Spittle-Fields:* No Pen can describe, no Words can express, *I say,* the strange Impression which this thing made upon my Spirits; I felt something shoot thro' my Blood; my Heart flutter'd; my Head flash'd, and was dizzy, and all within me, *as I thought,* turn'd about, and much ado I had, not to abandon myself to an Excess of Passion at the first Sight of her, much more when my Lips touch'd her Face; I thought I must have taken her in my Arms, and kiss'd her again a thousand times, whether I wou'd or no.[36]

Although Defoe never seems overly concerned with parsing sentences, this single long one is extraordinary. Each of the "clauses" reworks and refines emotion that could not be held, complete, in the clause that preceded it: "a Secret Horror upon my Mind"; "yet it was a secret inconceivable Pleasure"; "my own Child; my own Flesh and Blood"; "and who I had never kiss'd since"; "No Pen can describe . . . *I say*"; "shoot thro' my Blood; my Heart flutter'd; my Head flash'd," and so forth. Roxana cannot seem to let the sentence go, and even the invocation of the inexpressibility topos is not an admission of literary or linguistic defeat. She redescribes sensations as she narrates a tumultuous sequence of events. No story can be told, the sentence barely completed, because the intensity of the moment resists resolution into the temporal sequence of narrative and into descriptive precision. Her repeated return to the subject is the result of an insistent desire to reach beyond given forms, to prolong the moment of description and narration, and thus to approximate the intensity of experience.

Moments like these suggest that the roundness of a character may be incidental or subsequent to questions of emotional representation. These representations are selective: Roxana does not lament the loss of her children with the same strength that underlies her recognition of Susan; Moll may briefly relate her separation from a child, then forget about it; Fanny Hill glosses over her parents' deaths but gives detailed accounts of other "emotional" events. Moments of connection with the fictional world of a novel seem full (or have a "depth" of their own), not necessarily because they reveal something about a character, but because the reader may enter the text through them. In considering the effects of Haywood's *Love in Excess*, for example, it does not matter whether one can see Melliora walking down the streets of a French city but whether readers can enter into a given construction of thought or feeling; to return for a moment to the question of lyric, Haywood's use of Donne marks the rhetorical production of subjectivity as shared, reconstructed emotional experience, on a lyric model. There is every reason to believe that Haywood's representations were indeed moving for readers, and not just on the evidence of Savage's puff: the popularity of her fiction speaks to readers' satisfaction with her representations of passion, and Haywood figures reading about passion as itself passionate experience.[37] If access to the emotional world of the text is contingent upon moments of intensity, as it often is, the concept of literary subjectivity that arises is more rhetorical than mimetic — subjectivity is a literary site of exchange, a way of crossing into the text.

This rhetorical construction can have very real effects on readers. *Fanny Hill, or Memoirs of a Woman of Pleasure* (1748–49) shows how moments of intensity can create illusions of completeness as well as extreme forms of chiasmus between reader and text. Cleland provides vivid portraits of feeling that demonstrate the power of novelistic approaches to consciousness. Even while Fanny, like Marivaux's Marianne or Richardson's Pamela, may sometimes lose consciousness, she does not lose (for readers like me) the sense of inner life conveyed by moments like her first encounters with her future husband: "To find myself in the arms of that beauteous youth was a rapture that my little heart swam in. Past or future were equally out of the question with me. The present was as much as all my powers of life were sufficient to bear the transport of without fainting. . . . Time was now annihilated with me."[38] Cleland's representation of a woman's self-narration links access to her inner life to her sexual availability (with serious political and literary connotations); bringing the mind's body (the space of eroticism) into contact with the bodies of reader and heroine makes for a powerful reading experience, one that insists on the centrality of the "I" and bases its construction in a set of pivotal moments.[39]

Examples of this kind of discontinuity are abundant, and enumerating them would serve little purpose. I want to emphasize, however, the way in which intimate contact between reader and character may be built piecemeal, and how Haywood, often cited as one of the least interior of early novelists, employs this technique both early and late (cf. Hammond). Haywood's *History of Miss Betsy Thoughtless* (1751) reveals the degree to which painful self-spectacle may become a site of crossing into literary interiority. If readers did not know the struggles Trueworth endures over his love and disapproval of Miss Betsy or his progressively falling in love with Harriot; if they did not see the distress Miss Betsy feels lying awake after one of many scrapes, her grief at losing Trueworth, or most importantly, the shame that leads to her reform, the story would not exist.[40] Not only is this novel a Bildungsroman of inner life — how to go from being Miss "Thoughtless" to gaining "True worth" — the most important events in the novel take place entirely on the inside;[41] no matter how "flat" the characters may otherwise be, these moments make it true that from *Roxana* to *Pamela*, *Fanny Hill*, or *Miss Betsy Thoughtless*, intensity is the prime value. Even in novels that focus exclusively on an individual, the novelistic self is discontinuous; part of its illusion of wholeness comes in the supplementary response offered by its readers. The *Pamela* event, as Warner shows, gives perfect evidence for this.[42]

By the end of the century, such techniques of inner vision would be normalized, and while we feel the vibrancy of privileged contact with and simultaneous creation of a mind other than our own, little or nothing marks the shift from representing action to narrating interior events so hidden that even their subjects are often unaware of them. These techniques are so much a part of the novel as most readers now understand it that it seems almost pointless to recount them; but awareness of the novel's newness and of the patterns it set for competing forms requires such reminders. Burney's *Cecilia* (1782) begins when the narrator presents the heroine's "secret prayer," plunging readers into her inner life.[43] While the completeness with which the narrator gives access to Cecilia's thoughts and feelings may seem banal in technical terms, it has only become so through a two-hundred-year accumulation:

> Time with Cecilia now glided on with such rapidity, that before she thought the morning half over, the evening was closed, and ere she was sensible the first week was past, the second was departed for ever. . . . Her heart, deeply wounded of late by unexpected indifference, and undeserved mortification, was now, perhaps, more than usually susceptible of those penetrating and exquisite pleasures which friendship and kindness possess the highest powers of bestowing. Easy, gay, and airy, she only rose to happiness, and only retired to rest; and not merely heightened was her present enjoyment by her past disappointment, but carrying her retrospection to her earliest remembrance, she still found her actual situation more peculiarly adapted to her taste and temper, than any she had hitherto at any time experienced. (241)

There is no difference here between recounting habitual behaviors and daily events and recounting retrospection and meditation. All of these events are equally accessible. Not only does inner life fall under the absolute power of narration, but even time can be folded within a complete power of organization and revelation. Memory, immediate perception, and futurity are combined by Burney in a way that removes subjective intensity from the limitations subjectivity itself imposes; the narrator's keen mind can create a completion of experience that, at any moment, her object, Cecilia, does not attain. Readers' experience of time and revelation holds a truth that is completely "inauthentic" but that has a power authenticity (truth to Cecilia's experience) could not, here, equal.

The relationship produced by the narrator between readers and the heroine's inner life is of absolute perspicuity; such a degree of transparency is heightened by the complete ignorance of the heroine's true self, which marks the other characters and drives the plot (almost on the model of *Clarissa*). No one knows Cecilia as do you or I—so we learn again and again. Where but in the novel is there, at this point in time, not only such a layered and complex rendering of the present and the past, but an emphasis on the techniques of perspicuity as signifiers of genre and the ethics of genre reading?[44] Indeed, our access to thought signals an ethics of community and judgment. The robust quality of Burney's internal narrations is not her own invention — it seems as much part of the genre as words on a page and can be traced from Pamela to Betsy Thoughtless to Fanny Price. By citing *Cecilia*, I wish to indicate rather that as the novel reached the 1770s, a period (and for some, the period) that helps to define its "rise" (in terms of publication and the theorization of its tradition), the representation of inner life as subject to the keenness of narrative vision may be effectively taken for granted.[45] This is not because every novel reveals round characters and soulful meditations but because narration in the genre seems so powerful as to be unrestricted by the boundaries of the self. It is through the episodic narration of intense moments of consciousness that readers build the worlds and minds they might step into.

Description has its powers, too. The rhetorical play surrounding genre, decorum, and ekphrasis has significance for novelistic subjectivity. If poetry and painting were sister arts in the eighteenth century, it was in executing the virtuoso description that most literary artists would make their greatest aesthetic claims. This is of course true of loco-descriptive poetry — the genre on which most of the significant post-Augustan poets cut their teeth — it is also true of Richardson's carefully emblematic description of Clarissa's prison or of the descriptions of bodily passion (influenced by painting and theater) in early Haywood.

Novels and poetry share a logic of pictorialism; it governs Collins's mirroring of Fear—"Like thee I start / Like thee disorder'd fly"—and the kind of tableau-style theatrical description of the passions that appears in sentimental literature: "His dark auburn hair was undressed, unpowdered, and hung loosely over his face, and he wore a long military great coat over a white waistcoat; his whole appearance indicating that kind of neglect which is the effect of hopeless despondence."[46] This pictorialism is the more or less straightforward use of descriptive conventions to link emotion to proper visual manifestations.

Ekphrasis in novels also engages pictorialism in the service of subjective perception and heightened consciousness, as with Congreve's Aurelian and his vision of rococo cherubs.[47] Ekphrasis has different implications in late-century sentimental novels like those of Charlotte Smith. Along with Burney and Radcliffe, Smith, writing at a crux of the novel's generic solidification, was one of the most significant experimenters in the novel at the close of the century. Between 1788 and 1798, the year of *Lyrical Ballads*, she wrote ten novels; she also helped found a new kind of locodescriptive sonnet. In these two genres she would undertake complementary projects concerned with the self and its surroundings and with the ways that, through description, one can give access to the other.

In the epistolary *Desmond* (1792), the hero pursues an unconsummated love for a married woman, Geraldine Verney. It is almost a courtly passion; he proves his love for her through painful and extravagant services. Desmond also writes romantic, melancholy letters:

> I know this betrays a very gothic and exploded taste, but such is the force of early impressions, that I have still an affection for "the bowed roof"—the cathedral-like solemnity of long lines of tall trees, whose topmost boughs are interlaced with each other. —I do not, however, defend the purity of my taste in this instance; for nature certainly never planted trees in direct lines. —But I account for my predilection, by the kind of pensive and melancholy pleasure I used to feel, when in my childhood and early youth, I walked alone, in a long avenue of arbeal, which led from a very wild and woody part of the weald of Kent, to an old house my father, at that period of my life, inhabited. I remember the cry of the woodpeckers, or yaffils, as we call them in that country, going to roost in a pale autumnal evening, answered by owls, which in great numbers inhabit the deep forest-like glens that lye behind the avenue. —I see the moon rising slowly over the dark mass of wood,

and the opposite hills, tinged with purple from the last reflection of the sun, which was sunk behind them. —I recall the sensations I felt, when, as the silver leaves of the aspins trembled in the lowest breeze, or slowly fell to the ground before me, I became half frightened at the encreasing obscurity of the objects around me, and have almost persuaded myself that the grey trunks of these old trees, and the low murmur of the wind among their branches, were the dim forms, and hollow sighs of some supernatural beings; and at length, afraid of looking behind me, I have hurried breathless into the house.[48]

This ekphrastic passage, in blank verse, might be at home in *The Prelude*, with its languorous descriptions accelerating into a moment of fear, sudden shocks resonant with Wordsworthian spots of time.[49] Smith combines the landscape sensibility of Thomson (quoted—"the bowed roof") with the personal animation of memory. The remembered landscape and its avenues mark a path leading to affective experience located equally in imagined vistas of the past and in present emotion renewed in the instant of writing.[50]

Such intensive description is not reserved for landscape. In her first novel, *Emmeline* (1788), Smith inaugurates a pattern of employing *visibilia* to focus the relationship between the internal and the external:

Mrs. Stoddard saw, sleeping . . . , a very young woman, pale, but extremely beautiful; and her hand, of uncommon delicacy, lay on the white quilt—A sight, which gave her pain for herself, and pity for the unfortunate person before her, affected her so much, that having stood a moment in astonishment, she stepped back to the place where Emmeline sat, and burst into tears.

With deepened blushes, and averted eyes, she [Emmeline] at first sought for refuge in affecting to be intent on the netting she drew from her work box; but having spoiled a whole row, her trembling hands could no longer go on with it; and as totally her tongue refused to utter the answer, which, by the pause he made, she concluded Godolphin expected.[51]

Along with similar objects of vision in other sentimental novels—like the monk's snuffbox, the grisette's gloves, or the money passed between Yorick and the *fille de chambre* in Sterne's *Sentimental Journey* (1768)— these overcharged visibilia concentrate and exteriorize emotional experience; Smith's use of such images has a lot in common with her use of landscape as analogue and focus for emotion. Smith's visibilia—Emme-

line's netting, the white hand on the sill, the arched roof of the trees —
provide lines of sight enabling readers to trace lines of emotion. We
focus on these objects through the eyes of significant others; the objects
themselves focus the interaction of multiple threads of inner experience,
threads connecting the reader's surrogate (Desmond, Mrs. Stoddard,
Godolphin) to another person or time (Desmond in his past, the frail
woman in the woods, or Emmeline herself) and ultimately to the reader.

Such patterns of connection and crossing are the result of Smith's
attempt to satisfy in the novel a technical concern that arises in her
sonnets; they exemplify another way in which the histories of novel and
lyric may be supplementary.[52] The compression of the sonnet offered a
challenge to the premise of expansiveness, which had characterized
eighteenth-century descriptive poetry. If, because of the grandeur of its
object, *The Seasons* seemed to expand constantly and without shape, as
Johnson argued, what parts of the natural world could be adequately
represented in a sonnet? Like William Lisle Bowles, Smith created sonnets more ambitious than anything any of her contemporaries were
likely prepared to see: if natural description seems endlessly expansive,
what happens when, in fourteen lines, landscape is combined with the
almost equally expansive space of memory?

As a record kept by mind and body of itself, memory is an answer to
questions of self-definition, and with it, to questions of self-description
(at least in Lockean or Humean epistemologies). By bringing landscape
and memory together, the sonnet for Smith becomes the locus for a
meeting between the knowledge of self and of world. Smith's sonnets,
however, chronicle their own failure to make experience whole and to
restore loss, as in "To the South Downs" (1784):

> Ah! hills belov'd — where once a happy child,
>   Your beechen shades, "your turf, your flowers among,"
> I wove your blue-bells into garlands wild,
>   And woke your echoes with my artless song.[53]

Smith's quotation of Gray's "Eton College" ode (l. 2) points toward what
is significant about her development of the landscape-memory trope;
here lie the contours of her revision and expansion of poetic and novelistic traditions. Gray does not picture himself in the past he idealizes:
rather, he envisions others playing in a distant scene; he replaces his own
experience with abstract or impersonal representations. Smith seeks to
reconstruct or at least evoke a self that life's pressures have lost. She
partially succeeds: although she has lost her youthful self, her mature

physical presence (in stark contrast to Gray) remains in the scene, in the form of her throbbing, broken heart:

> Ah! hills belov'd — your turf, your flowers remain;
>> But can they peace to this sad breast restore;
> For one poor moment soothe the sense of pain,
>> And teach a breaking heart to throb no more?   (ll. 5–8)

The weight of trouble (a series of misfortunes she painstakingly recounts in prefaces to her poetry) has put the pleasures of landscape out of her reach. What compensatory pleasures does poetry offer? Little, in the sonnet's narrow cell. Gestures of quotation or allusion (typical of Smith) are a way of simultaneously pushing the boundaries of time, self, and fourteen lines; they are an attempt to access a plenitude whose loss Smith laments. The scene of meditation and memory is not evoked through observation but through quotation: description here escapes Smith's own poetry and is only recouped by a turn to a poetic vista that was, as we recall, deeply inhospitable to its original speaker. Smith's poem, like similar ones by Collins, is about the failure of poetry; like Gray's, it also evokes the failure of sight and of self, and her sonnet ends with a desire for dissolution:

> And you, Aruna! — in the vale below,
>> As to the sea your limpid waves you bear,
> Can you one kind Lethean cup bestow,
>> To drink a long oblivion to my care?
> Ah! no! — when all, e'en Hope's last ray is gone,
>> There's no oblivion — but death alone!

Smith seeks a mode of representation capable of providing evocative access to the present and the past as contexts for speech and self. If natural description figures the scene that surrounds and supports the self in space, memory, as the record of identity, provides an unmistakable "description" of the self in time. But memory seems to escape the poem, just as landscape escapes description: on one hand the past is placed at the borders of the piece through quotation of Gray's "Eton College" ode; on the other, Smith's gestures toward autobiography remain beyond the boundaries of the poetry, either in prefaces that record her sufferings or as oblique gestures to a story too capacious to find inclusion in only fourteen lines. In poem after poem in the *Elegiac Sonnets*, Smith settles for iterated, indescribable suffering. This is why her sonnets do not form a sequence, but are serial — one is not enough because the history of experience becomes flattened on the space that should evoke it. There are competing claims between landscape and memory, which seem irresolvable; they can only be deferred.[54]

There is no such difficulty in the passage from *Desmond*, implying that there is more to her sonnets' pattern of lacunae than could be satisfied by judgment of Smith's literary skill. The experience that Desmond narrates is apprehended in a completion of space and time; he has moved on in both dimensions. This completion seems produced by recollection, not in tranquillity, but in a context hospitable in its own way to exactitude and evocation. While financial pressures certainly influenced her decision to "go prose," questions of genre beyond those implied by facts of the market are significant too. What did Smith feel each genre was capable of or suited for? Focusing perception on an object or range of objects — aspen leaves, a dark mass of wood in *Desmond*; a row of netting or a white hand in *Emmeline* — enables a shift from external to internal perception where the speaker's body engages a palimpsest of emotion and sight. The novelistic concern with chiastic processes makes spaces of imagination and sympathy move into one another. "To the South Downs" does not create the web of unfolding vision that *Desmond* produces; the poem eschews what the novel embraces — perceptual narrative. In *Desmond* particular description is combined with the progress of its perceiver, so that autobiographical narrative, as the substance of meditation, unfolds the significance of vision and imagination together. It is not that sonnets cannot do this (of course they can); rather, it is that Smith assigns different labor to each genre.

The folding of time through memory in *Desmond* is a first-person version of the complexity of the passage from *Cecilia* above. In her novels, Smith combines the temporal mastery of Burney's narration of consciousness with the descriptive power of ekphrasis to evoke subjective plenitude. Moreover, the novel's form pushes Smith to capitalize upon the effect of epistolary address, the listening ear or reading eye, to provide another strain of stabilizing context; it stages recollection as the union between the speaker's recreation of self, his past, and the responsive ear of his listener. *Desmond* does what the sonnets do not; it successfully unites description of inner and outer worlds in terms both of a single subject (one person's memory and sight) and of representation itself (speech/writing and hearing/reading): none of the sonnets written before *Desmond* and addressed to a friend is descriptive or personal in her typical pattern.

Later in *Desmond*, the poetry of description again meets a listening ear, where (as in other novels by Smith's female contemporaries) Finch's "Nocturnal Reverie" is the model of meditation and memory Smith revises:

> It is now night—a calm, a lovely night! without a moon indeed, but with the canopy of heaven illuminated with countless myriads of "planetary fires!" such a night, my Fanny, as some of those in which we used, during the first year of my marriage, to be induced by Desmond to wander in the coppice-walks and shrubberies that surrounded the lawn at Linwell. —Alone, as I am here, I must not, venture so far from the house. But I may traverse the grass-plot before it, and listen to the nightingales, of which numbers salute me every evening with their song from the opposite woods—their delicious notes, softened and prolonged by the echoes from the bridge and the water. One, only one, seems to have taken up his lonely abode in the garden here—Alas! I could be romantic enough to fancy it the spirit of some solitary and deserted being like myself, that comes sympathetically to hear and sooth my sorrows.
>
> Let me tell them, then to this visionary visitant, rather than to my Fanny; and now, in wishing her a good night, wish too, that her slumbers may bring to her mind, without disturbing it, the image of her
>
> GERALDINE. (218–19)

Like Finch's speaker, Smith's Geraldine wanders abroad, alone, in "such a night," indulging in her melancholy musings. Whereas Finch postpones the introduction of her speaker until the final lines of the poem, Geraldine's memories as well as her body are the foundation of significance. Finch's "Nocturnal Reverie" delays intimacy in its lonely night, insisting instead on the community of cattle and other beasts of evening; Smith insists on a human intimacy installed by epistolary writing and distilled in the reciprocal illumination of self and surroundings. Intimacy is also grounded in the doubling of perception between vista and emotion, present and past. Finch's lyric is overwritten by and in the novel; Smith's own sonnets (a seeming paradox, given the sonnet's history of precision) also pale in comparison to the tightness and intensity of the passage from *Desmond.* The reference above to "planetary fires" is then significant, a direct quotation of a poem by Radcliffe, "Night," which is part of the novel *The Romance of the Forest* (1791). Instead of prefacing meditation in a purely poetic past, Smith signals her double allegiance to descriptive modes by beginning with a reference to a lyric embedded within a novel.[55]

There is signal importance in Smith's aesthetic practice: she develops strategies for making consciousness — understood as inner experience (memory, emotion, imagined vistas and futures) — available, usually through the presentation of some object of vision or contemplation that allows readers to "see" connections between people. This circles back to the question of the permeability of fictional worlds: Smith wishes to make *consciousness* permeable, for its boundaries to be penetrable under the pressure of imaginative vision.[56] The worlds of fiction and consciousness are not the same but exist in a relationship of mutual support. Smith's aesthetic reconstruction of consciousness is fictional but relies on principles other than those of the allegorical consciousness of Gray or Collins. Desmond's landscape is made available by memorial reconstruction and acute perception, and each space, of the inside and of out, is cross-implicated and interdependent.[57] This is a focalization of the techniques of chiasmus and contact, which I earlier associated with the questions of realism, fictionality, and fictional interiority. Smith's novels, even more than the poetry she wrote before them, have a sharp focus: in looking at things and amenable spaces (a correlate of the novel's attention to houses), Smith can look into minds and hearts as well. The space through which fiction enters our experience in these cases, the points of contact that the novel creates and exploits, are those of the imaginative perception of visual objects.

§ The techniques of narration and description that novelists used to create permeable consciousness through momentary, intense contacts expanded dramatically over the second half of the eighteenth century, going beyond the patterns set by lyric; most significant among these innovations was the development of free indirect discourse as a combination of narration and description, blending inner life and a contrasting outer world. It is generally imagined that Austen was the major innovator in this technique, but the history of free indirect discourse is older than this. Gérard Strauch traces it to Bunyan's *Grace Abounding* (1666),[58] and he, Anne Neumann, and John Dussinger also locate Richardson's novels at a crucial point in the tradition.[59]

The presence of free indirect discourse in novels of letters is highly significant. If, as Ira Konigsberg argues, the importance of first-person narration is linked to the novelistic concern with perception, then the development of free indirect discourse is crucial because it combines subjective representation with "the control and magnification of traditional third-person voice."[60] The kind of focus on subjectivity and perception facilitated by the epistolary novel gave way in this view to techniques that blend one consciousness with another and that signal the crossing of the boundaries of a single subject. In the history of the novel, letters gave way, in a broad sense, to free indirect discourse and associated techniques, from the epistolary *First Impressions* to its reincarnation using the newer tool of representation in *Pride and Prejudice*. One of the tools employed within the novel's rhetoric of realism to join fictional and real worlds, the letter, transformed, became a tool to join minds and sensibilities.

If free indirect discourse makes use of the boundaries between one imagination and experience and another, the transition between the two is not always happy. Provisionally locating its literary origins in Bunyan, Strauch notes that free indirect discourse mediates between Bunyan's "saved" present and his freely sinning past. Free indirect discourse may mark the presence of difference or dissonance, and its yoking of disparate minds or perceptions often results in irony or satire. Pope uses, if not free indirect discourse, something very like it in the "Epistle to Bathurst" — note, it is a letter:

> Old Cotta sham'd his fortune and his birth,
> Yet was not Cotta void of wit or mirth:
> What tho' (the use of barb'rous spit forgot)
> His Kitchen vy'd in coolness with his Grot?
> His court with nettles, moats with cresses stor'd,
> With soups unbought and sallads blest his board.
> If Cotta liv'd on pulse, it was no more
> Than Bramins, Saints, and Sages did before;
> To cram the Rich was prodigal expence,
> And who would take the Poor from Providence?   (ll. 179–88)

The last four lines ring with Cotta's reasoning, and in all likelihood with words from his own meager thoughts. Free indirect discourse has a history that crosses both generic and modal boundaries, functioning most frequently in this period by creating satiric disharmonies.

Brooke, in *The Excursion* (1777), uses free indirect discourse for this purpose, and with a flair no preceeding novelist can claim. The first instance of this technique in *The Excursion* is generically significant, used to summarize a letter from the heroine, Maria Villiers, to her sister Louisa:

> She had passed a delightful evening in the best company, at the house
> of a very respectable lady, the widow of a baronet; had been invited by

half a dozen ladies of the most estimable character, to parties where she should see only persons of the first fashion; had attracted the notice of the most amiable young nobleman in town, the heir of an immense fortune. — But his rank and fortune were the least considerations — she had found the man she should have chosen had she seen him in a cottage — the man on earth formed to make her happy — had found him possest of that bewitching delicacy of sentiment — that dear sensibility — that perfect honour — that noble simplicity of character — that dignity of manner — his looks exprest such benevolence of heart — such candour was painted on his countenance — it was Virtue adorned by the Graces — his eyes spoke the language of truth and tenderness — their souls were formed for each other — it was his least merit to be the most lovely of mankind.⁶¹

Readers know Lord Melvile to be none of this, and Brooke drives this home with a delicious barb at poetic style: "she would have filled a folio sheet in this Pindaric Style, the style of a girl bred in shades, who loves for the first time, if the bellman had not reminded her to seal and send away her letter" (26). This deflation is familiar from Brooke's earlier *Lady Julia Mandeville*, where the witty Lady Anne writes after her own flattering description of the hero, "But whither am I running? and where was I when this divine creature seduced me from my right path? Oh, I remember, at chapel: it must be acknowledged my digressions are a little Pindaric!" (56). These, like other satirical twists on poetic or quasi-poetic style (in, e.g., *The Delicate Distress*), register discomfort with the highly coded and overused nature of such writing.

The Excursion, however, links three significant categories. Lyric, letter, and free indirect discourse are united under the rubric of emotion and personal experience; the three formal or stylistic approaches come together as supplements as they gesture toward making consciousness permeable, toward allowing one set of thoughts and feelings to be permeated by another, and toward the blending of consciousness with objects or facts of form (voice, images, words, phrases). The patterns of Maria's mind and her linguistic possibilities fuse with the narrator's to form a composite image, half created and half perceived. Brooke makes use of free indirect discourse throughout the utterly delightful *Excursion*. For pages at a time, one-sentence paragraphs of free indirect discourse (appearing on the page not quite like lines of verse) let readers into a character's rapidly flowing thoughts. By blending and refracting consciousness free indirect discourse opens up the possibilities for literary subjectivity, figured primarily as access to experience and the sharing of that experience from one mind to another.

§ The structures and patterns of the novel concerned with crossing the boundaries between one mind and the world outside it tend toward chiasmus and include the typical devices of the rhetoric of novel realisms; the use of ekphrasis and imaginative vision to bring internal and external perceptions together in Smith, Brooke, or even Congreve; and the doubling and folding of time effected by Burney or Smith. Novelists use narration and description to pinpoint and rework moments of depth or emotional intensity that indicate the particularity of personal experience even without the completion of character: Defoe's Roxana is a nobody in particular, as Gallagher would term her, in part because she seeks linguistic control of emotional life. All of these work together in the novel as ways of making consciousness permeable; bursts of intensity bring readers into contact with the space of interiority. I have shown part of the great degree to which genres learn from one another as they accrete their status as models for composition. I have also shown the kind of contests of satire and irony that help shape the possibilities of generic crossover and the recursive way in which genres define themselves based on absorption and revision. In the next chapter, I explore the effects of these changes on romantic verse and show how lyric and novel would coevolve at the levels of technique and structure.

§ Six

The Novel and the New Lyricism

In midcentury British lyrics, personal speech and experience are shaped by a series of philosophical, moral, and generic challenges: What is the value of an individual's emotions? How are those emotions conveyed effectively and affectively? What conditions of representation enable readers, in imagination, to cross the boundaries between one man or woman and another? These questions concern literary subjectivity and its borders; the novel mediates such challenges through its rhetorical construction of relationships between reader and text. Novels create sites of crossing that bring the reader and the fictional world into close contact through five principal routes: the mechanics of rhetorical forms of realism; a careful focusing of perception and its corollary, description; new techniques for creating permeable and doubled consciousness; the refinement of constructs of ethical and sympathetic reading; and the use of moments of intensity to create "consciousness" as a site of literary exchange. In this chapter I argue that these strategies of chiasmus influenced romantic lyrics: the novel taught its readers new things about the literary self—things crucial to the mode of representing experience we now consistently call lyric.

The constructions of consciousness encountered in novels go beyond those of contemporary lyrics: individual consciousness is not, of course, equivalent to lyric representation. Similarly, in investigating the relationship of novelistic consciousness to constructions of self in romantic lyrics, I make no wholesale equation. Rather, I trace the interaction of representative lyrics with a matrix of genre history, which helps to define possibilities for literary subjectivity and to make a literary self accessible to readers.[1] This chapter connects the following features of the new varieties of romantic lyricism to the influence of novels: the cross-implication of domesticity and lyric consciousness, a Richardsonian pattern of enclosure and ideal address, a particular structure of sympathetic encounters, specificity of time and place, a novelistic concept of affective and ethical reading, and a colloquial language of self-construction.[2] Their appearance in lyrics depends upon two things: the novelistic pattern of chiasmus and the weight of the pressures exerted on the literary market by the novel's striking (and for many upsetting) ascendancy.

I focus on a small group of poems chosen primarily for their position in forming the early romantic mythology (or ideology) of lyric. The range of romantic poetry is so broad that any single set of conventions will not compass it; romanticism traces an arc from the compact yet dizzying poetry of Blake and the brusque beauty of Burns to the domestic poetry of Hemans and the collectivist lyrics of Thomas Spence, as well as the different models apparent in Wordsworth, Coleridge, or Keats.[3] Within this range, I examine a set of poems including *Poems on the Naming of Places*, "Resolution and Independence," "An Evening Walk," "Salisbury Plain," "Frost at Midnight," and "Ode to a Nightingale." These poems do not all address other important conventions (of public poetry, of Revolutionary fervor, and so forth); there are also many romantic lyrics that do not exhibit some of the conventions under consideration. This is as it should be. I seek to account for the reasons that at the end of the eighteenth century a distinct set of images of self in romantic lyrics were constructed in the specific, and—following the path marked out by poetic genre history alone—even surprising, shapes in which they appeared. In focusing on poems at the heart of canonical romanticism, I also intend to demonstrate how generically complicated romantic literary history must be, particularly a history concerned with form.

§ In the Preface to *Lyrical Ballads*, the literary reforms Wordsworth proposes are not restricted to the aesthetic ground of verse alone: contemporary literature as a whole poses a problem. He situates his vision of emotion recollected in tranquillity against the debased sensibility of the "frantic novel, sickly and stupid German Tragedies, and deluges of idle and extravagant stories in verse."[4] His project is one of taste first; literary forms become important as they shape aesthetic apprehension and regulate pleasure: meter, for example, "temper[s] and restrain[s] . . . passion," but what is essential to composition is entirely different. Indeed, Wordsworth's much-discussed allusion to the natural language of men locates him within a context of poetry conceived as an imaginative rather than a formal class, one that includes prose and that can set the ground for understanding the vital, if sometimes anxious, relationship between romantic lyrics and the novel.[5]

In the Preface, Wordsworth emphasizes the close relation between prose and metrical composition: "They both speak by and to the same organs; the bodies in which both of them are clothed may be said to be of the same substance, their affections are kindred, and almost identical, not necessarily differing even in degree; Poetry sheds no tears 'such as Angels weep,' but natural and human tears; she can boast of no celestial ichor that distinguishes her vital juices from those of prose; the same human blood circulates through the veins of them both" (736).

He carries the point further in his footnote to this statement: "I here use the word 'Poetry' (though against my own judgment) as opposed to the word Prose, and synonymous with metrical composition. But much confusion has been introduced into criticism by this contradistinction of Poetry and Prose, instead of the more philosophical one of Poetry and Matter of Fact, or Science. The only strict antithesis to Prose is Metre; nor is this, in truth, a *strict* antithesis, because lines and passages of metre so naturally occur in writing prose, that it would be scarcely possible to avoid them, even were it desirable" (736). Given the proximity of metrical and prosaic invention, Wordsworth chooses to write in verse because "few persons will deny, that, of two descriptions, either of passion, manners, or characters, each of them well executed, the one in prose and the other in verse, the verse will be read a hundred times where the prose is read once" (740). Wordsworth has compared "the distressful parts of 'Clarissa Harlowe'" to Shakespeare — and Shakespeare has won: he experiences too much "reluctance . . . [when] he comes to the re-perusal" of the untempered passages about Clarissa's woes (740). Meter and rhyme have advantages.

Wordsworth's comments on prose, especially the inevitability of meter, can be profitably read in the context of eighteenth-century theories and practices of prosody. From Aristotle to Sidney to Lowth's lectures on the Hebrew poets, poetry was not wedded so much to rhyme or meter as to imagery and the force of passion.[6] The poems of Ossian, immensely important in the development of romanticism, were themselves rendered in prose paragraphs of varying lengths without rhyme or consistent metrical pattern. Macpherson (who attended Lowth's lectures) relates this to "translation": "They are not set to music, nor sung. The versification in the original is simple; and to such as understand the language, very smooth and beautiful. Rhyme is seldom used: but the cadence, and the length of the line varied, so as to suit the sense. The translation is extremely literal. Even the arrangement of the words in the original has been imitated; to which must be imputed some inversion in the style, that otherwise would not have been chosen."[7] These poems, for Macpherson and his admirers, are poetic because they are moving and there are traces of an elevated imagination in the choice and arrangement of words and images, not because of characteristics of meter or rhyme. An essay appearing in the *Monthly Magazine* of July 1796, "Is Verse essential to Poetry?" is in line with this ancient tradition; the author asserts (in terms that influenced Wordsworth)[8] that, given "that fiction is the hallowed temple of poetry," verse is not essential, although it is "certainly the fairest dress of poetry" (456).[9]

As Clayton argues, even the doctrine of pure poetry could work against the exclusive claims of verse: "Romantic writers held that brief, intense passages of a longer work could be poetic, even if the rest of the piece were not. Shelley wrote, 'The parts of a composition may be poetical, without the composition as a whole being a poem.' Coleridge thought that no work, even a short lyric, could be all poetry."[10] Warton's test for pure poetry involves rewriting verse as prose, stripping away meter, rhyme, and poetic word order to see if a core of the truly poetic remains, and while Coleridge's claim that "a poem of any length neither can be, or ought to be all poetry" might seem to exclude long forms, it suggests that they may encompass the purely poetic within them.[11] In general terms, the germane distinction for the romantics had more to do with form than mode: while *Clarissa* is clearly neither ode nor sonnet, it is not clear that it is not at times poetic.[12]

In fact, there was contemporary debate over that possibility. Hazlitt addresses the topic in ambiguous terms: "It has been made a question whether Richardson's romances are poetry; and the answer perhaps is that they are not poetry because they are not romance."[13] He elaborates the unpoetic characteristics of *Clarissa*, *Pamela*, and *Grandison*, focusing on the too-minute nature of Richardson's descriptions and their inexorable emotional demands. He ends by suggesting that Richardson's "poetical genius is like Ariel confined in a pine tree, and requires an artificial process to let it out" ("Lectures," 5:15)—a model inferior for Hazlitt to Shakespeare's image of "poesy . . . as a gum / which issues whence 'tis nourished, our gentle flame / Provokes itself, and like the current flies" (*Timon* 1.1, quoted in Hazlitt, "Lectures," 5:15). At other points, however, these faults become virtues: Richardson's books "have the romantic air of a pure fiction, with the literal minuteness of a common diary. The author had the most matter-of-fact imagination that ever existed, and wrote the oddest mixture of poetry and prose" ("On the English Novelists," 6:117–18). Even Richardson's minuteness can be a gift: "This kind of high finishing from imagination is an anomaly in the history of human genius; and, certainly, nothing so fine was ever produced by the same accumulation of minute parts" ("Novelists," 6:118).

Hazlitt's praise focuses on emotional potential, so that Richardson's "real excellence" lay in "combining [features of human nature] in certain ideal forms of passion and imagination" ("Novelists," 6:119). The effects are so powerful that he "should suppose that never sympathy more deep or sincere was excited than by [Clarissa's woes] except by the calamities of real life" ("Novelists," 6:120). Richardson's ability to evoke the passions is what makes Bowles (the poet who, with Charlotte Smith, effected the late-century sonnet revival and strongly influenced Coleridge) argue for *Clarissa*'s poetical qualities. For Bowles, " 'the interest we take in the history of *Clarissa* is derived from PASSIONS. Its great characteristic is PATHOS; and this I have distinguished as a far more essential property than flowers and leaves! The passions excited make RICHARDSON so far, and no further, poetical' " (Clayton, *Romantic Vision*, 40).[14] Romantic poets read *Clarissa* and novels like it with an eye to the poetic possibilities.[15]

Literary interiority is closely implicated in Hazlitt's and Bowles's emphasis on the passions and the poetic in Richardson; they are concerned with possibilities for representations of inner life that are moving and affective. Hazlitt signifies that this is at the root of the pleasure readers take in *Pamela*: "The interest of the story increases with the dawn of understanding and reflection in the heroine: her sentiments gradually expand themselves, like opening flowers" ("Novelists," 6:118–19).[16] Subjectivity—having an inner world that can bloom—becomes a site of literary exchange. This blossoming of consciousness—the intensity of the representations of Pamela's or Clarissa's inner worlds—opens a widened field of possibility for romantic lyrics. "Pamela" blooms *into* the reader's consciousness.

This is tied in part, of course, to Richardson's epistolary method, which gives access to or approximates a kind of individual consciousness with extraordinary intensity. As Watt describes it, the minuteness of epistolary representation is key: "The daily experience of the individual is composed of a ceaseless flow of thought, feeling and sensation; but most literary forms—biography and even autobiography for instance—tend to be of too gross a temporal mesh to retain its actuality."[17] Richardson slowed down and amplified individual sensation, perception, and expression: his forays into the terrain of consciousness laid a path for both novelists and poets.

Richardson's constructions isolate subjectivity as communicative consciousness with a precision and an intensity that share significant features with lyrics such as "Ode to a Nightingale." Keats's bower is a figure of enclosure with ancient roots, reaching back to the *locus amoenus* in Virgil and through him to the line of Spenser, Pope, and Thomson;[18] more than a place of rest, the eighteenth-century space of retirement becomes increasingly that of self-fashioning — the dissenter's undertaking of self-analysis in isolation and before God or even that of Pope in Twickenham.[19] But the bower in Keats does more than this: it cradles a stripped-down version of the self whose most potent literary predecessor is *Clarissa*. As Frederick Garber has pointed out, the enclosures of *Clarissa*, from closet to coffin, are precursors of the romantic bower, safe spaces (even if desperately so) for self-expression; while Clarissa's enclosures become prisons, however, the romantics seek "a context of and for the self, . . . not only . . . the kind of place in which the self could function but also the best kind of place for it": Clarissa's signal failure (196).[20] Richardson is central, however, because with him the protected space can also be a place for successfully stabilizing the intercourse between one earthly heart and another, where the closed perspective of subjectivity is reified (as closet walls) and then transcended by the ideal presence of a friend. Richardson describes this vision of the self in isolation in his correspondence. Detailing a woman's proper mode of expression, he writes: "Silence indeed to me is a commendation, when worthy subjects offer not . . . ; for air and attention will shew meaning, beyond what words can, to the observing: but the pen will shew soul and meaning too. — Retired, the modest lady, happy in herself, happy in the choice she makes of the dear correspondent of her own sex (for ours are too generally designers), uninterrupted, her closet her paradise, her company herself, and ideally the beloved absent; there she can distinguish herself: by this means she can assert and vindicate her claim to sense and meaning."[21]

In Richardson's model the writer finds a way of blending public and private spaces through the force of the imagination, balancing the demands of reticence and modesty — much as does the poet in John Stuart Mill's model of lyric. For Mill, the reader of a lyric almost eavesdrops upon the poet's utterance — gaining access to subjective integrity and sincerity in a way that the author of *Pamela* and *Clarissa* would thoroughly approve. Richardson's letter writer makes "company" of her own self, turns "sense" into "meaning," and the purity of her enclosure produces the kind of happy happiness (happy in her self, happy in the choice she makes) that Keats envies in his bird — his surrogate, impossible self. Her domestic paradise is a groundbreaking stage for self- and other-consciousness.

In this sense the readings from Warton onward of "Eloisa to Abelard" as preromantic constrain literary history to account for an ideal of isolation that is more germane to Richardson than to Pope (and whose literary successors are at first more in novels than in poems). It is not hard to rewrite Richardson's description, or abstract from it, to show the contours of romantic self-revelation. Given the frequent appropriation of the feminine throughout "masculine Romanticism" (as Anne Mellor calls it), I suggest a reconfiguration of the elements of Richardson's scene:[22] for the closet, substitute the bower of "Ode to a Nightingale," of "This Lime-Tree Bower My Prison," or the "secluded scene" of "Tintern Abbey"; for the "correspondent," supply the friend (Coleridge) who stabilizes the monologia of the *Prelude*, the absent heart whose sympathy one shares or needs (Lamb in "This Lime-Tree Bower My Prison"), the "dearest Friend," the "dear dear friend" who is almost a better self (Dorothy in "Tintern Abbey"), or even Keats's nightingale.

Clarissa's isolation and self-representation get to the heart of certain limits of consciousness: the barriers of sensation, either of pain or of pleasure (and the problems of affectively communicating them); the limits of sympathetic exchange (when bodies and their experience are finite and bounded); the seductive appeal of dissolution (as a way of moving beyond sensual and communicative limits); the possibilities and problems of enclosure (protecting and imprisoning the self); and the both disruptive and constitutive presence of the social. Each of these is a movement in the progress of Clarissa's soul after the rape (she, like the nightingale, has violation in her past). In Keats these same components appear as aching numbness, trembling old men, dissolving and forgetting, an insulating bower, and the last forlorn bell that simultaneously tolls the sound of isolation and of the human world; these elements carry a legacy of defeat, bewilderment, and beauty that the most influential novel of the century gave them. Elements of older patterns of solace, desire and/or affection, moral verification and judgment, and the imagined possibility of an ideal world are present in romantic uses of isolation and enclosure tempered by the thought of an absent friend, but with the romantics these elements are joined to aspects or themes that are all

present in the Richardsonian model alone: domesticity, silent communication, and the filtering of perception by awakened consciousness.[23]
These additions to the structure of enclosure are crucial to the relationship between romantic lyric and novel; I address them in what follows.

§ In *Poetic Form and British Romanticism* Stuart Curran argues that form
is perception in the vast majority of romantic poems. M. H. Abrams
set out the prototypical version of this position in his typology of the
"Greater Romantic Lyric"; he argues for the relation between an imaginative excursion, a poetic epiphany, and a particular poetic form.[24] Curran claims a similar connection for a variety of poetic kinds. For example, "All the major Romantic poets who approach pastoral either in
terms of specific generic conventions or even as a mode tend to internal-
ize it, making it a psychological perspective or conceptual arena."[25] The
sonnet is subject to similar treatment, so that after its revival by Bowles
and Smith, it is deeply implicated in the relationship these poets posit
between memory or sentiment and landscape (often rendered one in
each of the sonnet's two parts). Moreover, as Curran points out, Smith
"justified her generic decorum by claiming that she had approached each
poem 'as no improper vehicle for a single sentiment' " (30), giving the
form a specific emotional frame. Miltonic sonnets, those in the style of
Michelangelo (both in Wordsworth's "Miscellaneous Sonnets" group)
or Petrarch (in Smith's collection), also take their places in this romantic
vision — a suture of perception and emotion with form.

There is another way to see the relationship between perception and
form, however. One day, sailing on Grasmere Lake, Hazlitt made a
suggestion that left Wordsworth somewhat piqued: "I . . . hinted . . . that
I thought he had borrowed the idea of his *Poems on the Naming of Places*
from the local inscriptions of the same kind in Paul and Virginia. He did
not own the obligation, and stated some distinction without a difference,
in defence of his originality. Any the slightest variation would be sufficient for this purpose in his mind; for whatever *he* added or omitted
would inevitably be worth all that any one else had done, and contain the
marrow of the sentiment" (17:115–16).

Hazlitt was not just taking the stuffing out of his elders (as was his
wont) in connecting Bernardin de St. Pierre's *Paul et Virginie* to a group
of Wordsworth's poems. He was suggesting that the myth of lived lyric
embodied in *Poems on the Naming of Places*, the myth of a poet's life as a
narrative punctuated by epiphanic moments of heightened perception
and lyric utterance, has a novelistic origin. In St. Pierre's novel, sibling-
like lovers live in an island paradise; they domesticate nature through

love and familial devotion, but also by the composition of poems dedicated to their experience of a world of plenty and of sorrow. Wordsworth's *Poems on the Naming of Places* are a series of short pieces memorializing sites around Grasmere important to his family; the poems bring together a sequence of lyric moments offered as if culled from the day-to-day life of domesticity (the life commemorated in Dorothy's journal), and it is not only Hazlitt who connects them to the novel. Jerome McGann and Elizabeth Fay argue that Wordsworth's myth of the poetic life and the idyllic community of St. Pierre are closely linked.[26] As Fay maintains, the Wordsworths and their friends frequently imagined themselves living out an ideal Bernardien narrative whose moments of perfection become lyric productions. It seems that a novel may have taught Wordsworth how poetry might be lived, how its formalization of perception and emotion could imprint itself on daily life, and how it could be presented as the product of domestic perception.

Romantic lyric has a powerful connection to narrative in the forms it engages, from ballad to romance or epic. But the significance of narrative in the romantic ethos goes beyond those questions of genre: the lived narrative of poetic production in which Wordsworth (or Coleridge, Hemans, or Keats) situates himself follows a novel script. In a way this has been long acknowledged, for the critically accepted ur-texts of romantic ideology include novels like *Paul et Virginie*, Rousseau's *Nouvelle Héloïse*, and Goethe's *Leiden des jungen Werthers*. More than this, however, the novel genre provides the groundwork of coherence (usually a domestic ground) that links one lyric moment to another.

The *Poems on the Naming of Places* offers one rationale as to why and how this is so. In the sixth piece, Wordsworth describes his brother John as "A *Silent* Poet," who "from the solitude / Of the vast sea didst bring a watchful heart / Still couchant, an inevitable ear, / And an eye practised like a blind man's touch" (ll. 80–83). Wordsworth finds a grove printed by John's step and by John's precedent sight; he discovers the poetry John's feet had already marked out. The John piece naturalizes the poet and the poetic enterprise and frees them both from the formal constraints of production. John is not Gray's mute inglorious Milton, a poet whom history or even literacy has passed by. It is possible for him to be a "silent" poet first because poetry in this period is redefined as something other than a particular kind of composition and is linked instead to particular acts of perceiving.[27] More than this, the poet figure becomes identified with a narrative of perceptual integrity and domestic affection; this is what Hazlitt adumbrates in his query about *Paul et Virginie*.

The move to associate poetic composition with inspired perception is not just in St. Pierre but can be traced in the novel from Haywood and Richardson through Charlotte Smith and Radcliffe. Clarissa writes an "Ode to Wisdom" in her distress, Pamela a psalm on her captivity by Mrs. Jewkes, and Mr. B. a love poem; each is written in response to a specific set of emotional conditions that determines the genre of poem written. Adeline in *The Romance of the Forest* (1791) writes "To the Visions of Family," an address to "commemorate" a moment "when her mind was tranquilized by the surrounding scenery";[28] in Smith's novels, almost every significant character composes poems of perception and reflection. The novel's surrounding prose sets the stage for the production of both poetic vision and poetry itself, and lyric emerges in the novel as a special form of speech with its own particular context.[29]

Smith's linkage of novel and poetry is intensive and bidirectional: if her novels absorb her poetry, her poems also absorb a novelistic ethos. Curran finds in her sonnets that

> the evocation of a momentary emotional state may have its fictive extension as well. . . . Whether deliberately or not, Smith prepared for her subsequent career as a novelist by capturing moments of emotional intensity within the sonnet. Her first edition contained five sonnets "Supposed to be written by Werter"; by the sixth edition she had incorporated another five-sonnet sequence from her own novel, *Celestina*. Even Smith's supposedly personal sonnets share in the tincture of novelistic emotions, shorn of the impedimenta of character, plot, and exposition. . . . Smith's singular achievement is to free established poetic discourse from its reliance on polished couplets, formal diction, and public utterances, and through centering on internal states of mind to realize an expressive and conversational intensity. (*Poetic Form*, 30–31)

Smith's privileged context for private utterance is that of the novel's domesticity: of 116 lyrics in *Elegiac Sonnets and Other Poems*, 29 are presented as the utterances of characters in novels. No reader of Smith's poetry, from Wordsworth to the present, could ignore the degree to which one genre implies the other.

This cross-implication of novel and lyric begins for Smith with another point of generic complexity. The structure of Smith's story relies on novelistic ideals: virtue in distress, the wounded mother, and the life, like Clarissa's or Sidney Biddulph's, whose true potential is cut short by the dastardly doings of rake and wastrel.[30] Smith's sufferings were certainly real, but as Sarah Zimmerman points out, they were given a recognizable form from fiction — that of the novel of sensibility.[31] In the several prefaces to the *Elegiac Sonnets*, Smith draws attention to the context of her personal poems on suffering, reminding her readers that she was in terrible financial straits because of the profligacy and cruelty of her husband. These statements range from the vague reference of the first and second editions, "Some very melancholy moments have been beguiled by expressing in verse the sensations those moments brought," to an extensive complaint in the preface to the sixth.[32] There, in the guise of a dialogue with a friend, she explains, "*You* know that when in the Beech Woods of Hampshire, I first struck the chords of the melancholy lyre . . . ! It was unaffected sorrows drew them forth: I wrote mournfully because I was unhappy — And I have unfortunately no reason yet, though nine years have since elapsed, to *change my tune*" (5). She goes on to exclaim against the slowness of those friends who endeavored, against her husband's suit, to help her obtain her father-in-law's fortune (secured to her in old Mr. Smith's will — or so he thought). Given this distress, she writes "all I am able to achieve — 'Toujours des Chansons tristes!' " (6). As a result of this self-description, Smith was as well known for her personal failures as for her literary successes. Cowper's description of her woes is typical: "I know not a more pitiable case . . . Chained to her desk like a slave to his oar, with no other means of subsistence for herself and her numerous children."[33] In the poems themselves, however, the references to actual events are few, the major exception being the death of one of her daughters (sonnets 65, 74, and 78). From the personal poems to those explicitly given fictional contexts (those supposed to be written by Werther or appearing in novels like *Emmeline, The Old Manor House,* or *Ethelinde*), Smith's sonnets operate within a framework of subjective experience given by the novel of sensibility.

This novelization of emotion — its suture to domesticity and sentimental grief — provides a context for better understanding later romantic lyrics, especially those of Wordsworth. It seems certain that Wordsworth knew Smith's novels as well as her poetry,[34] and we may trace, at the first level of influence, the echo of a sonnet from *Emmeline* (1788; no. 38 in the *Elegiac Sonnets*) in "A slumber did my spirit seal" (1799):

When welcome slumber sets my spirit free,
  Forth to fictitious happiness it flies,
  And where Elysian bowers of bliss arise,
I seem, my Emmeline — to meet with thee!
Ah! Fancy then, dissolving human ties,

> Gives me the wishes of my soul to see;
> Tears of fond pity fill thy soften'd eyes:
>   In heavenly harmony — our hearts agree.
> Alas! these joys are mine in dreams alone,
> When cruel Reason abdicates her throne!
>   Her harsh return condemns me to complain
> Thro' life unpitied, unrelieved, unknown!
>   And as the dear delusions leave my brain,
>   She bids the truth recur — with aggravated pain!

Wordsworth's ethereal lyric alters several linguistic features of the earlier poem:

> A slumber did my spirit seal;
>   I had no human fears:
> She seemed a thing that could not feel
>   The touch of earthly years.
>
> No motion has she now, no force;
>   She neither hears nor sees;
> Rolled round in earth's diurnal course,
>   With rocks, and stones, and trees.

Emmeline's lover, Godolphin, pens his sonnet convinced that they can never be united (the heroine's obligations to her cousin prevent their marriage). Wordsworth's speaker also contemplates loss, but it is much more final (although less extravagant in tone). Signified even by the inversion of ideas from the opening line of one poem to the other, at the levels of plot and mood there is a revisionary relationship between the two poems. The parallel language of the first lines suggests that the similarities between the two are not coincidental: the "dissolving of human ties" compares nicely to "a thing that could not feel / the touch of earthly years," the activated and mutual harmony of sight in Smith is a good contrast to Wordsworth's "neither hears nor sees," and the constant "harsh return" of reason and truth is echoed (with a difference) in the cyclical motion in Wordsworth's poem.

The differences between these two poems can be addressed in terms from the Preface to *Lyrical Ballads*. The move from personified abstractions (the abstract given fleshy terms) to the most concrete of objects (the thing-ness of the rocks and stones and trees is what counts) is a movement from what Wordsworth would describe as artificiality to "the natural language of men." Eighteenth-century poetic diction, whether in the form of abstractions, familiar phrases ("heavenly harmony," from Dryden; "Elysian bowers," from the Ancients; "bowers of bliss" from Spenser, etc.), or even poetic or sentimental cliché ("Tears of fond pity fill thy soften'd eyes"), is left behind. In stripping the poetic impedimenta of "When welcome slumber sets my spirit free" to create his own vision of loss, Wordsworth chooses a more prosaic form of language — measured based on one kind of eighteenth-century poetic criterion (the use and kind of imagery). This turn to the prosaic is a move inward toward the novel-home of Smith's poem, toward a kind of everydayness of representation.

One might imagine Wordsworth performing the same analysis on Smith's sonnet that he carried out on Gray's "Sonnet on the Death of West," cutting out the obvious poeticisms of the age (personification, stock diction) and leaving lines and phrases like "When welcome slumber sets my spirit free," "I seem, my Emmeline — to meet with thee," "dissolving human ties," and "condemns me to complain / Thro' life unpitied, unrelieved, unknown." Such language he preserves. The most conventional parts of Smith's repertoire then are inverted in Wordsworth's poem: personification (turning abstraction or object into person) becomes its opposite (the reduction of person into thing); the harmony of sight (from Donne and other love lyrics) is blinded ("she neither hears nor sees"); and the cycles of Reason and Fancy are transformed into the regular revolutions of the planet and all on it.

Hunt traces acute similarities between Wordsworth's and Smith's poetry: he pairs "Tintern Abbey" and *The Emigrants;* "It is a beauteous evening, calm and free" and "Far on the sands, the low retiring tide" (from *Emmeline*); the "Immortality" ode and "No more my wearied soul attempts to stray"; "An Evening Walk" and "What awful pageants crowd the evening sky"; and so on. Hunt argues that the resemblance is structural: "Charlotte Smith's sonnets consistently follow what we have come to recognize as the 'Wordsworthian' pattern: they proceed from visual observation to psychological commentary, from the description of an experience to the interpretation of it — with all the potential for irony inherent in the almost inevitable discrepancy between the external and the internal world, between what we see and do, and what we *think* we see and do" ("Wordsworth and Charlotte Smith," 92–93). This "Wordsworthian" pattern may be subsequent to and partially dependent on Smith's precedent, but it bears a similar connection to the novel as well.

In addition to the verbal and image-oriented convergence of "A slumber did my spirit seal" and "When welcome slumber sets my spirit free," there is a deeper structural link (as my analysis of inversions suggests). Paul de Man's reading of the Wordsworth poem identifies its most striking structural aspect as the narrative event elided between the two stanzas. The poem reveals "two stages of consciousness, one belonging to the past and mystified, the other to the *now* of the poem, presented as being in error."[35] The separation of these two moments is incomplete because of the double resonance of lines 3–4, but it appears on the page: "The 'now' of the poem, . . . the moment of death . . . lies hidden in the blank space between the two stanzas. The fundamental structure of allegory reappears here in the tendency of the language toward narrative, the spreading out along the axis of an imaginary time in order to give duration to what is, in fact, simultaneous within the subject" (225). While de Man argues that this tendency toward narrative is an effect of allegory, I argue from another direction. The abstraction of narrative is symbolic, and the novel becomes the symbol from which poetry draws its counterclaims to value.

This narrative abstraction involves in part the question raised by spots of time, the relation of the lyric moment to a ground that is both narrative and biographical.[36] Critics like Don Bialostosky and Jay Clayton have effectively explored the problem of voice and narration in Wordsworth's poetry, but what is at stake here is somewhat different: the gesture toward the tale, rather than the telling of it.[37] Implicit in many of these indicated narratives are references, elaborations, or manipulations of novelistic technique or structure. This extends as far as poems like "Resolution and Independence," "Salisbury Plain," and others I will discuss shortly. I wish to emphasize that this "Lucy" poem gains its inspiration from a poem embedded within a novel. Here, the relationship between the genres is somewhat parodic, but it is constructive rather than destructive; no one could claim that the artistic achievement of "A slumber did my spirit seal" is found in parody or pastiche.[38] What is key here is not just the presence of a hidden narrative; this is sufficiently accounted for, of course, by the ballad itself. What matters is that the narrative value around which the poetry eventually circles back is the culture's most powerful narrative form.

Poetry has here a vital relationship to novels, a relationship that is more than merely analogous to the Gestalt distinction that Barbara Herrnstein Smith uses to relate verse to prose: if "meter serves . . . as a frame for the poem, separating it from a 'ground' of less highly structured speech and sound," in Smith's oeuvre, novels are the ground in which poetry takes root, in which it takes on sense, and where it is made understandable in a literary version of lived experience.[39] If poetry is the name for or the shape of a kind of altered, enhanced perception, as it is for Wordsworth in *Poems on the Naming of Places*, a novel provides a base from which that vision begins.

§ Novelistic vision is often bounded by the walls of a house. But beyond the cliché, domesticity emerges in the eighteenth-century novel as a site of chiastic interchange between readers and the world of representation, bringing the two into close and vibrant contact. By the 1760s there is a shift in the weight of representation signified by the cumulative presence of works like *Roxana, Clarissa, Sir Charles Grandison, Humphry Clinker, Amelia, David Simple,* and *The History of Miss Betsy Thoughtless.* The domestic becomes increasingly associable with the novel's history in the eighteenth century, beginning with the influence of conduct books on the birth of the form and moving on to the developing fiction of sensibility.

Domesticity in the novel becomes a way of creating intimacy and giving access to individual consciousness: the novel teaches us that we may better know someone's modes of thinking and feeling, the contours of her desire, the patterns of his emotion, by knowing what goes on between siblings or from parent to child. This is the lesson of *Clarissa,* but also of *Jane Eyre, Mansfield Park,* or *What Maisie Knew.* It is not the only pattern that the novel offers — the barest mentions of family can be found in *Robinson Crusoe* or *Gulliver's Travels,* and the protonovel *Pilgrim's Progress* (part 1) requires the renunciation of the family — but nonetheless, the domestic pattern is given by the novel genre as part of its representational schema, of theme and of chiasmus and rhetorical realisms.[40] With the coming of the novel new kinds of occasional representation emerge involving the family. Responses to domestic events in the wake of the novel reach beyond the death of a child or one's distance from a spouse (in Bradstreet, Jonson, or Donne, e.g.) to include simple mundanities like a walk with one's sister or a conversation by a child's bedside. The domestic in the novel absorbs and goes beyond the adulterous intrigues or courtship plots of contemporary drama, and despite the occasional presence of the domestic world in epic, the ballad tradition (e.g., "The Wife of Usher's Well"), or the family elegy, the homely stuff of representation that Wordsworth adapts in his poetry (from the matter of individual poems throughout *Lyrical Ballads* or *Miscellaneous Sonnets* to groups like "Poems founded on the Affections" or "Poems

Referring to Childhood"), may be read as the outcome of a shift in representational focus brought about chiefly by the novel over a period of seventy or more years.

The diffusion of domesticity as literary structure that begins with the novel can be felt through the works of every significant romantic writer. For Coleridge an allegiance to domestic spaces helps defend against charges of Jacobin radicalism and freethinking.[41] Blake makes domesticity an important part of his symbolic, while in Wordsworth's poems, as in those of Hemans, Coleridge, or Baillie, the domestic is central in genres from which it had traditionally been tangential or excluded: Wordsworth's pastoral, for example, is often as much about domesticity as it is about shepherds, the ideal, or a relationship to landscape, focusing on family units and the disruption of them (as in "Michael," "Ruth," "The Thorn," or "We Are Seven"). Even nonnarrative poems, like "To a Butterfly" (1802) and "A Farewell" (1802), center on domestic possibilities, and in the latter poem (as in many by Coleridge), what makes the idyll ideal is the prospect of domestic tranquillity. In "An Evening Walk," as Robin Jarvis suggests, it is a domestic fantasy that enables the perceptual narrative of the walk to come to a hopeful close: a cottage to share with Dorothy, "that cottage . . . / (Sole bourn, sole wish, sole object of my way . . .)" (ll. 415–16).[42] Perhaps more oddly, "Salisbury Plain," with its murderer protagonist, combines the rogue biography of the novel's early history with the sentimental domesticity of its later years.[43] Intimacy in Wordsworth's lyrics hinges either on domestic enclosures or on the closeness, the imaginary protective unit, of familial relationships (Dorothy's presence is most important here), and although the majority of Wordsworth's poems take place outside the home, the domestic still prevails.[44] The domestic situations Wordsworth develops in lyrics or narrative poems have no parallel in Gray, Pope, Donne, Spenser, or Virgil, and though domestic tenderness figures in earlier eighteenth-century poems of sensibility, the domestic becomes literary, that is, achieves a specific representational status, first in *Moll Flanders*, *Pamela*, or *The Vicar of Wakefield*.[45] If by the end of the century a reorganization of family life (a tricky historical problem) was in fact under way, the new importance of domesticity in genres like drama and lyric is rooted in more than this. The mere presence of domesticity in lyric is one thing and may be explained in relation to larger cultural shifts; understanding its typical configuration in literary representation requires a literary-historical approach as well. Neither can replace the other.

The first significant wave of domestic verse, that of Leapor and

Collier starting around the 1740s, and the next wave, that of *The Deserted Village* (Goldsmith, 1770), *The Village* (Crabbe, 1783), and *The Task* (Cowper, 1785), follow historically upon the novel's successful indication of the literary virtues and possibilities of domesticity. I will address the other poets shortly, but Cowper's *Task* reveals much about the relationship between novels and poems when the self is at issue. Domesticity in the novel, I have argued, provides a compact version of the social in which to frame and make sense of personal experience; to restate this as synecdoche, in the novel, the house is the space that properly protects and exposes the self for view. The idea that the home shapes the self is part of the late-eighteenth-century episteme; that it is the space that enables the self to speak its experience with propriety is the novel's gift. As pathology, this is the entrapment of *Clarissa*; as iconic health, it is the drawing-room community of *Grandison*. The intimacy of the domestic brings the readers of novels into close contact with the world and minds of the fiction. Cowper's approach to domesticity, and to the personal through it, owes much to this tradition.

A deflated epic invocation — of domesticity — opens *The Task* by making small room for the self:

> I SING the SOFA. I, who lately sang
> Truth, Hope, and Charity, and touch'd with awe
> The solemn chords, and with a trembling hand,
> Escap'd with pain from that advent'rous flight,
> Now seek repose upon an humbler theme;
> The theme though humble, yet august and proud
> Th'occasion — for the Fair commands the song.[46]

In line with earlier eighteenth-century poets like Shenstone or Prior, Cowper introduces self first as an object of laughter, disarming possible accusations of egotism; Cowper, however, stakes a claim to self-presentation by providing a limiting space to house it. The domestic is the context that enables self-vision. Domestic space, evoked by the literal support of the SOFA, provides a safe enclosure from which the poet's song can be heard. Cowper's speaker, unlike that of Collins in the "Ode to Evening" (for example), is not confused, split, or divided by the space he calls home. In latching on to domesticity (as distinct from Collins's merely pastoral hut, abandoned, unmarked by family or the comforts of home), Cowper finds room for autobiography. The poem proceeds from the furnishings of the house to the pleasures of memory:

> ... The SOFA suits
> The gouty limb, 'tis true; but gouty limb,
> Though on a SOFA, may I never feel:
> For I have lov'd the rural walk through lanes
> Of grassy swath, close cropt by nibbling sheep,   (bk. 1, ll. 106–10)
>
> E'er since a truant boy I pass'd my bounds
> T'enjoy a ramble on the banks of Thames;
> And still remember, nor without regret
> Of hours that sorrow since has much endear'd.   (ll. 114–17)

The walk of locodescriptive poetry becomes linked to the story of self only after the domestic sets the scene of recollection — lying on the SOFA in repose.

Throughout the poem, many if not most of its personal moments are linked to domesticity, as at the opening of book 3, where echoes of the more personal parts of Thomson (Cowper's speaker rests "beneath elm or vine, / My languid limbs, when summer sears the plains" [ll. 29–30]) are ratified by contemplation of "Domestic happiness, thou only bliss / Of Paradise that has surviv'd the fall!" (ll. 41–42). If the absence of lyric marks the fall in *The Seasons* ("Spring," ll. 242–74), homely presence brings paradise back for Cowper; it both cradles the body within it and sets the stage for the poetry of the self. In *The Task*, the poet's body, that striking absence in much poetry of the early and midcentury, makes a vivid appearance, coaxed into presence by a combination of sympathy and domestic relations:

> ... What's the world to you? —
> Much. I was born of woman, and drew milk,
> As sweet as charity, from human breasts.
> I think, articulate, I laugh and weep,
> And exercise all functions of a man.
> How then should I and any man that lives
> Be strangers to each other? Pierce my vein,
> And catechise it well; apply thy glass,
> Search it, and prove now if it be not blood
> Congenial with thine own: and, if it be,
> What edge of subtlety canst thou suppose
> Keen enough, wise and skilful as thou art,
> To cut the link of brotherhood, by which
> One common Maker bound me to the kind?   (bk. 3, ll. 195–209)

As with this passage, book 4 of *The Task* draws personal scenes through domestic ones, as if the metonymy the novel introduced were now to be taken for granted.

The Winter Evening is announced not by a personification on a silver car but by the horn of the postman; the nocturnal comforts of home are signaled by an epistolary turn, a turn to the mode of the most significant domestic fiction of the era. The postman's letters bear novel news:

> Houses in ashes, and the fall of stocks,
> Births, deaths, and marriages, epistles wet
> With tears, that trickled down the writer's cheeks
> Fast as the periods from his fluent quill,
> Or charg'd with am'rous sighs of absent swains,
> Or nymphs responsive . . .   (bk. 4, ll. 16–21)

Whatever the daily experience of eighteenth-century readers with letters of their own, the experience of epistolary spectatorship that these lines evoke is that of the reader of novels in letters, a reader who, whether sympathetic like Cowper or uninterested like the postman, reads from some remove. The novel's treatment of letters lays the background to this scene, from the sentimental epistolarity of tears to the heroical (and often pastoral) epistles of amatory fiction. The vision of a postman's bag filled with letters, represented at the distance of sympathy—and no closer—is the legacy of novelists from Charles Gildon (*The Post-Man Robb'd of his Mail; or, the Packet broke open*) to Behn, Haywood, Richardson, and on.

Cowper does not assimilate novelistic matter without indigestion; in turning to the domestic through the (painful) mundanities of epistolary life, he empties out the humanity of his letters, placing them in the carefree hands of the carrier (bk. 4, ll. 12–15). He quickly moves on to balance private with public through the less personal medium of the newspaper. With it in hand he shuts himself into the safe space of home, the enclosure that the novel made a literary prerequisite of the self (ll. 36–41). The novel is Cowper's silent partner—he refers only to romance (bk. 3, l. 116). Given the language that dominated discussion of the novel, "romance" is all but a shibboleth for its contested sibling: one term, as McKeon demonstrates, is incomprehensible without the other; and the two occupy the same semantic field (as Hazlitt's comments on Richardson, which we saw earlier, show). When Cowper uses "romance," then, he evokes the field of prose fiction while suppressing the prime generic mover, the novel, in a move that would prefigure the romantic elevation of romance as the novel's imaginative superior. While the novel paves the way for Cowper's domestic approach to the personal, it does so as subaltern or subsidiary.

Genres are employed to rewrite one another, and georgic also enables Cowper to take the novelistic topos of domestic intimacy into the public space of poetry, to move from home (*oikos*) and letter to economy (*oikonomia*) and news, to match the humble cucumber against grape or grain. Dustin Griffin points out that *The Task* holds a central place in shaping eighteenth-century georgic, "redefining labor . . . as a virtually spiritual activity, and shifting . . . attention from the public sphere to the private."[47] The eighteenth-century ascendance of a domesticated georgic extends back to the poetry of Collier and Leapor.[48] What matters for Cowper, however, is not household labor (cf. "Crumble Hall") so much as the household's intimate space. The sublimation of domestic labor into domestic space is key to a genre where servant girls like Pamela trade wage labor for bourgeois domesticity.

The novel connection to a domesticated georgic where labor is redefined is explicit in Brooke's 1777 *Excursion*. Brooke opens in the pastoral retreat of Colonel Dormer, guardian of two teenage sisters: the girls "were leaning over the terrace wall of their uncle's garden admiring the radiant lustre of the setting sun, the mixed gold and azure which played on a rustic temple . . . , praising the heart-felt pleasures of retirement, and the tranquil joys of a rural life," when a wealthy woman passes by, sparking ambition in the heart of one sister, Maria (5). Colonel Dormer's life of otium makes him negligent. Maria is allowed to go alone to London, where misadventures leave her almost without reputation. She is finally saved and returns to the country at the end of the tale: a violent storm strikes while the heroine and her friends are wandering from the villa where they have lodged. Suddenly in the darkness, they "hear a clock strike, and . . . see, through a coppice of trees, a glimmering light at a little distance" (147). That light comes from Maria's own home; she has unwittingly wandered back to where she began. This is a different rural retreat, "a neighborhood of persons endeared to each other by the most tender ties"; there, says the reformed guardian, "We will build a little, plant a great deal, and above all, garden to infinity," cultivating both "vegetative beauty" and domestic bliss (153). Such domestic cultivation is for Brooke the ultimate goal of the female novelist: altering a quotation from Thomson's georgic "Spring," she argues that women make the best novelists because it is their task "to expand (as well by writing as conversation) the bud of reason, 'And teach the young idea how to shoot' " (2). Brooke's *Excursion* makes concrete the ideas of literary labor advanced in the novel genre. Novels (not just through manipulating conduct literature) participate in a georgic writerly project: domestic cultivation. This project is one to which *The Task* owes allegiance.[49]

The effect of the novel genre on Cowper's range of representation involves both creativity and ambivalence. Cowper's wry yet fascinated relationship to the world of the home, and by my extension to its literary agent, sets what would become a standard for romantic poets trying to claim a space of eminence for poetry in a culture whose love affair with novels was becoming notorious. Wordsworth's turn-of-the-century disgust at "frantic novels" (1800 Preface) is delivered in the voice of a man who knew what people bought and what the public read. When J. S. Mill tries, thirty years after *Lyrical Ballads,* to define poetry, he situates it in regard to novels in a hierarchical relationship whose contours had already been established: "Many of the greatest poems are in the form of novels; and, in almost all good serious fictions, there is true poetry. But there is a radical distinction between the interest felt in a novel as such, and the interest excited by poetry; for the one is derived from *incident,* the other from the representation of *feeling.* In one, the source of the emotion excited is the exhibition of a state or states of human sensibility; in the other, of a series of states of mere outward circumstances."[50] The generic status of poetry no longer depends, as it did for Sidney, upon a distinction between truth of fact and the "truth" of a Golden nature; for Mill it is a contest over how imaginative "truth" may be subdivided generically. Such classification became impassioned statement only after the romantics had redefined the poetic through what might be called shrewd literary politics — absorbing and reworking the novel and its matter within the frame of a set of claims about poetic purity. Both aesthetically (from the viewpoint of a literary tradition that could never be generically exclusive, whatever one's desires) and pragmatically (from the viewpoint of a literary market where reading was promiscuous and novels highly popular), poetry was compelled to define its relationship to the novel.[51]

If no earlier, from the moment that claims to canonicity were made in the name of the novel (by Fielding, Clara Reeve, or Anna Barbauld), literary history hit a major turning point: whatever had been its popularity, whatever had been its literary value, the novel now had claims to sequence, development, and a self-defined tradition. It was also subject to fierce competition and even open war from writers who, like Wordsworth, felt a growing sense of their duties as newly professionalized poets and the pressures of what Siskin calls "novelism." These duties were not just to literature ("extravagant stories in verse") or to nation ("sickly and stupid German Tragedies"); in a time when literature was becoming distinct from other belles lettres, they encompassed the foundations of what it meant to be a "poet" and not just "an author."[52]

§ It is time to return to *Poems on the Naming of Places*, for with these poems one may begin to determine what Wordsworth — as self-proclaimed prophet — took to be the work of lyric in the new literary economy. The *Poems on the Naming of Places* first appeared in the 1800 *Lyrical Ballads*. Originally, there were five poems; a sixth was added in the 1815 *Works*, and a final piece (first published in 1845) appeared as part of the group in 1849. The series contains a number of elements from the Wordsworthian repertoire: in all but the last a walk culminates in a realization; the city is frequently contrasted with the life-giving expanse of nature; pastoral conventions organize patterns of perception (especially in the first poem); an elegiac impulse moves all the *Poems* (but is most important in the two last); the *Poems* also employ novelistic tones and conventions in an eminently Wordsworthian fashion.

Jonathan Bate has observed the truly synthetic character of the *Poems*, arguing that they attempt to unite naive and sentimental views of nature: "naming . . . acts for Wordsworth as a kind of mediation . . . resolving the tension that exists between the 'lived, illiterate and unconscious' [experience of nature] and the 'learned, literate and conscious'" experience.[53] At the level of the individual poems, there are multiple acts of mediation. Bate argues that "It was an April morning: fresh and clear" marks "a transitional, liminal [moment] . . . : it pauses between winter and summer. [Bate uses] the term liminal to suggest the idea of a threshold, a margin between two worlds, for 'margin' is an important word in two of the other place-name poems. Three times the poet uses the word 'yet': such qualifications are emblematic of his uncertainty and confusion" (204).

In the wake of deconstruction it may be all too easy to identify competing or dialectically related moments in a poem, modes that the poem tries to synthesize or mediate, but *Poems on the Naming of Places* are deeply involved in such a pattern. The *Poems* repeatedly employ strategies of transition and mediation, whether it is to unify two perspectives, as Jonathan Bate argues; two moments (the lost past, elegized in the present moments of writing and reading); or, as I argue, two modes.

The *Poems* attempt to reconcile two modes of experience, the flights of the imagination and everyday domesticity (a version of the high and the low), and two modes of representation, the poetic and the novelistic. This is clear in the second poem of the series, "To Joanna." This piece is conversational, even leaning toward the Coleridgean mode, but it is also epistolary:

> Amid the smoke of cities did you pass
> The time of early youth; and there you learned,
> From years of quiet industry, to love
> The living Beings by your own fire-side,
> With such a strong devotion, that your heart
> Is slow to meet the sympathies of them
> Who look upon the hills with tenderness,
> And make dear friendships with the streams and groves.
> Yet we, who are transgressors in this kind,
> Dwelling retired in our simplicity
> Among the woods and fields, we love you well,
> Joanna! and I guess, since you have been
> So distant from us now for two long years,
> That you will gladly listen to discourse
> However trivial, if you thence be taught
> That they, with whom you once were happy, talk
> Familiarly of you and of old times.

The poem opens in tension between two kinds of domestically oriented affection, "love [for] / The living Beings by [Joanna's] own fire-side" and that of the Grasmere friends, who wish to create a written substitute for intimacy in two parallel acts of inscription — the poem-as-letter and the poem-as-epitaph, the "uncouth" chiseling of her name upon "the native rock / Above the Rotha, by the forest-side" (ll. 80–81). The poem cultivates this intimate exchange in the epistolary language of the novel:

> While I was seated, now some ten days past,
> Beneath those lofty firs, that overtop
> Their ancient neighbour, the old steeple-tower,
> The Vicar from his gloomy house hard by
> Came forth to greet me; and, when he had asked,
> "How fares Joanna, that wild-hearted Maid!
> And when will she return to us?" he paused;
> And, after short exchange of village news,
> He with grave looks demanded for what cause,
> Reviving obsolete idolatry,

> I, like a Runic Priest, in characters
> Of formidable size had chiselled out
> Some uncouth name upon the native rock.   (ll. 18–30)

Wordsworth gives several clues that lines 18–26 should be read differently from those that immediately follow; besides a shift in diction, this narrative interlude is metrically muddy compared to the strongly accented sequel. We may be tempted to ascribe the epistolary tone to the familiar letter itself, the *soi-distant* object of reference for the novel in letters and sometimes of the verse epistle. However, choosing to see only the familiar letter behind the poem poses a delicate problem: verisimilitude in one genre, the novel, seems to indicate that it represented everyday experience in the way that most signifies its generic success; verisimilitude in poetry might merely signify a faithfulness of representation and not a conventional aspect of literary form.[54]

Such a position would be naive. As Bialostosky points out, none of the elements of everyday life that appears in Wordsworth does so "simply in the primary sphere of communication from which it is taken"; even and especially the "natural language of man" appears in line with generic codes.[55] The first test is one of formal grouping: for an educated reader of the present or for a culturally competent reader of Wordsworth's era, the composite image, with its churchyard, old Vicar, village gossip, and the confessedly "trivial" (l. 15) matter (in line with the village scenes of *Pamela* or *The Vicar of Wakefield*), has a novelistic tint phrased with conventional novelistic modesty (like Clarissa's apologies for her minuteness or the ironic self-deprecation of Jane Austen's ivory miniatures). The ideal of a community of letter writers as elaborated domesticity — the household fractured by distance but united by epistolary tact — is that valorized most powerfully by *Grandison*, the apotheosis of a private-public web of domestic conversation and community. It is not that everyday life is not the (pen)ultimate object of reference in the poem, but rather that everyday life is grouped and filtered as the novel would have it, and presented by a shift in representational mode.

There are many such shifts in mode in "To Joanna," from the pastoral contrasts of the first verse paragraph to the epistolary notes of the second, the romance flavor of lines 26–30 or 51–65, the visionary language around line 70, and the final domestic tone of the closing inscription:

> there,
> In memory of affections old and true,
> I chiselled out in these rude characters

Joanna's name deep in the living stone:
And I, and all who dwell by my fireside,
Have called the lovely rock, JOANNA'S ROCK.

These shifts in literary language correspond to shifts in subject, suggesting that Wordsworth not only associated matter with form (as he certainly did) but that he also had modal or generic reference in mind, not a verisimilitude or realism without root. These modes in juxtaposition move the poem from one fireside, "amid the smoke of cities," to another, in the purity of the dale; one model of intimacy is substituted for another, and this substitution is effected by noticeable and complete alterations in style.

Rooted in the domestic, the conversational, and the domestically intimate, the poem opens to invoke the subject matter and conventional styles of the novel-as-genre, not the matter of pastoral, topographical, elegiac, or descriptive poems (the other literary and modal referents of the piece); there are also echoes of Cowper in Wordsworth's adaptation of the novel's domestic and epistolary ideals. That this sense of home and self is the offspring of the novel as genre is apparent in comparing Wordsworth's Vicar to the closest of his poetic kin: none is so close as his novelistic forebears. Goldsmith's *Deserted Village* has closeups of a vicar and a schoolmaster, but these are quite different from Wordsworth's conversational moment. Goldsmith's *Village* vicar (as opposed to his *Wakefield* one) is primarily emblematic; he is an object of description (never does he speak) and a site of mourning; his actions are repetitive, not particular, and he is not the active character of Wordsworth's *Poems*. It is the *Wakefield* vicar, with his fluid speech and nosy concern, who seems closer on the canonical tree. The other germane verse *Village* is by a poet — Crabbe — who is remarkable for his reception as a novelistic craftsman. An anonymous essay on Crabbe in the *Saturday Review* (1864), "Fiction — in Prose or Verse?" makes this connection: "Epic poets choose subjects great enough for epics, and idyllic poets choose such subjects as are suitable for idyls [*sic*] — that is, tales of human adventure or suffering where the interest is not quite up to the higher level of the epic. Of these subjects none are more natural to the modern mind than tales of contemporary life. The same feelings which prompt us to depict ourselves in prose fiction also lead us to describe verse incidents chosen from that daily life in which we take so strong an interest."[56] Again (although later), critics posit a modal connection between the domestic in verse and in the novel. Crabbe's matter-of-factness put him occasionally at odds with romantics like Wordsworth, but his poetry, like Wordsworth's, focuses on the communal and the everyday, by way of a novelistic style.[57]

In "To Joanna," the shift in styles from pastoral to conversational and back registers a shift in mode that can be deemed to refer as much to objects (from woods and field to warm firesides) as to genres or modes (from Virgilian or Theocritan eclogues to domestic novels). To argue that the first (reference to the simplicity of woods and field) is self-conscious reference to a poetic style and the second (invocation of the domestic) is mere chronicling of the real is, ironically, to slip as readers quite fully into the world of novelistic naturalization (the concealment of convention, which marks much novel realism); it is to take for faithful record what is artful representation. The novel has a set of convenient references for its kind of representation, including (at this historical moment), chatty letters, country vicars, village news, and absent friends who need to be kept in touch. The epistolary language of "To Joanna" in the context of this literary history invites comparisons to the language of the epistolary novel, the storytelling tone of a letter from, let us say, Pamela to her absent parents, Harriet Byron to her aunt, or even Matt Bramble to his friend the doctor. Wordsworth's decision to include this kind of material in his poetry is a gesture supported by the novelistic impulse (as it is identified by Watt or the anonymous Crabbe partisan in the *Saturday Review*), not only to chronicle the everyday, but to bring the minutiae of daily existence into the realm of art. Wordsworth here enters a novelistic field of representation, even though part of the problem with identifying the field as novelistic is the fact that the novel's conventions tend to erase their status as conventions all but entirely, hiding in realism and its rubrics. The battles waged in novels over how to tell the truth (those identified by McKeon) seem to have been (provisionally) won, and poetry would take the lesson to heart.

Domestic intimacy is represented in *Poems on the Naming of Places* through novelistic strategies and in a novelistic context (that of *Paul et Virginie*); it is also materially connected to what Wordsworth identifies as the essential and oldest form of written poetry, the epitaphic inscription. Geoffrey Hartman argues that the epitaph is the base genre from which Wordsworthian nature poetry develops, and Jonathan Bate locates it at the root of the place-name poems.[58] *Poems on the Naming of Places*, in fact, bring the novelistic under the rubric of the poetic (in the sense of the originary epitaph), mediating between one form's representations and the other's — the domesticity of the novel and of letters with the purity of epitaphic inscription.

The placement of the *Poems* in the 1849 edition strongly suggest such a relation, situating them between the "Poems Founded on the Affections" on one side and the "Poems of the Fancy" and "Poems of the Imagination" on the other; between the domestic — the subject of novelistic inquiry — and the imaginative, the object as well as the source of poetic production.[59] That the placement of these poems is significant can be deduced from Wordsworth's account of his organizational plans. As W. J. B. Owen notes, "In a letter of May 1809 we find him drafting for Coleridge's inspection a scheme of which elements remain in the edition of 1815 and later editions."[60] In this plan *Poems on the Naming of Places* follow " 'Natural objects and their influence on the mind either as growing or in an advanced state, . . . [and] as a transition to . . . those poems relating to human life' " (Owen, *Wordsworth as Critic*, 151, quoting Wordsworth). This is part of a chronological scheme that Wordsworth partly abandons in his later editions, but it demonstrates his feeling that the *Poems* (a) could not be subsumed under a larger rubric (even that of the inscription, as is apparent in the 1815 edition) and (b) were transitional in some important sense. In the 1815 edition, this transitional character is partially lost, as the *Poems* "appear between 'Sonnets Dedicated to Liberty' and 'Inscriptions' " (155), but even there their oddity and categorical integrity are maintained. In the final edition of the *Works*, when the chronological scheme is partially replaced, they appear again to mediate between categories — this time between modes of representation and aspects of experience (the two are related).

As lyrics, *Poems on the Naming of Places* are as difficult to classify as they might be to defend if not for the novel — if they are not inscriptions, what are they, and why and how should they be read? The charge of egotism or self-indulgence frequently leveled at Wordsworth by contemporaries like Anna Seward (and later, Keats), a charge familiar from eighteenth-century criticism of lyric (and implicit in the lyric paradigm discussed in Chapter 3), could rarely be so clearly laid as in response to the *Poems*, written by a private gentleman about a group of people distinguished only by the attention they receive. Wordsworth creates interest by relying on domestic intimacy as an essential way of giving access not only to interiority and to personal experience but to the *essential* — the monadic building blocks of the true reality (spots of time, lyric revelations, etc.). It is through the domestic that, as in the novel, the affective space of representation can be imaginatively fleshed out. However, the novel's structural influence is of greater extent.

If *Poems on the Naming of Places* adopt domesticity as a means of opening up interiority and guiding readers inside it, they also adopt other features of novel-style rhetorical realisms. The near-sacralization of space in these poems is rooted in epitaphic consecration, but the fixation of time and space upon which these poems are centered goes beyond this poetic pattern. Their specificity — the invocation of a unique moment in which Joanna's name is carved, the blending of unique moments past and present when William, following John's footsteps, discovers the tight little poet's grove — makes concrete (as inscription) the invocation of temporal and spatial specificity involved in "Lines Composed a Few Miles above Tintern Abbey, on Revisiting the Banks of the Wye during a Tour, July 13, 1798," or many of Smith's sonnets "Written on the Sea Shore. — October, 1784"; "To melancholy. Written on the banks of the Arun, October 1785"; or "Written in Farm Wood, South Downs, in May 1784." In pieces like these, the poem as document has treble "reference" (however fictional): to the thoughts and feelings of the speaker, to the surrounding place, and to the time of utterance.

Unlike their midcentury counterparts, Smith and Wordsworth represent a figure in a coordinately unique landscape and simultaneously offer a model of emotional involvement; their model, however, is the one on which novelists stake their representational venture. Novels often specify, chiastically, the framework of interaction between the reader's world and that of the representation. This kind of contextual specificity is a signpost in the careful mapping between texts and reader at the foundation of the novel's rhetorical identity. The success of this tactic has cross-generic results, so that even if the epitaph is the poetic model upon which Wordsworth builds, it is by following the novelistic mode of St. Pierre that in *Poems on the Naming of Places* Wordsworth is able to mold the epitaph to provide a proper context for lyric self-representation and personal speech: *Sic Viator* can become an epistolary address, a domestic greeting, and a unique statement of here and now, because the epitaphic tradition is reborn into the novel's brave new world.

These poems are a case in point — but far from being the entire body of evidence — for the thesis that strategies of novelistic representation provide a groundwork for figuring personal experience in romantic lyrics. The *Poems* share several novelistic attributes, from the Werther-like promenade of the first poem (Werther-like because of its elegiac motivation and sentiments) to the Richardsonian enclosure that shapes the poem most elegiac in tone, that for Wordsworth's brother John. This piece is the emotional climax of the *Poems;* there we may underscore the most important aspect of the connection between lyric and novel. As described above, John is identified as a poet *avant la lettre*, "A *silent* Poet" (l. 80). Wordsworth brings latent poetry into being by retiring to a space where, to quote Richardson with a gendered difference, "with his pen, he can shew soul and meaning, too. . . . Uninterrupted . . . in his paradise, his company himself, and . . . his brother, the beloved absent; . . . he can distinguish himself: by this means he can assert and vindicate his claim to sense and meaning."

This claim to sense and meaning goes beyond the love of two brothers, the specificity of trees, birds, or footprints in the snow, to something of greater significance—the creation of a space for lyric and for the professional poet. John's absence and silence mark the space in which Wordsworth finds a permanence of speech and of creation, where he turns silent poetry into words, and elevates the lyric to the mystical status of indelible inscription. The Richardsonian image of the absent loved one creates a writerly self, here ratifying the poet's vocation and his love in a movement of sympathy and inscription (the pathway worn by John's feet is the equivalent of the poet's words).[61] The poems follow the principle of consciousness-as-chiasmus as moments of intensity produce a sense of depth around the seemingly inconsequential mapping of one space onto another. In effect, the novelistic is brought under the rubric of the poetic; it is rendered as a mode ultimately under poetic control.

§ The use of novelistic convention as a ground for the ideal poetic endeavor is also fundamental to "Resolution and Independence," a poem with a long critical history as a statement of the problems of the romantic poetic persona, and a poem central to the tradition of the romantic pedestrian excursion. "Resolution and Independence" offers a familiar pensive Wordsworth, walking as he contemplates his status as poet and as man:

> My whole life I have lived in pleasant thought,
> As if life's business were a summer mood;
> As if all needful things would come unsought
> To genial faith, still rich in genial good;
> But how can He expect that others should
> Build for him, sow for him, and at his call
> Love him, who for himself will take no heed at all?

As pressing as the problem of the poet's isolation in an economic world of labor is the problem of his isolation in a social world of meaning:

> I thought of Chatterton, the marvellous Boy,
> The sleepless soul that perished in his pride;
> Of Him who walked in glory and in joy
> Following his plough, along the mountain-side:
> By our own spirits are we defied:
> We Poets in our youth begin in gladness;
> But thereof come in the end despondency and madness.   (ll. 8–14)

Walking and wondering, the poet has an experience sent as if "by pecu-liar grace, / A leading from above, a something given" (ll. 50–51). He encounters an old man who tells him a story. The tale at first seems so much noise for the poet; it is told twice over at the speaker's somewhat distracted request, and the poet-walker tunes out its teller in favor of an internal moment:

> The old Man still stood talking by my side;
> But now his voice to me was like a stream
> Scarce heard; nor word from word could I divide.   (ll. 106–8)

Having retreated into thought, Wordsworth experiences a poetic epiph-any, but his strategic deafness can be embarrassing. What seems shock-ing is his lack of immediate sympathetic response to the old man's plight — his selective listening. He stands absorbed by his own fears and an internal vision, overwriting the old man's anguish with his poetic hopes.

The double lapse in the speaker's attention has been a crux in the poem's critical history.[62] Recent scholarship has examined the history of walking in poetry and travel narratives partly in order to resolve some of the problems the poem raises for romanticism. Celeste Langan's *Romantic Vagrancy* connects walking to liberalism in an arc that spans from Rous-seau to Wordsworth, and she describes Wordsworthian encounters as "collision[s] between the social and political dimensions of liberalism."[63] When these encounters break down, as here, words lose logical force and become murmurs; romantic lyric rewrites Enlightenment liberalism to bring the individual subject into a chaotic social world. In tracing this genealogy, Langan focuses on Rousseau's *Rêveries*, which "demonstrates how the epistemological subject of Enlightenment thought is an asocial subject, [while] the Romantic project, by contrast, restores that subject to a social setting, the encounter with another subject" (15). Langan identi-fies the crux of "Resolution and Independence" as a thwarted or manipu-lated convention from Rousseauvian walks. There is a gap in this genealogy, for in fact the encounter at the heart of this poem is a generic convention of novels: novel protagonists, out on a walk, often encounter a stranger who volunteers his or her history: this is the leitmotif of Henry Fielding's novels and a significant component of works by Sarah Fielding, Defoe, Haywood, Lennox, Smollett, Smith, and even Richardson.[64] Moreover, in novels, such encounters are fundamentally concerned with social or political commitment. In the Man of the Hill episode in *Tom Jones*, a classic such moment, the encounter stages the superiority of Tom's ethical and political commitments (to the King, to a woman being threatened by murder) over the Old Man's seclusion from social forces and obligations.

The convention that is thwarted in "Resolution and Independence" is one of response; the poet-walker ought exhibit something more than abstraction. The expectation that the tale of the sick and wasted old man will elicit a sympathetic response in the hearer and a corresponding change in his life is one in which we are trained by a literary history shaped by the novel. Hunter points out that novels, like whales, will swallow anything, from didactic treatises, conduct tracts, and newspaper accounts to often digressive tales. He differentiates the "stories within" of novels from those in romance and epic: "there [in the earlier genres] they have neat and tidy borders that divide them from previous and subsequent action. Hearers may applaud or otherwise show approval of the story and the storyteller, but seldom do they interact with the telling. In novels, however, there tends to be emphasis on the telling itself—the tone of voice, facial expressions, body movement—and on the varieties of response that are elicited" (*Before Novels*, 48).

Chief among those responses, especially toward the late century, is sympathy, the appropriate return for tales of suffering in Mackenzie, Sterne, Radcliffe, or Charlotte Smith. The origins of these tales and the increasingly common sympathetic response are fuzzy. Stories in periodicals like the *Spectator* often rely on representations of moral souls struck by sympathy, and characters in plays respond sympathetically as well, but it is in the novel that the pattern of walk-meeting-story-response emerges as a key convention of representation (in *Tom Jones*, *Joseph Andrews*, *David Simple*, *A Sentimental Journey*, Smith's *Emmeline*, and too many others to name). Hunter's definition enables us to differentiate novelistic uses of narrative sympathy from pictures of suffering in the poetic tradition, such as in Crabbe's *Village*. There, the old man who complains of his woes "to the winds that blow" is alone (ll. 180–227), no one sees or hears, and there is no possibility of reaction other than from the reader (though this is expected).[65] Theories of moral sentiments in the eighteenth century from Shaftesbury to Smith motivate the refinement of the story-within technique in the novel to focus on sympathetic response, but narrative plays little role in these theories.[66]

A moment from Smith's *Emmeline* is both typical of the encounter in the novel genre (in its reliance on sympathetic involvement) and innovative (in its affective use of landscape). Emmeline and a friend go for a stroll in Woodbury Forest:

> the deep shade of the beech trees with which it is covered, is broken by wild and uncultured glens; where, among the broom hawthorn and birch of the waste, a few scattered cottages have been built upon sufferance by the poor for the convenience of fewell. . . . The two friends were enjoying the softness of a beautiful April morning in these woods, when, in passing near one of the cottages, they saw, at a low casement half obscured by the pendent trees, a person sitting, whose dress and air seemed very unlike those of the usual inhabitants of such a place. (217)

The frail woman appears to be in distress, and she poses a mystery the friends must solve; they pursue her and ask, in the romance tradition, for her history. Her story of adulterous passion, pregnancy, and despair is indeed interesting to the two friends whose sympathies are engaged in her favor — in the novelistic vein. (They respond only audibly, with words of comfort, but it is common in other novels to respond visibly, most often with tears of compassion.)

In "Resolution and Independence," the leech gatherer's story follows these conventions only to upend them. As in Smith's tale, readers are guided along a changing natural perspective from background to figure, focusing finally on the telling of a tale that should stir the heart. Because Wordsworth follows a path of discovery whose most frequent eighteenth-century appearance was in the novel, well-read contemporaries might expect the speaker of the poem to utter the conventional novelistic sympathetic response; what they get instead is silence — twice. As Laurence Lockridge points out, in most of Wordsworth's poems of encounter, "the emphasis is as much on the quality of the observer's response as it is on the suffering" he encounters (*Ethics of Romanticism*, 214); Wordsworth encourages his readers, in line with Hunter's description of novelistic practice, to focus on the responses of listener to tale. However, Wordsworth disappoints if we expect the novel's idea of an appropriate sympathetic sequel. The penultimate stanza offers a miniaturized version of "The Solitary Reaper":

While he was talking thus, the lonely place,
The old Man's shape, and speech — all troubled me:
In my mind's eye I seemed to see him pace
About the weary moors continually,
Wandering about alone and silently.
While I these thoughts within myself pursued,
He, having made a pause, the same discourse renewed.

Here, as in the later poem, the silenced speech and motion of a figure in the landscape combine with the viewer's contemplation to form the core of the lyric moment. The poem's resolution finds a place for a poetic labor in which the memory of the old man will always link the poet to sanity and vitality. Wordsworth bends or inverts the novel's conventions to produce, at the moment of inversion (the expected visible or audible sympathetic response), a lyric moment (which, given the emphasis on the poet as professional, as class representative, is almost *the* lyric moment as generic instance). The novelistic narrative is replaced by a poetic one; the novel, represented synecdochally by its conventions, disappears at the point where the professional poet solidifies his position in the world.[67]

Like the old man, who "with this [his tale] . . . other matter blended," Wordsworth blends generic matter: this pattern pleased him enough that it reappears in "The Ruined Cottage," "The Old Cumberland Beggar," and "Simon Lee."[68] The oddity of these encounters stands out yet more starkly in "An Evening Walk." As Jarvis points out, the encounter with the Female Beggar and her sentimental tale has proven troublesome, as it does not fit the conventional structure of pedestrian poetry: "in contrast to the poem's accustomed mode of quickfire accumulation of balanced, opposing images . . . in turning to the Female Beggar the pedestrian observer is expressly turning *away from* observation" (*Romantic Writing*, 94, emphasis original). Jarvis argues that the speaker turns toward "fully-internalised walking" — a substantive analogue for poetry; I argue that the anomaly signified by the turn from observation to the sentimental narrative of a stranger is a generic interruption, a turn toward the novel. The same kind of interruption marks "Salisbury Plain," where the sailor hears the woman's tale of domestic grief and responds with "True sympathy" (l. 451). These tales of domestic grief appear as poetic visions, but visions that absorb the sentimental novel both as narrative and, in the case of "An Evening Walk," in its idyllic end in a homely cot. The horrors of "An Evening Walk" can be salved by the contemplation of domestic retreat; but as Jarvis and Anne Wallace assert, the resolution domesticity offers is not absolute, for the owl sobs, the dog howls, and hooves echo eerily (Jarvis, *Romantic Writing*, 95–96; Wallace, *Walking*, 146). A comparison to Cowper is again illuminating: novelistic matter is not easily absorbed in romantic poetry; the competing pressures of genre create an uneasy vision.

In "Resolution and Independence," Wordsworth opted for a scenario of generic inversion. In effect, as in the Lucy poems and the *Poems on the Naming of Places* (or to a lesser degree *The Task*), in "Resolution and Independence" novelistic convention is placed in the service of the verification and justification of poetry. The lyric's main literary rival, the novel, is placed — firmly — in the background.[69] The triumph of lyric in "Resolution and Independence" relies on the manipulation of novelistic conventions of response. Two aspects of the poem are especially significant: first, compared to earlier novels, the sympathetic response of Wordsworth's speaker is interior — it is not visible, marked on the speaker's body as tears, nor is it audible, emerging as sighs or speech (the mainstays of sensibility); second, compared to the midcentury lyrics examined in Chapter 3, even if the key moment of experience here is internal, the presence of the poet-speaker, both physically and emotionally, is powerfully clear (cf. Winchilsea, Collins, Gray, etc.) In Wordsworth's poetry, the "return" of the poet's body and the melding of sympathy and lyric come about through manipulating novelistic codes of responsiveness (as it was in Cowper).[70]

Eighteenth-century novels posit an ideal location for their readers based on a privileged type of moral response. Sympathetic tears belong not just to characters but, more fundamentally for the popularity of the genre, to its readership: "Novelists . . . position each private reader as the exceptional connoisseur of commendable sympathies, and to imply such a reader's understanding of the communication of sentiments and the special capacities of sensibility. It is as if the very form of the novel in the eighteenth century implied a contract, by the terms of which a reader was set apart from the anti-social vices or insensitivities which the novels were able to represent."[71]

The novel, as critics including Janet Todd, John Mullan, Deirdre Lynch, and William Warner argue, trained its public in a new kind of reading.[72] The moral contract of literature had been previously entrammeled by quasi-Horatian demands for delight and instruction or the Aristotelian models of pity and fear; the ethical contract of sympathetic reading created a bond that expanded these principles. Novels gave processes of reading a new cultural significance and a place in a reader's techniques of self-knowledge and self-fashioning; they made reading imaginative literature matter both ethically and physically. To follow Warner's excellent argument in *Licensing Entertainment*, the *Pamela* phenomenon of partisan bickering, heated contest, and deep-seated allegiance was the first major event in this new culture of reading: emotional and moral responsiveness, as shaped by the novel, centered reading in an expanded didacticism. Whereas sermons and the Bible had once shared a near monopoly on the demand for moral assent, imaginative literature became a site where complex forms of ethical and emotional response challenged readers to prove their worthiness and gain admittance to a community of well-meaning, right-feeling people. As the century progressed, alongside and in conjunction with characters like Pamela or Mr. B., readers become special kinds of subjects through their literary experience.

This matrix of reading is a prerequisite to the kind of engaged reading that is a fundamental expectation of the lyrics of Wordsworth, Coleridge, or Keats. Langan describes the reading Wordsworth promotes in terms of chiasmus: he seeks a "model" that includes "both a casually affective reading and a reading that itself affects the text, leaving, as it were, the impression of a footprint across its surface. This is the point of the chiasmatic metaphors that structure" "Expostulation and Reply" and "The Tables Turned" (*Romantic Vagrancy*, 83).[73] For Wordsworth, poetic texts enable exchanges; the activity of poetry — its *poiesis*, or making — is a kind of pure vision that, when shared by poet and reader, creates a broadened ethical, affective, and political community. These kinds of readerly communities, formed by crossing in and through texts, were forged by novels and placed at the basis of literary experience. Such a concept of reading is, as I will show, key to Wordsworth's instructions for reading his sonnets in "Nuns fret not." The novel did not invent intense affective reading, but it centered it in private response and in a literary architecture of sympathy, chiasmus, and creative vision.

Novels also place the fiction of a community of responsiveness at the basis of lyric experience. In *Clarissa* and *Pamela* both heroines use lyric models as writers who were readers first: Clarissa reads and imitates Job, Pamela the Psalms. The consensus that lyric brings about begins as a readerly sensibility that emphasizes criteria of response. First, the heroines conform themselves to lyric models, creating the imaginative illusion (or literary fiction) that they are no longer isolated in their emotional experiences: they feel as and with Job or David and the Israelites.

Second, their own artistry is presented in the context of the consensus that it, in turn, creates: Clarissa's self-elegy equally foregrounds the work of art and the emotional response it generates in those who read it; Mr. B.'s passion is solidified by his response to Pamela's correspondence and imitations of lyric.[74] Genres or modes (more proper here) become constructed in terms of readerly community.

This novelistic dynamic of response provides a clue to the insertion of the body of the poet in romantic lyrics. The inversion of conventions of response may produce a poem like "Resolution and Independence"; the observance of these conventions produced a quite different piece. Wordsworth's first published poem, the "Sonnet on Seeing Miss Helen Maria Williams Weep at a Tale of Distress" (1787), appeared under the pseudonym "Axiologous" and was never reprinted by the author:

> She wept. — Life's purple tide began to flow
> In languid streams through every thrilling vein;
> Dim were my swimming eyes — my pulse beat slow,
> And my full heart was swell'd to dear delicious pain.
> Life left my loaded heart, and closing eye;
> A sigh recalled the wanderer to my breast;
> Dear was the pause of life, and dear the sigh
> That call'd the wanderer to my breast;
> That tear proclaims — in thee each virtue dwells,
> And bright will shine in misery's midnight hour;
> As the soft star of dewy evening tells
> What radiant fires were drown'd by day's malignant pow'r
> That only wait the darkness of the night
> To cheer the wand'ring wretch with hospitable light.

The poem presents the speaker's body as enlivened and sensually defined by the sight of another poet's body, viewed as she responds to a "Tale." Williams is portrayed in line with the leitmotif of novels of sensibility (the recurring theme of response fundamental within the novels as well as in relation to their readers). The sonnet does not boast a coherent set of bodily images; as Pinch remarks, the physical motions it depicts do not clearly reveal either the speaker's body or Williams's own (slow pulse, full heart, and thrilling veins seem not entirely compatible). But, "This appeal to a visual fantasy of a woman weeping is the trope that enables Wordsworth's apprenticeship to the literary" (*Strange Fits of Passion*, 80).

The Wordsworth of sensibility is largely forgotten because he eventually surpasses his models; we never again encounter a mawkish moment so extreme as in the Williams sonnet.[75] In the view of some of his most influential readers (like Abrams, Hartman, or, more recently, Marshall Brown), Wordsworth's poetry was successful partially because he was able to temper the excesses of a culture of emotion, to distill and purify the culture of sensibility. Part of the essence that Wordsworth purifies is the tradition of emotional response; for him, response becomes a matter of inner life, not exterior markings (words, tears, etc.). This is the pattern of "Resolution and Independence," "We are Seven," "Ruth," or *Poems on the Naming of Places*, and it is significant that Wordsworth, even under a pseudonym, introduces himself poetically as a body enthralled in the mechanics of responsiveness.[76] He appears as poet and body through internalizing (literally, physically) the marks on the body of another poet: we see someone else first, and by confused degrees (like the repeated motions in and out of the self in the second quatrain) end up in the poet's breast. The Williams sonnet may be a poem of barely mediated conventionality, but that is the point; Wordsworth appears, disguised, using *conventions* popularized by the novel. When he appears in *propria persona*, it is by refining his techniques of appropriation and revision.

Novelistic patterns, then, are deeply embedded in romantic poetic practice, and there are other traces of the novel in the lyrics of the end of the century. In "This Lime-Tree Bower My Prison," Coleridge presents a version of sympathetic involvement that evokes a process, à la Bakhtin, of novelization. Coleridge tries insistently to break free of his double prison — that of the lime-tree bower and his own pain (the terrible scalding he received when Sarah spilled boiling milk on his foot, preventing his partaking in the stroll). The process is halting; we encounter breaks of insistence, repeated exclamations ("Yes!" "Ah!"), which might correspond to renewed pain (or the awareness of it) and the necessity of increasing the completeness of his imagined escape. In this process, Coleridge tries out several possibilities for imagining the joy of his friends, and each involves a marked shift in diction:

> Yes! they wander on
> In gladness all; but thou, methinks, most glad,
> My gentle-hearted Charles! for thou hast pined
> And hungered after Nature, many a year,
> In the great City pent, winning thy way
> With sad yet patient soul, through evil and pain

> And strange calamity! Ah! slowly sink
> Behind the western ridge, thou glorious sun!
> Shine in the slant beams of the sinking orb,
> Ye purple heath-flowers! richlier burn, ye clouds!
> Live in the yellow light, ye distant groves!
> And kindle, thou blue ocean!   (ll. 26–37)

In shifting the focus of sympathy to Charles, Coleridge also shifts the focus to an elided narrative — the story of Lamb's sister, who in a frenzied moment killed their mother and seriously wounded their father with a knife. He does so beginning with an oblique reference to Milton's Satan (*Paradise Lost*, 9.445, "long in populous city pent"), but this is not a Miltonic interlude. With this simile, Coleridge situates Satan not in epic but rather in something like a Bildungsroman. Milton's fallen angel does not win his way through evil, pain, and strange calamity; that is the story of a Tom Jones, David Simple, Amelia Booth, or Evelina Anville, whose lives are turned upside down by the metropolis and its strange people and events.[77] Epic has entered a new, novelized world. The distinctness of this moment is emphasized by the sudden shift to Miltonic pastoral (in the vein of *Lycidas*) in the next few lines ("Ah! slowly sink"). Sympathy, crucial to the novelistic encounter, comes with an imagined encounter with Charles's story. Casting Charles in a novelized epic leads directly to impassioned poetic description; Coleridge, inspired by a more complete imaginative identification with Charles, sees what Lamb might see even more clearly.

I have focused in this chapter on a number of lyrics that have a narrative cast — recounting a walk one evening or an encounter with an old man. But the importance of the novel to lyric goes beyond the question of narration; it illuminates questions of poetic form. When Wordsworth introduces a group of sonnets with "Nuns fret not," he is concerned with the way readers come into poetic space. I argued in the last chapter that a similar concern about the relationship between a reader's world and the world of a text was at the heart of the novelistic enterprise in the preceding century. "Nuns fret not" suggests one poetic response:

> Nuns fret not at their convent's narrow room;
> And hermits are contented with their cells;
> And students with their pensive citadels;
> Maids at the wheel, the weaver at his loom,
> Sit blithe and happy; bees that soar for bloom,

High as the highest Peak of Furness-fells,
Will murmur by the hour in foxglove bells:
In truth the prison, unto which we doom
Ourselves, no prison is: and hence for me,
In sundry moods, 'twas pastime to be bound
Within the Sonnet's scanty plot of ground;
Pleased if some Souls (for such there needs must be)
Who have felt the weight of too much liberty,
Should find brief solace there, as I have found.

This poem is about the problem of space in the sonnet form and the difficulty of making expansive perceptions (from cells to citadels, from tall peaks to narrow buds) fit into elegant constraint: part of the answer to this is Miltonic—the delay of the volta until the ninth line. But the poem is also concerned with how poetic space can be made to encompass both the poet and his readers. When Wordsworth literalizes the etymology of sonnet-as-stanza as a narrow room, he does more than sonneteers before him by focusing on the relationship between literary space (the sonnet's size), visual space (from nun to bee), and the reader's space as imagination. He begins by echoing the pretty rooms that Donne reserves for his mistress and himself, but Wordsworth offers to bring the reader into the room with him: like the nuns, like the bees, and like the poet, the poem's reader will be bound within the space of the sonnet on the page. Wordsworth maps us, our reading, our experiences, both onto the space the sonnet marks out (blossom, vale, cells) and onto the literal space of the sonnet itself. This poem attempts to make the sonnet's form the very site of crossover between the spaces of reading and the read; the form of the sonnet is the point of chiasmus, the thing shared by all parties. If novels provide points of contact that exist as particular spaces (Bow Street, London), rhetorical directions (the logic of names is the same in the fictional and the real worlds), or documents like letters, Wordsworth suggests that the link between worlds is the shape of poetry itself. Like "Resolution and Independence," "Nuns fret not" suggests the preeminence of poetry; the rhetorical structure of chiasmus that relates novels to the discursive worlds of their readers is marked over by the forms of lyric, the one set of markers that irremediably separate the two genres in the eighteenth century. My argument here is about reading, beginning with Wordsworth's consciousness (in the Preface to *Lyrical Ballads*) of reading as an activity shaped by the presence of novels, and continuing through his visions of chiastically affective reading in "Expostulation and Reply" and "The Tables Turned." Knowing how novels operate rhetorically in the eighteenth century can enable us to look more carefully at the rhetorical innovations of romantic poetry.

What is critically important in all of the instances I have addressed is the use of representational practices pioneered in the novel to bridge the gap between one person's lived experience and that of another — to bring experience, finally, *home*. After the novel, pity, fear, and the canonical passions no longer hold a monopoly on literary affect; now the domestic affections are part of the literary topography of emotion, and they help form the chiastic sites that mediate between one body and its closed perspective and another, between a world mapped out on the page and a world mapped out in and through a reader's body: a rhetorical relation. This is perhaps the legacy of novels because the novel is the one literary form that comes into its majority when the silent reading of relatively sterile print is a dominant experience of the literary.[78] The new novel, as the form that must negotiate this isolation almost from its appearance, carried with it much of what became the new lyricism.

♭ Coda: Generic Difference and Genre Futures

A wide range of eighteenth-century novels absorbed and adapted lyric conventions in representing private experience. Patterns from the ode, elegy, epithalamium, and courtly lyric were used to structure emotional events and individual perception. In this process, a melding of conventions would take place. The novel's chiastic realism, its insistence on domestic intimacy, the domestic occasion, and sympathetic response, all influenced the future of the lyric. If clusters of lyric conventions would appear in novels (around visions of marriage, images of the beloved, or the moments of death), clusters of novelistic conventions (e.g., inversions or internalizations of response, the importation of Richardsonian enclosure and address, the staple realist images of village life) or the specificity of fictional context associated with novelistic realisms would punctuate and even help form lyric moments.

In examining lyric absorption in the novel I have focused primarily on the epistolary tradition because it most explicitly engaged the concerns of sensible (or felt) subjectivity. However, there were other strains of novelistic invention and other novelistic influences in the romantic tradition: in addition to the genre-scale impact of the rhetoric of realisms, Smollett certainly was influential, and *Tristram Shandy* was cited by Wordsworth as a favorite novel.[79] The qualities of subjective perception and delicate irony in these novels, qualities that make *Tristram Shandy* or *A Sentimental Journey* the only eighteenth-century novels considered "lyrical" by Ralph Freedman, doubtless had their effect.[80] Isolating every novelistic influence on the literary landscape would be a hopeless (and thankless) task. I have only begun to identify the broad categories of such influence, to think about how the novel as a dominant genre left marks on the lyric. What should be apparent, however, is that any history of genre must be a history of genres as well. For scholars of the novel, this means attending to the marks the novel left on its generic successors and the ways it encourages our rereading of those genres that had gone before. For historians of romanticism, it means taking seriously the lesson of *The Prelude* and asking, to alter Tilottama Rajan's statement, "what happens [when] the . . . lyrical voice is [re]situated in the prose of the world."[81] In focusing simultaneously on poetry and prose as complex, interrelated, formal structures, I write against the division between the two often maintained on both sides in the methodological wars between formalists and historicists. By historicizing forms, I hope to offer common ground for critics concerned with the intricacies, contradictions, beauties, and survival of the literary enterprise.

In closing, there remains — at the very least — one major question to be addressed: the disappearance from the novel of some of the factors that, I argue, have been highly influential in the lyric. The interruptive narrative or story-within participated in a paradigm of emotional responsiveness crucial to romantic lyrics, but this often clumsy, interruptive feature would fade in the nineteenth century. In part, the novelistic future of this practice can be found in the carefully handled subplots of a *Middlemarch*; however, as Hunter argues, more close kin to the embedded narrative is the flashback.[82] Instead of a character recounting his or her history, we have an internalized version of the older technique. Just as Wordsworth interiorized the response that inserted tales generate, the later novel often interiorized the act of telling through remembering.

In the same vein, the epistolary novel's constructions of interiority helped shape the romantic lyric, but the letter all but died in the novel at about the same time lyric underwent its vigorous renewal. The convenient ideal location for the relative disappearance of letter fiction is in Jane Austen — the oft-told tale that *Pride and Prejudice* was the revision of an earlier epistolary work, *First Impressions*. The letter as self-revelation gave way to techniques of free indirect discourse.[83] As I showed in Chapter 5, some of the earliest uses of free indirect discourse would occur in epistolary novels (or even verse epistles), and advances in the technique would also take place in the context of letters (as in Brooke's *Excursion*). In Jane Austen's shift to free indirect discourse (although she did not entirely give up letters), inner life was opened up to dual vision, the doubling of self and other signified by the narration of thought.[84]

A focus on the boundaries of inner life and the methods for crossing, redrawing, and revealing them was common to the future of both novel and lyric in the nineteenth century, whether in "Ode to a Nightingale" or *Emma*. This was frequently achieved through structures of doubling: the patterns of address in Wordsworth or Coleridge (to Nature, Dorothy, or an absent friend), techniques of narration (in the free indirect discourse of Austen, Brooke, or Burney), and the layering of perception (synesthesia in Keats, memory in Austen or Wordsworth). Free indirect discourse in the novel and the romantic lyric have something important in common: both connected consciousness to the facts of literary form, blending consciousness into words, phrases, and the controlling factors of representation, moving both genres toward techniques that emphasize what is half-created and what perceived. It is not an unwarranted conclusion that the evolution of the letter underpinned both generic innovations, for the verse epistle fell away in poetry as well as in the novel. While the epistle was dominant in Augustan poetry, it gave way to the lyric in the romantic era. Dowling argues that the lonely scene of composition of the Augustan verse epistle developed into the isolation of a Chatterton, Collins, or Gray, and Alan Liu maintains that "the Romantic friend . . . is the outer, objective . . . identity whose correspondence (literally, his letters) communicates" and buttresses the romantic self (*Wordsworth*, 284). Again, there are parallel phenomena in verse and in prose: the address of the epistle was pressed outward to a public frame and inward toward the imagination in the colloquy of *The Prelude* or the conversation poem, and the self-revelation and articulate speech in the letter were internalized as thought and revealed through the public agency of the narrator as free indirect discourse in the novel.[85] In seeking a literary model that would ground and mediate the conflicts involved in speaking personal experience, both novel and lyric relied on techniques (of double voice, of doubled address, of rhetorical realisms) that would forge a link between the worlds of reading and the read.

Because I focus so closely on the interaction and sometime coevolution of the novel and lyric toward the end of the eighteenth century, it may seem that I have occasionally fallen into the temptation or trap of similitude, that I have collapsed one thing into the other and have traced likeness at the expense of difference. It is fitting to close, then, by affirming the distinctions that separate one genre from the other. To do this, I will say a few, largely symbolic, words about Austen — whose works are stunningly, beautifully, fittingly, novels — and Wordsworth, whose poetry, to my great delight, is just that. Novels and poems are differing objects of experience, objects we encounter in different ways because they "ask" us to do so. Between *Persuasion* and "Nutting" there are distinctions too pleasant to be slighted. Wordsworth and Austen have repeatedly been paired; critics have fruitfully examined parallel uses of memory, scene, the senses, and the emotional significance of the seemingly insignificant.[86] Austen's last novel, *Persuasion*, is an especially useful place for describing the union of many of the kinds of doubling I have here discussed, the layering of lyric and letter, the incredible possibilities of free indirect discourse, and the sensual uses of memory. Other critics have pursued these connections; I have in view something smaller.

In setting Austen against Wordsworth as an illustration of generic difference I am not concerned with issues of compactness, the explicit contours of form (lines, rhymes, or the patterns of sonnet or ode), or the amount and kind of narration. Such distinctions between lyric and novel seem never to address the unique and hardly inferior pleasures one has in reading each. The point where we may suggestively consider the difference between the two is in the relationships between structures of feeling and the whole in novel and poem. In her last two novels, Austen writes about characters who tend to be erased in the world around them. No one notices Fanny Price or Anne Elliot; their feelings and mortifications are shared only by a select few (including, most importantly, us readers). If the world erases Austen's heroines, Wordsworth's speakers illuminate their surroundings. Emotions in *Mansfield Park* and *Persuasion* appear as punctuations in a larger fabric, pinprick holes that, if one is close enough and looks in the right way, open up to extraordinary vistas. They always exist, below the surface, waiting to be seen. Austen always preserves that surface; for Wordsworth, however, it is a veil to be torn away or lifted for a moment that is forever preserved.

Such remarks would seem to have little generic applicability, extending only to novels or poems like the ones at hand (*Villette* or *Tess of the D'Urbervilles*, as well as *Persuasion*, "Ode to the West Wind," "As Kingfishers Catch Fire," or "Tintern Abbey"); each poet or novelist approaches his or her craft in different ways at different times. When we do attempt to describe the relations between genres, however, we may use similar terms — of surfaces and tiny, pinprick marks. Novel and lyric tend to approach or contain each other piece by piece — by the exchange of conventions, the borrowing of a phrase, the importation of subject or mood. They do not meet as strangers, for they have long been in contact, and in an encounter with one, we may see the other in fragments, in parts, and in constant revision.

Notes

Introduction

1. Marshall Brown, in *Preromanticism* (Stanford: Stanford University Press, 1991), gives a cogent overview of these histories and reclaims the term to describe "styles different from, yet dialectically related to "romanticism (2). His history of the romantic episteme follows moments of dis-ease in the economy of sensibility as visible in Gray, Collins, Sheridan, Goldsmith (as both novelist and poet), and Sterne. For him, the emergence of romanticism is about a new relationship between "Nature . . . history . . . [and] mind" (299). Brown analyzes "the rites of passage that chasten and subdue sensibility into romantic humanism. The conception of a transcendental time and space and of a transcendental ego, the birth of an aesthetic imagination, the mastery of plot and character development, the assemblage of an order of the organic, the emergence of will and of action as the primary categories of selfhood, the disposition of the multiple temporality of the event, [and] the elements of a life according to the coordinates of human consciousness," key components in the romantic ideology, are formed as the results of the practices of poetry, but also of novels and plays (359–60). I extend the concerns Brown raises to consider generic relations themselves, and I owe a great debt to his work.

2. Anne Janowitz, *Lyric and Labor in the Romantic Tradition* (Cambridge: Cambridge University Press, 1998), is a good example of the way in which recent scholarship has taken as its object an archaeology of romantic tradition, recapturing the vital diversity of poetic production in the period. Other notable studies include Brown, *Preromanticism;* Jerome McGann, *The Poetics of Sensibility: A Revolution in Literary Style* (Oxford: Clarendon Press, 1996); Nicholas Roe, *John Keats and the Culture of Dissent* (Oxford: Clarendon Press, 1997); Paul Magnuson, *Reading Public Romanticism* (Princeton: Princeton University Press, 1998); and Clifford Siskin, *The Work of Writing: Literature and Social Change in Britain, 1700–1830* (Baltimore: Johns Hopkins University Press, 1998), to name only a few significant recent works.

3. Jacques Derrida, "The Law of Genre," in *Acts of Literature*, ed. Derek Attridge (New York: Routledge, 1992), 227.

4. Michael McKeon, *The Origins of the English Novel, 1600–1740* (Baltimore: Johns Hopkins University Press, 1987), 1.

5. Nigel Smith, *Literature and Revolution in England, 1640–1660* (New Haven: Yale University Press, 1994), ch. 8.

6. William Wordsworth, "1802 Preface," in *Poetical Works*, rev. ed., ed. Ernest de Selincourt (New York: Oxford University Press, 1936), 735.

7. W. J. Bate, *The Burden of the Past* (Cambridge: Harvard University Press, Belknap Press, 1970).

8. Wordsworth comments on the *Reliques* in the "Essay Supplementary to the Preface," *Poetical Works:* "as to our country, its poetry has been absolutely redeemed by it. I do not think that there is an able writer in verse of the present day who would not be proud to acknowledge his obligations to the 'Reliques'; I know that it is so with my friends; and for myself, I am happy in this occasion to make a public avowal of my own" (749). He singles out "Sir Cauline" and quotes admiringly from "The Child of Elle" (748).

9. See Albert B. Friedman, *The Ballad Revival: Studies in the Influence of Popular on Sophisticated Poetry* (Chicago: University of Chicago Press, 1961): Friedman notes that Coleridge was strongly influenced by "The Child of Elle," "The Marriage of Sir Gawaine," and "Sir Cauline," all poems "substantially reworked by Percy" (210). Percy frequently added tearful scenes and reworked or invented elements of plot for emotional effect (206).

10. Thomas Percy, *Reliques of Ancient English Poetry, Consisting of Old Heroic Ballads, Songs, and Other Pieces of Our Earlier Poets, Together with Some Few of Later Date.* 3 vols., ed. Henry B. Wheatley (London, 1876), 1:132–39, ll. 173–76.

11. In Percy's youth, his library contained "Behn's novels, *Gulliver's Travels, Robinson Crusoe, Moll Flanders,* and . . . *Pamela,*" according to Bertram H. Davis, *Thomas Percy: A Scholar-Cleric in the Age of Johnson* (Philadelphia: University of Pennsylvania Press, 1989), 5. Percy seemingly valued *Pamela;* when he later cleared out his library, selling or giving away more than half of the volumes, he kept the novel. I have not found any direct indication of Percy's reading *Clarissa,* but I consider it likely, based on Percy's regard for Richardson's fiction (not, notably, his *Aesop's Fables*) and the phenomenal popularity of *Clarissa.* Nick Groom, in *The Making of Percy's Reliques* (Oxford: Clarendon Press, 1999), gives a strong account of Percy's composition, arguing that it is rooted in what he calls "Percy's bibliolatry" — the absolute dependence of the *Reliques* on what Percy read. Groom does not consider the impact of novels on the *Reliques,* but his extensive investigation of Percy's other sources is first-rate.

12. Samuel Richardson, *Clarissa* (New York: Penguin Books, 1980), 890.

13. *The Percy Letters,* ed. Cleanth Brooks (New Haven: Yale University Press, 1977), 7: 201.

14. See McKeon, *Origins of the English Novel*, ch. 1.

15. Mikhail Bakhtin, *The Dialogic Imagination*, trans. Caryl Emerson and Michael Holquist (Austin: University of Texas Press, 1981), 39. The effect of the novel on other genres is not "their subjection to an alien generic canon; on the contrary, novelization implies their liberation from all that serves as a brake on their unique development" (29). The novel opens a "new zone . . . for structuring literary images, namely, the zone of maximal contact with the present (with contemporary reality) in all its openendedness" (11). The idea of proximity to the present as time and as place is crucial to my rethinking of formal realism later on in this project — I focus not so much on what the novelistic "present" appears to be but on how we are brought into contact with it.

16. I take this idea of eighteenth-century culture as media culture from William Warner, *Licensing Entertainment: The Elevation of Novel Reading in Britain, 1684–1750* (Berkeley: University of California Press, 1998).

17. See *Reconsidering the Rise of the Novel*, a special issue of *Eighteenth-Century Fiction* 12, nos. 2–3 (2000).

18. Linda Colley, in *Britons: Forging the Nation, 1707–1837* (New Haven: Yale University Press, 1991), argues that following the Act of Union, inhabitants of England, Scotland, and Wales, newly "Britons," struggled, in terms of wars and rebellions as well as political, social, and economic fragmentation, to create a new national community.

19. William Dowling, *The Epistolary Moment: The Poetics of the Eighteenth-Century Verse Epistle* (Princeton: Princeton University Press, 1991).

20. Richard Feingold, *Moralized Song: The Character of Augustan Lyricism* (New Brunswick, N.J.: Rutgers University Press, 1989), 93.

21. See Anne Williams, *The Prophetic Strain: The Greater Lyric in the Eighteenth Century* (Chicago: University of Chicago Press, 1984): she examines "The Vanity of Human Wishes," Job, and other examples of expanded lyric in longer poetry. Williams also documents the influence of biblical poetry in this expansion. She insists, rightly, that the move of lyric outward into satires, epistles, and elsewhere is a kind of "generic appropriation" that is "the distinctive mark of the eighteenth-century greater lyric" (35).

22. Norman Maclean, "From Action to Image: Theories of the Lyric in the Eighteenth Century," in *Critics and Criticism*, ed. R. S. Crane (Chicago: University of Chicago Press, 1952), 414.

23. Henry Home, *Elements of Criticism*, quoted in Alistair Fowler, *Kinds of Literature: An Introduction to the Theory of Genres and Modes* (Oxford: Clarendon Press, 1982), 37.

24. Joseph Warton, *Essay on the Genius and Writings of Pope*, 2 vols. (London, 1806), 1: iv–v.

25. James Beattie, *Essays: On Poetry and Music, As They Affect the Mind, on Laughter, and Ludicrous Composition; On the Usefulness of Classical Learning*, 3d ed. (London, 1779), 36.

26. *Lives of the English Poets*, ed. George Birkbeck Hill, 3 vols. (Oxford: Clarendon Press, 1905), 1: 6.

27. M. H. Abrams, "Structure and Style in the Greater Romantic Lyric," in *From Sensibility to Romanticism: Essays Presented to Frederick A. Pottle*, ed. Frederick Hilles and Harold Bloom (New York: Oxford University Press, 1965), 527.

28. John Sitter, *Literary Loneliness in Mid-Eighteenth-Century England* (Ithaca: Cornell University Press, 1982), 13.

29. Brean S. Hammond, *Professional Imaginative Writing in England, 1670–1740* (Oxford: Clarendon Press, 1997), 108. Hammond's expansion of the Bakhtinian perspective into drama and amatory fiction is an important contribution to recent efforts to expand the story of the rise of the novel to include more than prose forms.

30. There are other kinds of epistolary novels, but for reasons that should become clear, the focus here is on novels where letters are used for their affective possibilities.

31. Janet Altman, *Epistolarity: Approaches to a Form* (Columbus: Ohio State University Press, 1982), 127–28.

32. Donald Davie, *Purity of Diction in English Verse* (London: Routledge and Kegan Paul, 1967), 13–14.

33. Ralph Freedman, *The Lyrical Novel: Studies in Hermann Hesse, André Gide, and Virginia Woolf* (Princeton: Princeton University Press, 1963), argues that "lyrical fiction . . . is not defined essentially by a poetic style" (1). "In the lyrical mode, [the literary world] is conceived, not as a universe in which men display their actions, but as a poet's vision fashioned as a design. The world is reduced to a *lyrical point of view*, the equivalent of the poet's 'I': the lyrical self" (8). Calling *To the Lighthouse* a lyrical novel is something different from calling *Clarissa* one; lyric means different things to Woolf and to Richardson.

34. Cf. Ian Watt in *The Rise of the Novel* (Berkeley: University of California Press, 1957): "Since the novelist's primary task is to convey the impression of fidelity to human experience, attention to any pre-established formal conventions can only endanger his success" (13). My argument, on the contrary, is that convention, by employing familiar codes and structures, enables the *effet du réel*.

35. See Wlad Godzich and Jeffrey Kittay, *The Emergence of Prose: An Essay in Prosaics* (Minneapolis: University of Minnesota Press, 1987). The authors call it "prose's subterfuge: not to be recognized for what it is, but for the way things are. Verse will take prose as matter to its form" (175). This works out in more ways than one, as we will see.

36. This idea began with Bakhtin's concept of the "zone of contact," which the novel initiates between genre and world, but instead of arguing that this contact functions primarily around the "plane of laughter" (23), I

suggest that it works by organizing a range of affective and cognitive readerly responses.

37. On the subordination of the novel, see Stuart Curran, "Romantic Poetry: Why and Wherefore?" *The Cambridge Companion to British Romanticism*, ed. Curran (Cambridge: Cambridge University Press, 1993), 216–35. For Wordsworth, see above, n. 6.

Chapter 1. *Clarissa* and the Lyric

1. See Watt's *Rise of the Novel* (Berkeley: University of California Press, 1957). Important accounts of the epistolary genealogy of Richardson's novels are Linda Kauffman, *Discourses of Desire* (Ithaca: Cornell University Press, 1986), Ruth Perry, *Women, Letters, and the Novel* (New York: AMS, 1980), and Robert Day, *Told in Letters: Epistolary Fiction before Richardson* (Ann Arbor: University of Michigan Press, 1966).

2. *Clarissa* (New York: Penguin Books, 1980), 141.

3. See, for example, Margaret Anne Doody, *A Natural Passion: A Study of the Novels of Samuel Richardson* (Oxford: Clarendon Press, 1974), Mark Kinkead-Weekes, *Samuel Richardson: Dramatic Novelist* (Ithaca: Cornell University Press, 1973), Christina Marsden Gillis, *The Paradox of Privacy: Epistolary Form in "Clarissa"* (Gainesville: University Presses of Florida, 1984), and Kauffman, *Discourses of Desire*.

4. Jocelyn Harris, "Richardson: Original or Learned Genius?" in *Samuel Richardson: Tercentenary Essays*, ed. Margaret Anne Doody and Peter Sabor (Cambridge: Cambridge University Press, 1989), 188–202. There has been some debate over the extent of Richardson's literary knowledge, but recent critics have been arguing in favor of more, rather than less. Michael Connaughton seems to believe that, even given Richardson's use of collections of quotations, Richardson's acquaintance with Herbert, for example, was more than that given by a commonplace book. "Richardson's Familiar Quotations: *Clarissa* and Bysshe's *Art of English Poetry,*" *Philological Quarterly* 60, no. 2 (1986): 191.

5. Nigel Smith, *Perfection Proclaimed: Language and Literature in English Radical Religion, 1640–1660* (Oxford: Clarendon Press, 1989), 299. For "radical religious writers. . . . 'poetry' refers to the manner in which radical religious language represents the internal" (230).

6. Smith, *Literature and Revolution in England, 1640–1660* (New Haven: Yale University Press, 1994), 4. On generic fluidity, see Michael McKeon, *The Origins of the English Novel, 1600–1740* (Baltimore: Johns Hopkins University Press, 1987), and Ralph Cohen, "On the Interrelations of Eighteenth-Century Literary Forms," in *New Approaches to Eighteenth-Century Literature*, ed. Phillip Harth (New York: Columbia University Press, 1974). For biblical genres, see Barbara Lewalski's *Protestant Poetics* (Princeton: Princeton University Press, 1979). About the debates on pastoral, see Pope and Johnson.

Ode is canvassed by Watts, Young, and Congreve, among others. Drama offered its own range of exemplary emotional statements — Congreve's *Mourning Bride* and Dryden's *Tyrannick Love* provide model passionate outbursts. It
is important to note that in finding appropriate quotations for his novels,
Richardson often relied on sources like Bysshe's *Art of English Poetry*, which
arranged exemplary quotations under headings (often emotional categories
like "Fear"). Connaughton points out that whatever affinities Richardson felt
for the drama, "Only slightly over half of the quotations from *Clarissa* are
from plays. . . . Had Richardson's objective been to recreate theatrical types,
he would have been more likely to turn for help to the *Thesaurus Dramaticus* or
its later version, *Beauties of the English Stage*. Even in Bysshe, moreover, he
does not deliberately seek out dramatic sources" ("Richardson's Familiar
Quotations," 193).

    7. See Lewalski's *Protestant Poetics*, Louis Martz's *Poetry of Meditation: A
Study in English Religious Literature of the Seventeenth Century* (New Haven:
Yale University Press, 1954), Helen Vendler's *Poetry of George Herbert* (Cam-
bridge: Harvard University Press, 1975), Anne Williams's *Prophetic Strain:
The Greater Lyric in the Eighteenth Century* (Chicago: University of Chicago
Press, 1984), and Nigel Smith's *Perfection Proclaimed. Clarissa* relies on a
tradition of Protestant religious verse that includes Anglican figures like
Herbert, but also on a nonconformist literary tradition investigated by N. H.
Keeble, among others. I focus on Herbert, Donne, and Job here because, as I
will show, Herbert is an important figure both in the early eighteenth century and for Richardson, Job is a central text in *Clarissa* and to religious verse,
and Donne's lyrics provide a model for understanding the mechanics of elegy
in *Clarissa*. See N. H. Keeble, *The Literary Culture of Nonconformity in Later
Seventeenth-Century England* (Athens: University of Georgia Press, 1987). In
Literature and Revolution, Smith argues that religious dissent ended the
"metaphysical" tradition in poetry (274) but it has an afterlife in novels, as I
show.

    8. William E. Stephenson, introduction to *Select Hymns, Taken out of Mr.
Herbert's Temple, and Turn'd into the Common Metre* (1697), *Augustan Reprint
Society* 98 (1962): 1. Quoting Simon Browne, "a clergyman interested in
hymns," around 1720.

    9. See Helen Wilcox, "Entering *The Temple*: Women, Reading, and De-
votion in Seventeenth-Century England," in *Religion, Literature, and Politics
in Post-Reformation England, 1540–1688*, ed. Donna B. Hamilton and Richard Strier (Cambridge: Cambridge University Press, 1996), 187–207. On
Dunton and the novel, see J. Paul Hunter, *Before Novels: The Cultural Contexts of Eighteenth-Century English Fiction* (New York: Norton, 1990), especially 99 ff.; on conduct books like Allestree's and the novel, see Nancy
Armstrong, *Desire and Domestic Fiction: A Political History of the Novel* (New
York: Oxford University Press, 1987).

10. W. Mears's *The Grove; or, a collection of original poems, translations &c. By W. Walsh, Esq; Dr. J. Donne. Mr. Dryden and other eminent hands* (1721, 2d ed. 1732), included a misattributed poem called "Absence," the only piece ascribed to Donne in the collection.

11. All biblical quotations are from the 1611 Authorized Version.

12. Williams discusses Job's place in regard to the sublime: "Symon Patrick, bishop of Ely, remarks in his popular commentary on Job (1678) that the poetry has a 'grandeur [that] is as much above all other poetry, as thunder is louder than a whisper,' a remark quoted by Edward Young in the introduction to his own paraphrase" (*Prophetic Strain*, 60).

13. For the cultural and literary importance of Job, see Williams, Young's preface to his paraphrase of the book, and Watts's preface to the *Horae Lyricae*. Nigel Smith shows how Job was used by seventeenth-century radical religious writers to construct a sense of self in *Perfection Proclaimed*.

14. On prayer and religious poetry as public forms, see Ramie Targoff, *Common Prayer: The Language of Public Devotion in Early Modern England* (Chicago: University of Chicago Press, 2001).

15. Robert A. Erickson, " 'Written in the Heart': Richardson and Scripture," *Eighteenth-Century Fiction* 2, no. 1 (1989). Jonathan Lamb analyzes the Job connection in *The Rhetoric of Suffering: Reading the Book of Job in the Eighteenth Century* (Oxford: Clarendon Press, 1995).

16. This survey is based on the LION English Full-Text Poetry Database. Job's complaint and God's response are the two most popular subjects of paraphrase. Most are in rhymed couplets, but Elizabeth Rowe's *Philomela* (1737), an expansion upon 19:26, and several hymns by Watts and Wesley are in other lyric verse forms. The hymns use the pronouns "I" and "We," emphasizing the personal nature of suffering and complaint (even if each must be overcome). Paraphrases published after 1785 (notably William Mason's and Edward Perronet's) tend to be in stanzaic lyric forms.

17. Tom Keymer discusses Clarissa's meditations in "Richardson's *Meditations:* Clarissa's *Clarissa,*" in *Samuel Richardson: Tercentenary Essays*, ed. Margaret Anne Doody and Peter Sabor (Cambridge: Cambridge University Press, 1989), 89–109. Through her use of Scripture, Clarissa's "experience . . . takes on a certain intelligibility: by lifting it to a level of intense poetic abstraction, Clarissa sheds the specific and local and begins to explain it in the larger moral terms of darkness and evil" (96).

18. As Keymer point out, Clarissa's meditations come after her rape and the ensuing period of madness. She for this time gives up narrative altogether: "like the rape itself, the fragmentation of discourse which accompanies it prepares Clarissa for the redefinition of self and experience in a new literary form, marking the point of a shift from realism to abstraction, and from epistolary narrative to meditation" ("Richardson's *Meditations,*" 93–94).

19. *Meditations,* Thomas Keymer, ed., in *Prefaces, Postscripts, and Related Writings,* vol. 1 of *Samuel Richardson's Published Commentary on "Clarissa," 1747–1765,* (London: Pickering and Chatto, 1998), 170.

20. See Norman Maclean, "From Action to Image: Theories of the Lyric in the Eighteenth Century," in *Critics and Criticism,* ed. R. S. Crane (Chicago: University of Chicago Press, 1952), 408–60. This occurs especially in regard to the Pindaric; Dryden's *Alexander's Feast* is the early century's primary example of the congruence of lyric and emotion.

21. Patricia Meyer Spacks, *The Poetry of Vision* (Cambridge: Harvard University Press, 1967), 121.

22. Scott Elledge, ed., *Eighteenth-Century Critical Essays,* 2 vols. (Ithaca: Cornell University Press, 1961), 2: 690.

23. Elledge, *Eighteenth-Century Critical Essays,* 1: 151–52.

24. Clarissa's use of the second person indicates how deeply disturbed and internally fragmented she is: not only is she completely overthrown by the experience of rape, but she had been constantly concerned about the status of her own experience throughout the novel. She is dealing here, as she puts it, with her "hated self" (L 295, 974). In others of the mad papers, she does use the first person, but it is not until she faces death and composes a self-elegy that she is able to speak more clearly of herself through her conflicts and divisions.

25. See, e.g., Watt, *Rise of the Novel,* or Kinkead-Weekes, *Samuel Richardson.* Richardson's "plainness" is often seen in counterdistinction to the floridness of romance or the epic complexities of Fielding. For an interesting counterargument, see Irwin Gopnik, *A Theory of Style and Richardson's "Clarissa"* (The Hague: Mouton, 1970).

26. Nigel Smith, *Perfection Proclaimed,* 328, 308.

27. Both laments rewrite Job 10:

> My soule is weary of my life, I will leave my complaint upon my self; I will speake in the bitternesse of my soule.   (1)

> Thine hands have made me and fashioned me together round about; yet thou doest destroy me.
> Remember, I beseech thee, that thou hast made me as the clay, and wilt thou bring me into dust againe?
> Hast thou not powred me out as milke, and cruddled me like cheese?
> Thou hast cloathed me with skin and flesh, and hast fenced me with bones and sinewes.   (8–11)

28. The extent of Richardson's literary knowledge has been under substantial debate. See n. 4. Richardson quotes from *The Temple* in a letter to Lady Bradshaigh and in *Clarissa.* See *Selected Letters of Samuel Richardson,* ed. John Carroll (Oxford: Clarendon Press, 1964), 91.

29. Lawrence Stone, *The Family, Sex, and Marriage in England, 1500–1800* (New York: Harper, 1997), 124–27.

30. Leah Marcus shows some of the complexity of religious ideas of childhood in late-seventeenth-century poetry in *Childhood and Cultural Despair* (Pittsburgh: University of Pittsburgh Press, 1978). Mary Leapor's "Cruel Parent" may also have some connection here. Richardson was a subscriber to her two posthumous volumes of collected poetry: "But [I] cannot leave my hated Self behind; / And am — oh am I — by my Parent curs'd; / Of all my woes the deepest and the worst." *Poems upon Several Occasions,* 2 vols. (London, 1748), 2:277.

31. Michael Schoenfeldt, *Prayer and Power: George Herbert and Renaissance Courtship* (Chicago: University of Chicago Press, 1991). Clarissa shares Herbert's "scrupulous attention to the affinity between obedience and opposition, between placating authority and challenging it" (25).

32. Helen Vendler, *The Art of Shakespeare's Sonnets* (Cambridge: Harvard University Press, 1997), 2.

33. Nigel Smith points out the frequency of the fragmentation of self in seventeenth-century radical religious poetry in *Perfection Proclaimed,* part 1. For Richardson's knowledge of Herbert, see above, nn. 4, 6, and 28.

34. Not all of the papers rely on lyric models as closely as Papers 2, 3, and 7. The juxtaposition of standard models of lyric expression with other kinds of speech is suggestive: if Richardson is working within a generalized concept of the lyric involving emotional expression and emotional consensus, intimacy, community, and the fragmentation of these ideals, the other papers can be seen as experiments in expanding the lyric mode beyond its received constructions. In this regard, Clarissa's papers are similar to devotional writing by seventeenth-century women combining lyric, autobiographical narrative, and biblical quotation. Wilcox notes that Herbert's poetry was especially conducive to women's use, because as "another David," his poetry spoke deeply and acceptably of religious experience, but also because he adapts a discourse of femininity in manipulating the love lyric and because of the autobiographical cast of his poems. Wilcox, "Entering the *Temple,*" 189; see also Nigel Smith, *Perfection Proclaimed,* and Elaine Hobby, *Virtue of Necessity: English Women's Writing, 1649–1688* (Ann Arbor: University of Michigan Press, 1988), on women's devotional writing and its genres.

35. The ten postrape papers bear an analogical relationship to the sonnet sequence. Sonnet sequences can compartmentalize emotion and event, separate moods and feelings for contemplation, and offer each moment up as shareable aesthetic and sensual experience (even if the pain of isolation is a theme of a given sonnet, the principle behind these expressions remains the same). Peggy Samuels writes that "the sonnet has a tendency to make a definitive statement; it leans toward or ingests the epigram. However, . . . within a sequence, the attempt at totalization or definitive statement and the

closure of the individual sonnet are placed in question. . . . the mere act of beginning another sonnet retrospectively pronounces the previous sonnets on the same subject incomplete." "Milton's Use of Sonnet Form in *Paradise Lost*," *Milton Studies* 24 (1988): 142–43.

36. Robert Alter, *The Art of Biblical Poetry* (New York: Basic Books, 1985), 6.

37. Alter sees a connection between biblical poetry and certain aesthetic strategies in the novel:

> in many instances that literary prose is influenced by contemporary or antecedent poetry in the same language, often seeking knowingly or unwittingly to achieve for itself a quasi-poetic status without the formal constraints of verse. Fielding's splendid satiric style, with its pointed antitheses and prized symmetries, surely owes something to his experience of Pope's handling of the heroic couplet, and Melville, striving to shape a prose of the sublime, is famous (or notorious) for his Miltonic and Shakespearean effects, sometimes producing whole passages that almost scan as blank verse. (6–7)

38. For women's commonplace books, see Carol Barash, *English Women's Poetry, 1649–1714: Politics, Community, and Linguistic Authority* (Oxford: Clarendon Press, 1996), 20; on devotional writing, especially by women, see Wilcox, "Entering the *Temple*," Hobby, *Virtue of Necessity*, and Nigel Smith, *Perfection Proclaimed*.

39. Williams samples discussions of the power of poetry: "Sir Richard Blackmore writes, 'Tis in the power of poetry to insinuate into the inmost Recesses of the Mind, to touch any Spring that moves the Heart, to agitate the Soul with a sort of Affection, and transform it into any Shape or Posture it thinks fit.' Or [Charles] Gildon: 'I think it may easily be made out, that there is nothing has a greater Power or Influence on the Heart than Poetry. . . . There is indeed no manner of Question but that true Poetry has Force to raise the Passions and to allay them, to change and to extinguish them'" (*Prophetic Strain*, 51).

40. Of Ovid's *Heroides*, Kauffman writes that they "interweave rhetoric and poetry, narrative and myth" (*Discoveries of Desire*, 23). James Wellington states in the context of "Eloisa to Abelard" that "a genre comparable to the heroic epistle in poetry enjoyed a distinguished parallel in music during the seventeenth and eighteenth centuries, and that Pope, in 1717, was writing in the midst of a musical tradition already well established throughout Europe and destined to continue unabated for the remainder of the century." Introduction to *Eloisa to Abelard* (Coral Gables, Fla.: University of Miami Press, 1965), 29.

41. Cf. Samuel Johnson's famous split decision: on the one hand his comment to Mrs. Thrale: "In a Man's Letters you know, Madam, his soul lies

naked, his letters are only the mirrour of his breast, whatever passes within him is shown undisguised in its natural process. Nothing is inverted, nothing distorted, you see systems in their elements, you discover actions in their motives"; on the other, his remarks in the "Life of Pope": "Very few can boast of hearts which they dare lay open to themselves, and of which, by whatever accident exposed, they do not shun a distinct and continued view; and certainly what we hide from ourselves we do not shew to our friends. There is, indeed, no transaction which offers stronger temptations to fallacy and sophistication than epistolary intercourse." Tom Keymer, *Richardson's "Clarissa" and the Eighteenth-Century Reader* (Cambridge: Cambridge University Press, 1992), 1.

42. Compare, for example, Clarissa's distress that her "ink runs nothing but gall" (225).

43. Janet Altman, *Epistolarity: Approaches to a Form* (Columbus: Ohio State University Press, 1982), 4.

44. Other critics have found poetic traces around Clarissa's death. In *Romantic Vision and the Novel* (Cambridge: Cambridge University Press, 1987), Jay Clayton notes that the romantics felt *Clarissa* had claims to the status of poetry. He finds the primary locus for poetic possibility in the last half of the novel: "the novel shifts from the conventions of narrative genres — the bourgeois courtship novel, the rape and seduction novel, the Restoration tragedy — to those more characteristic of lyric, poetic forms. Louis Martz has described the extensive use that poets such as Donne and Herbert made of traditional devotional material to create what he calls 'the poetry of meditation.' And Margaret Doody wonders why readers of *Clarissa* do not respond to the same techniques in Richardson's novel that they are so willing to admire in the 'Metaphysical poets'" (43). For Clayton *Clarissa* exemplifies a problem fundamental to romantic ideology: the position and representation of transcendent experience. If romantic-era "readers [felt] that the 'elevated scenes' which deal with Clarissa's preparation for death are 'poetic'" (43), they were for Clayton focusing on the possibilities for transcendent individual experience, possibilities that stretch the capacities of pure narrative.

45. For theorists of sympathy, this makes perfect sense. James Beattie, in his *Essay on Poetry and Music, As They Affect the Mind*, 3d ed. (London, 1779), writes, "With the dead we sympathise, and even with those circumstances of their condition whereof we know that they are utterly insensible; such as, their being shut up in a cold and solitary grave, excluded from the light of the sun, and from all the pleasures of life, and liable in a few years to be forgotten for ever" (182).

46. See Terry Castle's *Clarissa's Cyphers* (Ithaca: Cornell University Press, 1982) for an alternative reading of the interpretative crux caused by the coffin's elaborate ornamentation (141 ff.).

47. Clarissa apologizes for the apparent singularity of her behavior: "She excused herself to the women, on the score of her youth, and being used to draw for her needleworks, for having shown more fancy than would perhaps be thought suitable on so solemn an occasion" (L 451, 1306). The intrusion of artistry in her design seems indeed an intrusion; she makes a feeble attempt to defuse and domesticate her choice by finding its roots in mundane female accomplishments. However, Clarissa cannot reduce her virtuosic final statement to a mere exercise of "fancy."

48. Lamb notes: "Nowhere is the book of Job more frequently reproduced in the eighteenth century than on tombstones, vaults, and mausoleums. Its popularity as a source of epitaphic sentiments is reflected in James Hervey's *Meditations upon the Tombs* (1746), where the author marks almost every pause before the dead with a quotation from Job, ranging from the common choices for graveyard inscription ('Here even the Wicked cease from troubling' and 'This is the House appointed for all living') to rather more vociferous passages, such as 'I shall never more see God in the Land of the living'" (274). As Lamb describes Job's wish, "It sets the point of determination in the future when matters of fact will be read with intensity, and when the force of an event will be deeply and suddenly familiar" (*Rhetoric of Suffering*, 49).

49. In *John Donne: Life, Mind, and Art* (New York: Oxford University Press, 1981), John Carey executes a similar count concerning the frequency of the appearance of death in *Songs and Sonets* and finds that thirty-two of fifty-four sonnets "find some means of fitting death in" (201).

50. In other words, I here disagree with Carey's analysis. He argues that Donne's preoccupation with death is the outgrowth of a form of megalomania: "The endeavour is, persistently, to treat death as a form of life, or to vivify it by giving it an active role in poems which are passionately concerned with living. . . . Donne nurses the egocentric delusion that when he dies it will be the world, not he, that will perish" (202).

51. Although there are no fatalities in "The Extasie," the intimate union it depicts is predicated on bodies that "like sepulchrall statues lay" (l. 18), dead insofar as they are bereft of the souls that "negotiate there" above them (l. 17). It too, partakes of the imaginative paradigm of the self-elegies.

52. R. C. Bald, *John Donne: A Life* (Oxford: Clarendon Press, 1970), 169. Quoted in Christopher Ricks, "Donne after Love," in *Literature and the Body: Essays on Populations and Persons*, ed. Elaine Scarry (Baltimore: Johns Hopkins University Press, 1989), 50.

53. Dayton Haskin notes: "The first edition of his *Poems* (1633) contained nine letters by Donne which seem to have been included as 'examples of epistolary elegance.' David Novarr [*The Making of Walton's Lives*] has observed that they were 'printed not for what they tell of Donne's life and insights, not as informal and personal revelations of the writer, [but] . . . for their art and grace.' They seem to have constituted a sort of manual of letter

writing." "A History of Donne's 'Canonization' from Izaak Walton to Cleanth Brooks," *Journal of English and Germanic Philology* 92 (1993): 17–36, at 23.

54. Ricks, "Donne after Love," 50.

55. We do well to be wary of Donne's penchant for mockery. Whatever he offers in the way of intimacy, he himself holds somewhat cheap. "The Extasie," for example, is marked by the irony of his suggestion that we part far purer than we came. He believes in the power of lyric to make us feel, to transform us, but he retains a healthy suspicion of it as well.

56. Donne's problems with intimacy and his combination of powerful affection for and violent feelings toward women have a parallel in Lovelace. Harris traces Donne's influence on Lovelace's mourning of Clarissa, particularly in regard to the "Nocturnall upon S. Lucie's Day" ("Richardson," 194).

57. Lamb describes an eighteenth-century engraving of Job's monument, which shows writing flowing across Job's skin onto a rock: "The graphemes on the book are imagined as a palimpsest which will cover and rebut the meaning of the under-text [the running sores] on his body. They will be wrapped around his broken body like a second skin, and he will wear them" (*Rhetoric of Suffering*, 46).

58. *Walton's Lives* (London, 1884), 74–75. Carey calls this Donne's "way of fashioning his dying into a work of art" (*John Donne*, 214). Doody points out this similarity in *A Natural Passion;* she goes on to connect *Clarissa* to the seventeenth- and eighteenth-century literatures of holy dying, and in general terms to the Metaphysical poets (174–87).

59. The self-elegies can be grouped in two schemes. Those like "The Canonization" begin with images of union and end in death. Others, like "The Funerall," begin with death's relic, the body, on the verge of dissolution, and use that to catapult the mind to another form of disruption and decay — that of intimacy. "The Extasie" straddles this divide.

60. The bracelets of hair are emblematic and not merely symbolic, partaking of the (at least) bipartite structure of the traditional emblem, icon/image joined to explication. They are objects of perception whose initial appearance is enigmatic — they are heavily coded as carrying symbolic import but require an accompanying text to deliver a message about the relationship between the visible world and the world of invisible meaning. Although these particular images would not be encountered in any emblem book, their cultural currency is such that they partake of their own canonical resonance.

61. Carey writes of this line: "The point of junction of the feeling with the felt, of the dead with the alive, attracts [Donne's] scrupulous attention. . . . When he speaks of the gravedigger unearthing 'A bracelet of brite haire about the bone,' the line startles us by its suggestion of death and life coiled together" (*John Donne*, 140).

62. Murray Brown argues that "Clarissa's funerary emblems . . . and her

corpse, conjoin the text, the spirit, and the flesh in a single visual statement" (468). Brown argues that the power of Clarissa's final use of emblems comes from the reification of the deployment of emblems as mere commonplace. In *"Emblemata Rhetorica:* Glossing Emblematic Discourse in Richardson's *Clarissa," Studies in the Novel* 27, no. 4 (1995), he maintains that part of Richardson's didactic project is to demonstrate that emblems schematize truths that experience can be made to verify. Clarissa's death is one of those verifications: "The emblematic commonplaces which we have been conditioned to understand with rhetorical topicality break those nominal boundaries, and we are confronted with emblems-made-actual" (457). Brown also adumbrates a connection between Richardson's use of emblems and that of Donne: "Richardson intends that our interpretative sensibilities rebound from inner to outer worlds in the metaphysical fashion [of Donne]" (468). Other critics have analyzed Richardson's use of emblems as well. Doody examines the prison scene in *A Natural Passion* (217–18) and notes that Richardson's emblems are largely "subjective: i.e., they are seen in the mind's eye of one of the characters, either recalled, imagined, or dreamed" (229), and that "his technique is to use an image consistently but in several different ways, so that meanings multiply; the effect is that of a play upon ideas" (188).

63. It is Lovelace's darling wish to have Clarissa live "the life of honor" with him, bearing his children (and nursing them) as his kept mistress (see the pornographic close of letter 220).

64. Recall that Richardson was familiar with *The Temple* — see above, n.4.

65. I here break from Brown's interpretation of the function of emblems in the novel. He writes, "Whereas Clarissa uses emblems and emblematic language to register her spiritual idealism, Lovelace appropriates these images in his attempts to facilitate and justify his agenda" (*"Emblematica Rhetorica,"* 455). Lovelace abuses emblems, trying to "twist [them] into any shape he desires, but because they are not neutral counters, they do not serve him long" (456). In the end, the emblems return to their rightful meanings, according to Brown, functioning as a clear "metalanguage" through which didacticism can function.

66. This is also perhaps why Richardson separates the introduction to the coffin from the emotional scene it creates (by almost one hundred pages) — it gives time to analyze it, absorb it, before the emotional *anschlauss.*

67. Cf. Lamb's description of Job's desire to have his story engraved on a rock: "This writing will act as a bandage to soothe, or as a garment to hide, the pain of the other writing, whose message he will never understand, which is inscribed in his boils and ulcers. It will be writing upon writing, a phylactery worn over the marks on his skin, whose efficacy will transpire as a future even taking place as the redeemer's mediation before God" (*Rhetoric of Suffering,* 46).

Chapter 2. Modes of Absorption

1. Linda Kauffman, *Discourses of Desire* (Ithaca: Cornell University Press, 1986), and Robert Day, *Told in Letters: Epistolary Fiction before Richardson* (Ann Arbor: University of Michigan Press, 1966).

2. Critics whose work is not limited to Britain have been more aware of this issue. In *The Dialogic Imagination*, trans. Caryl Emerson and Michael Holquist (Austin: University of Texas Press, 1981), Bakhtin argues that Menippean satire, a mixed form, is one of the most important precursors to the novel. He also explores the relation between lyric and novel in *Eugene Onegin*. ("Epic and Novel" and "From the Prehistory of Novelistic Discourse," in *The Dialogic Imagination*.) Friedrich Schlegel also argues for the interrelation of novel and lyric in *Dialogue on Poetry*, trans. Ernst Behler and Roman Struc [University Park, Pa.: Pennsylvania State University Press, 1968), focusing on the contributions of the novel to the aesthetic ideal and episteme of romanticism. Although he sees drama as the origin of the novel, he "can scarcely visualize a novel but as a mixture of storytelling, song, and other forms" (102). Doody, also working within a wider scope of literary history, mentions the presence of lyric in the novel in *The True Story of the Novel* (New Brunswick, N.J.: Rutgers University Press, 1996) but does not pursue the connection.

3. Wlad Godzich and Jeffrey Kittay, *The Emergence of Prose: An Essay in Prosaics* (Minneapolis: University of Minnesota Press, 1987). Godzich and Kittay argue that the earliest prose marks a difficult translation from verse originals, inaugurating a competition over the relative capabilities of the two literary practices. They are absolutely on target in their insistence that we not read prose merely as an unformed base of language on top of which verse and its rules may be imposed.

4. R. S. White. "Functions of Poems and Songs in Elizabethan Romance and Romantic Comedy," *English Studies* 68, no. 5 (1987): 393.

5. Maureen Barry McCann Boulton, *The Song in the Story: Lyric Insertions in French Narrative Fiction, 1200–1400* (Philadelphia: University of Pennsylvania Press, 1993).

6. White, "Poems and Songs," 393. While the majority of White's discussion of lyric in prose romance centers around issues of emotion, he also argues that in Elizabethan drama the situation is somewhat different; in particular, lyric in Shakespeare's or Lyly's comedies tends toward the ironic.

7. Phillip Sidney, *The Countess of Pembroke's Arcadia* (New York: Penguin Books, 1977), 651.

8. This practice is less frequent in heroic than in pastoral romance. Still, see for example *Amadis of Gaul:* Book 1 contains both Belterebus's song "made in his passion" and Leonoreta singing "that song which Amadis . . . made for [her] love" (Robert Southey's translation, 1872, vol. 1, 298; vol. 2, 15).

9. The practice of lyric insertions in English prose narratives is largely the result of Continental influence. However, although British romances do not contain lyric insertions until well into the Renaissance, parallel lyric insertions appear in other kinds of British literature. In metrical romance, for example, lyrics make an appearance: the Song of Troilus in book 1 of Chaucer's *Troilus and Criseyde* (c. 1382) is taken from Petrarch's Sonnet 88. The overall highly literary tone of *Troilus* is related to its frequent imitation of Continental sources and conventions. Derek Pearsall has been so good as to point out to me the regular use of lyrics in allegorical love visions in the Middle Ages. Again, all these uses are related to the concentration of emotion in virtuoso expressions.

10. The three uses are as monologue, message, and in the *dit* — a first-person narrative form in which the poet is hero. Boulton's approach is truly impressive: "After compiling what I hope is a nearly exhaustive list of narrative works that include inserted lyrics, I examined every lyric insertion in each of seventy-two narratives composed between 1200 and 1405 that I found to contain such insertions . . . , and have attempted to determine the literary function or functions of that lyric within the work" (*Song in the Story*, 18–19).

11. Boulton cites Paul Zumthor's argument that "the 'psychology' of romance characters is often no more than a rhetorical expansion of the central *formulae* of the *chanson* applied to either past or future action" (*Song in the Story*, 24). This line of reasoning can be traced to W. P. Ker's *Epic and Romance* (1896). When Boulton resumes this argument, she expands it to suggest that romance sometimes has structural underpinnings in lyric strategies. Of the *Roman de la Rose*, she writes that "Guillaume de Lorris assumed the voice of the lyric 'I' and elaborated the themes of the chanson in an allegorical narrative" (272). Nichols, in contrast, argues that genre distinctions between lyric and romance are irreducible: "Amorous Imitation: Bakhtin, Augustine, and *Le Roman d'Enéas*," in *Romance: Generic Transformations from Chrétien de Troyes to Cervantes*, ed. Kevin Brownlee and Martina Schordilis Brownlee (Hanover, N.H.: University Press of New England, 1985), 43–73. He substitutes Augustine's *Confessions* for troubador lyrics as the model of romance subjectivity. Although there are traces of *The Confessions* in romance, that pattern is not the only influence on the tradition.

12. Edith Rickert, introduction to *Early English Romances of Love* (New York: Cooper Square Publishers, 1966), xii.

13. In *Inescapable Romance* (Princeton: Princeton University Press, 1979), Pat Parker gives a solid discussion of the connection between certain strains of lyric (especially by Keats, Mallarmé, Stevens, and Valéry) and romance tradition.

14. Like the letter, of course, lyrics do not always work this way. It would be naive to assume that the song of a Cleophila, as in the *Arcadia*, is automat-

ically a sincere and accurate revelation of emotion, merely because it shifts the register from prose to poetry. The presence of poetic language or diction in a prose form is nonetheless significant: the effort required to produce an overtly lyric artifact (the difference in "register," to use Boulton's term) signals the need for increased (or at least different) readerly attention. Even if we, as savvy readers and critics, are on guard against fallacies of sincerity, we do well to note that being taken in—or at least along—by expectation and illusion is part of the pleasure of art, and the strategy of artists.

15. Arthur Marotti, "Manuscript, Print, and the Social History of the Lyric," in *The Cambridge Companion to English Poetry: Donne to Marvell*, ed. Thomas N. Corns (Cambridge: Cambridge University Press, 1993), 52.

16. Ilona Bell, "The Lyric Dialogue of Courtship," in *Representing Women in Renaissance England*, ed. Claude J. Summers and Ted-Larry Pebworth (Columbia: University of Missouri Press, 1997), 82. Bell also puts an epistolary poem at the heart of the women's lyric tradition in Elizabethan England.

17. R. C. Bald, *John Donne: A Life* (Oxford: Clarendon Press, 1970), 169.

18. J. Paul Hunter, *Before Novels: The Cultural Contexts of Eighteenth-Century English Fiction* (New York: Norton, 1990), 41.

19. The debate over whether Behn or Defoe was the first English novelist has slowed in recent years. On *Nobleman* in particular, see Maximilian Novak, "Some Notes toward a History of Fictional Forms: From Aphra Behn to Daniel Defoe," *Novel* 6 (winter 1973): 120–33, Judith Keagan Gardiner, "The First English Novel: Aphra Behn's *Love Letters*, the Canon, and Women's Tastes," *Tulsa Studies in Women's Literature* 8 (fall 1989): 201–22, and Paula Backscheider, "Sex, Sin, and Ideology: The Drama's Gift to the Genesis of the Novel," *Selected Proceedings from the Canadian Society for Eighteenth-Century Studies* 12 (1993): 1–15. I am tempted to (and do) call *Nobleman* a novel, but a novel with close ties to romance.

20. Carol Barash, in *English Women's Poetry, 1649–1714: Politics, Community, and Linguistic Authority* (Oxford: Clarendon Press, 1996), writes that her "discussion of Behn attempts to show the overlap between the novel and a particularly women's poetic tradition based on Continental heroic models" (2). Barash's chapter on Behn, however, makes little mention of the novels. She emphasizes the generic mixtures found in Behn's oeuvre, reading the *Voyage to the Isle of Love* as a novel/romance in meter that includes lyric segments—songs and an epithalamium (113). In the present chapter I attempt to link Behn's use of lyric conventions (and that of other novelists) to a poetic tradition in which women figure, but which goes beyond gender into the arena of genre, as well.

21. On the seventeenth-century popularity of the *Arcadia*, see Charlotte Morgan, *The Rise of the Novel of Manners* (New York: Columbia University Press, 1911): "During the forty years preceding the outbreak of the war, it

was printed no less than nine times, three times more by the end of the century, and shortly thereafter 'modernized' by a certain Mrs. Stanley" (15). Moreover, "References to the Arcadia are legion. We all know Milton's acknowledgment that the 'vain and amatorious poem' was a book 'in that kind full of worth and wit.' Waller, Cowley, Sir William Temple, and Bishop Hurd all read it with pleasure. Finally, Addison, it will be remembered mentioned it among the books in 'Leonora's Library' " (15).

22. Aphra Behn, *Love-Letters between a Nobleman and His Sister* (New York: Penguin Books, 1993), 34–35.

23. Janet Todd, introduction to *The Works of Aphra Behn* (London: William Pickering, 1992), 1:xxxix.

24. See, for example, Spenser's *Epithalamion,* Jonson's *Celebration of Charis,* or Lovelace's "To Althea, from Prison," among others.

25. See Nigel Smith, *Literature and Revolution in England, 1640–1660* (New Haven: Yale University Press, 1994), 234 ff., and Blair Worden, *The Sound of Virtue* (New Haven: Yale University Press, 1996), on romance and politics.

26. There is a range of political implications of women's use of the pastoral, which, while intriguing, is outside the scope of this study. On these implications, see Barash, *English Women's Poetry,* and Maureen Duffy, *The Passionate Shepherdess* (London: Cape, 1977), among others.

27. Montague Summers, introduction to *The Works of Aphra Behn* (London: William Heinemann, 1915), 1:liv.

28. The second "hexameter line" could also be read as two trimeter ones, given the strong caesura after "flower."

29. See Janet Todd's introduction to *Nobleman,* xxvi. In *The Sign of Angellica* (New York: Columbia University Press, 1989), Todd also links *Nobleman* to the poems, largely in terms of Behn's life: "Some of the letters are similar to her seemingly autobiographical poems concerning the value of sexual love when sincere and some of her problems over respectability when sexual nature has been acknowledged and expressed in Sylvia's anxiety; these problems also inform the pattern of action, the repeated arousals and disappointments of the lovers" (79).

30. William Congreve, "A Discourse on the Pindaric Ode," in *Eighteenth-Century Critical Essays,* ed. Scott Elledge (Ithaca: Cornell University Press, 1961), 1:143.

31. Such remarks (though not Congreve's) were often directed against women poets. See Steele's famous comment in *The Spectator* (no. 366) about "Numbers . . . as loose and unequal, as those in which the *British* Ladies sport their *Pindariques.*" Also note Edward Young's dictum in his later essay "On Lyric Poetry": "Judgment, indeed, that masculine power of the mind, in ode, as in all compositions, should bear the supreme sway; and a beautiful imagination, as its mistress, should be subdued to its dominion. Hence, and hence

only, can proceed the fairest offspring of the human mind." In Elledge, *Eighteenth-Century Critical Essays*, 1:412.

32. Young, "On Lyric Poetry," 411.

33. Todd, *Sign of Angellica*, 82.

34. See, for example, Backsheider, "Sex, Sin, and Ideology," and Rose Zimbardo, "Aphra Behn: A Dramatist in Search of the Novel," in *Curtain Calls: British and American Women and the Theater, 1660–1820*, ed. Mary Anne Schofield and Cecelia Machesky (Athens: Ohio University Press, 1991), 371–82.

35. Zimbardo points out a change in the use of the soliloquy at the end of the seventeenth century: "in the 1690s, soliloquy was changed from its earlier iconic function (i.e., to arrest action and provide, in emblematic declamation, a gloss upon it) to be a device by which a playwright could present a character 'thinking out loud' " ("Aphra Behn," 377). This does not fundamentally change the shape of most soliloquies, however, especially in the terms I employ.

36. In *The Rover*, for example, Blount's speech in act 3, scene 2 summarizes past action and poses a future course: "I am a dull believing English country fop—but my comrades! death and the devil! there's the worst of all—then a ballad will be sung tomorrow on the Prado, to a lousy tune of the enchanged 'squire, and the annihilated damsel—but Fred that rogue! and the colonel, will abuse me beyond all Christian patience—had she left me my clothes, I have a bill of exchange at home, would have saved my credit—but now all hope is taken from me—well, I'll home (if I can find the way)." *Oroonoko, The Rover, and Other Works*, ed. Janet Todd (New York: Penguin Books, 1992), 200.

37. The queen's short soliloquy in *The Widow Ranter* is a perfect example of this: "The more I gaze upon this English stranger, the more confusion struggles in my soul; oft I have heard of love, and oft this gallant man (when peace had made him pay his idle visits) has told a thousand tales of dying maids. And ever when he spoke, my panting heart, with a prophetic fear in sighs replied, I shall fall such a victim to his eyes." *The Widow Ranter*, in *Oroonoko, The Rover, and Other Works*, 270. Although the diction here is elevated and the speech shows internal rhyme and recognizable rhythm, it does not have the structural complexity and extension of metaphor of the "lyric" segments of *Nobleman*, nor is it a declaration of love to the beloved. Such a moment also allows the differentiation of Behn's language from euphuism, a sixteenth-century English version of *préciosité*. Euphuism changes rhetorical figures with great frequency, shifting from trope to trope even within a single sentence. The preferred form of ornamentation in this kind of speech is aural; assonance or alliteration is used to buttress antitheses that themselves are "pursued regardless of sense," as the *Oxford Companion to English Literature*, ed. Margaret Drabble (New York: Oxford University

Press, 2000), 338, explains. While I discuss lyric segments, not whole letters, I am only identifying as lyric substantial chunks that are grammatically cogent and intellectually more or less complete, fragments that form discrete units of sense.

38. L'Estrange's translation is in *The Novel in Letters: Epistolary Fiction in the Early English Novel*, ed. Natascha Würzbach (Coral Gables, Fla.: University of Miami Press, 1969), 1–21. Morgan has identified *The Portuguese Letters* as "the greatest single influence of the [seventeenth] century" and has argued that their legacy is felt largely as a groundbreaking exploration of emotion (*Rise of the Novel of Manners*, 73). Würzbach notes that "the sentimental analysis of the *Portuguese Letters* provided the strongest single impetus to the rise of epistolary narrative" (xxx–xxxi).

39. "There was no narrative whatever in the conventional sense, almost no *mise-en-scène* or suggestion of the antecedent action. The reader was presented with page after page of the most rareified subjectivity" (Day, *Told in Letters*, 34). Given the text's emotional concern, however, it is odd that Day describes the most prominent influence of these letters as dramatic: "The suffering mind of the Nun occupied the entire picture. . . . fiction had reached the technique of the drama at its most refined level — the tirade" (34). Guilleragues's letters are inflected by the language of heroic tragedy and contain allusions to Racine, but they are much more deliberative and measured than such a comparison would suggest. To be fair, the association of passionate speech by women with drama is warranted at least by the numbers: with the exceptions of Sappho and a few others (Behn, Phillips, Wroth, etc.), lyric was an overwhelmingly male genre; women's passions (especially those of amorous rage) found an early representation in dramatic form. Ros Ballaster argues that the language of the letters is connected to "the language of religious experience, and spiritual autobiography" and is marked by "linguistic disorder and logical inconsistency." *Seductive Forms: Women's Amatory Fiction from 1684–1740* (Oxford: Clarendon Press, 1992), 63. L'Estrange's translation gives this "disorder" a particular, lyric order.

40. Gabriel Joseph de Lavergne Guilleragues, *Lettres de la religieuse portugaise* (Paris: Livres de poche, 1993), 63; Würzbach, *Novel in Letters*, 5.

41. The French is "Cette absence . . . me privera donc pour toujours de regarder *ces yeux dans lesquels je voyais tant d'amour* et *qui me faisaient connaître des mouvements qui me comblaient de joie, qui me tenaient lieu de toutes choses* et *qui enfin me suffisaient?*" (Guilleragues, *Lettres*, 63; emphasis mine).

42. On argument in the *Letters* and other heroides, see Kauffman, *Discourses of Desire*.

43. Anonymous, *New Miscellaneous Poems: With Five Love-Letters from a Nun to a Cavalier, Done in to Verse* (London: J. Morphew, 1713).

44. *Love-Letters to a Gentleman*, in *Oroonoko, The Rover, and Other Works*, 154.

45. Most critics accept the autobiographical link to the letters: see Morgan, *Rise of the Novel*, Todd, *Sign of Angellica*, and Angeline Goreau's *Reconstructing Aphra: A Social Biography of Aphra Behn* (New York: Dial Press, 1980).

46. Behn's characters share a theory of the letter with Donne, thinking letters mingle souls. In *Nobleman*, Philander writes to Sylvia, "thy letter I confess is dear, it contains thy Soul and my happiness" (36), and Sylvia responds, "for while I write methinks I'm talking to thee, I tell thee thus, my soul, while thou methinks art all the while smiling and listening by" (37).

47. Leo Damrosch has kindly pointed out to me the resonance between this financial metaphor and those Shakespeare uses in the sonnets.

48. Anne Williams, *The Prophetic Strain: The Greater Lyric in the Eighteenth Century* (Chicago: University of Chicago Press, 1984), 35.

49. James Wellington, introduction to Pope's *Eloisa to Abelard* (Coral Gables, Fla.: University of Miami Press, 1965), 29.

50. John Dryden, *Essay of Dramatic Poesy*, quoted in Wellington, *Eloisa to Abelard*, 31. In *The Epistolary Moment: The Poetics of the Eighteenth-Century Verse Epistle* (Princeton: Princeton University Press, 1991), William Dowling also notes the lyric affinities of the Ovidian epistle (27).

51. Sylvia writes: "Thou wert gone, — that very word yet strikes a terrour to my Soul, disables my trembling hand, and I must wait for reinforcements from some kinder thoughts. But, Oh! from whence shou'd they arrive?" (145). For characteristics of heroides, see Kauffman, *Discourses of Desire*, 35–44.

52. There are two other heroical epistles in *Nobleman*. In the second of these, with the certainty of abandonment and the desire for revenge, the pitch of tragedy rises: "Look to't *Philander* — she that had the courage t'abandon all for Love, and faithless thee, can when she finds her self betray'd and lost, Nobly revenge the ruin of her fame, and send thee to the other world with, *Sylvia*" (190).

53. Tonson appended an introduction by Dryden to the collection: Œnone to Paris, is in Mr. Cowley's way of imitation only [giving latitude to translator to embellish, staying within form but manipulating sense]. I was desired to say that the author, who is of the Fair Sex, understood not Latin. But if she does not, I am afraid she has given us occasion to be asham'd, who do." *Ovid's Epistles: With His Amours. Translated into English Verse by Mr. Dryden, Mr. Pope, and others* (1751).

54. Œnone was published in 1680, Amintas in 1688. Composition dates are questionable.

55. An aesthetic evaluation of this passage might also focus on the conventionality of the language. Too, it might investigate the radical volta that follows the apostrophe, "*Sylvia!*" and explore the revision of convention and melding of styles that this change implies.

56. Barash, *English Women's Poetry*, 11. See especially Jane Barker, *A Patch-Work Screen for the Ladies* (1723). This "novel" — I'm unsure what else to call it — links meditative and descriptive poems to a prose narrative frame. Galesia, the heroine, is in a chaise full of storytellers, and after a series of traveler's mishaps, ends up visiting a lady who is making a patchwork screen. Galesia contributes scraps of paper from her trunk, which constitute her artistic oeuvre, ranging from landscape lyrics to an elegy, a poem about scientific discovery, and a versified recipe.

57. Eliza Haywood, *Love in Excess; or, The Fatal Enquiry* (Peterborough, Ontario: Broadview Press, 1994), 86.

58. Anna Nardo, "The Submerged Sonnet As Lyric Moment in Miltonic Epic," *Genre* 9 (1976): 22. On the invocations, see John Mulder, "The Lyric Dimension of *Paradise Lost*," *Milton Studies* 23 (1987): 145–63; the epithalamium is canvassed in Sara Thorne-Thomsen, " 'Hail Wedded Love': Milton's Lyric Epithalamium," *Milton Studies* 24 (1988): 155–85; on sonnets, see also Peggy Samuels, "Milton's Use of Sonnet Form in *Paradise Lost*," *Milton Studies* 24 (1988): 141–54.

59. Ros Ballaster argues in *Seductive Forms* that scenes like this act out hysteria (172 ff.). The heroine "mimics" the landscape while her body signals desire without her will; her body is then "opaque" and "uninterpretable" and enacts a refusal of inscription. In relying on lyric, however, Haywood is insisting on the connection of shared emotion to writing.

60. Haywood is skilled at writing traditional descriptions of the body agitated by passion. For period discussion of the passions, see, for example, Aaron Hill, *The Art of Acting* (1746). For criticism, see Alan Mackenzie, *Certain, Lively Episodes: The Articulation of Passion in Eighteenth-Century Prose* (Athens: University of Georgia Press, 1990), and Adela Pinch, *Strange Fits of Passion: Epistemologies of Emotion, Hume to Austen* (Stanford: Stanford University Press, 1996).

61. Cf. Donne:

Our soules, (which to advance their state,
      Were gone out,) hung 'twixt her, and mee.

And whil'st our soules negotiate there,
      Wee like sepulchrall statues lay;
All day, the same our postures were,
      And wee said nothing, all the day.   (ll. 15–20)

62. This is certainly a description that tastes of *Paradise Lost:*

God! with what an air he walked! What new attractions dwelt in every motion — And when he returned the salutes of any that passed by him, how graceful was his bow! How lofty his mein, and yet, how affable! — A sort of an inexpressible awful grandeur, blended with tender languishments, strikes the amazed beholder at once with fear and Joy! — Something beyond humanity shines round him! Such looks descending angels wear, when sent on heavenly embassies to some favorite mortal! Such is their form! Such radient beams they dart and with such smiles they temper their divinity with softness! (180)

63. On the construction of Pope's persona, see Dustin Griffin, *Alexander Pope: The Poet in the Poem* (Princeton: Princeton University Press, 1978).

64. Pope finds part of these sentiments in the Hughes text: letters "have Souls, they can speak, they have in them all that Fire which expresses the Transports of the Heart; they have all the Fire of our Passions, they can raise them as much as if the Persons themselves were present; they have all the Softness and Delicacy of Speech, and sometimes a Boldness of Expression beyond it" (Wellington, *Eloisa to Abelard*, 68–69). Perhaps the ascription of souls to letters here led Pope to recall Donne's idea of their intermingling. The Donne is cited in Chapter 1, above.

65. Leopold Damrosch, Jr., *The Imaginative World of Alexander Pope* (Berkeley: University of California Press, 1987), 49.

66. Reuben Brower, *Alexander Pope: The Poetry of Allusion* (Oxford: Clarendon Press, 1959), 78.

67. There are a few exceptions. For example, Ovid's complaints about exile in the *Tristia* are not, properly speaking, lyrics.

68. It is an interesting fact of literary history that Cowley wrote a verse romance (in the Ovidian style). *Constantia and Philetus* (1633) includes songs, complaints, and amorous epistles.

69. Samuel Johnson, *Lives of the English Poets*, ed. George Birkbeck Hill, 3 vols. (Oxford: Clarendon Press, 1905), 1:14–15.

70. Jonathan Lamb, in *The Rhetoric of Suffering: Reading the Book of Job in the Seventeenth Century* (Oxford: Clarendon Press, 1995), suggests that this is a feature of much eighteenth-century literature, where we find "the reluctance of the community to enter into the sharpness of an individual's suffering" when it is styled as a first-person complaint (176). This will be addressed more fully in the next chapter.

71. See Griffin, *Pope*, on Pope's use of antiselves, 172 ff. On Bolingroke, see 202.

Chapter 3. Lyric Tensions

1. Norman Maclean leveled the first blow against the idea of the eighteenth century as "a 'non-lyrical age'" in "From Action to Image: Theories of the Lyric in the Eighteenth Century," in *Critics and Criticism*, ed. R. S. Crane (Chicago: University of Chicago Press, 1952), 408.

2. See Donald Davie, *The Eighteenth-Century Hymn in England* (Cambridge: Cambridge University Press, 1993), Margaret Doody, *The Daring*

Muse: Augustan Poetry Reconsidered (Cambridge: Cambridge University Press, 1985), and Madeleine Forell Marshall and Janet Todd, *English Congregational Hymns in the Eighteenth Century* (Lexington: University Press of Kentucky, 1982).

3. Akenside's "Ode on Lyric Poetry" (1745) refers to all of these figures. On patriotic lyric models see Dustin Griffin, *Patriotism and Poetry in Eighteenth-Century Britain* (Cambridge: Cambridge University Press, 2002), 63–71.

4. On the richness of Anacreontic, see Marshall Brown, "Passion and Love: Anacreontic Song and the Roots of Romantic Lyric," *ELH* 66 (1999): 373–404. For a useful survey of midcentury poetry that emphasizes the looseness and irregularity of generic distinctions, see John Butt, *The Mid-Eighteenth Century*, ed. Geoffrey Carnall (Oxford: Clarendon Press, 1979), 57–92.

5. Several miscellanies give a sense of this. The *Flowers of Parnassus; or, The Lady's Miscellany, for the Year M.DCC.XXXV. Containing Great Variety of Original Pieces in Prose and Verse; and many Curious Particulars published since the Year One Thousand Seven Hundred and Thirty-Four* (London: J. & T. Dormer, 1736) includes several interesting seventeenth-century and contemporary works. There are poems by Jonson and Stephen Duck, amorous lyrics, poems seemingly in imitation of Finch, heroides, epistles, epigrams, satires, political poems, pastorals, an epyllion, some occasional poetry, and so on. Another anthology, *The Cupid* (1739), reveals highly dramatic love poems (often excerpted from plays like *The Conquest of Granada*). Studying such miscellanies would prove highly interesting, but there is no space for it here. They do suggest that amatory lyrics, though not significant enough for their authors, if contemporaries, to be named, maintained popularity in the period.

6. Anthony Cooper Shaftesbury, "Soliloquy, or Advice to an Author" (1710), in *Characteristics of Men, Manners, Opinions, Times*, ed. John M. Robertson (Indianapolis: Bobbs-Merrill, 1964), 1:205. N. H. Keeble argues for the continuation of an introspective tradition in late-seventeenth-century nonconformist writing in *The Literary Culture of Nonconformity in Late Seventeenth-Century England* (Athens: University of Georgia Press, 1987).

7. Doody, *Daring Muse*, 57–61; Nigel Smith, *Literature and Revolution in England, 1640–1660* (New Haven: Yale University Press, 1994), 250–94. Smith points out several developments during the wane of lyric in the Republic, including the rise of women poets, the importance of religious lyrics (dissenting and otherwise), and transformations in panegyric (especially in Cowley's odes).

8. Anne Williams describes the development of the greater ode in *The Prophetic Strain: The Greater Lyric in the Eighteenth Century* (Chicago: University of Chicago Press, 1984).

9. See Maclean's argument in "From Action to Image." Note also the emphasis on emotion in the St. Cecelia odes by Dryden and Pope.

10. See Williams, *Prophetic Strain*, Richard Feingold, *Moralized Song: The Character of Augustan Lyricism* (New Brunswick, N.J.: Rutgers University Press, 1989), and William Dowling, *The Epistolary Moment: The Poetics of the Eighteenth-Century Verse Epistle* (Princeton: Princeton University Press, 1991).

11. The versions of the romantic tradition I have in mind are those of M. H. Abrams, notably in *Natural Supernaturalism* (New York: Norton, 1971), the work of Josephine Miles, especially *Eras and Modes in English Poetry* (Berkeley: University of California Press, 1964), Geoffrey Hartman's work on Wordsworth, W. J. Bate on Keats, and James Engell's *Creative Imagination* (Cambridge: Harvard University Press, 1981), among others. In revisionist modes, a wealth of scholars have produced remarkable work (of whom I'll name only a few): Anne Mellor, Stuart Curran, Donna Landry, and others have aimed to expand the romantic canon to include women's poetry; Jerome McGann has written on the poetry of sensibility; and Marshall Brown has made significant contributions, first in *Preromanticism* (Stanford: Stanford University Press, 1991), which is the most important treatment to date of romantic poetry as the offspring of multiple genres, and in "Passion and Love," among other pieces.

12. Eric Partridge, *Eighteenth-Century English Romantic Poetry* (Folcroft, Pa.: Folcroft Press, 1924), 13.

13. Partridge makes strong initial claims, which fall by the wayside: "By 1753 there had been formed a body of novel-literature large and important enough to compel the attention of the English reading public . . . , and by 1771 the masterpieces of Johnson, Sterne, and Goldsmith, along with the already famous works of Richardson, Fielding, and Smollett, thus consolidating the strong position of the novel" (24). Such works were important partly because "they treated a great variety of themes, provided food for the imagination and matter for thought; they analysed character and developed situation beyond what was artistic in drama or desirable in poetry; they whetted curiosity and aroused all sorts of emotions. . . . these novels made for liberty in literature" (24). Partridge assigns the greatest impact of the novel to its break with classicism: "It was inevitable that poets, actual or potential, should . . . lose no time in taking possession of this new material and transmuting it, by the magic of their verse, into something rarer and finer. They did not, at first, realise fully its possibilities: they felt diffident as to how such and such an emotion, situation or scene would fit into poetry of the best kind" (25). His ultimate claim is that the novel did "not quite . . . revolutionise English poetry, — for the germs of Romanticism had sent forth shoots long before the appearance of Richardson's first story —, but to hasten and to strengthen the revolt implied in the work of Ramsay, Thomson, and lesser men" (*English Romantic Poetry*, 26).

14. All references to *The Seasons* are from James Sambrook's edition based on that of 1746 (Oxford: Clarendon Press, 1972).

15. "Life of Thomson," in Samuel Johnson, *Lives of the English Poets*, ed. George Birkbeck Hill, 3 vols. (Oxford: Clarendon Press, 1905), 3:285. Cf. John Barrell, *The Idea of Landscape and the Sense of Place, 1730–1840: An Approach to the Poetry of John Clare* (Cambridge: Cambridge University Press, 1972), 33–34.

16. See, for example, the foundationally important anthology *English Romantic Poetry and Prose*, ed. Russell Noyes (New York: Oxford University Press, 1956).

17. My discussion of landscape owes a conceptual debt to John Dixon Hunt's *Figure in the Landscape: Poetry, Painting, and Gardening during the Eighteenth Century* (Baltimore: Johns Hopkins University Press, 1976).

18. Hunt notes that in *The Seasons*, "the person who actually registers the details of the natural world is often . . . rather impersonal. The 'lonesome muse,' like the 'lone Quiet on her silent walks' whom he meets later, is too general and too structurally eloquent of a universal condition to bring to its encounter with landscape any very personal energy"(*Figure in the Landscape*, 124–25).

19. Patricia Meyer Spacks, *The Poetry of Vision* (Cambridge: Harvard University Press, 1967), 16.

20. Barrell, *Idea of Landscape*, 21, emphasis original.

21. Finch's "*Nocturnal Reverie*" appears in *The New Oxford Book of Eighteenth-Century Verse*, ed. Roger Lonsdale (New York: Oxford University Press, 1984). Hunt writes of this poem that "[a] personal observation . . . is modulated into a social, public relation . . . , and this reluctance to record the working of private sensibilities among the pastoral scenery has, of course, a strong hold on the Augustan poet" (180).

22. There are seeming exceptions as well: Dyer's "Grongar Hill" (1726) and Parnell's "Hymn to Contentment" (1714) have repeated insertions of the poet-speaker's "I" over the course of the work. These poems place a strong emphasis on the moral qualities of the landscape, and both end, interestingly enough, with a "you" — something like the epistolary address of moral satire. Barrell links the question of the distance between speaker and landscape to the "commanding height" from which the land is viewed (*Idea of Landscape*, 24–25).

23. Ernest Tuveson traces the early modern roots of English theories of sympathy to the seventeenth-century divine Isaac Barrow, and they continue through Hume's 1739 *Treatise on Human Nature* until the end of the century. "Shaftesbury and the Age of Sensibility," in *Studies in Criticism and Aesthetics, 1660–1800*, ed. Howard Anderson and John Shea (Minneapolis: University of Minnesota Press, 1967), 76–77. For overviews of sympathy, see W. J. Bate, *From Classic to Romantic: Premises of Taste in Eighteenth-Century England*

(Cambridge: Harvard University Press, 1949), ch. 5, and Engell, *Creative Imagination*. Bate suggests that Smith's *Moral Sentiments* was more the summary of an episteme than a directing influence (135), and Engell describes the wide range of treatises on sympathy as the century progresses: "In 1753 James Balfour's *A Delineation of the Nature of the Obligations of Morality* appeared, followed the next year by two works that also illustrate the rise of sympathy, David Fordyce's *Elements of Moral Philosophy* and James Bergh's *The Dignity of Human Nature*. Thirty years after his first influential book, Hutcheson published *A System of Moral Philosophy* which mentions sympathy as a permanent quality of man's nature" (149).

24. Many years later, James Beattie was to identify anthropomorphic sympathy as a key component of georgic: "There are few passages of descriptive poetry into which we enter with a more hearty fellow-feeling, than where Virgil and Lucretius paint so admirably, the one the sorrow of a steer for the loss of his fellow, the other the affliction of a cow deprived of her calf." *Essays: On Poetry and Music, As They Affect the Mind; On Laughter, and Ludicrous Composition; On the Usefulness of Classical Learning*, 3d ed. (London, 1779), 182.

25. On Thomson and empire, see Suvir Kaul, *Poems of Nation, Anthems of Empire: English Verse in the Long Eighteenth Century* (Charlottesville: University Press of Virginia, 2000).

26. *Summer, Autumn*, and *Winter* end with a plea for or exhortation to moral certainty based on awareness of the natural order. Knowing "that this dark State, / In wayward passions lost and vain pursuits, / This infancy of being cannot prove / The Final issue of the works of God" (*Summer*, ll. 1800–1830), we may either beg, with the poet, that nature "Enrich me with the knowledge of thy works!" (*Autumn*, l. 1352) or heed the poet's call to moral optimism: "bear up a while, / And what your bounded view, which only saw / A little part, deemed evil is no more" (*Winter*, ll. 1065–67).

27. "The Adventurous Muse," l. 22, in Lonsdale, *New Oxford Book of Eighteenth-Century Verse*, 71. On community and the political turmoil of the emerging British nation, see Linda Colley, *Britons: Forging the Nation, 1707–1837* (New Haven: Yale University Press, 1991).

28. See, for example, Stephen Cox, *The Stranger within Thee: Concepts of Self in Late-Eighteenth-Century Literature* (Pittsburgh: University of Pittsburgh Press, 1980), 8. Concepts of national identity also help poets escape solipsism, as Griffin argues in *Patriotism and Poetry*. Sympathy is also key in negotiating the relationship between British subjects and the subjects of empire. For significant arguments in this regard, see Srinivas Aravamudan, *Tropicopolitans: Colonialism and Agency, 1688–1804* (Durham, N.C.: Duke University Press, 1999), ch. 3, and Laura Brown, *Fables of Modernity: Literature and Culture in the English Eighteenth Century* (Ithaca: Cornell University Press, 2001).

29. Shaftesbury, "Soliloquy, or Advice to an Author," in Robertson, *Men, Manners, Opinions, Times*, 1:131. On this subject, see David Marshall, *The Figure of the Theater: Shaftesbury, Defoe, Adam Smith, and George Eliot* (New York: Columbia University Press, 1986), ch. 2.

30. Autobiography seems an exception to this rule, as does the first-person novel. One of my aims in this chapter is to explore how constraints on personal utterance have genre-specific effects. In "The Poetry of Thomas Gray: Versions of the Self," in *Modern Critical Interpretations: Thomas Gray's "Elegy Written in a Country Churchyard,"* ed. Harold Bloom (New York: Chelsea House, 1987), 19–37, Roger Lonsdale notes: "The cautious progress of autobiography in the eighteenth century in itself indicates suspicion of introspection as morbid or egocentric. (Introspective or confessional autobiography in England before 1740 was almost entirely religious in character, a purposeful scrutiny of private experience for spiritual ends.)" (27). I treat autobiography in greater depth in the next chapter.

31. Dowling explicitly connects the concern with solipsism to the wane of lyric in the period. He argues that although the Renaissance lyric "harbor[ed] a certain threat of solipsism, [it] had so far been able to banish that threat through its promise of consummation in the world of the body" (*Epistolary Moment*, 23). In the eighteenth century, however, "Lockean epistemology, with its dissolution of the physical world into private or mental impressions, dissolves this premise of lyric as well" (24). While Locke's theories are only part of the story, they are a powerful aspect of a cultural climate where a lone voice reaching out from one body to others is often deprived of stabilizing ground or authority.

32. Often in these cases either sympathy is the subject of the representation or it is antecedent; in that case, the poet/speaker is a "we" or someone else altogether.

33. The last of *Summer*'s extended references to the poet-self similarly ends in an invocation for a view of the greater natural presence:

> Beside the dewy border let me sit,
> All in the freshness of the humid air,
> There on that hollowed rock, grotesque and wild,   (ll. 622–24)

> Now, while I taste the sweetness of the shade,
> While Nature lies around deep-lulled in noon,
> Now come, Bold fancy, spread a daring flight
> And view the wonders of the torrid zone.   (ll. 629–32)

34. Feingold notes that there is a "double effort to represent the experience of inwardness and at the same time speak to an audience imagined as present to [the poet]. . . . What it marks is the writer's insistent interest in the intersection of social and inward experience, an interest he reveals in his

articulated and enacted wish to be seen as speaking with public authority even at the represented moment of self-absorption" (*Moralized Song*, 1).

35. See, e.g., Leapor, "The Beauties of the Spring," or "The Sacrifice," in *Poems upon Several Occasions* (London, 1748), and Masters, "Returned in Answer to a poetical Complaint from Miss —," in *Familiar Letters and Poems on Several Occasions* (London, 1755).

36. Hunt points out that "like all Augustan poets, Thomson . . . relies . . . usually upon organizing his ideas and feelings in some available artificial structure — the deliberate imitation of classical poets, for example" (*Figure in the Landscape*, 113). As Feingold and Janice Haney have shown, the early-eighteenth-century lyric most often appears as a version of Horace's, Virgil's, Pindar's, or Anacreon's voice. Janice Haney, "Eighteenth-Century Lyrical Models and Lyrical Languages: Essays toward a Theoretical History of the Lyric" (Ph.D. diss., Stanford University, 1978). See also Howard Weinbrot, *The Formal Strain: Studies in Augustan Imitation and Satire* (Chicago: University of Chicago Press, 1969).

37. Ralph Cohen argues that "each season . . . is composed of eulogies, elegies, hymns, prospect view, narratives, historical catalogs, and descriptive scenes." *The Unfolding of "The Seasons"* (London: Routledge and Kegan Paul, 1970), 105. He notes the segment addressed "to the 'ALL-PERFECT HAND'" in *Summer* (32–42), as well as the hymn above.

38. In the hunted hart section, the poet is replaced structurally via his sympathetic involvement with the animal. This is a special kind of lyric of substitution, as it might be called: the poet tries to lose himself in another identity. Cohen notes the fluidity of personal pronouns in the concluding "Hymn": "Although the *Hymn* is a public poem, the poet introduces himself at the end of the fourth stanza . . . and the poet suddenly particularizes what had been a general hymn. The introduction of the first person in a third person address is one of the characteristic procedures of Thomson" (*Unfolding*, 319).

39. Cf. Doody's *Daring Muse*, 75. Donald Davie notes: "In Book 10 of the *Republic* Socrates is willing to admit only two genres of poetry into the state: 'hymns to the gods and encomia to good men.' And Aristotle in Poetics 4 concurs. When Edmund Spenser wrote his *Fowre Hymnes* . . . he was appealing to that ancient Greek precedent, as was James Thomson when he published 'Hymn on Solitude.'" *Eighteenth-Century Hymn*, 16–17.

40. At least one of Thomson's poems has been popularly sung — "Rule, Britannia."

41. In *The Unfolding of "The Seasons,"* Cohen challenges the traditional version of Shaftesbury's influence on *The Seasons*, arguing rightly that many other sources contributed to Thomson's moral position. More recently, however, Robert Inglesfield has emphasized Shaftesbury's *aesthetic* influence by demonstrating formal connections between Thomson's poetry and *The*

Moralists. It is fairly certain that Thomson was well acquainted with and admired the piece, as Inglesfield notes: "A crude blank-verse poem ["The Works and Wonders of Almighty Power"], almost certainly a very early poem of Thomson's, and consisting entirely of a paraphrase of Theocles's 'Meditation,' was printed in Aaron Hill's London periodical *The Plain Dealer* in 1724." "Shaftesbury's Influence on Thomson's 'Seasons,'" *British Journal for Eighteenth-Century Studies* 9, no. 2 (Autumn 1986): 143. The prototypical discussion of Shaftesbury's influence is C. A. Moore, "Shaftesbury and the Ethical Poets in England, 1700–1760," *PMLA* 31 (1916): 264–325. Moore describes a vast arc of influence over the eighteenth century, a view challenged by other critics. Tuveson's description of Theocles' hymn in "Shaftesbury and the Age of Sensibility" could as well be a description of *The Seasons:* "Although there are traces of lyric, especially pastoral, and even epic in it, nevertheless it was truly a new departure in literature; it dealt a disastrous blow to the system of genres so long accepted by literary theorists. Pope pointed out that it could be written in blank verse — no accident, probably, for Philocles enthusiastically speaks of his 'number'd Prose.' Description, tableaux, scenes, which previously had been subordinate to the argument of any longer poem at least, now become ends in themselves" (86).

42. In *An Essay on the Genius and Writings of Pope* (1756–82), Joseph Warton compares Shaftesbury's sublime description of mountains to Pope's passage on the Alps in the latter's *Essay on Criticism.* Shaftesbury wins for his poetical tones ([London, 1806], 1:134–35). Shaftesbury touts Theocles' hymn: "Tomorrow, when the eastern sun as poets describe with his first beams adorns the front of yonder hill, there, if you are content to wander with me in the woods you see, we will pursue those loves of ours by favour of the sylvan nymphs; and invoking first the genius of the place, we will try to obtain at least some faint and distant view of the sovereign genius and first beauty" (*Moralists*, 2:40). Philocles responds: "And with the advantage of the rural scene around us, his numbered prose, I thought, supplied the room of the best pastoral song. For in the manner I was now wrought up, 'twas as agreeable to me to hear him, in this kind of passion, invoke his star and elements, as to hear one of those amorous shepherds complaining to his flock, and making the woods and rocks resound the name of her whom he adored" (2:115).

43. Cf. Dowling, *Epistolary Moment*, and Marshall, *Figure of the Theater*, 19–29. Marshall connects the problems with personal speech in Shaftesbury and his age to sympathy in a theatrical model. He does not discuss lyric but instead addresses philosophical inquiry, novels, and the metaphor and structure of address of drama in his analysis, revealing the cross-generic relation of formal and thematic concerns. His emphasis on the theater, like mine on the lyric, does not provide a "key" to Shaftesbury or the culture of sympathy — if we imagine there is only one way to open the box. Marshall does,

however, require us to remember the importance not only of genres but also of the interactions between them as "theaters" for cultural concerns and as ways of negotiating questions and problems of expression.

44. See Robert Marsh, "Shaftesbury's Theory of Poetry: The Importance of the 'Inward Colloquy,' " *ELH* 28, no. 1 (1961): 54–69. Marsh argues that for Shaftesbury, "All human souls are essentially a duality in unity" and that "the history of poetry clearly reveals the importance of this principle of 'duality' " (59).

45. Cf. Cox, "Shaftesbury is so concerned with the question of moral significance that he fails to deal with the equally important question of identity" (*Stranger within Thee*, 19), and Marshall, "The outlines of a real and true self, the character of a self-same person, seem less distinct as Shaftesbury performs his dramatic method on himself"; his concern is not self-definition (*Figure of the Theater*, 50). Marshall describes the "radical instability" of Shaftesbury's notion of self (40–67).

46. Cf. Marshall, "Can [the self] be seen as anything other than a textual indicator whose name has no value in itself but whose reference never can be ascertained?" (64).

47. James Engell notes the fluidity of the poet for Shaftesbury: "The poet is 'annihilated' by throwing himself into the object or person he imitates, and thus the poet's own subjective nature is absorbed into the objective world, creating a work of art that captures the fullest possible human perception" (*Creative Imagination*, 146).

48. Shaftesbury presents no coherent single voice, even if he proposes a kind of meditation that seems on the surface quite similar to (though much less detailed than) the tradition underpinning some of the most powerful lyrics of the preceding era. Martz has described the close relationship between Renaissance religious meditation and the poetry of figures like Donne or Herbert in *The Poetry of Meditation: A Study in English Religious Literature of the Seventeenth Century* (New Haven: Yale University Press, 1954). Like these works, *The Moralists* sketches an image of the world and the self in a form that adapts lyric conventions (as well as those of theater, as Marshall explains); however, the distance of *The Moralists* from *The Temple* extends more deeply than the shift from poetry to prose. Shaftesbury separates meditation from religious tradition, even arguing that the early practice of catechism has soured his contemporaries on self-questioning (*Characteristics*, 1.198–99); he also distances himself from enthusiastic divines ("Advice," 1:110). This is part of a larger secular tradition that seeks to eschew the "taint" of religious enthusiasm, and, as Hunt notes, Shaftesbury "refurbishe[s]" the micro- macrocosm equation "with scientific thinking" (*Figure in the Landscape*, 65). In view of the wide range of popular (and arcane) religious meditations available to him, Shaftesbury's refusal to link his practice to religion is of a piece with his distrust of enthusiasm. Martz's insistence

on the isolation of meditative poetry has been challenged by Anthony Low in *Love's Architecture: Devotional Modes in Seventeenth-Century English Poetry* (New York: New York University Press, 1978), Michael Schoenfeldt, and Ramie Targoff, among others; Shaftesbury's meditative poetry does not even evoke a coherent sense of self.

49. Much of what has been described as Shaftesburian in Thomson could have come from other sources. However, hymnal language in *The Seasons* is close to that of Theocles in *The Moralists* (see n. 41). While C. A. Moore may overestimate the extent of Shaftesbury's influence, it is broad: "The *Characteristics* went into a fourth English edition in 1727, a fifth in 1732, and by 1790 reached the eleventh. It was translated into French and German, and was referred to constantly by English and European writers" ("Ethical Poets," 275). Moore states that "with the possible exception of John Locke, Shaftesbury was more generally known in the mid-century than any English philosopher" (277). This, perhaps, an exaggeration, and even if he was well known, not everyone felt well inclined toward Shaftesbury's philosophy—his "free-thinking" was unacceptable in many circles.

50. Barrell has suggested that the tortuous syntax of the first twenty lines results from tension between "allegorical" and "descriptive" methods of vision and representation (the two terms come from Collins's 1746 collection, *Odes on Several Descriptive and Allegorical Subjects*). Critics (among them A. S. P. Woodhouse) have argued that the two terms are not in conflict but in apposition; in view of any allegorical subject or figure, Collins insists on a descriptive approach; still, however, we may agree with Barrell as to the potential for conflict involved in the two terms. There are fundamental tensions underlying the poem's evocation of vision; if we ask what the poet's visual and sensual relationship to his subject may be, the question of conflict (or apposition) between allegory and description, personification and the natural, takes on a different cast. See Barrell, *The Birth of Pandora and the Division of Knowledge* (London: Macmillan, 1992), ch. 2, and A. S. P. Woodhouse, "The Poetry of Collins Reconsidered," in *From Sensibility to Romanticism: Essays Presented to Frederick A. Pottle*, ed. Frederick W. Hilles and Harold Bloom (New York: Oxford University Press, 1965), 93–137.

51. On literary pictorialism and personification, see particularly Jean Hagstrum, *The Sister Arts: The Tradition of Literary Pictorialism and English Poetry from Dryden to Gray* (Chicago: University of Chicago Press, 1958). Earl Wasserman's 1950 article on personification is comprehensive: "The Inherent Values of Eighteenth-Century Personification" *PMLA* 65, no. 4 (1950): 435–63. Other critics have found Collins's approach to personification especially fleshy in this poem. Merle Brown writes, "In the 'Ode to Evening' Collins has not merely draped a generalisation with a person, he has actually created an 'abstraction blooded.'" "On William Collins' 'Ode to Evening,'" *Essays in Criticism* 11, no. 2 (1961): 136.

52. Paul Sherwin, *Precious Bane: Collins and the Miltonic Legacy* (Austin: University of Texas Press, 1977), 118.

53. Cf. Steven Knapp, *Personification and the Sublime: Milton to Coleridge* (Cambridge: Harvard University Press, 1985), on sublime personification. He argues that in the eighteenth century, personifications almost always imply the kind of doubling of the "Ode to Evening," and with that doubling, the denial of absolute agency for speaker, poet, or allegorical figure. The separation of agency from the poetic persona that Knapp describes is analogous to the disappearance or fracturing of self I analyze here. As John Crider notes, "In Collins's odes the personification is no longer a means but an end, . . . an object which is also a subject and therefore [of] which the poet feels himself an object." "Structure and Effect in Collins' Progress Poems," *Studies in Philology* 60 (1963): 60.

54. Richard Wendorf describes a similar process of dissolution and fragmentation in "Pity." In the last lines, "The poet not only expresses his sacred declaration to Pity but literally gives himself up (devotes himself) to this emotional force. This devotion approximates virtual dissolution: he will 'melt away' into the dreams of passion he has created within the splendors of his temple. But Pity's shrine, after all, is located within the poet's mind." *William Collins and Eighteenth-Century English Poetry* (Minneapolis: University of Minnesota Press, 1981), 99–100.

55. Cf. Doody, *Daring Muse:* "Characteristically, . . . an ode goes through a number of transient descriptions, unfixed alternatives which replace but do not cancel each other out . . . as Collins does . . . in the 'Ode to Evening,' with the various types and phases of evenings. In its rapid superimposed catalogue the Ode deals with all that might be said and provides an effect of fullness, but, except perhaps in the 'Ode to Evening,' the sense of amplitude is in some way countered by a sense of anxiety as to local and contemporary possibilities" (255). As I have argued, this is *especially* true of the "Ode to Evening." Christopher R. Miller gives a similar reading of the end of "Evening" from the perspective of Evening's longevity, in his forthcoming book, *The Poetics of Evening: Perception and Time in the Romantic Lyric.*

56. Patricia Meyer Spacks, "The Eighteenth-Century Collins," *Modern Language Quarterly* 44, no. 1 (1983): 16.

57. Marshall Brown points out the drastic shift caused by the replacement of "Peace" in the earlier version for "Health" in the last, arguing that Collins moves toward personal bodily experience (*Preromanticism*, 50–51). I argue that personal bodily experience is asymptomatic in this poem. He also argues that Eve as personification is replaced by evening over the course of the poem: "Evening becomes herself by outgrowing her fictive body," "She begins small enough to be served by tiny elves and ends large enough for the leafy earth to be her lap" (54). I believe that Eve persists as personification throughout, but Brown does point out the instability in Collins's imagina-

tion of the physical. By the end, what breaks down is the idea of physical presence in any way proper to the speaker—his own or that of his desire. Merle Brown traces the multiple absences of the poet and concludes that the poet is not "a finite person" and hence is "essentially identical with his muse, Eve" ("Ode to Evening," 145). I argue, somewhat to the contrary, that identity with the muse, especially conceived as oneness or unity, is precisely what the poem cannot sustain; however, Collins's refusal of the "finite" can certainly be read as a refusal of the physical. I believe that the latter approach is more accurate, however, because physical representations are emphasized from the first moments of the poem.

58. Feingold, *Moralized Song*, 16.

59. See Karen Weisman, "The Aesthetics of Separation: Collins's 'Ode Occasioned by the Death of Mr. Thomson,'" *Style* 28, no. 1 (1994): 55–64: "Collins . . . does not want to denigrate the inherent value of the abstract by utterly submerging it within the perceptually concrete. . . . It is therefore entirely appropriate that the highest concentration of personal abstractions . . . occurs near the center of the poem, which marks Collins's closest proximity to the grave of Thomson in his imaginary journey down the Thames" (60). Personifications—imaginary bodies—substitute for Collins's own.

60. Cf. Knapp, *Personification and the Sublime*, on the "Ode to Fear."

61. Graveyard poetry, from Parnell to Blair or Doddridge, is an interesting case. In meditating on the vanity of human wishes, it emphasizes disjunction between the body (the remnants lying beneath the tomb) and the moral voice or spirit. Janet Todd notes of meditative verse in general that "the poet, usually male, contemplates death in a darkening world, having retreated from public life into a region that provides no social and almost no physical context for the self." *Sensibility: An Introduction* (New York: Methuen, 1986), 51. I argue as this chapter proceeds that the paradigm of sympathy requires social contextualization even in isolation.

62. Although we might normally think of the world left to the poet as his landscape, it is not one that he comfortably inhabits or that is proper to him. The older debate over the location of the "churchyard" of the poem has given way to alternate interpretations. As early as 1950, F. W. Bateson was arguing for a "symbolic village," rather than a real one, in *English Poetry: A Critical Introduction* (New York: Longmans, Green, 1950), 189. In *Preromanticism*, Marshall Brown goes so far as to argue that the space in the poem is "space" itself, some approximation of a Kantian manifold of perception. Among the spaces/topoi that the poem refuses is also that of the georgic as history—the plowman is gone, the poet remains. On this, see Griffin, *Patriotism and Poetry*, 164–70.

63. Adam Smith, *The Theory of Moral Sentiments* (Indianapolis: Liberty Press, 1984), 12–13.

64. See Engell, *Creative Imagination*. The difference between romantic aesthetic sympathy and its Augustan moral precursor also lies in part in the position of the subject's body, as I will show in the final chapter.

65. From a slightly different angle, we see this concern in a contemporary critic's account of the "Elegy": "At least one of [Gray's] contemporaries was shocked even by the *Elegy:* 'Delicacy and taste recoil at the publication of internal griefs. They profane the hallowedness of secret sadness; and suppose a selected and decorated expression compatible with the prostration of the soul." Bateson, *English Poetry*, 187, quoting *A Criticism on the Elegy Written in a Country Churchyard*. See also David Marshall: Smith's "theory of sympathy presupposes a certain instability of self, it depends upon an eclipsing of identity, a transfer of persons in which one leaves oneself behind and tries to take someone else's part" (*Figure of the Theater*, 177).

66. Roger Lonsdale describes it thus: "the poet has found an acceptable escape route from the self in the growing contemporary doctrine of the ethical centrality of sympathy" ("Poetry of Thomas Gray," 26). However, what is important to remember is the delicacy of this transaction: "If there is uncertainty in both the syntax and the broader movement in . . . [the conclusion of] the poem it perhaps betrays the poet's uneasiness as he tries to bridge the gap between the impersonal assurance of the earlier stanzas and what he is now intent on describing: the memorial and sympathy he can imagine himself receiving after his own death" (23).

67. W. Hutchings points out the extraordinary degree to which in the *Elegy* the grammatical structure confuses object and subject, and at the end, "the elegist's transformation into object appears complete. It is emphasized by the fact that the only time in the poem that the first person singular pronoun occurs in the nominative is in the swain's narration: 'One morn I missed him on the customed hill'" (109). "Syntax of Death: Instability in Gray's *Elegy Written in a Country Churchyard*," in Bloom, *Modern Critical Interpretations*, 83–99. Cf. also Smith on the importance of the object: "A son, upon the death of an indulgent and respectable father, may give way to [grief] without much blame. His sorrow is chiefly founded upon a sort of sympathy with his departed parent; and we readily enter into this humane emotion. But if he should indulge the same weakness upon account of any misfortune which affected himself only, he would no longer meet with any such indulgence" (*Theory of Moral Sentiments*, 49).

68. On the value of bodies of color for liberal utopias, see Aravamudan, *Tropicopolitans*, and for modernity, Laura Brown, *Fables of Modernity*. On poetic dimensions of this problem, see Kaul, *Poems of Nation*.

69. *Wordsworth's Preface to Lyrical Ballads*, ed. W. J. B. Owen (Copenhagen: Rosenkilde and Bagger, 1957), 119.

70. On Gray's propensity to mix levels of diction, see Spacks's *Poetry of Vision*, ch. 3.

71. A survey of contemporary British elegies in the British Library re-
veals a concern with sympathy and benevolence. I quote the final lines of one
representative poem, "ON THE VERY MUCH LAMENTED DEATH of the truly
NOBLE, and universally Respected, LORD BASIL HAMILTOUN, SON TO THE
DECEAST *WILLIAM* Duke of *HAMILTOUN,* GRAND-CHILD TO JAMES *Duke of*
HAMILTOUN, AND WILLIAM *Marquess of DOWGLAS; Who was unfortunately
Drown'd* August 27, 1701, Aetat: 29: *by endeavouring to rescue his Servant*":

> His SYMPATHY continu'd to the last;
> Ah me! that at this time it mov'd so fast.
> When he attempt'd his Servant's Life to save,
> And lost his own: yet the DESIGN was BRAVE.

72. As many critics have pointed out, Gray's experience at Eton wasn't
quite so painless. See Vincent Newey, "The Selving of Thomas Gray," in
Thomas Gray: Contemporary Essays, ed. W. B. Hutchings and William Ruddick (Liverpool: Liverpool University Press, 1993), 29.

73. Hugh Blair, *Lectures on Rhetoric and Belles Lettres*, ed. Harold F. Harding (Carbondale: Southern Illinois University Press, 1965), 1:325.

74. Wasserman quotes James Beattie in emphasizing the almost organic
(or at least irreducible) connection supposed to exist between emotion and
figure: "Hyperbole, apostrophe, and prosopopeia, wrote James Beattie, are
among the most passionate figures; and 'some violent passions are peculiarly
inclined to change things into persons'" ("Inherent Values," 441).

75. Cf. the moral landscape in Gray's poem and that of Dyer's "Grongar
Hill" or Parnell's "Hymn to Contentment": in both of those poems, we find
a powerful speaking "I," but as the landscape becomes more inflected by
moral precepts, the "I" is succeeded by a monitory address to a "you," which
offers comparison between two kinds of vision and experience. Parnell's
poem, for example, ends, "Go search among your idle dreams, / Your busy or
your vain extremes; / And find a life of equal bliss, / Or own the next begun
in this."

76. Spacks argues for a temporal interpretation. For her, both the rosy-
cheeked children and the pageant of woes are equally removed from the
speaker: "The pervasive artifice of presentation, the unrelieved insistence of
the rhetorical distancing, keep the reader conscious of the poet as manipula-
tor of reality" (*Poetry of Vision*, 100). In line with this reasoning, "If a man's
perceptions about maturity are essentially insights into its horrors, it follows
that he may need to glamorize his perceptions about childhood; if beauty
cannot be located in the present, it must be asserted of the past or the future"
(101). Beauty is placed firmly out of reach, but the crux of the poem, the
fundamental imaginative pattern, has more to do with questions anterior to
that of beauty: the physical presence of either object or subject and the
source in it of passion. Physical presence is incompatible with emotional

experience in his scheme of representation. The sonnet on West may appear to be a significant counterexample of Gray's use of bodily reference, with its "These Ears, alas! for other Notes repine, / A Different Object do these Eyes require" (ll. 5–6). What the poet's Eyes and Ears reject seems to be the landscape with its "smileing Mornings," "redning Phoebus," "Birds in . . . amorous Descant," and so on (ll. 1–4). On closer inspection, however, it is more, for as Lonsdale points out, all of these images are taken from Milton, Virgil, Ovid, and Pope. Poetic descriptions made by the masters allow, as Vincent Newey explains, the poet to "find contact with the external world only at second-hand" ("Selving of Gray," 24). The trajectory works both ways: if we come close to nature through the filter of convention, it is thus that we approach the poet's body as well. His own words cannot come close; his own emotions are denied him.

77. That this was still a struggle some fifty years later can be seen in Keats's *Ode on a Grecian Urn* (1819).

78. Charles Rzepka argues that Gray erases the speaker's body in the "Elegy" in order to enter "an imagined world of invisible lives." *The Self As Mind: Vision and Identity in Wordsworth, Coleridge, and Keats* (Cambridge: Harvard University Press, 1986), 4. I would agree with this, except that Rzepka argues that this absence of the body is an indication of solipsism, stating that the ploughman's retreat signals the "felt absence of the other" (4), and that the eradication of the social facilitates the imagination of the villager's woes. Rzepka's argument does not jibe with contemporary theory, however, because social pressures (coupled with instinct) are precisely those that produce sympathetic involvement.

79. Mary Leapor, *Poems upon Several Occasions*, vol. 1. Donna Landry argues for the challenges in this stanza to working women's (particularly erotic) self-expression in *The Muses of Resistance: Laboring-Class Women's Poetry in Britain, 1739–1796* (Cambridge: Cambridge University Press, 1990), 84. Leapor cannot be Sappho because such passion violates sexual decorum and her claims to classical learning are always a matter of contention.

80. The 1730 text, in *Eighteenth-Century Poetry*, ed. David Fairer and Christine Gerard (London: Blackwell, 1999), ll. 64–69. John Goodrige's readings of this poem and of Collier's "Woman's Labour," in *Rural Life in Eighteenth-Century English Poetry* (Cambridge: Cambridge University Press, 1995), and Landry's *Muses of Resistance* influenced my thinking about these poems. Although Roxann Wheeler, in *The Complexion of Race: Categories of Difference in Eighteenth-Century British Culture* (Philadelphia: University of Pennsylvania Press, 2000), argues that color became central only late in the century, in Duck's poem, skin color and nation are allied.

81. Collier's elegy on Duck also introduces the poet's "I" only via a move to extended metaphor. Cf. Landry, *Muses of Resistance*, 76.

82. Margaret Anne Doody, "Sensuousness in the Poetry of Eighteenth-

Century Women Poets," in *Women's Poetry in the Enlightenment: The Making of a Canon, 1730–1820*, ed. Isobel Armstrong and Virginia Blain (New York: St. Martin's Press, 1999), 3–32, at 26.

83. Landry connects Collier and Leapor in these terms, arguing, "Both seem to find [here] . . . a necessary poetic license for their criticism of the dominant order" (*Muses of Resistance*, 106).

84. Marshall Brown, "Passion and Love," 383, 377.

85. Matthew Prior, "A Better Answer to Cloe Jealous," in Lonsdale, *New Oxford Book*, 57.

86. See Watts's "Hurry of Spirits, in a Fever and Nervous Disorder" (1734), Smart's "Hymn to the Supreme Being on Recovery from a Dangerous fit of Illness" (1756), or Chandler's "My Own Epitaph" (1736). This pattern of fragmentation and pain enabling a subject who ought to be silent to speak is visible in seventeenth-century women's religious poetry. A woman like Elizabeth Major can write lyric because she seeks God's grace, and also because "She constructs a new self [in her poetry] . . . broken by suffering and made up only of permissible feminine elements." Elaine Hobby, *Virtue of Necessity: English Women's Writing, 1649–1688* (Ann Arbor: University of Michigan Press, 1988), 66.

87. Fairer and Gerard, *Eighteenth-Century Poetry*, 257–62, ll. 11–12.

88. Akenside's "Ode on Leaving Holland" does focus more than others on the poet's imaginative involvement with the landscape, but this is a rare exception. Another exception, though not an ode, is Joseph Warton's "Dying Indian," mentioned above, where a wounded Indian gives his farewell speech — and indeed, it sounds like a fragment of a drama with lyric overtones, rather than the other way around. This poem, like others we have encountered ("Eloisa to Abelard," most notably), approaches the sorrows of the self outside of the *propria persona*.

89. John Sitter, *Literary Loneliness in Mid-Eighteenth-Century England* (Ithaca: Cornell University Press, 1982). Griffin challenges Sitter's idea of solitude in *Patriotism and Poetry*; following Griffin, I argue that poets often have company, imagined or otherwise.

90. It would be intriguing, though outside the scope of this project, to pursue a comparison between midcentury mainstream poets like Gray and Quaker poets of the preceding century. Nigel Smith points out the instability of self in this radical poetry and argues that it "transcend[s] the 'fleshy' finite self by means of the elaboration of allegories which describe the self in natural imagery." *Perfection Proclaimed: Language and Literature in English Radical Religion, 1640–1660* (Oxford: Clarendon Press, 1989), 26.

91. Barrell, following Wasserman, notes the lack of particularity of place in Dyer and links it to moralizing tendencies (*Idea of Landscape*, 35). See also Robin Jarvis, *Romantic Writing and Pedestrian Travel* (New York: St. Martin's Press, 1997), 72–74.

92. For Cockburn, see *Poems by Eminent Ladies* (London, 1755).

Chapter 4. Rhetorical Realisms

1. Roger Lonsdale, "The Poetry of Thomas Gray: Versions of the Self," in *Modern Critical Interpretations: Thomas Gray's "Elegy Written in a Country Churchyard,"* ed. Harold Bloom (New York: Chelsea House, 1987), 27, quoting Henry Pemberton.

2. Robert Day gives a rough "estimate that a thousand works of fiction, new or revived, appeared in something like forty-five hundred editions or issues between the Restoration and 1740. Of these, over two hundred works in five hundred editions or issues were letter fiction." *Told in Letters: Epistolary Fiction before Richardson* (Ann Arbor: University of Michigan Press, 1966), 2. He cites Frank Black's 1933 assessment that from 1740 to 1800, the ratio of epistolary fiction to all fiction was 1:6 (213, n. 2). Numbers for other first-person fiction are harder to ascertain. My own surveys of print catalogs (estimates based on titles and personal knowledge, so in no way perfect) suggest that around 20 percent of published novels were nonepistolary first-person works. James Raven, examining the period between 1750 and 1770, writes, "Although the number of new 'memoirs' is variable over the decade, some of the most popular are from this category. Increasingly during the 1760s these memoirs are written as 'adventures' and 'genuine histories' in the first person." *British Fiction, 1750–1770: A Chronological Check-List of Prose Fiction Printed in Britain and Ireland* (Newark: University of Delaware Press, 1987), 12. Catalogues consulted include *Eighteenth-Century Short-Title Catalogue*, Leonard Orr, *A Catalogue Checklist of English Prose Fiction, 1750–1800* (Troy, N.Y.: Whitson, 1979), Jerry C. Beasley, *A Check List of Prose Fiction Published in England, 1740–1749* (Charlottesville: University Press of Virginia, 1972), and William H. McBurney, *A Check List of English Prose Fiction, 1700–1739* (Cambridge: Harvard University Press, 1960).

3. Felicity Nussbaum, *The Autobiographical Subject: Gender and Ideology in Eighteenth-Century England* (Baltimore: Johns Hopkins University Press, 1989), 24.

4. J. Paul Hunter notes, "A few autobiographies, like that of Bunyan, had appeared in print in the seventeenth century, but it was well into the eighteenth century before even major figures could confidently propose their own lives to the public. . . . Observers like Pope and Fielding . . . stand stunned in amazement at the audacity, self-interest, and public narcissism of someone who could autobiographically offer *An Apology for the Life of Colley Cibber, Comedian.*" "The Insistent 'I,' " *Novel* 13 (fall 1979): 21. There are still those, like John Dunton, who just do not care about such rules of taste. For a good sampling of women's autobiographical writings, see Carolyn A. Barros and Johanna M. Smith, eds., *Life-Writings by British Women, 1660–1815: An Anthology* (Boston: Northeastern University Press, 2000).

5. Raven, *British Fiction, 1750–1770.*

6. Patricia Meyer Spacks, *Imagining a Self: Autobiography and Novel in*

Eighteenth-Century England (Cambridge: Harvard University Press, 1976), 22.

7. See J. Paul Hunter's *Before Novels: The Cultural Contexts of Eighteenth-Century English Fiction* (New York: Norton, 1990), Lennard Davis's *Factual Fictions: The Origins of the English Novel* (Philadelphia: University of Pennsylvania Press, 1996), and William Warner's *Licensing Entertainment: The Elevation of Novel Reading in Britain, 1684–1750* (Berkeley: University of California Press, 1998) on these last two points. On literacy and novel reading, see Isabel Rivers, ed., *Books and Their Readers in Eighteenth-Century England* (Leicester: Leicester University Press, 1982). On the rise of consumerism, see John Brewer and Roy Porter, eds., *Consumption and the World of Goods* (New York: Routledge, 1993). An essay in that collection by Colin Campbell, "Understanding Traditional and Modern Patterns of Consumption in Eighteenth-Century England: A Character-Action Approach," examines the relationship between ideals of sensibility and consumer patterns, looking at dandy figures, pseudo-aristocrats, and others. Joyce Appleby's article "Consumption in Early Modern Social Thought," also in this collection, is a useful consideration of contemporary reactions to the rise of consumerism. For a thorough account of most of these aspects, see Michael McKeon, *The Origins of the English Novel, 1600–1740* (Baltimore: Johns Hopkins University Press, 1987).

8. Samuel Johnson, "Life of Thomson," in *Lives of the English Poets*, ed. George Birkbeck Hill (Oxford: Clarendon Press, 1905), 3:299–300.

9. Cf. Nussbaum on eighteenth-century autobiography: "In short, eighteenth-century works of self-biography are less quests toward self-discovery in which the narrator invents herself or himself than repetitive serial representations held together by the narrative 'I'" (*Autobiographical Subject*, 18). She goes on to note that "Baptists and Methodists, as well as Quakers, demonstrate uncertainty about rendering a whole or fixed identity in the narrative forms they adopt. John Wesley commonly took notes hour by hour as well as day by day" (20).

10. Deirdre Lynch, "Personal Effects and Sentimental Fictions," *Eighteenth-Century Fiction* 12, nos. 2–3 (2000): 348.

11. Deirdre Lynch, *The Economy of Character: Novels, Market Culture, and the Business of Inner Meaning* (Chicago: University of Chicago Press, 1998), 6. Lynch focuses mainly on criticism and metatexts to work through the implications of "character" and characterization in the early century; in the process, literary representation may occasionally fall out of view. Her discussion of *Roxana*, for example, traces the word *character* in the novel somewhat at the expense of Roxana's powerful self-representation. Moreover, in arguing that character description is criticized in financial or economic terms, Lynch does not mention that almost all literary description is assessed by contemporaries in this way, in terms of how much is enough and how much

is too much (especially important for landscape and botanical description), and this may overemphasize the fiduciary metaphor. This quibble aside, Lynch's book is persuasive, and I have found it useful (as my discussion of late-eighteenth-century novels in the next chapter testifies). Like Lynch, but in a different mode, I am inquiring into how character — as selfhood — is created on the page, and how it is a question of public and private (cf. Lynch, "Personal Effects," 352–53). I also argue in Chapter 5 that a sense of literary interiority may be achieved by representing emotional intensity at particular moments, even if that emotion belongs to a character, like Moll Flanders or Robinson Crusoe, who may seem contradictory, incomplete, or even, some-times, flimsy: it does not always require temporal extension.

12. For Watt's classic statements about formal realism, see *The Rise of the Novel: Studies in Defoe, Richardson, and Fielding* (Berkeley: University of California Press, 1957), ch. 1. His most succinct description of formal realism defines it as "the premise, or primary convention, that the novel is a full and authentic report of human experience, and is therefore under an obligation to satisfy its reader with such details of the story as the individuality of the actors concerned, the particulars of the times and places of their actions, details which are presented through a more largely referential use of lan-guage than is common in other literary forms" (32). Ira Konigsberg puts this in terms of perception: "The novel became the major literary form during this period . . . because it . . . dramatized a significant awareness of the individual's relationship to reality developing in the culture of the time: the novel most directly confronted the problem of perception in both its narra-tive technique and subject matter." *Narrative Technique in the English Novel: Defoe to Austen* (Hamden, Conn.: Archon Books, 1985), 9–10.

13. Davis, *Factual Fictions*, 188. Davis identifies one of the fundamental characteristics of the news/novel matrix (the complex of media from which the novel emerged) as an "emphasis on forcibly decreasing the distance between the reader and the text" (58).

14. Warner, *Licensing Entertainment*, ch. 5, on the *Pamela* event.

15. She gives a touchingly jumbled picture of her suffering: "I arose; but was so stiff with my hurts, so cold with the dew of the night, and the wet grass on which I had sat, as also with the damps arising from so large a piece of water, that with great pain I got from this pond, which now I think of with terror; and bending my limping steps toward the house, took refuge in the corner of an outhouse, where wood and coals are laid up for family use: there, behind a pile of fire-wood, I crept, and lay down, as you may imagine with a heart just broken; expecting to be soon found out by cruel keepers, and to be worse treated than ever I yet had been" (214) Cf. John Dussinger on this point in *The Discourse of Mind in Eighteenth-Century Fiction* (The Hague: Mouton, 1974): "Topographically the description of this episode has the effect of juxta-posing the most trivial physical details with momentous reflections on human

suffering and divine providence" (61). The scene establishes an "equivalence . . . between mind and body, between spiritual and material" (62).

16. Strictly speaking, Pamela's consciousness is the sum of those things
presented as filtered through "it": this is my point. Some cognitive scientists
would argue this to be the case for all of us.

17. As Catherine Gallagher argues, the proliferation of detail that characterizes early novels served its readers as a signal of its status as fiction;
sparse detail, such as one finds in the scandal chronicles of Delarivier Manley, indicated a real person being described under the thin veil of allegory: as
the novel became differentiated from market competitors, "realism . . . [be-
came] the mark, the code of the explicitly fictional." "Nobody's Story: Gender, Property, and the Rise of the Novel," in *Eighteenth-Century Literary
History: An MLQ Reader*, ed. Marshall Brown (Durham, N.C.: Duke University Press, 1999), 32. See also McKeon, *Origins of the English Novel*, for a
similar argument about codes of fictionality and competing modes of verisimilitude.

18. Nancy Armstrong, *Desire and Domestic Fiction: A Political History of the
Novel* (New York: Oxford University Press, 1987), and Christopher Flint,
Family Fictions: Narrative and Domestic Relations in Britain, 1688–1798 (Stanford: Stanford University Press, 1998). While most scholars accept the principle that the novel takes hold of the domestic in a new and important way,
few have done the careful work required to prove it. Flint's book is an excellent step in this direction. Other recent studies include Betty A. Schellenberg, *The Conversational Circle: Rereading the English Novel, 1740–1775* (Lexington: University Press of Kentucky, 1996), Jacqueline Elaine Lawson,
Domestic Misconduct in the Novels of Defoe, Richardson, and Fielding (Lewiston, Wales: Mellen University Press, 1994), and Caroline Gonda, *Reading
Daughters' Fictions, 1709–1834: Novels and Society from Manley to Edgeworth*
(Cambridge: Cambridge University Press, 1996). In *The Imaginary Puritan,
Literature, Intellectual Labor, and the Origins of Personal Life* (Berkeley: University of California Press, 1992), Nancy Armstrong and Leonard Tennenhouse
note that the relationship between domesticity and individuality is usually
privileged in historical analyses of the period surrounding the emergence of
the novel: "Even the most sophisticated scholars and critics tend to assume
that consciousness enters history and takes up a definitive relationship with
the world by means of the family. . . . It is in this area that historians join the
nomenclature of class and status to that of emotion and moral character,
hallmarks of the enclosed and individuated consciousness" (70). They go on
to state, succinctly, that "the family is where modern consciousness receives a
body" (85). Tennenhouse and Armstrong argue that this ideological nexus is
a product of literature as a privileged form of intellectual work.

19. I distinguish the treatment of domesticity in the novel and in
eighteenth-century drama in terms given by Arthur Sherbo in *English Senti-*

mental Drama (East Lansing: Michigan State University Press, 1957) and Laura Brown in *English Dramatic Form, 1660–1760: An Essay in Generic History* (New Haven: Yale University Press, 1981). Sherbo argues that sentimental plays, the form primarily associated with the domestic in drama, are subject to the same criticism leveled against romance: they violate probability (5–7). He finds that "the improbable, the illogical, the exaggerated or the artificial . . . is an inevitable concomitant of sentimentalism" in its dramatic incarnation (32). The absence of interiority is also a hallmark of the style (Brown concurs in this). The complex of issues that surrounds the domestic in the novel is not found in drama. However, there are ways in which novel and drama have an interesting relationship around the domestic — predictably, this occurs in the latter part of the century. It is noticeable, Sherbo comments, that "sentimental comedies were relatively more successful in the sale of printed copies than in the record of performances on the stage" (144); the *London Magazine* complains of one such comedy, Frances Sheridan's 1763 *Discovery*, "The last act is rather a Richardsonian narration than part of a dramatic action" (cited in Sherbo, 148).

Drama seems to have imitated the novel. Laura Brown argues that the novel may not be the origin of domestic realism in the eighteenth century, but it was the most successful literary form in developing and effecting domestic realism (146). She contends, "Where Steele in *The Conscious Lovers* resorts to irrelevant stage business to sustain his plot, Richardson progressively educes Pamela's activity and even her physical freedom" (192), and concludes that "Richardson embraces the stasis of the moral plot, and makes a virtue of that necessity. The energy and engagement of *Pamela* and *Clarissa* arise not from the external reversals of a lively action, but from the internal tensions of a complex psychology. With this simple innovation, Richardson solves the fundamental problem of moral form and avoids the fatal weaknesses that destroy the drama" (191). See also T. G. A. Nelson's discussion of the largely iconographic significance of children in Restoration and Augustan comedy in *Children, Parents, and the Rise of the Novel* (Newark: University of Delaware Press, 1995). He argues as well for flatness of characterization in domestic drama. By the time of *Tom Jones*, "novels . . . are expected to pursue many of those narrative threads which in stage plays could not be followed to the end" (175); in effect, novels demand and enact the expansion of the domestic. Richard Gill connects country-house poems to the eighteenth-century novel in *Happy Rural Seat: The English Country House and the Literary Imagination* (New Haven: Yale University Press, 1972), 227–47.

20. I am leaving aside the question of verisimilitude here — enough work has been done on this subject for me. I am subordinating the what of representation to the how. By shifting the focus to rhetoric, I am also making room for an important characteristic of the novel as a print form — its concern with connecting readers and writers separated by large distances of

space and or culture, a characteristic that critics from Robert Darnton to J. Paul Hunter have explored.

21. Bruce Robbins, *The Servant's Hand: English Fiction from Below* (New York: Columbia University Press, 1986), 95. Robbins uses *Turcaret* as a test case of the more general principle, which servants effect.

22. Any chiasmus between the worlds of reading and the read may, instead of orienting the reader, disorient him or her, especially if there are questions as to the status of the text as fiction. This effect was exploited by wily or sophisticated authors as a way of controlling the reader's imagination of the text and his or her affective involvement with the world the text evokes. This is a separate issue from that created by a reader's experience, regardless of knowledge, of the text as if it were real—the suspension of disbelief. The early encounters of readers with works like *Moll Flanders*, wondering whether these tales were true or not, were facilitated by chiasmus—whether the world of the text were seen to be fictional or not, the encounter would be guided and governed by the same rhetorical means.

23. Catherine Gallagher, *Nobody's Story: The Vanishing Acts of Women Writers in the Marketplace, 1670–1820* (Berkeley: University of California Press, 1994).

24. On the relationship of houses to novels, see a range of books including Christina Marsden Gillis, *The Paradox of Privacy: Epistolary Form in "Clarissa"* (Gainesville: University Presses of Florida, 1984). On the relationship of conduct books to the novel, see Armstrong's *Desire and Domestic Fiction*, as well as Flint. In *Family Fictions*, Flint traces this connection at length and, in a particularly convincing example, notes that "a number of [nineteenth-century] conduct books, such as *The Domestic Instructor*—which was 'selected principally from celebrated authors'—simply extracted particularly effective exhortatory material from domestic prose fiction" (13).

25. My focus on the relationship between the domestic and the work of narration means that I can treat the two novelistic "traditions" of Richardson and Fielding together. Fielding's focus on domestic mock-epic is an important case in point. Following Elizabeth Kraft, I identify the narrator as the central consciousness in *Tom Jones*, and believe that the process of narration is linked to that of interpretation in creating ethical identity for both reader and narrator. See *Character and Consciousness in Eighteenth-Century Comic Fiction* (Athens: University of Georgia Press, 1992), 65 ff., 74. The manipulation of convention through the lens of domesticity connects consciousness, narration, the fictional, and the real quite neatly.

26. In amatory fiction like that of Haywood, solipsism is the greatest threat to the ideology of love. Cf. John Richetti, *Popular Fiction before Richardson: Narrative Patterns, 1700–1739* (Oxford: Clarendon Press, 1969). Novels "mediate" generic concerns, but not always with uniform success (as with the challenges to *Pamela*).

27. Gallagher writes: "Henry Fielding, for example, defined 'No Body' as 'All the People in Great Britain, except about 1200.' Hogarth also seems to have intended his Nobody to stand for the common man, and 'opposed him . . . to the pretentious Somebody.' Somebody was used throughout the seventeenth and eighteenth centuries as Nobody's foil; the two figures were common enough, for example, to form a pair in a deck of playing cards and were stock masquerade characters. . . . Hence, just as Nobody might be seen as the prototype of fictional characters, Somebody might be seen as the prototype of scandalous reflections" (*Nobody's Story*, 207).

28. Gallagher argues, "Fiction, then, stimulates sympathy because, with very few exceptions, it is easier to identify with nobody's story and share nobody's sentiments than to identify with anybody else's story and share anybody else's sentiments" (*Nobody's Story*, 172). The key is not primarily that "fiction allowed readers to be, in Burke's words, 'acquisitive without impertinence'" (Gallagher, "Gender, Property," 36). Gallagher argues that in sympathizing with others, we blur the boundaries between them and ourselves "in a way that obscures the 'otherness' of the original sufferer" (*Nobody's Story*, 169). Fictional characters are not "others," in her view; they are the property of the reader's imagination, and this erases ethical problems of appropriation. Gallagher's twentieth-century emphasis on the ethics of sympathy, however, does not fit with the contrary ethics of eighteenth-century moral philosophers. Because sympathy, for Hume, Smith, or its other theorists, is never perfect, no matter how much an emotion may become our own, we are still aware of the separation between our own identities and those of sympathetic others: identity is more than the experience of a particular emotion at a particular time. Hume's idea of identity as the continual presence of the idea of the self to the mind is appropriate here, but there is no reasonable definition of identity that argues that the experience of a single emotion can change it—though some versions of Stoicism might make me reconsider this.

29. Steven Knapp, *Personification and the Sublime: Milton to Coleridge* (Cambridge: Harvard University Press, 1985), 98–99. Knapp also argues that "Collins stands at the center . . . of eighteenth-century attitudes toward poetic fiction" (87).

30. The sonnet in the later century, by parceling out space and time (often in the form of rivers), begins to achieve its own scheme for making landscape or context fit feeling, but that looks, for the moment, too far ahead.

31. The editor-didactic narrator, when she or he is our fundamental means of access to the tale and its emotions, may seem something like the speaker of a poem like Gray's "Eton College" ode, separate from but implicated by the space of sympathetic imagination. But the novel's editor persona functions almost explicitly in service of chiasmus, moving us toward the

space of sympathy. The editor orchestrates a scene that is depicted as if it were independent of him (rarely her); the claims to truth that the editor makes place him at the margins of a fictional universe where both reality and the imagination lend him substance. He is the point through which experience appears as fiction. If editors disappear or are marked over by the stories they tell, readers usually feel no loss, because they are a part of the machinery that produces experience. They become functionally equivalent to other formal aspects of representation such as dates and times. This is not to say they are inherently without personality (Fielding's, Defoe's, and Richardson's personae certainly are peculiar), but rather that they provide a framework of vision that renders them a part of, as Baudry might argue, the apparatus. The speaker of the "Eton" ode, by contrast, makes no claims to truth, and as such, he is fragmented by the pressures of fiction: a paradox that should begin to make sense by now.

32. The moments of chiasmus that the editor-narrator figure creates usually come very early on. For example, even more than with his prefaces, Fielding effects chiasmus (characteristically, with tongue in cheek) in book 1, chapter 4, when he describes the land around Paradise Hall: "Reader, take care, I have unadvisedly led thee to the top of as high a hill as Mr. Allworthy's, and how to get thee down without breaking thy neck, I do not well know" (31). Fielding reminds us that just because we can "map" the fictional world enough to enter it does not mean we know it, that it is entirely transparent to us.

33. See, most explicitly, book 8, chapter 1, of *Tom Jones:* "For tho' every good author will confine himself within the bounds of probability, it is by no means necessary that his characters, or his incidents, should be trite, common, or vulgar. . . . Nor must he be inhibited from shewing many persons and things, which may possibly have never fallen within the knowledge of great part of his readers. If the writer strictly observes the rules above-mentioned, he has discharged his part; and is then intitled to some faith from his reader, who is indeed guilty of critical infidelity if he disbelieves him" (329). This contractual ideal of representation is eminently neoclassical in Richard Kroll's terms: "If neoclassical texts . . . habitually reveal and examine the terms under which they construct themselves, perhaps their most distinctive device is to allude to and dramatize the reader's necessarily contingent activity when faced with the text. . . . The topos serves directly to reiterate those distinctions among constituent textual elements, features, or signs, which only the reader's judgment and sagacity can provisionally reassemble and articulate." *The Material Word: Literate Culture in the Restoration and Early Eighteenth Century* (Baltimore: Johns Hopkins University Press, 1991), 53. Kroll is not making this argument about novels in particular but about a range of contemporary writing. If, however, we apply the idea to the novel, we may put the convenient example of *Tristram Shandy* as resistant work against this scheme and notice the congruity.

34. The ellipsis in this quote removes the phrase "projective identification." The idea of chiasmus I am pursuing involves something like identification, but I do not use this word because I wish to avoid the idea of putting oneself in the place of a character—I think this is *not* what is happening. Rather, chiasmus suggests points of contact, rather than the taking on of a temporary identity. We move in the fictional world while rooted at the same time in our own.

35. Epithalamia have also been written in prose, as Virginia Tufte points out in *The Poetry of Marriage: The Epithalamium in Europe and Its Development in England* (Los Angeles: Tinnon-Brown, 1970).

36. Samuel Richardson, *Sir Charles Grandison*, 3 vols., ed. Jocelyn Harris (New York: Oxford University Press, 1972), 3:220–21.

37. Heather Dubrow, *A Happier Eden: The Politics of Marriage in the Stuart Epithalamium* (Ithaca: Cornell University Press, 1990).

38. While in Richardson's view Harriet's bashfulness is an added beauty, it produces underlying discord. The fact that Harriet's "heart misgives her" (3:219) is related to the story of Clementina—the Italian woman whom Sir Charles first loved, but from whom he was divided by religious scruples. Their failed romance is mirrored and evoked by Emily's thwarted affection for her guardian, Sir Charles; she attends the wedding with her "heart . . . very heavy" and speaks sorrowfully of poor Clementina (3:234).

39. Susan Lamb, in a paper delivered at a NEASECS conference at Williams College (September 20, 1998), argues convincingly that *Grandison* is also very much concerned with national unification. Sir Charles's marriage with Harriet reflects the concerns, after the 1745 Jacobite rebellion, with the integration of the warring parties in Hanoverian Britain (Sir Charles's father is coded as a Jacobite).

40. Based on the division of the letter into four dated sections, there is another connection with epithalamia. Richardson moves from the call to awakening to the epideictic topoi traditionally part of an epithalamium when Mr. B. pays Pamela a morning visit. Mr. B. praises his bride: "I am not now so much the admirer of your beauty, all charming as you are, as of your virtue. My love therefore must increase, even should this perishable beauty fail, as the station of life you are now entering upon, will afford you augmented opportunities to display your virtue!" (372). Pamela also gives her share of praise, twice including encomia based on the fundamental equality of herself and her groom; this is in line with an epithalamium like Donne's "Eclogue," where one section is devoted to the "Equality of Persons." What is significant is not that such words are implausible without taking into account poetic traditions; it is the order of the words and moments that is most intriguing. The first stanzas of epithalamia usually begin with the break of day, and it is there that Scaliger and others locate the appropriate position for praise of both celebrants; the first division of Pamela's letter groups events in the same way. The other three divisions of the letter suggest that their

patterning and closure have formal import: the last two in particular close with a structural device inherited from the poetic tradition. Cf. the praise of bride and groom to Mary Masters's "On Miranda's Marriage," in *Poems on Several Occasions* (London, 1733).

41. Sheppard explicitly places the epithalamium as tribute to "the affection [he bears] to [the] memories" of his hero and heroine (*The Loves of Amandus and Sophronia* [London, 1650], 140); Richardson's use of the epithalamium suggests a similar kind of tribute to Pamela's worthiness. Richardson tends to use lyric conventions to emphasize Pamela's right to or fitness for her new state in high life, as we will see shortly.

Chapter 5. The Limits of Lyric and the Space of the Novel

1. Henry Fielding, *Tom Jones* (New York: Penguin Books, 1966), 121.

2. There are two other quotations, both from lyrics: Donne's "Second Anniversarie" (elegy being the twin of epithalamium in terms of their mutual reliance on social events that mark changes in state, but also because elegies often use epithalamial conventions to speak of death) and Horace's Ode i.xix, on the charms of Glycera (a woman, like Sophia, who has a comely forwardness).

3. The poem is truly charming — for those unfamiliar with it, here are two stanzas, one of description:

> Her feet beneath her Petticoat
> Like little mice stole in and out,
>   As if they fear'd the light;
> But oh! she dances such a way,
> No Sun upon an Easter day
>   Is half so fine a sight. (ll. 43–48)

And one showing the moments just after retirement:

> When in he came (*Dick*) there she lay
> Like new-faln snow melting away,
>   ('Twas time I trow to part);
> Kisses were now the onely stay,
> Which soon she gave, as who would say,
>   God b'w'y'! with all my heart. (ll. 115–20)

The Works of Sir John Suckling, vol. 1, *The Non-Dramatic Works*, ed. Thomas Clayton (Oxford: Clarendon Press, 1971), 79–84.

4. In *A Natural Passion*, Margaret Doody relates this scene to the ballad-opera tradition, with its "cue for a song" (62). She also argues, rightly, that poetry here signals a class allegiance and the perfection of romantic love: "Once [the] hero and heroine are placed in the correct relationship, the traditional language of love is appropriate" (62). The novel, for her, registers

a shift in language "at its half-way mark. Richardson strives for a more 'poetic' rendering of love and fulfillment. He deliberately invokes poetry. . . . Richardson is concerned to show, not only that Pamela is equal to the life of the drawing-room, but also that the love between Mr. B. and Pamela is truly romantic" (61).

5. The use of lyric as a means of amorous rapprochement is common. There is a parallel instance in Congreve's 1691 *Incognita*, in *The Complete Works of William Congreve*, ed. Montague Summers (London: Nonesuch, 1923), 1:107–53, where a lover overhears a maiden singing of her griefs and realizes he is her beloved (148–49). In Charlotte Lennox's first published novel, *The Life of Harriot Stuart, Written by Herself* (1750), ed. Susan Kubica Howard (Madison, N.J.: Fairleigh Dickinson University Press, 1995), there are several cases where the heroine's skill at poetic composition convinces men of her feeling heart (69–70, 129, 148–49). Another similar moment occurs in Elizabeth Griffith's *Delicate Distress* (1769), ed. Cynthia Booth Ricciardi and Susan Staves (Lexington: University Press of Kentucky, 1997), when the heroine's husband reveals, unwittingly, his love for another woman by way of a song (64). This is the inverse of the moments above; the soliloquy-like use of lyric in Griffith points toward a dramatic use.

6. Summers, *Complete Works of Congreve*, 1:26.

7. Jean Hagstrum, *The Sister Arts: The Tradition of Literary Pictorialism and English Poetry from Dryden to Gray* (Chicago: University of Chicago Press, 1958), 31, 34.

8. Brian Vickers, *Classical Rhetoric in English Poetry* (Carbondale: Southern Illinois University Press, 1989), 36.

9. Literary prose has close historical relations to poetry. Marbury Bladen Ogle, in "Some Aspects of Medieval Latin Style," *Speculum* 1 (1926), writes: "Since . . . poetry was to such a large extent the subject of study, the language not only of school exercise but of prose generally tended more and more to become poetic; ordinary language was tabooed, and its place was taken by a prose which was adorned with all the artifices of poetry. And not only was the style of prose made poetic, but the matter which in the best period had belonged to the province of poetry, found treatment in prose, especially descriptions — descriptions of objects of nature, objects of art, . . . and panegyrics of great men and praises of their deeds" (175–76). Quoted in Wlad Godzich and Jeffrey Kittay, *The Emergence of Prose: An Essay in Prosaics* (Minneapolis: University of Minnesota Press, 1987), 146.

10. Thomas Sprat, *History of the Royal Society* (1667), ed. Jackson I. Cope and Harold Whitmore Jacobs (St. Louis, Mo.: Washington University Press, 1958), 112.

11. On the discursive mists and uncertainties of the Royal Society themselves, see Michael McKeon, *The Origins of the English Novel, 1600–1740* (Baltimore: Johns Hopkins University Press, 1987), 68–73.

12. For the connection between the Royal Society and the novel, most famously, see Ian Watt, *The Rise of the Novel* (Berkeley: University of California Press, 1957). Revisionist accounts of the influence and meaning of the Royal Society's take on rhetoric can be found in Richard Kroll's *Material Word: Literate Culture in the Restoration and Early Eighteenth Century* (Baltimore: Johns Hopkins University Press, 1991) and Vickers's "English Royal Society and English Prose Style: A Reassessment," in *Rhetoric and the Pursuit of Truth: Language Change in the Seventeenth and Eighteenth Centuries*, ed. Brian Vickers and Nancy S. Streuver (Los Angeles: William Andrews Clark Memorial Library, 1985), 3–76. For a nuanced analysis of religious "plain style," see N. H. Keeble, *The Literary Culture of Nonconformity in Later Seventeenth-Century England* (Athens: University of Georgia Press, 1987), 240 ff.; he argues that plainness has as much or more to do with meaning than with style.

13. See Alistair Fowler, *Kinds of Literature: An Introduction to the Theory of Genres and Modes* (Oxford: Clarendon Press, 1982): "Almost any feature . . . can become genre-linked and belong more or less regularly to a kind's repertoire. This applies equally to what used to be called content, as opposed to form. Images, motifs, and tropes in the stratum of represented objects all form a part of a repertoire. And, conversely, a work's genre can affect its constituents' stratification. Thus graphemes may have quite different functions in concrete poems and in elegies, and images of the seasons are significant at different levels in georgics, haiku, and Romantic odes" (58).

14. *The Works of Thomas Gray*, ed. Edmund Gosse (London: Macmillan, 1903), 2:108, quoted in John Guillory, *Cultural Capital: The Problem of Literary Canon Formation* (Chicago: University of Chicago Press, 1993), 120.

15. Cf. Cleanth Brooks in *The Well Wrought Urn* (London: Dennis Dobson, 1968): "The 'Elegy' is a tissue of allusions, and half-allusions. If the materials of which it is composed are 'poetic,' they have been made poetic by other poets" (86).

16. Donald Davie, *Purity of Diction in English Verse* (London: Routledge and Kegan Paul, 1967).

17. Compared to Mr. B's use of amorous lyric, Harriot's is inflected by the gender concerns that face women's use of similar language. A collection of love lyrics, *The Cupid. A Collection of* LOVE SONGS, *In Twelve Parts. Suited To Twelve Different Sorts Of Lovers, Viz. The Female Lover, The Admiring Lover, The Slighted Lover, The Modest Lover, The Constant Lover, The Jealous Lover, The Tender Lover, The Whining Lover, The Saucy Lover, The Merry Lover, The Pressing Lover, The Happy Lover* (London, 1739), reprints, anonymously, poems by both well-known (like Suckling) and unknown authors. Of the twelve divisions, "The Female Lover" shows women overwhelmingly speaking powerful passions and engaging in illicit sex (which they come to regret when their lovers, inevitably, leave them).

18. Frances Brooke, *Lady Julia Mandeville* (London: Scholartis Press, 1930), 65.

19. Margaret Doody, *The Daring Muse: Augustan Poetry Reconsidered* (Cambridge: Cambridge University Press, 1985), 199–200.

20. Donald Davie argues that some of the best poetry from 1750 or so on shares this prosaic flavor: it "has the virtues of good prose and yet is good poetry. I shall think that [such poems] have the virtue of prose if I can establish that their diction is chaste; and I shall think them good poetry if they have the metaphorical richness and force we associate with poetry of quite another source" (*Purity of Diction*, 28).

21. See the second half of Deirdre Lynch's *Economy of Character: Novels, Market Culture, and the Business of Inner Meaning* (Chicago: University of Chicago Press, 1998) for a more extraliterary account of character and taste. See also Jay Clayton, *Romantic Vision and the Novel* (Cambridge: Cambridge University Press, 1987): "Narrative . . . was an ethical form . . . because it was 'impure', it had the capacity to reflect . . . the conflictual, heterogeneous, and dialogical position of an individual in the social order" (104).

22. E. Phillips Poole, in his introduction to *Lady Julia Mandeville*, writes, "Mrs. Brooke's ability as a lyric poet is illustrated, apart from the songs in her two operettas, by the fragments included in her volume of 1756, and by some verses on the death of Mrs. Yates that appeared in the *Gentleman's Magazine*. At her best she attains a certain facile tunefulness reminiscent of the songs of Dryden: seldom is there anything to hold the attention of the reader, and on the whole she must be pronounced a versifier in no way distinguished from the herd of those who adorned the pages of eighteenth-century periodical literature" (25–26).

23. Ian Watt links Lovelace to "the Cavalier attitude to sex" in *Rise of the Novel* (227).

24. Spenser's "Lacking my love, I go from place to place," from *Amoretti* (1595), rewrites a moment from the Song of Songs. Note the attention to place and the absent image (literalized in Richardson's mirror):

> And seek eachwhere, where last I saw her face,
> Whose image yet I carry fresh in mind.
>
> Yet nor in field nor bower I her can find,
> Yet field and bower are full of her aspect.
>
> Cease then, mine eyes, to seek herself to see;
> And let my thoughts behold herself in me.

Richardson's rake does not experience the resignation of Spenser's final couplet, but Lovelace does rely on visions of the past as he raves. See also an eighteenth-century version of this kind of poem (post-*Clarissa*), Aaron Hill's "Whitehall Stairs" (1753).

25. The palm image also appears in a fourth-century epithalamium by Claudian, "Honorious et Maria."

26. This is one of many elements in *Clarissa* of the anti-epithalamium: "Instead of expressing joy over a proper union, the anti-epithalamium expresses lamentation or foreboding over a union which for some reason is improper or unsanctioned, and thus presages tragedy, death, dissension, revenge, murder, war, or other disruptions of order and nature. . . . In addition, pastoral funeral elegy also occasionally associates epithalamic devices with death, but the epithalamium here usually symbolizes triumph over death by means of rebirth in nature or mystical union in heaven. However, elegies use both normal and negative epithalamic imagery." Virginia Tufte, *The Poetry of Marriage: The Epithalamium in Europe and Its Development in England* (Los Angeles: Tinnon-Brown, 1970), 38. This is true in Clarissa's self-elegy, where Lovelace describes Clarissa as a "half-broken stalked lily." That misuse of emblem can be read as symbolic of Clarissa's false marriage (to Lovelace) and her true one (to God); Sappho's image of the bride as a 'trampled flower whose crumpled beauty adorns the earth" would become highly popular with later writers of marriage poetry (12). The use of epithalamia to describe the marriage of women/virgins to Christ has roots in England stretching to the medieval period; readings of the Song of Songs as an allegory of the marriage of Christ and the Church remain current today.

27. On Lovelace's manipulation of language see Murray L. Brown, "*Emblemata Rhetorica:* Glossing Emblematic Discourse in Richardson's *Clarissa,*" *Studies in the Novel* 27, no. 4 (1995): 455–76; on his insistence on returning comedy to Clarissa's tragedy, see Doody, *Natural Passion,* 114–15. Doody argues that Lovelace violates the rules and limits placed on comic rakes and steps into the world of tragedy, and although he should know what lies at the end of that road (death), he constantly fools himself into believing he has the power to switch genres at will, to enter the world of comedy, with its reformed rakes and happy marriages.

28. Cf. the fire scene (L 228, 740–41) with Sidney's "Have I caught my heavenly jewel":

> Have I caught my heavenly jewel
> Teaching sleep most fair to be?
> Now will I teach her that she,
> When she wakes is too too cruel. (ll. 1–4)
>
> Her tongue waking still refuseth,
> Giving frankly niggard 'no'
> Now will I attempt to know
> What 'no' her tongue sleeping useth.
>
> See, the hand, which, waking, guardeth,
> Sleeping, grants a free resort;

Now will I invade the fort;
Cowards Love with loss rewardeth. (ll. 9–16)

O sweet kiss — but ah, she is waking,
Louring beauty chastens me;
Now will I away hence flee;
Fool, more fool, for no more taking. (ll. 25–28)

29. Doody also argues that Clarissa's ultimate transcendence "is foreign to the heroines of the tragic dramas" (*Natural Passion*, 122).

30. One text useful in exploring an answer would be *Tristram Shandy* — a novel that takes the questions of genre to be those of an ethics of imagination and judgment and that refuses, with a vengeance, closure as the limit of the self. *Tristram*, however, would take us down diversionary paths; I keep him here as an important digression. I return, with a flourish of my cane, to Brooke.

31. Cf. the letter Lady Woodville sends to her sister immediately following the passages above:

> Fanny Weston is *à la mort*, at Sir James Thornton's quitting us. That love is the cause of her mourning, I well know, but I begin now to apprehend that Sir James, and not lord Seymour, is the object of her passion. She has a much better chance, in this case, than the other, for I am persuaded if Thornton knew of her affection for him, he would endeavour to make her happy.
>
> Alas! If he loves another, how impossible! I fancy he is enamoured, of one of the miss Withers's. — His fortune and family are such, that I do not believe he would be rejected; yet I could not wish him success, for poor Fanny Weston's sake.
>
> Men more easily triumph over an unhappy passion, than women. Dissipation, change of place, and objects, all contribute to their cure; while perhaps the poor sighing fair one is absolutely confined to the same spot, where she first beheld her charmer, and where every object reminds her, that here he sat, and walked, or talked.
>
> I am persuaded there is a great deal more in these local memento's, than lovers are willing to allow. I therefore shall not oppose Fanny Weston's going to London, if she should again propose it. (143–44)

Even though this letter revisits some of the same matter, its style is different. The pastoral fair one remains, the resonance with Lady Woodville's own despair producing elaborate language, but overall, the relative absence of intense personal emotion gives a different texture to the prose and draws Griffith away from lyric expressions.

32. I cannot resist mentioning a Blakean prolepsis in Griffith's *Delicate*

Distress: "Is it not strange, that nature should vary, so much, in the human genus, as to create a Lucy Straffon, and a Mary Fanning? . . . The animal creation do not differ thus, from their own species. . . . Hapless variety! Sad source of misery! the tiger, and the lamb, are not less similar, than the betrayer, and the betrayed — yet both wear the same form, and only by experience, is the difference found. — Nay, sometimes, we have seen the fairest face conceal the vilest heart; as lurks the serpent, underneath the rose" (165).

33. The pastiche of bad novels in Charlotte Smith's *Desmond* (1792) is instructive as well: " 'the beautiful, the soft, the tender Iphigenia closed not, during the tedious hours, her beauteous eyes, while the glorious flambeau of silver-slippered day sunk beneath the incrimsoned couch of coral-crowned Thetis, giving up the dormant world to the raven-embrace of all-o'er clouding night.' " Janet Todd and Antje Blank, eds., *Desmond* (London: Pickering and Chatto, 1997), 199. The faults of this passage are the faults of Dunces, updated for the close of the century: incoherence, the indiscriminate use of imagery, fine-sounding contradiction, etc. — all in lightness, though, not dark. These are all to say that the faults of bad description in the novel are those of bad poetry.

34. Tobias Smollett, *Peregrine Pickle*, ed. James L. Clifford (New York: Oxford University Press, 1964), 12. Elizabeth Kraft points out Smollett's use of lyric in *Character and Consciousness in Eighteenth-Century Comic Fiction* (Athens: University of Georgia Press, 1992): "Smollett understood the novel's propensity to occupy the consciousness of the reader, and to fully exploit that propensity, he realized, the novelist must be prepared to acknowledge the other things that occupy that consciousness. Those things, of course, are innumerable, and so the individual consciousness always remains to an extent separate from the communal concerns. However, there is, occasionally, fusion, and that fusion produces the lyric moment of shared consciousness. Such is the moment documented by *Peregrine Pickle*" (136).

35. Cf. Lynch, *Economy of Character.* Lynch argues that early novels do not rely on "round" characters so much as on an economy of description. See also n. 11, Ch. 4.

36. Daniel Defoe, *Roxana, or The Fortunate Mistress,* ed. Jane Jack (Oxford: Oxford University Press, 1964), 277.

37. See William Warner, *Licensing Entertainment: The Elevation of Novel Reading in Britain, 1684–1750* (Berkeley: University of California Press, 1998), 118 ff.

38. John Cleland, *Fanny Hill, or Memoirs of a Woman of Pleasure* (London: Penguin Books, 1985), 75.

39. One might read the politics of this move through Nancy Armstrong's *Desire and Domestic Fiction: A Political History of the Novel* (New York: Oxford University Press, 1987): Femininity *is* bourgeois interiority.

40. Eliza Haywood, *The History of Miss Betsy Thoughtless* (New York: Oxford University Press, 2000), 194–95, 206–7.

41. See, for example, Trueworth imagining Miss Betsy to be free with her favors (210) or Miss Betsy receiving Trueworth's letter of departure and, like Lizzie Bennet after her, undergoing shades of response from anger to extreme, consciousness-giving shame (248–49).

42. Warner, *Licensing Entertainment*, ch. 5.

43. Frances Burney, *Cecilia* (1782), ed. Margaret Anne Doody and Peter Sabor (New York: Oxford University Press, 1988), 5.

44. Lynch, *Economy of Character*, 167 ff., on the ethical significance of reading characters.

45. On the importance of the period from the 1770s on in the novel's history, see, for example, Lynch, *Economy of Character*; Clifford Siskin, "Eighteenth-Century Periodicals and the Romantic Rise of the Novel," *Studies in the Novel* 26, nos. 1–2 (1994): 26–42, and J. A. Downie, "Mary Davys's 'Probable Feign'd Stories' and Critical Shibboleths about 'The Rise of the Novel,'" *Eighteenth-Century Fiction* 12, nos. 2–3 (2000): 324. Siskin summarizes the facts thus: "From an annual rate of only about four to twenty new titles through the first four decades, and remaining—despite Fielding's and Richardson's popularity—within a range of roughly twenty to forty for the next three, new novel production peaked briefly near sixty in 1770 before a steep decline to well below forty during the latter half of that decade. Within the next seven years, however, the output jumped—more than doubled—to close to ninety, and to increase sharply into the next century" (26).

46. Charlotte Smith, *Ethelinde, or the Recluse of the Lake*, 5 vols. (London, 1790), 3:35.

47. Cf. Doody's account of ekphrasis in *The True Story of the Novel* (New Brunswick, N.J.: Rutgers University Press, 1996), chs. 17 and 18. She emphasizes the importance of a reader's or character's interpretation of these rhetorical episodes.

48. Smith, *Desmond*, 81.

49. Compare also the rising moon with that in "Strange Fits of Passion" and the focus on minute motions of trees with Coleridge's "This Lime-Tree Bower My Prison," or the precedent section from *The Task*, book 1, ll. 338–49.

50. Lynch thinks of such attention to objects and landscapes as typical of "romantic-period characters"; it is used "to suggest an inner consciousness that seems to exist independent of exchange relations" (*Economy of Character*, 118). Depth is recognized through connoisseurship or skilled reading. This attention to objects and to space is indeed a component of the emerging consumer culture, but it is also a trope with an extensive precapitalist history in poetry and prose, as we may recall from the charged landscapes of Spenser or Haywood's *Love in Excess* (see Ch. 2). See Lynch, "Personal Effects and Sentimental Fictions," *Eighteenth-Century Fiction*, 12, nos. 2–3 (2000): 345–68, for an examination of keepsakes and other possessions as emotional foci

at midcentury and beyond. The general technique is of great importance in, for example, Sophia Lee's *Recess* (1783–85), where the descriptive skill with which Matilda renders her friend's wet white dress floating in the breeze creates a powerful emotional moment (Lexington: University Press of Kentucky, 2000), 134.

51. Charlotte Smith, *Emmeline* (London: Pandora Press, 1987), 291, 472.

52. Walter Francis Wright also connects Smith's poetry to the pattern of fragmented descriptive passages in her novels. *Sensibility in English Prose Fiction, 1670–1814: A Reinterpretation* (Urbana: University of Illinois Press, 1937), 69.

53. "To the South Downs," ll. 1–4, in *The Poems of Charlotte Smith*, ed. Stuart Curran (New York: Oxford University Press, 1993), 15.

54. Smith's sonnets offer serial repetition of a state of loss; her novels similarly function through deferral. The hero and heroine typically meet and fall in love early on, and the bulk of the novel chronicles events that impede their marriage. Because the future is uncertain and the present involves frustration, memory is paramount—scenes of contemplation and remembered joy are the primary emotional markers, and it is in these moments that landscape description as well as lyric insertions appear. The context of emotional intensity is the blockage of resolution and plot. Cf. Curran and Zimmerman on Smith's sonnets and prefaces as serial.

55. The use of landscape in poetry of the early nineteenth century has strong roots in the Gothic novels of the later eighteenth, like those of Radcliffe. The protagonists of Gothic and sensibility are avatars of a mode of feeling that romantic poets would deliberately come to imitate. On the relationship of the Gothic to the romantic, see Robert Kiely, *The Romantic Novel in England* (Cambridge: Harvard University Press, 1972). Kiely argues for the poetic characteristics of Gothic, though at the expense of earlier novels; John Dixon Hunt, in *The Figure in the Landscape: Poetry, Painting, and Gardening during the Eighteenth Century* (Baltimore: Johns Hopkins University Press, 1976), argues for a parallel between late-century poetry and Gothic prose fiction as well (185). See also Wright, *English Prose Fiction*, A. D. Harvey, *English Prose in a Changing Society* (London: Allison and Busby, 1980), and Marilyn Gaull, *English Romanticism: The Human Context* (New York: Norton, 1988). These accounts focus on the interaction of novel and poetry in a chain from Thomson/Collins/Gray to Gothic and then the romantics. Gothic is often seen as the weak link and its debts greater than its contributions (with the exception of *Otranto*).

56. Cf. the moment in Ann Radcliffe's *Romance of the Forest* when La Motte, preparing to perpetrate violence against the heroine, is stopped by the sound of "her sing[ing] in her sleep. . . . The low and mournful accent . . . expressed too well the tone of her mind" (New York: Oxford University

Press, 1986), 230. There, the unimaginative villain needs the help of lyric to see within the soul. There is no simple developmental story going on here — lyric may be germane to novelistic concerns but it is so in varying degrees in different works written at the same time.

57. Cf. Dorrit Cohn, *Transparent Minds: Narrative Modes for Presenting Consciousness in Fiction* (Princeton: Princeton University Press, 1978). I owe a great deal to this stunning work. My project, and in particular the last part of this chapter, is in some ways an attempt to specify, for one country and one period, the way in which mental "transparency" is a concept nurtured by generic interactions.

58. Gérard Strauch, "Dialogue intérieur et style indirect libre dans *Grace Abounding*," *Bulletin de la Société de Stylistique Anglaise* 2 (1980): 33–48.

59. Gérard Strauch, "Richardson et le style indirect libre," *Recherches Anglaises et Nord-Americaines* 26 (1993): 87–101; Anne Waldron Neumann, "Free Indirect Discourse in the Eighteenth-Century English Novel: Speakable or Unspeakable? The Example of *Sir Charles Grandison*," in *Language, Text, and Context: Essays in Stylistics*, ed. Michael Toolan (London: Routledge, 1992), 113–35; John Dussinger, " 'The Language of Real Feeling': Internal Speech in the Jane Austen Novel," in *The Idea of the Novel in the Eighteenth Century*, ed. Robert W. Uphaus (East Lansing, Mich.: Colleagues Press, 1985), 97–115. Margaret Doody finds something approaching free indirect discourse in some Restoration ballads and calls this version of the "technique 'ventriloquism'; the voice of the 'real' speaker (speaking for the poet, and his audience) is momentarily cast into the personification of the Opposite or Other; a dummy or puppet-speaker is given a strange voice" (*Daring Muse*, 44). Strauch estimates that in *Clarissa*, the most intensely interior of all Richardson's novels, 82 percent of the pages involve free indirect discourse. Figures for *Pamela* and *Sir Charles Grandison* are 38 and 46 percent, respectively.

60. Ira Konigsberg, *Narrative Technique in the English Novel: Defoe to Austen* (Hamden, Conn.: Archon Books, 1985), 7.

61. Frances Brooke, *The Excursion*, ed. Paula Backscheider and Hope D. Cotton (Lexington: University Press of Kentucky, 1997), 26.

Chapter 6. The Novel and the New Lyricism

1. Subjectivity here is at base an analytical construct — it indicates a set of frameworks for understanding the relationship of a human being to those things that define the possibilities of experience. It is the name for several (sometimes contradictory) groupings, descriptions, even proscriptions for the self and its surroundings. As such, subjectivity has no proper synonym; "consciousness" and "interiority" are the ones I use, but such change of terms indicates the slant of my approach. Subjectivity as an analytical category, however, goes beyond the phenomenal experience of self, and it includes a range of things it will always surpass — from questions of class to

concepts of identity. Subjectivity links multiple ways of defining the self: it is not necessarily individualistic, but it may be; it is not necessarily communitarian, conservative, or liberal, Cartesian, Kantian, or Hegelian, but it may be any of these.

2. Andrea K. Henderson looks at the multiplicity of romantic models of identity in literary and nonliterary genres in *Romantic Identities: Varieties of Subjectivity* (Cambridge: Cambridge University Press, 1996). Her study is a needed corrective to the tendency to assume that the Wordsworthian self is the only romantic model there is. The book ranges from medical literature and concepts of maternity to drama, narrative, and lyric in the Shelleys, and to questions of revolution in *The Borderers*. As I state above, however, identity and subjectivity are not congruent, and blurring the two may create the danger of category mistakes. In focusing on literary models of subjectivity as they are influenced by genre, I hope to adhere to an ideal of specificity and to avoid bleeding over into adjacent cultural space as much as possible. I focus thus not because I think the larger cultural space is unimportant: influences beyond the "purely" literary contribute to and even largely define literary models of subjectivity. Work that identifies those relations and describes and analyzes them is indispensable; my work casts its net over a smaller beast. I am indebted to Kevin Gilmartin for referring me to Henderson's work.

3. This project may be profitably understood in conjunction with other recent work on understanding the history of the romantic period as a key moment in the history of canon formation. Anne Janowitz, for example, in *Lyric and Labor in the Romantic Tradition* (Cambridge: Cambridge University Press, 1998), has emphasized the presence of a collectivist lyric voice that competes with that of the more egotistical sublime; recent work in the history of the novel (William Warner, *Licensing Entertainment: The Elevation of Novel Reading in Britain, 1684–1750* [Berkeley: University of California Press, 1998], Deirdre Lynch, *The Economy of Character: Novels, Market Culture, and the Business of Inner Meaning* [Chicago: University of Chicago Press, 1998], Clifford Siskin, "Eighteenth-Century Periodicals and the Romantic Rise of the Novel," *Studies in the Novel* 26, nos. 1–2 (1994): 26–42, and others) increasingly identifies the romantic period as that in which the novelistic canon is defined, and so forth. I believe it extremely important to think about genre as it is constructed through a plurality of genres and the relationships and competitions among them.

4. 1802 Preface, in *Wordsworth: Poetical Works*, ed. Thomas Hutchinson, rev. Ernest de Selincourt (Oxford: Oxford University Press, 1936), 735.

5. Gene W. Ruoff explicitly connects Wordsworth's strictures on natural language to the novel in "1800 and the Future of the Novel: William Wordsworth, Maria Edgeworth, and the Vagaries of Literary History," in *The Age of William Wordsworth*, ed. Kenneth R. Johnston and Gene W. Ruoff (New Brunswick, N.J.: Rutgers University Press, 1987), 291–314. Ruoff links the

natural language of man and the focus on "low" subjects to the use of dialect in novels, especially in Edgeworth's groundbreaking *Castle Rackrent,* published the same year as the first Preface. As will become apparent, the germ of Wordsworth's shift to lived experience is in the novel; not only because of his chosen objects of representation (especially the domestic) but also because of how those objects are represented (the natural language of men and novelistic plain style).

6. The claim that poetry is identifiable as a kind of fiction can be traced also to Sidney's *Defense of Poesy* (1595), but before this, to Quintilian, Cicero, and Aristotle. Lowth and his contemporaries are important because they focus on prosodic aspects of this question (see Ch. 1, above). Cf. Hugh Blair in *Lectures on Rhetoric and Belles Lettres* (1783), ed. Harold F. Harding (Carbondale: Southern Illinois University Press, 1965): "There is also a species of Prose, so measured in its cadence, and so much raised in its tone, as to approach very near to Poetical Numbers. . . . The truth is, Verse and Prose, in some occasions, run into one another" (2:313).

7. James Macpherson, *The Poems of Ossian and Related Works*, ed. Howard Gaskill (Edinburgh: Edinburgh University Press, 1996), 6.

8. See W. J. B. Owen, *Wordsworth As Critic* (Toronto: University of Toronto Press, 1969), 118.

9. In the essay, in addition to Ossian, novelists like Cervantes and Sterne are cited as writers of poetic prose (455). The anonymous author adduces a list of earlier critics who fall on his side of the question, rebuts those whose positions do not agree, and argues that based on criteria of mimesis, imaginative facility, pleasurableness, and sensibility, a novel or comedy is as poetic as an epic.

10. Jay Clayton, *Romantic Vision and the Novel* (Cambridge: Cambridge University Press, 1987), 39.

11. *Biographia Literaria*, ed. James Engell and W. J. Bate (Princeton: Princeton University Press, 1983), 2:15 (ch. 14). For the Warton, see the Introduction, above.

12. In *Forming the Critical Mind* (Cambridge: Harvard University Press, 1989), James Engell points out the complicated nature of the prose-poetry distinction: "The fact that Johnson . . . refuses to define poetry says a good deal about the metamorphoses in ideas of poetry at large" (228). In trying to define the poetic, given these odds, poets have recourse to language and structure: "The only way to account for an essential commonality of specific words in both poetry and prose, yet a disjunction in paths to knowledge expressed through different species of composition, requires elevating combinations of words to a new level of importance, seeing figuration as no longer an ornament or embellishment of meaning and knowledge. What is being newly emphasized is not poetic language considered as isolated words, but as special structure of words embodying a distilled, heightened form of

awareness" (222). Poetry becomes a special kind of perception given special verbal form. This does not exclude passages from novels.

13. William Hazlitt, "Lectures on the English Poets," in *The Complete Works of William Hazlitt*, ed. P. P. Howe (London: J. M. Dent, 1933), 5:14.

14. Clayton notes, "In the course of making his argument 'that *passions are more poetical* than *manners*,' Bowles turns to the example of Richardson" (*Romantic Vision*, 40). The text under consideration is Bowles's *Letters to Lord Byron on a Question of Poetical Criticism*. The counterpart to Richardson's partial and conditional elevation is Pope's extraordinary devaluation; the context of Bowles's statement is a debate over Pope's right to be called a poet.

15. As Mark Kinkead-Weekes points out, "Blake said Richardson 'won his heart,'" according to Geoffrey Keynes, *A Bibliography of William Blake* (New York, 1921), 64. Kinkead-Weekes, *Samuel Richardson: Dramatic Novelist* (Ithaca: Cornell University Press, 1973), 237 n. 1. Kinkead-Weekes writes that he "used to read" Clarissa's descriptions of violated sexuality after her rape as a source of Blake's poem from *Songs of Experience*, "The Sick Rose," but that he gives this up as "both superficial and significantly mistaken" (237). I think such a connection is neither superficial nor mistaken. Clayton notes, "The parts of *Clarissa* that, for Romantic readers, might have qualified Richardson for a place on the slopes of Parnassus are the very scenes that modern readers often find the most tedious: the heroine's suffering and transfiguration in the last third of the novel" (*Romantic Vision*, 39). My approach differs significantly from Clayton's in that he focuses on character, not style, language, or structure: "In particular, *Clarissa* anticipates the Romantic problem of how to accommodate a transcendent dimension of character within the formal conditions of narrative" (27–28).

16. Hazlitt's evident love for Richardson's novels makes him uneasy; or so I interpret the mixture of adoration and asperity in his comments. See especially the description of the erotic qualities of his response: "I admire the Clementinas and Clarissas at a distance: the Pamelas and Fannys [*Joseph Andrews*] of Richardson and Fielding make my blood tingle. I have written love-letters to such in my time, *d'un pathetique à faire fendre les rochers*" ("Table Talk: On Great and Little Things," in *Complete Works*, 8:236).

17. Ian Watt, *The Rise of the Novel* (Berkeley: University of California Press, 1957), 191–92.

18. On the *locus amoenus*, see Ernst Robert Curtius, *European Literature and the Latin Middle Ages*, trans. Willard R. Trask (Princeton: Princeton University Press, 1953), 192–200.

19. On Pope, see Maynard Mack, *The Garden and the City* (Toronto: University of Toronto Press, 1969). "Epistle to Arbuthnot" begins with a plea for enclosure—"Shut the door," but as we saw in Chapter 2, Pope is more concerned about an escape from the self than to it (an idea shocking in its Duncity), and in his self-revelation he eschews lyric expression, often

describing himself as object, not subject. Pope's is the retreat of defeat; Clarissa makes retreat a triumph.

20. Major discussions of *Clarissa* occur in the first two chapters of Frederick Garber's *Autonomy of the Self from Richardson to Huysmans* (Princeton: Princeton University Press, 1982). He begins with *Clarissa* but argues that Rousseau's *Nouvelle Héloïse* offers the major link to the romantics. *Julie* is something of a *locus classicus* for studies of the rise of romanticism. Significant readings include Paul de Man's "Intentional Structure of the Romantic Image," in *The Rhetoric of Romanticism* (New York: Columbia University Press, 1984), 1–17. Rousseau's main influence in *Julie* was *Clarissa*.

21. *Correspondence of Samuel Richardson*, ed. Anna Barbauld (London: Richard Phillips, 1804), 252–53. Garber connects this scene of "paradisal enclosure" (*Autonomy of the Self*, 7) to the romantics' bowers by way of Rousseau's *Nouvelle Héloïse*: "the enclosure of consciousness becomes the subject of one of Rousseau's ultimate ironies, a revealing twist to the consequences of the Richardsonian world. . . . The series of incarcerations in Richardson's novel become a series of asylums in Rousseau's enclosures" (26); "though Clarissa was a necessary step toward Julie, she could not show the way toward subsequent romantic developments" (30). He does not, as I will shortly, trace the particular components of Richardsonian enclosure into a generalized romantic pattern. Rousseau's *Julie* was highly important in the development of romanticism, but I do not agree that Richardson's main importance was to provide a model of enclosure that was ironized by followers. The individual components of Richardson's image of the self in retirement are not themselves new, and many, as I have shown, come from the Renaissance religious lyric. What is significant, however, are Richardson's particular configuration, the use to which it is put, his extraordinary popularity, and the consequent popularization of his model of the speaking, feeling subject.

22. Diane Long Hoeveler, *Romantic Androgyny* (University Park, Pa.: Pennsylvania State University Press, 1979), Anne Mellor, *Romanticism and Gender* (New York: Routledge, 1993), and Elizabeth Fay, *Becoming Wordsworthian* (Amherst: University of Massachusetts Press, 1995), have all argued that male romantic poets often took a position coded as feminine in their work, appropriating the traditional ground of the feminine through their focus on emotional expressiveness. I agree with this analysis in part; however, the modern gendered coding of emotion had not been completed in the late eighteenth century, and even if it had, I strongly disagree with Mellor's seeming indication that masculine appropriation is a usurpation, leaving women nowhere to run, no field of action or experience.

23. In examining the construction of personal space and isolation mediated by ideal presence, which underpins much romantic lyric, scholars have traced the influence of a variety of traditions: the "lady" who presides over

courtly lyric, the Friend who is in colloquy with Herbert, or an ideal companion and sympathizer such as Stella is to Swift. Elizabeth Fay traces Wordsworth's addresses to Dorothy to the courtly tradition in *Becoming Wordsworthian*, 9–12. Swift, of course, does not transcend enclosure, whether of the body or of the sickroom, in his poems to Stella. Joel Haefner identifies other important scenes of romantic writing in "The Romantic Scene(s) of Writing," in *Revisioning Romanticism: British Women Writers, 1776–1837*, ed. Carol Shiner Wilson and Joel Haefner (Philadelphia: University of Pennsylvania Press, 1994), 256–73: the poet's garret (taken from Chatterton), the Bluestocking salon, and the Sapphic agora. The poet's garret, the most germane site here, does not include the ideal friend or the question of domesticity. The friendship poetry of Katherine Phillips is a possible source, and the relationship of Montaigne and La Boétie is intriguing as well. In the *Essais*, Montaigne invokes his dead friend in his attempts at self-definition. Charles Taylor argues that "he attributed his undertaking the study [of himself] to the loss of his friend, La Boétie, as though it were second best: . . . 'He alone partook of my true image, and carried it off with him. That is why I so curiously decipher myself.' The self is both made and explored with words; and the best for both are the words spoken in the dialogue of friendship. In default of that, the debate with the solitary self comes limping far behind." *Sources of the Self: The Making of the Modern Identity* (Cambridge: Harvard University Press, 1989), 183. The *Nicomachean Ethics* had also proffered friendship as a way of self-knowledge (see books 8 and 9); again, the significance of Richardson's proposition comes in the preference given to imagined presence and the idealized isolation of enclosure.

24. M. H. Abrams's "Structure and Style in the Greater Romantic Lyric" can be found in *From Sensibility to Romanticism*, ed. Frederick W. Hilles and Harold Bloom (New York: Oxford University Press, 1965), 527–60. Christopher R. Miller's forthcoming book, *The Poetics of Evening*, follows this path, arguing that Wordsworth, Keats, and Coleridge stabilize their perceptual wanderings through the conventions of the evening poem.

25. Stuart Curran, *Poetic Form and British Romanticism* (New York: Oxford University Press, 1986), 111.

26. Jerome McGann, in *The Poetics of Sensibility: A Revolution in Literary Style* (Oxford: Clarendon Press, 1996), argues that the influence of St. Pierre was greater than that of Rousseau (124–25); Elizabeth Fay notes that "both William and Dorothy were much impressed by . . . Saint-Pierre's romantic idyll and that their life at Alfoxden was faithfully modeled on this French pastoral of collaborative existence" (*Becoming Wordsworthian*, 54).

27. This is partially to restate Abrams's thesis in *The Mirror and the Lamp* (New York: Oxford University Press, 1953) about the shift from mimetic to expressive theories of art. I focus on one part of that change in choosing the terms above.

28. Ann Radcliffe, *The Romance of the Forest* (New York: Oxford University Press, 1986), 35. There are several other poems, including "To the Lilly," "Night," "Song of a Spirit," "Air," "Sunrise," etc.

29. The lyric insertion, as shown in Chapter 2, has roots reaching back to the thirteenth-century romance (and beyond), but novel versions of this practice show their own development. In novels, poems shape perception by giving it a shape suitable for presentation. More broadly, poetic quotation and style usually enter the novel via a concern with perception and in particular ways: first (but not chronologically so), as chapter or volume epigraph, a practice taken from the Latin or Greek epigraph in poetry; second, as an exemplary statement of a moral sentiment or moment of wisdom (Pope is often the culprit here); third, via a move of analogy that establishes mood or moral outcome (Shakespeare is the favored referent); fourth, as an expression of emotion (as in *Love in Excess*); and fifth (perhaps a subcategory of the previous one), for indicating a change in or crystallization of the way of seeing in character or story, literally or metaphorically. This last category includes Clarissa's poignant conclusion, signing off to Anna in tears and unable to continue, with "mistiness of all the colours in the rainbow twinkling upon my deluged eye" (L 45, 205). This poetic language is distinguished from the surrounding speech by the use of metaphor, but here specifically by metaphors that indicate Clarissa's shift from reporting experience to living it; a shift from description distanced from the immediate moment and seen as such, to a moment where expression and feeling move into closer proximity, not so much temporally as linguistically (cf. Pamela's epithalamium or the letters in Smith's *Desmond*).

30. See Patricia Meyer Spacks, *Imagining a Self: Autobiography and Novel in Eighteenth-Century England* (Cambridge: Harvard University Press, 1976), for a good account of the interrelation between the novel and the autobiography in the eighteenth century. See also Felicity Nussbaum, *The Autobiographical Subject: Gender and Ideology in Eighteenth-Century England* (Baltimore: Johns Hopkins University Press, 1989).

31. See Sarah Zimmerman, "Charlotte Smith's Letters and the Practice of Self-Presentation," *Princeton University Library Chronicle*, 53, no. 1 (1991): 50–77: "By offering an account of indigence in the language of sensibility, Smith presented herself as a sympathetic figure to a public familiar with tales of women's suffering from the sentimental novels that followed the example of Samuel Richardson's *Clarissa*. In *Elegiac Sonnets*, Smith assumed a role that was already available — the heroine of sensibility — but she revitalized the story by providing her readers with details from her own life — an on-going plot. The prefaces that open most of her works become in effect, a serialized autobiographical narrative" (59–60).

32. *The Poems of Charlotte Smith*, ed. Stuart Curran (New York: Oxford University Press, 1993), 3.

33. Quoted in Janet Todd's introduction to *The Old Manor House* (London: Pandora Press, 1987), xi.

34. In "Wordsworth and Charlotte Smith," *Wordsworth Circle* 1 (1970): 85–103, Bishop Hunt states: "At some point Wordsworth no doubt saw or heard about Charlotte Smith's second novel, *Ethelinde, or the Recluse of the Lake* (1789), which centers on the family seat of 'Sir Edward' at Grasmere, and which received high praise for its description of the scenery of the lakes. . . . Certainly by 1820, and perhaps much earlier, he knew Charlotte Smith's prose well enough to refer to it casually in conversation, with an air of knowing what he was talking about" (100). Fay argues for an early acquaintance with the novels, *Ethelinde* would become an important model for what Fay terms the "Wordsworthian Life" (*Becoming Wordsworthian*, 27–30), a kind of romantic self-fashioning whereby the poet situates him- or herself in a close and sustaining relationship to a natural ground — Grasmere for both Smith and Wordsworth.

35. Paul de Man, "The Rhetoric of Temporality," in *Blindness and Insight: Essays in the Rhetoric of Contemporary Criticism* (Minneapolis: University of Minnesota Press, 1983), 224.

36. The spot of time comes, of course, from book 11 of the 1805 *Prelude* (ll. 257–78). It is an effect of memory, the return of those moments that have "distinct prominence," "nourish" our minds, and carry a "beneficent influence." As Geoffrey Hartman remarks, "Poetry, in Wordsworth, names that ideal moment of 'blended night' or 'interchangeable supremacy.' " "Words, Wish, Worth," in *The Unremarkable Wordsworth* (Minneapolis: University of Minnesota Press, 1987), 114. Spots of time function in part as the lived equivalent of poetry in the *Prelude*.

37. See Don Bialostosky, *Making Tales: The Poetics of Wordsworth's Narrative Experiments* (Chicago: University of Chicago Press, 1984), Clayton, *Romantic Vision*, ch. 5, and also Karl Kroeber, *Romantic Narrative Art* (Madison: University of Wisconsin Press, 1960). Bialostosky argues that "Wordsworth distinguishes 'narrative' without reference to storytelling. For him the mark of narrative is not the narrator's telling of events but his speaking of himself and repeating the speech of his characters" (12).

38. Other critics have argued for a close relationship between novels of sensibility and the Lucy poems (and poems like Coleridge's "Eolian Harp." Adela Pinch relates the "misfittings" in "Strange fits of passion" — the seeming disproportion between event and emotion, the lack of an objective correlative — to Wordsworth's rewriting of the sensibility tradition. That tradition blends poetry, drama, and novels. *Strange Fits of Passion: Epistemologies of Emotion, Hume to Austen* (Stanford: Stanford University Press, 1996), 107. See also McGann, *Poetics of Sensibility*, ch. 2.

39. Barbara Herrnstein Smith, *Poetic Closure: A Study of How Poems End* (Chicago: University of Chicago Press, 1968), 24.

40. As Elizabeth Heckendorn Cook points out, domestic possibilities are not the only ones in epistolary novels. *Epistolary Bodies* (Stanford: Stanford University Press, 1996).

41. Paul Magnuson, *Reading Public Romanticism* (Princeton: Princeton University Press, 1998), 91.

42. Robin Jarvis, *Romantic Writing and Pedestrian Travel* (New York: St. Martin's Press, 1997), 96.

43. On rogue biographies, see John Richetti, *Popular Fiction before Richardson: Narrative Patterns, 1700–1739* (Oxford: Clarendon Press, 1969).

44. In *Wordsworth, the Sense of History* (Stanford: Stanford University Press, 1989), Alan Liu notes the foundational importance of domestic friendship to Wordsworth's concept of self: "the Romantic friend . . . is the outer, objective, or exogamous identity whose correspondence (literally, his letters) communicates to a family its own inner identity. Rhetorically: a friend is the metonymic medium in which a family writes its intuition that it is itself structured by communications of metaphorical identity closer than mere metonymy or 'liking' " (284).

45. One exception to this general rule is the pastoral of Milton's Eden, which contains the elements of a dyadic domestic bliss. Children and siblings, however, come with the destruction of Eden, rather than with its fulfillment.

46. *Cowper: Poetical Works*, ed H. S. Milford, 4th ed. (London: Oxford University Press, 1967), 1:1–7.

47. Dustin Griffin, "Redefining Georgic: Cowper's *Task,*" *ELH* 57 (1990): 865–79, at 876.

48. On the ascendance of georgic, see Anthony Low, *The Georgic Revolution* (Princeton: Princeton University Press, 1985), and three essays in *The Country and the City Revisited: England, the Politics of Culture, 1550–1850*, ed. Gerald Maclean, Donna Landry, and Joseph P. Ward (Cambridge: Cambridge University Press, 1996): Karen O'Brien, "Imperial Georgic, 1660–1789," 160–79; John Barrell, who traces the domestication of georgic onward to Wordsworth and, following Elizabeth Heckendorn Cook, to Burney's novels, in "Afterword: Moving Stories, Still Lives" (231–50); and Cook, "Crown Forests and Female Georgic: Frances Burney and the Reconstruction of Britishness" (197–212). Anne Wallace argues for the abstraction of labor in late-eighteenth- and nineteenth-century georgic in *Walking, Literature, and English Culture: The Origins and Uses of Peripatetic in the Nineteenth Century* (Oxford: Clarendon Press, 1993). Collier's domestic poetry centers on work; Leapor also evokes domestic scenes that are not georgic, as in "The Cruel Parent" or "Mopsus," but that could be at home in novels.

49. On the relation of georgic to a complex generic history of writerly labor, see Clifford Siskin, *The Work of Writing: Literature and Social Change in Britain, 1700–1830* (Baltimore: Johns Hopkins University Press, 1998).

50. "What Is Poetry?" in *Mill's Essays on Literature and Society*, ed. J. B. Schneewind (New York: Collier Books, 1965), 102–17, at 104.

51. For Mill, narrative is juvenile, and "Passing now from childhood, and from the childhood of society, to the grown-up men and women of this grown-up and unchildlike age — the minds and hearts of greatest depth and elevation are commonly those which take greatest delight in poetry; the shallowest and emptiest, on the contrary, are, by universal remark, the most addicted to novel-reading" ("What Is Poetry?" 105).

52. Cf. Clifford Siskin, "The Lyric Mix: Romanticism, Genre, and the Fate of Literature," *Wordsworth Circle* 25, no. 1 (1994): 7–10: "To assume that these writers were only finding their personal voice in the lyric . . . is to erase a layer of representation that was crucial to the use of the lyric at the time. The very act of writing in that form represented one's participation in a larger discursive project . . . in which lyrics effectively functioned as data in hypothetical narratives of knowledge linking past to present" (8). On novelism, see *The Work of Writing* (21–22). Siskin also argues: "The lyric . . . came into its own *as* it came to form the new body of knowledge called Literature" (*Work*, 133).

53. Jonathan Bate, "Wordsworth and the Naming of Places," *Essays in Criticism* 39, no. 3 (July 1989): 196–216, at 199.

54. Cf. Barthes's discussion of realism in *S/Z*, trans. Richard Miller (New York: Hill and Wang, 1974): "realism . . . consists not in copying the real but in copying a depicted copy of the real: this famous *reality* . . . is *set farther away*, postponed, or at least captured through the pictorial matrix in which it has been steeped before being put into words: code upon code" (55).

55. Don Bialostosky, "Genres from Life in Wordsworth's Art: 'Lyrical Ballads' 1798," in *Romanticism, History, and the Possibilities of Genre, 1789–1837*, ed. Tilottama Rajan (Cambridge: Cambridge University Press, 1998), 109–21, 118.

56. *Saturday Review*, 28 September 1864, 394–96. Included in *Crabbe, The Critical Heritage*, ed. Arthur Pollard (London: Routledge and Kegan Paul, 1972), 415. The critic goes on to compare Crabbe and Austen.

57. See Wordsworth's comments on Crabbe's realism in the Pollard collection (290–93). Beth Nelson points out the similarities between Crabbe's poems and the novels of Godwin, Inchbald, and Holcroft, noting his three never-published (destroyed) novels as well: *George Crabbe and the Progress of Eighteenth-Century Narrative Verse* (Lewisburg, Pa.: Bucknell University Press, 1976).

58. Geoffrey Hartmann, "Wordsworth, Inscriptions, and Romantic Nature Poetry," in *From Sensibility to Romanticism*, ed. Frederick W. Hilles and Harold Bloom (New York: Oxford University Press, 1965), 389–413.

59. On the increasing connection of "imagination" to poetry, see James Engell, *The Creative Imagination* (Cambridge: Harvard University Press, 1981).

60. W. J. B. Owen, *Wordsworth As Critic*, 151.

61. Miller, *Poetics of Evening*, notes that John's feet form a parallel inscription.

62. See Steven Knapp, *Personification and the Sublime: Milton to Coleridge* (Cambridge: Harvard University Press, 1985), on the speaker's failures of attention: "Corresponding to the slipperiness or inadequacy of the central image in 'Resolution and Independence' is the speaker's well-known but still mysterious inability to concentrate on what he himself wants to interpret as a providential answer to his needs. This is the point, of course, of Lewis Carroll's brilliant parody 'The White Knight's Song,' in which the speaker keeps asking an old man how he makes his living and then instantly lapses into reverie about his own self-interested schemes, thinking, for example, 'of a way / To feed oneself on batter, / And so go on from day to day / Getting a little fatter' " (116).

63. Celeste Langan, *Romantic Vagrancy: Wordsworth and the Simulation of Freedom* (Cambridge: Cambridge University Press, 1995), 192.

64. J. Paul Hunter, *Before Novels: The Cultural Contexts of Eighteenth-Century English Fiction* (New York: Norton, 1990), 47–52.

65. George Crabbe, *Selected Poetry*, ed. Jem Poster (Manchester: Carcanet, 1986).

66. The inserted tale and call for sympathetic response have a complex history. Sympathy had since Shaftesbury and Arbuckle been deemed a key component in aesthetic and moral theory, but it was not until the 1750s or so that it would become a primary principle of representation. In fact, theorists of sympathy focused on its literary possibilities in a restricted manner, usually considering the communication of passions from one body to another: Hill, for example, in a theatrical context, details the proper presentation of the body under the influence of passion, using this as a method of inducing sympathy in viewers; Kames, Beattie, and Blair explore the speech and language proper to the passions in similar terms (usually as exemplified by Shakespeare or other dramatists, but later writers mention Ossian frequently as well). These models suggest that the proper expression of passion is the key to its sympathetic reproduction in viewer or reader. These kinds of representation became increasingly ancillary in the later century — they were not merely the trappings and the suits of woe, but they were not the core of literary sympathy either. In the novel of sentiment the sufferer's narrative becomes the locus for sympathetic involvement. The embedded tales that drive the experience of protagonists in Sarah Fielding, Charlotte Smith, or Mackenzie can be traced to romance, but in the later eighteenth century they were state-of-the-art loci for demonstrating a character's moral sensibilities and providing melancholy pleasures. Given this context, it is striking that the leading theoretical accounts of sympathy do not consider narrative a primary model for eliciting sympathetic involvement, in part an effect of the status of

the novel in the period. Their most memorable hypothetical scenes (Burke's execution of a criminal or the destruction of London; Smith's vision of a man on the rack, etc.) are images rather than narratives of events and are syncretic. Smith's example of "our brother . . . upon the rack" is typical: "By the imagination we place ourselves in his situation, we conceive ourselves enduring all the same torments, we enter as it were into his body, and become in some measure one with him, and thence form some idea of his sensations" (*Moral Sentiments*, 9). As Lockridge argues in *The Ethics of Romanticism* (Cambridge: Cambridge University Press, 1989), the British tradition of moral philosophy offers an inadequate way of accounting for Wordsworth and other romantic poets in their approach to sensibility.

67. Again, novel and georgic intersect. Wallace argues that walking replaces cultivation for Wordsworth (*Walking*, 118 ff.). But in encounters, it is where walking *stops* that the poetic process is solidified; georgic is overwritten by novelistic encounters, and both are placed in service of a lyric project.

68. Lockridge argues that the "lyrical repossession" of loss in "Resolution and Independence" and "The Solitary Reaper" is characteristic of the early poetry but disappears after 1805 (*Ethics of Romanticism*, 216). This makes sense in terms of the question of generic solidification; once Wordsworth has redefined lyric against novels, the generic anxiety need no longer manifest in this way.

69. In "Wordsworth and the Forms of Poetry," Stuart Curran identifies a larger generic inversion in Wordsworth's poetry: "Wordsworth's greatest innovation . . . may have been his decision to collapse the traditional hierarchy altogether: his epic breadth is contained within a familiar epistle, a verse letter to Coleridge. The epistolary fiction controls the intimacy of tone, the associative logic, and internal rumination of the poem, but on a larger plane it also establishes the work's purposes in a bond of communication between writer and reader" (in Johnston and Ruoff, *Age of Wordsworth*, 115–32, at 131).

70. Liu argues that before 1796, Wordsworth's poetry "is essentially anonymous in its concerns with the politics of collective consciousness. Where 'I' or 'mind' occurs, it is as stiffly conventional as any personification from a descriptive or sensibility poem" (*Wordsworth*, 222). As the poet develops an "ideology of self," he does so through troping off and refining questions of domesticity and tragedy, in Liu's view; this requires the elision of narrative agency, or "history." Liu's readings of the generic intricacies of *The Borderers*, *The Ruined Cottage*, and *The Prelude* can be supplemented by investigating the other generic concern surrounding domesticity, self, and narrative at the basis of his self-definition. That is, in part, my project here. Clayton, in *Romantic Vision*, also argues for a mixing of modes; for him this is Wordsworth's attempt to counter the "threatening quality of narrative itself" (115). Narrative is interrupted by a visionary turn.

71. John Mullan, *Sentiment and Sociability: The Language of Feeling in the Eighteenth Century* (Oxford: Clarendon Press, 1988), 13–14.

72. Most critics point to the later part of the century and the sentimental novel as the time and genre in which emotional contracts of reading become conventional. Janet Todd, in *Sensibility: An Introduction* (New York: Methuen, 1986), uses Mackenzie's *Man of Feeling* as an exemplar of the practices of sentimental fiction, where readers are given "a course in the development of emotional response, whose beginning and end are literary. The reader learns how to respond to fictional or narrated misery and how to read the tale" (93). Lynch argues that ethical, emotive reading is the product of changes in novels circa 1770, and that "the project of these readers and writers . . . involved rendering reading an occasion when readers got to know themselves and their feelings" (*Economy of Character*, 126). Warner rightly argues in *Licensing Entertainment* that this kind of reader-novel relationship originated earlier. Formula fiction by Behn, Haywood, or Manley posits the reader as a subject marked off and defined most significantly by the pressures of desire; these novelists teach readers what to want and how to want it within the privacy of the scene of reading. This kind of readerly relationship is then remolded by ethical pressures to create readers so involved in the dynamics of ethical and emotional response that the *Pamela* phenomenon becomes possible (223). With *Pamela*, the reader is placed at the center of a doubled or even trebled world composed, one, of the plane of the fiction; two, of the web of fellow readers (Pamelists and Anti-Pamelists) committed to reading in a way that had never been previously seen; and three, of the world of everyday life in which these other strands are based. In this context, readerly response becomes a basis for self-evaluation and community judgment. The reading enacted in *Pamela* goes beyond the moral affirmation involved in *The Spectator* or other periodicals to involve readers in careful, eager exegesis, close reading, emotional response, and self-assessment. On the relationship between moral sensibility and the romantics, see Lockridge, *Ethics of Romanticism*.

73. Chiasmus for Langan refers to the exchange of values and terms associated with nature and books: light and spirit.

74. In novels, the inserted lyric—coffin-as-elegy, psalm imitations—is usually less important as an aesthetic object than as an object that allows expression for the author and evokes response from the audience. Romantic lyric, of course, focuses more intently on the aesthetic object.

75. On the vexed relationship of the romantic poets to sensibility, see especially Jerome McGann's reading of Coleridge's "Eolian Harp" in *The Poetics of Sensibility*, ch. 2.

76. Cf. "Salisbury Plain," where it is the Sailor, not Wordsworth, who speaks.

77. Janet Todd points out the prevalence of this pattern in sentimental

novels: "The average sentimental novel opposing vice and virtue took the virtuous hero to the horrors of London; it then allows him to escape into the rural provinces to find a happy ending" (*Sensibility*, 14). On the mixture of genres in "Lime-Tree Bower" and the conversation poems in general, see James Engell, "Imagining into Nature: *This Lime-Tree Bower My Prison*," in *Coleridge, Keats, and the Imagination*, ed. J. Robert Barth, S.J., and John L. Mahoney (Columbia: University of Missouri Press, 1990), 81–96: "In *This Lime-Tree Bower My Prison* we find elements of pastoral, landscape or loco-descriptive, meditative spiritual or religious, lyric, and didactic forms. Blank verse grandeur and epic diction surface at moments, but in proximity to a domestic, colloquial style; philosophical issues are couched in something akin to an epistle form. Some passages attain the voice of an ode, others of a hymn" (81).

78. This complex of issues has received full critical attention in recent years. See, for example, Hunter, *Before Novels*, 41 ff. See also Robert Darnton, "First Steps toward a History of Reading," in *The Kiss of Lamourette* (New York: Norton, 1990), 154–87.

79. Ernest de Selincourt suggests that a passage from *Tristram Shandy* is behind part of *The Waggoner* in Wordsworth, *Poetical Works*, ed. de Selincourt, 1:498–99, quoted in Duncan Wu, *Wordsworth's Reading, 1800–1815* (Cambridge: Cambridge University Press, 1995), 205. Wu notes what evidence there is for Wordsworth's novel-reading.

80. Ralph Freedman, *The Lyrical Novel: Studies in Hermann Hesse, André Gide, and Virginia Woolf* (Princeton: Princeton University Press, 1963).

81. Tilottama Rajan, "Romanticism and the Death of Lyric Consciousness," in *Lyric Poetry: Beyond New Criticism*, ed. Chaviva Hosek and Patricia Parker (Ithaca: Cornell University Press, 1985), 194–207. The unaltered quotation reads, "Wordsworth's decision to absorb 'There was a boy' into *The Prelude* is a paradigm for what happens throughout the prehistory of the longer poem, as the still unwritten lyrical voice is situated in the prose of the world" (200).

82. Hunter, *Before Novels*, 47–52. Hunter also lists the "inset, . . . anecdote, . . . [and] pretended exposition" (47).

83. See Ira Konigsberg, *Narrative Technique in the English Novel: Defoe to Austen* (Hamden, Conn.: Archon Books, 1985).

84. See Roy Pascal, *The Dual Voice* (Totowa, N.J.: Rowman and Littlefield, 1977).

85. In *Reading Public Romanticism*, Magnuson argues that many romantic lyrics are readable as public letters and suggests that the paratext with which publication surrounds romantic lyrics gives them a public frame in which address is encoded. I add that colloquy also internalizes epistolary address by making it imaginary; the two pressures coexist.

86. To begin, see Pinch, *Strange Fits of Passion*, Gene Ruoff, "Anne

Elliot's Dowry: Reflections on the Ending of *Persuasion*," in *Modern Critical Views: Jane Austen*, ed. Harold Bloom (New York: Chelsea House, 1986), 61–74, Stuart Tave, "Jane Austen and One of Her Contemporaries," in *Jane Austen: Bicentenary Essays*, ed. John Halperin (Cambridge: Cambridge University Press, 1975), 61–74, and A. Walton Litz, *"Persuasion:* Forms of Estrangement," in Halperin, *Jane Austen*, 221–32.

§ Bibliography

Primary

Akenside, Mark. *The Poetical Works of Mark Akenside.* Ed. Robin Dix. Madison, Wis.: Fairleigh Dickinson University Press, 1996.

Barker, Jane. *A Patch-Work Screen for the Ladies; or, Love and Virtue Recommended: In a Collection of Instructive Novels. Related after a Manner Intirely New, and Interspersed with Rural Poems, describing the Innocence of a Country-Life.* London, 1723.

Behn, Aphra. *Love-Letters between a Nobleman and His Sister.* New York: Penguin Books, 1993.

———. *Oroonoko, The Rover, and Other Works.* Ed. Janet Todd. New York: Penguin Books, 1992.

———. *The Works of Aphra Behn.* Vol. 1, *Poetry.* Ed. Janet Todd. London: Pickering and Chatto, 1992.

Brooke, Frances. *The Excursion.* Ed. Paula Backsheider and Hope D. Cotton. Lexington: University Press of Kentucky, 1997.

———. *Lady Julia Mandeville.* London: Scholartis Press, 1930.

Burney, Frances. *Cecilia.* Ed. Margaret Anne Doody and Peter Sabor. New York: Oxford University Press, 1988.

Cleland, John. *Fanny Hill, or Memoirs of a Woman of Pleasure.* New York: Penguin Books, 1985.

Coleridge, Samuel Taylor. *The Complete Works of Samuel Taylor Coleridge.* Ed. E. H. Coleridge. Oxford: Clarendon Press, 1912.

Collier, Mary. *Poems on Several Occasions.* Winchester, 1762. BL, shelfmark 11632 f. 12.

Congreve, William. *The Complete Works of William Congreve.* 4 vols. Ed. Montague Summers. London, Nonesuch, 1923.

Cowley, Abraham. *The Collected Works of Abraham Cowley.* 2 vols. Ed. Thomas O. Calhoun et al. Newark: University of Delaware Press, 1989.

Cowper, William. *Cowper: Poetical Works.* Ed. H. S. Milford. 4th ed. London: Oxford University Press, 1967.

Crabbe, George. *Selected Poetry*. Ed. Jem Poster. Manchester: Carcanet, 1986.

The Cupid. A Collection of LOVE SONGS, *In Twelve Parts. Suited To Twelve Different Sorts Of Lovers. Viz. The Female Lover, The Admiring Lover, The Slighted Lover, The Modest Lover, The Constant Lover, The Jealous Lover, The Tender Lover, The Whining Lover, The Saucy Lover, The Merry Lover, The Pressing Lover, The Happy Lover.* London, 1739.

Defoe, Daniel. *Roxana, or The Fortunate Mistress*. Ed. Jane Jack. New York: Oxford University Press, 1964.

Donne, John. *The Complete Poetry and Selected Prose of John Donne*. Ed. Charles Coffin. New York: Modern Library, 1952.

———. *Poems on Several Occasions*. London, 1719.

Fielding, Henry. *Tom Jones*. New York: Penguin Books, 1966.

Fielding, Sarah. *The Adventures of David Simple and Volume the Last*. Ed. Peter Sabor. Lexington: University Press of Kentucky, 1998.

The Flowers of Parnassus; or, The Lady's Miscellany, for the Year M.DCC.XXXV. Containing Great Variety of Original Pieces in Prose and Verse; and many Curious Particulars published since the Year One Thousand Seven Hundred and Thirty-Four. London: J. & T. Dormer, 1736.

Goldsmith, Oliver. *The Collected Works of Oliver Goldsmith*. 5 vols. Ed. Arthur Friedman. Oxford: Clarendon Press, 1966.

Griffith, Elizabeth. *The Delicate Distress*. Ed. Cynthia Booth Ricciardi and Susan Staves. Lexington: University Press of Kentucky, 1997.

The Grove: Or a Collection of Original Poems, Translations, &c. by W. Walsh, Esq., Dr. J. Donne. Mr. Dryden and other eminent hands. London, 1721.

Guilleragues, Gabriel Joseph de Lavergne. *Lettres de la religieuse portugaise*. Paris: Livre de poche, 1993.

Haywood, Eliza. *The History of Miss Betsy Thoughtless*. New York: Oxford University Press, 2000.

Love in Excess; or, The Fatal Enquiry. Peterborough, Ontario: Broadview Press, 1994.

Herbert, George. *Select Hymns, Taken out of Mr. Herbert's Temple, and Turn'd into the Common Metre* (1697). *Augustan Reprint Society* 98 (1962).

———. *The Works of George Herbert*. Ed. F. E. Hutchinson. Oxford: Clarendon Press, 1941.

Herrick, Robert. *The Complete Poetry of Robert Herrick*. Ed. J. M. Patrick. New York: Anchor Books, 1963.

Keats, John. *Complete Poems*. Ed. Jack Stillinger. Cambridge: Harvard University Press, Belknap Press, 1978.

Leapor, Mary. *Poems upon Several Occasions*. 2 vols. London, 1748. BL, shelf-mark 79 a. 10, 79 a. 11.

Lee, Sophia. *The Recess*. Lexington: University Press of Kentucky, 2000.

Lennox, Charlotte. *The Life of Harriot Stuart, Written by Herself*. Ed. Susan

Kubica Howard. Madison, N.J.: Fairleigh Dickinson University Press, 1995.

L'Estrange, Roger. *Five Love-Letters from a Nun to a Cavalier.* In *The Novel in Letters: Epistolary Fiction in the Early English Novel,* ed. Natascha Würzbach, 1–21. Coral Gables, Fla.: University of Miami Press, 1969.

Lobeira, Vasco. *Amadis of Gaul.* Trans. Robert Southey. 3 vols. London, 1872.

Lonsdale, Roger, ed. *Gray and Collins: Poetical Works.* New York: Oxford University Press, 1977.

———. *The New Oxford Book of Eighteenth-Century Verse.* New York: Oxford University Press, 1984.

Macpherson, James. *The Poems of Ossian and Related Works.* Ed. Howard Gaskill. Edinburgh: Edinburgh University Press, 1996.

Masters, Mary. *Familiar Letters and Poems on Several Occasions.* London, 1755. BL, shelfmark 993 k. 22.

———. *Poems on Several Occasions.* London, 1733. BL, shelfmark 11631 e. 42.

Milton, John. *Complete Poems and Major Prose.* Ed. Merrit Y. Hughes. Indianapolis: Odyssey, 1957.

New Miscellaneous Poems: With Five Love-Letters from a Nun to a Cavalier, Done in to Verse. London: J. Morphew, 1713.

Noyes, Russell, ed. *English Romantic Poetry and Prose.* New York: Oxford University Press, 1956.

"ON THE VERY MUCH LAMENTED DEATH of the truly NOBLE, and universally Respected, LORD BASIL HAMILTOUN, SON TO THE DECEAST WILLIAM Duke of HAMILTOUN, GRAND-CHILD TO JAMES *Duke of* HAMILTOUN, AND WILLIAM *Marquess of* DOWGLAS; *Who was unfortunately Drown'd August* 27, 1701, Aetat: 29: *by endeavouring to rescue his Servant.*" BL, shelfmark 11633 i 9/4.

Ovid. *Ovid's Epistles: With His Amours. Translated into English Verse by Mr. Dryden, Mr. Pope, and others.* London, 1751.

Poems by Eminent Ladies. 2 vols. London, 1755.

Percy, Thomas. *Reliques of Ancient English Poetry, Consisting of Old Heroic Ballads, Songs, and Other Pieces of Our Earlier Poets, Together with Some Few of Later Date.* Ed. Henry B. Wheatley, 3 vols. London, 1876.

Pope, Alexander. *The Poems of Alexander Pope.* Ed. John Butt. New Haven: Yale University Press, 1963.

Radcliffe, Ann. *The Romance of the Forest.* New York: Oxford University Press, 1986.

Richardson, Samuel. *Clarissa.* New York: Penguin Books, 1980.

———. *Correspondence of Samuel Richardson.* Ed. Anna Barbauld. London: Richard Phillips, 1804.

———. *Meditations.* Ed. Thomas Keymer. *Samuel Richardson's Published Commentary on "Clarissa,"* 1747–1765. London: Pickering and Chatto, 1998. Vol. 1.

——. *Pamela, or Virtue Rewarded.* New York: Penguin Books, 1980.

——. *Selected Letters of Samuel Richardson.* Ed. John Carroll. Oxford: Clarendon Press, 1964.

——. *Sir Charles Grandison.* Ed. Jocelyn Harris. 3 vols. New York: Oxford University Press, 1972.

Sheppard, Samuel. *The Loves of Amandus and Sophronia, Historically Narrated. A Piece of rare Contexture, Inriched with many pleasing Odes and Sonnets, occasioned by the Jocular, or Tragicall occurrence, happening in the progresse of the* HISTORIE. London, 1650.

Sidney, Phillip. *The Countess of Pembroke's Arcadia.* New York: Penguin Books, 1977.

Spenser, Edmund. *The Works of Edmund Spenser: A Variorum Edition.* 9 vols. Ed. Charles Osgood et al. Vol. 2, *The Minor Poems.* Baltimore: Johns Hopkins Press, 1947.

Smith, Charlotte. *Desmond.* Ed. Janet Todd and Antje Blank. London: Pickering and Chatto, 1997.

——. *Emmeline.* London: Pandora Press, 1987.

——. *Ethelinde, or The Recluse of the Lake.* 5 vols. London, 1790.

——. *The Old Manor House.* London: Pandora Press, 1987.

——. *The Poems of Charlotte Smith.* Ed. Stuart Curran. New York: Oxford University Press, 1993.

Smollett, Tobias. *Peregrine Pickle.* Ed. James L. Clifford. New York: Oxford University Press, 1964.

Sterne, Laurence. *The Life and Opinions of Tristram Shandy.* New York: Oxford University Press, 1983.

Suckling, John. *The Works of Sir John Suckling.* 2 vols. Ed. Thomas Clayton. Vol. 1, *The Non-Dramatic Works.* Oxford: Clarendon Press, 1971.

Thomson, James. *The Seasons and The Castle of Indolence.* Ed. James Sambrook. Oxford: Clarendon Press, 1972.

Wordsworth, William. *Poetical Works.* ed. Thomas Hutchinson, rev. Ernest de Selincourt. 5 vols. New York: Oxford University Press, 1936.

Secondary

Abrams, M. H. *The Mirror and the Lamp.* New York: Oxford University Press, 1953.

——. *Natural Supernaturalism.* New York: Norton, 1971.

——. "Structure and Style in the Greater Romantic Lyric." In *From Sensibility to Romanticism: Essays Presented to Frederick A. Pottle*, ed. Frederick Hilles and Harold Bloom, 527–60. New York: Oxford University Press, 1965.

Alter, Robert. *The Art of Biblical Poetry.* New York: Basic Books, 1985.

Altman, Janet Gurkin. *Epistolarity: Approaches to a Form.* Columbus: Ohio State University Press, 1982.

Aravamudan, Srinivas. *Tropicopolitans: Colonialism and Agency, 1688–1804.* Durham, N.C.: Duke University Press, 1999.

Armstrong, Nancy. *Desire and Domestic Fiction: A Political History of the Novel.* New York: Oxford University Press, 1987.

Armstrong, Nancy, and Leonard Tennenhouse. *The Imaginary Puritan, Literature, Intellectual Labor, and the Origins of Personal Life.* Berkeley: University of California Press, 1992.

Backscheider, Paula. "Sex, Sin, and Ideology: The Drama's Gift to the Genesis of the Novel." *Selected Proceedings from the Canadian Society for Eighteenth-Century Studies* 12 (1993): 1–15.

Bakhtin, Mikhail. *The Dialogic Imagination.* Trans. Caryl Emerson and Michael Holquist. Austin: University of Texas Press, 1981.

Bald, R. C. *John Donne: A Life.* Oxford: Clarendon Press, 1970.

Ballaster, Ros. *Seductive Forms: Women's Amatory Fiction from 1684 to 1740.* Oxford: Clarendon Press, 1992.

Barash, Carol. *English Women's Poetry, 1649–1714: Politics, Community, and Linguistic Authority.* Oxford: Clarendon Press, 1996.

Barrell, John. "Afterword: Moving Stories, Still Lives." In *The Country and the City Revisited: England, the Politics of Culture, 1550–1850,* ed. Gerald Maclean, Donna Landry, and Joseph P. Ward, 231–50. Cambridge: Cambridge University Press, 1996.

———. *The Birth of Pandora and the Division of Knowledge.* London: Macmillan, 1992.

———. *The Idea of Landscape and the Sense of Place, 1730–1840: An Approach to the Poetry of John Clare.* Cambridge: Cambridge University Press, 1972.

Barros, Carolyn A., and Johanna M. Smith, eds. *Life-Writings by British Women, 1660–1815: An Anthology.* Boston: Northeastern University Press, 2000.

Barthes, Roland. *S/Z.* Trans. Richard Miller. New York: Hill and Wang, 1974.

Bate, Jonathan. "Wordsworth and the Naming of Places." *Essays in Criticism* 39, no. 3 (1989): 196–216.

Bate, W. J. *The Burden of the Past.* Cambridge: Harvard University Press, Belknap Press, 1970.

———. *From Classic to Romantic: Premises of Taste in Eighteenth-Century England.* Cambridge: Harvard University Press, 1949.

Bateson, F. W. *English Poetry: A Critical Introduction.* New York: Longmans, Green, 1950.

Beasley, Jerry C. *A Check List of Prose Fiction Published in England, 1740–1749.* Charlottesville: University Press of Virginia, 1972.

Beattie, James. *Essays: On Poetry and Music, As They Affect the Mind; On Laughter, and Ludicrous Composition; On the Usefulness of Classical Learning.* 3d ed. London, 1779.

Bell, Ilona. "The Lyric Dialogue of Courtship." In *Representing Women in Renaissance England*, ed. Claude J. Summers and Ted-Larry Pebworth, 76–92. Columbia: University of Missouri Press, 1997.

Bialostosky, Don. "Genres from Life in Wordsworth's Art: 'Lyrical Ballads' 1798." In *Romanticism, History, and the Possibilities of Genre, 1789–1837*, ed. Tilottama Rajan, 109–21. Cambridge: Cambridge University Press, 1998.

———. *Making Tales: The Poetics of Wordsworth's Narrative Experiments*. Chicago: University of Chicago Press, 1984.

Blair, Hugh. *Lectures on Rhetoric and Belles Lettres*. 2 vols. Ed. Harold F. Harding. Carbondale: Southern Illinois University Press, 1965.

Boulton, Maureen Barry McCann. *The Song in the Story: Lyric Insertions in French Narrative Fiction, 1200–1400*. Philadelphia: University of Pennsylvania Press, 1993.

Brewer, John, and Roy Porter, eds. *Consumption and the World of Goods*. New York: Routledge, 1993.

Brooks, Cleanth. *The Well Wrought Urn*. London: Dennis Dobson, 1968.

Brower, Reuben A. *Alexander Pope: The Poetry of Allusion*. Oxford: Clarendon Press, 1959.

Brown, Laura. *English Dramatic Form, 1660–1760: An Essay in Generic History*. New Haven: Yale University Press, 1981.

———. *Fables of Modernity: Literature and Culture in the English Eighteenth Century*. Ithaca: Cornell University Press, 2001.

Brown, Marshall. "Passion and Love: Anacreontic Song and the Roots of Romantic Lyric." *ELH* 66 (1999): 373–404.

———. *Preromanticism*. Stanford: Stanford University Press, 1991.

Brown, Merle. "On William Collins' 'Ode to Evening.'" *Essays in Criticism* 11, no. 2 (1961): 136–53.

Brown, Murray L. "*Emblemata Rhetorica*: Glossing Emblematic Discourse in Richardson's *Clarissa*." *Studies in the Novel* 27, no. 4 (1995): 455–76.

Butt, John. *The Mid-Eighteenth Century*. Ed. Geoffrey Carnall. Oxford: Clarendon Press, 1979.

Carey, John. *John Donne: Life, Mind, and Art*. New York: Oxford University Press, 1981.

Castle, Terry. *Clarissa's Cyphers*. Ithaca: Cornell University Press, 1982.

Clayton, Jay. *Romantic Vision and the Novel*. Cambridge: Cambridge University Press, 1987.

Cohen, Ralph. "On the Interrelations of Eighteenth-Century Literary Forms." In *New Approaches to Eighteenth-Century Literature*, ed. Phillip Harth, 33–78. New York: Columbia University Press, 1974.

———. *The Unfolding of "The Seasons."* London: Routledge and Kegan Paul, 1970.

Cohn, Dorrit. *Transparent Minds: Narrative Modes for Presenting Consciousness in Fiction*. Princeton: Princeton University Press, 1978.

Coleridge, Samuel Taylor. *Biographia Literaria.* Ed. James Engell and W. J. Bate. Princeton: Princeton University Press, 1983.

———. *The Collected Works.* 16 vols. Ed. Carol Woodring. Vol. 2, *Table Talk.* Princeton: Princeton University Press, 1990.

Colley, Linda. *Britons: Forging the Nation, 1707–1837.* New Haven: Yale University Press, 1991.

Congreve, William. "A Discourse on the Pindaric Ode." In vol. 1 of *Eighteenth-Century Critical Essays,* ed. Scott Elledge, 143–47. Ithaca: Cornell University Press, 1961.

Connaughton, Michael. "Richardson's Familiar Quotations: *Clarissa* and Bysshe's *Art of English Poetry.*" *Philological Quarterly* 60, no. 2 (1986): 183–95.

Cook, Elizabeth Heckendorn. "Crown Forests and Female Georgic: Frances Burney and the Reconstruction of Britishness." In *The Country and the City Revisited: England, the Politics of Culture, 1550–1850,* ed. Gerald Maclean, Donna Landry, and Joseph P. Ward, 197–212. Cambridge: Cambridge University Press, 1996.

———. *Epistolary Bodies.* Stanford: Stanford University Press, 1996.

Cox, Stephen. *The Stranger within Thee: Concepts of Self in Late-Eighteenth-Century Literature.* Pittsburgh: University of Pittsburgh Press, 1980.

Crider, John. "Structure and Effect in Collins' Progress Poems." *Studies in Philology* 60 (1963): 57–72.

Curran, Stuart. *Poetic Form and British Romanticism.* New York: Oxford University Press, 1986.

———. "Romantic Poetry: Why and Wherefore?" In *The Cambridge Companion to British Romanticism,* ed. Curran, 216–35. Cambridge: Cambridge University Press, 1993

———. "Wordsworth and the Forms of Poetry." In *The Age of William Wordsworth,* ed. Kenneth R. Johnston and Gene W. Ruoff. New Brunswick, N.J.: Rutgers University Press, 1987.

Curtius, Ernst Robert. *European Literature and the Latin Middle Ages.* Trans. Willard R. Trask. Princeton: Princeton University Press, 1953.

Damrosch, Leopold, Jr. *The Imaginative World of Alexander Pope.* Berkeley: University of California Press, 1987.

Darnton, Robert. *The Kiss of Lamourette.* New York: Norton, 1990.

Davie, Donald. *The Eighteenth-Century Hymn in England.* Cambridge: Cambridge University Press, 1993.

———. *Purity of Diction in English Verse.* London: Routledge and Kegan Paul, 1967.

Davis, Bertram H. *Thomas Percy: A Scholar-Cleric in the Age of Johnson.* Philadelphia: University of Pennsylvania Press, 1989.

Davis, Lennard. *Factual Fictions: The Origins of the English Novel.* Philadelphia: University of Pennsylvania Press, 1996.

Day, Robert. *Told in Letters: Epistolary Fiction before Richardson*. Ann Arbor: University of Michigan Press, 1966.

de Man, Paul. *Blindness and Insight: Essays in the Rhetoric of Contemporary Criticism*. Minneapolis: University of Minnesota Press, 1983.

——. *The Rhetoric of Romanticism*. New York: Columbia University Press, 1984.

Derrida, Jacques. "The Law of Genre." In *Acts of Literature*, ed. Derek Attridge, 221–52. New York: Routledge, 1992.

Diehl, Huston. *An Index of Icons in English Emblem Books, 1500–1700*. Norman: University of Oklahoma Press, 1986.

Doody, Margaret Anne. *The Daring Muse: Augustan Poetry Reconsidered*. Cambridge: Cambridge University Press, 1985.

——. *A Natural Passion: A Study of the Novels of Samuel Richardson*. Oxford: Clarendon Press, 1974.

——. "Sensuousness in the Poetry of Eighteenth-Century Women Poets." In *Women's Poetry in the Enlightenment: The Making of a Canon, 730–1820*, ed. Isobel Armstrong and Virginia Blain, 3–32. New York: St. Martin's Press, 1999.

——. *The True Story of the Novel*. New Brunswick, N.J.: Rutgers University Press, 1996.

Dowling, William. *The Epistolary Moment: The Poetics of the Eighteenth-Century Verse Epistle*. Princeton: Princeton University Press, 1991.

Downie, J. A. "Mary Davys's 'Probable Feign'd Stories' and Critical Shibboleths about 'The Rise of the Novel.'" *Eighteenth-Century Fiction* 12, nos. 2–3 (2000): 309–26.

Drabble, Margaret, ed. *Oxford Companion to English Literature*. New York: Oxford University Press, 2000.

Dubrow, Heather. *A Happier Eden: The Politics of Marriage in the Stuart Epithalamium*. Ithaca: Cornell University Press, 1990.

Duffy, Maureen. *The Passionate Shepherdess*. London: Cape, 1977.

Dussinger, John. *The Discourse of the Mind in Eighteenth-Century Fiction*. The Hague: Mouton, 1974.

——. "'The Language of Real Feeling': Internal Speech in the Jane Austen Novel." In *The Idea of the Novel in the Eighteenth Century*, ed. Robert W. Uphaus, 97–115. East Lansing, Mich.: Colleagues Press, 1985.

Elledge, Scott, ed. *Eighteenth-Century Critical Essays*. 2 vols. Ithaca: Cornell University Press, 1961.

Engell, James. *The Creative Imagination*. Cambridge: Harvard University Press, 1981.

——. *Forming the Critical Mind*. Cambridge: Harvard University Press, 1989.

——. "Imagining into Nature: *This Lime-Tree Bower My Prison*." In *Coleridge, Keats, and the Imagination*, ed. J. Robert Barth, S.J., and John L. Mahoney, 81–96. Columbia: University of Missouri Press, 1990.

Erickson, Robert A. "'Written in the Heart': Richardson and Scripture." *Eighteenth-Century Fiction* 2, no. 1 (1989): 17–52.

Fay, Elizabeth. *Becoming Wordsworthian*. Amherst: University of Massachusetts Press, 1995.

Feingold, Richard. *Moralized Song: The Character of Augustan Lyricism*. New Brunswick, N.J.: Rutgers University Press, 1989.

Flint, Christopher. *Family Fictions: Narrative and Domestic Relations in Britain, 1688–1798*. Stanford: Stanford University Press, 1998.

Fowler, Alistair. *Kinds of Literature: An Introduction to the Theory of Genres and Modes*. Oxford: Clarendon Press, 1982.

Freedman, Ralph. *The Lyrical Novel: Studies in Hermann Hesse, André Gide, and Virginia Woolf*. Princeton: Princeton University Press, 1963.

Friedman, Albert B. *The Ballad Revival: Studies in the Influence of Popular on Sophisticated Poetry*. Chicago: University of Chicago Press, 1961.

Gallagher, Catherine. "Nobody's Story: Gender, Property, and the Rise of the Novel." In *Eighteenth-Century Literary History: An MLQ Reader*, ed. Marshall Brown, 27–42. Durham, N.C.: Duke University Press, 1999.

———. *Nobody's Story: The Vanishing Acts of Women Writers in the Marketplace, 1670–1820*. Berkeley: University of California Press, 1994.

Garber, Frederick. *The Autonomy of the Self from Richardson to Huysmans*. Princeton: Princeton University Press, 1982.

Gardiner, Judith Keagan. "The First English Novel: Aphra Behn's *Love Letters*, the Canon, and Women's Tastes." *Tulsa Studies in Women's Literature* 8 (fall 1989): 201–22.

Gaull, Marilyn. *English Romanticism: The Human Context*. New York: Norton, 1988.

Gillis, Christina Marsden. *The Paradox of Privacy: Epistolary Form in "Clarissa."* Gainesville: University Presses of Florida, 1984.

Godzich, Wlad, and Jeffrey Kittay. *The Emergence of Prose: An Essay in Prosaics*. Minneapolis: University of Minnesota Press, 1987.

Gonda, Caroline. *Reading Daughters' Fictions, 1709–1834: Novels and Society from Manley to Edgeworth*. Cambridge: Cambridge University Press, 1996.

Gopnik, Irwin. *A Theory of Style and Richardson's "Clarissa."* The Hague: Mouton, 1970.

Goreau, Angeline. *Reconstructing Aphra: A Social Biography of Aphra Behn*. New York: Dial Press, 1980.

Griffin, Dustin. *Alexander Pope: The Poet in the Poems*. Princeton: Princeton University Press, 1978.

———. *Patriotism and Poetry in Eighteenth-Century Britain*. Cambridge: Cambridge University Press, 2002.

———. "Redefining Georgic: Cowper's *Task*." *ELH* 57 (1990): 865–79.

Groom, Nick. *The Making of Percy's Reliques*. Oxford: Clarendon Press, 1999.

Guillory, John. *Cultural Capital: The Problem of Literary Canon Formation*. Chicago: University of Chicago Press, 1993.

Haefner, Joel. "The Romantic Scene(s) of Writing." In *Revisioning Romanticism: British Women Writers, 1776–1837*, ed. Carol Shiner Wilson and Joel Haefner, 256–73. Philadelphia: University of Pennsylvania Press, 1994.

Hagstrum, Jean. *The Sister Arts: The Tradition of Literary Pictorialism and English Poetry from Dryden to Gray*. Chicago: University of Chicago Press, 1958.

Hammond, Brean S. *Professional Imaginative Writing in England, 1670–1740*. Oxford: Clarendon Press, 1997.

Haney, Janice. "Eighteenth-Century Lyrical Models and Lyrical Languages: Essays toward a Theoretical History of the Lyric." Ph.D. diss., Stanford University, 1978.

Harris, Jocelyn. "Richardson: Original or Learned Genius?" In *Samuel Richardson: Tercentenary Essays*, ed. Margaret Anne Doody and Peter Sabor, 188–202. Cambridge: Cambridge University Press, 1989.

Hartman, Geoffrey. *The Unremarkable Wordsworth*. Minneapolis: University of Minnesota Press, 1987.

———. "Wordsworth, Inscriptions, and Romantic Nature Poetry." In *From Sensibility to Romanticism: Essays Presented to Frederick A. Pottle*, ed. Frederick W. Hilles and Harold Bloom, 389–413. New York: Oxford University Press, 1965.

———. *Wordsworth's Poetry, 1787–1814*. Cambridge: Harvard University Press, 1987.

Harvey, A. D. *English Prose in a Changing Society*. London: Allison and Busby, 1980.

Haskin, Dayton. "A History of Donne's 'Canonization' from Izaak Walton to Cleanth Brooks." *Journal of English and Germanic Philology* 92 (1993): 17–36.

Hazlitt, William. *The Complete Works of William Hazlitt*. 21 vols. Ed. P. P. Howe. London: J. M. Dent, 1933.

Henderson, Andrea K. *Romantic Identities: Varieties of Subjectivity*. Cambridge: Cambridge University Press, 1996.

Hill, Aaron. *The Art of Acting*. London, 1746.

Hobby, Elaine. *Virtue of Necessity: English Women's Writing, 1649–1688*. Ann Arbor: University of Michigan Press, 1988.

Hoeveler, Diane Long. *Romantic Androgyny*. University Park: Pennsylvania State University Press, 1979.

Hunt, Bishop C. "Wordsworth and Charlotte Smith." *Wordsworth Circle* 1 (1970): 85–103.

Hunt, John Dixon. *The Figure in the Landscape: Poetry, Painting, and Gardening during the Eighteenth Century*. Baltimore: Johns Hopkins University Press, 1976.

Hunter, J. Paul. *Before Novels: The Cultural Contexts of Eighteenth-Century English Fiction*. New York: Norton, 1990.

———. "The Insistent 'I.' " *Novel* 13 (fall 1979): 19–37.

Hutchings, W. "Syntax of Death: Instability in Gray's *Elegy Written in a Country Churchyard.*" In *Modern Critical Interpretations: Thomas Gray's "Elegy Written in a Country Churchyard,"* ed. Harold Bloom, 83–99. New York: Chelsea House, 1987.

Inglesfield, Robert. "Shaftesbury's Influence on Thomson's 'Seasons.' " *British Journal for Eighteenth-Century Studies* 9, no. 2 (1986): 141–56.

Janowitz, Anne. *Lyric and Labor in the Romantic Tradition.* Cambridge: Cambridge University Press, 1998.

Jarvis, Robin. *Romantic Writing and Pedestrian Travel.* New York: St. Martin's Press, 1997.

Johnson, Samuel. *Lives of the English Poets.* Ed. George Birkbeck Hill. 3 vols. Oxford: Clarendon Press, 1905.

———. *Selected Essays from the "Rambler," "Adventurer," and "Idler."* Ed. W. J. Bate. New Haven: Yale University Press, 1968.

Kauffman, Linda. *Discourses of Desire.* Ithaca: Cornell University Press, 1986.

Kaul, Suvir. *Poems of Nation, Anthems of Empire: English Verse in the Long Eighteenth Century.* Charlottesville: University Press of Virginia, 2000.

Keeble, N. H. *The Literary Culture of Nonconformity in Later Seventeenth-Century England.* Athens: University of Georgia Press, 1987.

Keymer, Tom. *Richardson's "Clarissa" and the Eighteenth-Century Reader.* Cambridge: Cambridge University Press, 1992.

———. "Richardson's *Meditations:* Clarissa's *Clarissa.*" In *Samuel Richardson: Tercentenary Essays,* ed. Margaret Anne Doody and Peter Sabor, 89–109. Cambridge: Cambridge University Press, 1989.

Kiely, Robert. *The Romantic Novel in England.* Cambridge: Harvard University Press, 1972.

Kinkead-Weekes, Mark. *Samuel Richardson: Dramatic Novelist.* Ithaca: Cornell University Press, 1973.

Knapp, Steven. *Personification and the Sublime: Milton to Coleridge.* Cambridge: Harvard University Press, 1985.

Konigsberg, Ira. *Narrative Technique in the English Novel: Defoe to Austen.* Hamden, Conn.: Archon Books, 1985.

Kraft, Elizabeth. *Character and Consciousness in Eighteenth-Century Comic Fiction.* Athens: University of Georgia Press, 1992.

Kroeber, Karl. *Romantic Narrative Art.* Madison: University of Wisconsin Press, 1960.

Kroll, Richard. *The Material Word: Literate Culture in the Restoration and Early Eighteenth Century.* Baltimore: Johns Hopkins University Press, 1991.

Lamb, Jonathan. *The Rhetoric of Suffering: Reading the Book of Job in the Eighteenth Century.* Oxford: Clarendon Press, 1995.

Landry, Donna. *The Muses of Resistance: Laboring-Class Women's Poetry in Britain, 1739–1796.* Cambridge: Cambridge University Press, 1990.

Langan, Celeste. *Romantic Vagrancy: Wordsworth and the Simulation of Freedom*. Cambridge: Cambridge University Press, 1995.

Lawson, Jacqueline Elaine. *Domestic Misconduct in the Novels of Defoe, Richardson, and Fielding*. Lewiston, Wales: Mellen University Press, 1994.

Lewalski, Barbara. *Protestant Poetics*. Princeton: Princeton University Press, 1979.

Litz, A. Walton. "*Persuasion:* Forms of Estrangement." In *Jane Austen: Bicentenary Essays*, ed. John Halperin, 221–32. Cambridge: Cambridge University Press, 1975.

Liu, Alan. *Wordsworth, the Sense of History*. Stanford: Stanford University Press, 1989.

Lockridge, Laurence. *The Ethics of Romanticism*. Cambridge: Cambridge University Press, 1989.

Lonsdale, Roger. "The Poetry of Thomas Gray: Versions of the Self." In *Modern Critical Interpretations: Thomas Gray's "Elegy Written in a Country Churchyard,"* ed. Harold Bloom, 19–37. New York: Chelsea House, 1987.

Low, Anthony. *The Georgic Revolution*. Princeton: Princeton University Press, 1985.

———. *Love's Architecture: Devotional Modes in Seventeenth-Century English Poetry*. New York: New York University Press, 1978.

Lowth, Robert. From *Lectures on the Sacred Poetry of the Hebrews*. In *Eighteenth-Century Critical Essays*, ed. Scott Elledge. Vol. 2, 687–703. Ithaca: Cornell University Press, 1961.

Lynch, Deirdre. *The Economy of Character: Novels, Market Culture, and the Business of Inner Meaning*. Chicago: University of Chicago Press, 1998.

———. "Personal Effects and Sentimental Fictions." *Eighteenth-Century Fiction* 12: nos. 2–3 (2000): 345–68.

Mack, Maynard. *The Garden and the City*. Toronto: University of Toronto Press, 1969.

Mackenzie, Alan. *Certain, Lively Episodes: The Articulation of Passion in Eighteenth-Century Prose*. Athens: University of Georgia Press, 1990.

Maclean, Norman. "From Action to Image: Theories of the Lyric in the Eighteenth Century." In *Critics and Criticism*, ed. R. S. Crane, 408–60. Chicago: University of Chicago Press, 1952.

Magnuson, Paul. *Reading Public Romanticism*. Princeton: Princeton University Press, 1998.

Marcus, Leah. *Childhood and Cultural Despair*. Pittsburgh: University of Pittsburgh Press, 1978.

Marotti, Arthur. "Manuscript, Print, and the Social History of the Lyric." In *The Cambridge Companion to English Poetry: Donne to Marvell*, ed. Thomas N. Corns, 52–79. Cambridge: Cambridge University Press, 1993.

Marsh, Robert. "Shaftesbury's Theory of Poetry: The Importance of the 'Inward Colloquy.'" *ELH* 28, no. 1 (1961):54–69.

Marshall, David. *The Figure of the Theater: Shaftesbury, Defoe, Adam Smith, and George Eliot.* New York: Columbia University Press, 1986.

Marshall, Madeleine Forell, and Janet Todd. *English Congregational Hymns in the Eighteenth Century.* Lexington: University Press of Kentucky, 1982.

Martz, Louis. *The Poetry of Meditation: A Study in English Religious Literature of the Seventeenth Century.* New Haven: Yale University Press, 1954.

McBurney, William H. *A Check List of English Prose Fiction, 1700–1739.* Cambridge: Harvard University Press, 1960.

McGann, Jerome. *The Poetics of Sensibility: A Revolution in Literary Style.* Oxford: Clarendon Press, 1996.

McKeon, Michael. *The Origins of the English Novel, 1600–1740.* Baltimore: Johns Hopkins University Press, 1987.

Mellor, Anne K. *Romanticism and Gender.* New York: Routledge, 1993.

Miles, Josephine. *Eras and Modes in English Poetry.* Berkeley: University of California Press, 1964.

Mill, John Stuart. "What Is Poetry?" In *Mill's Essays on Literature and Society,* ed. J. B. Schneewind, 102–17. New York: Collier Books, 1965.

Moore, C. A. "Shaftesbury and the Ethical Poets in England, 1700–1760." *PMLA* 31 (1916): 264–325.

Morgan, Charlotte. *The Rise of the Novel of Manners.* New York: Columbia University Press, 1911.

Mulder, John. "The Lyric Dimension of *Paradise Lost.*" *Milton Studies* 23 (1987): 145–63.

Mullan, John. *Sentiment and Sociability: The Language of Feeling in the Eighteenth Century.* Oxford: Clarendon Press, 1988.

Nardo, Anna. "The Submerged Sonnet As Lyric Moment in Miltonic Epic." *Genre* 9 (1976): 21–35.

Nelson, Beth. *George Crabbe and the Progress of Eighteenth-Century Narrative Verse.* Lewisburg, Pa.: Bucknell University Press, 1976.

Neumann, Anne Waldron. "Free Indirect Discourse in the Eighteenth-Century English Novel: Speakable or Unspeakable? The Example of *Sir Charles Grandison.*" In *Language, Text, and Context: Essays in Stylistics,* ed. Michael Toolan, 113–35. London: Routledge, 1992.

Newey, Vincent. "The Selving of Thomas Gray." In *Thomas Gray: Contemporary Essays,* ed. W. B. Hutchings and William Ruddick, 13–38. Liverpool: Liverpool University Press, 1993.

Nichols, Stephen G. "Amorous Imitation: Bakhtin, Augustine, and *Le Roman d'Enéas.*" In *Romance: Generic Transformations from Chrétien de Troyes to Cervantes,* ed. Kevin Brownlee and Martina Schordilis Brownlee, 47–73. Hanover, N.H.: University Press of New England, 1985.

Novak, Maximilian. "Some Notes toward a History of Fictional Forms: From Aphra Behn to Daniel Defoe." *Novel* 6 (winter 1973): 120–33.

Nussbaum, Felicity A. *The Autobiographical Subject: Gender and Ideology in*

Eighteenth-Century England. Baltimore: Johns Hopkins University Press, 1989.

O'Brien, Karen. "Imperial Georgic, 1660–1789." In *The Country and the City Revisited: England, the Politics of Culture, 1550–1850*, ed. Gerald Maclean, Donna Landry, and Joseph P. Ward, 160–79. Cambridge: Cambridge University Press, 1996.

Orr, Leonard. *A Catalogue Checklist of English Prose Fiction, 1750–1800*. Troy, N.Y.: Whitson, 1979.

Owen, W. J. B. *Wordsworth As Critic*. Toronto: University of Toronto Press, 1969.

Parker, Pat. *Inescapable Romance*. Princeton: Princeton University Press, 1979.

Partridge, Eric. *Eighteenth-Century English Romantic Poetry*. Folcroft, Pa.: Folcroft Press, 1924.

Pascal, Roy. *The Dual Voice*. Totowa, N.J.: Rowman and Littlefield, 1977.

Percy, Thomas. *The Percy Letters*, ed. Cleanth Brooks. Vol. 7. New Haven: Yale University Press, 1977.

Perry, Ruth. *Women, Letters, and the Novel*. New York: AMS, 1980.

Pinch, Adela. *Strange Fits of Passion: Epistemologies of Emotion, Hume to Austen*. Stanford: Stanford University Press, 1996.

Pollard, Arthur, ed. *Crabbe, the Critical Heritage*. London: Routledge and Kegan Paul, 1972.

Rajan, Tilottama. "Romanticism and the Death of Lyric Consciousness." In *Lyric Poetry: Beyond New Criticism*, ed. Chaviva Hosek and Patricia Parker, 194–207. Ithaca: Cornell University Press, 1985.

Raven, James. *British Fiction, 1750–1770: A Chronological Check-List of Prose Fiction Printed in Britain and Ireland*. Newark: University of Delaware Press, 1987.

Richetti, John. *Popular Fiction before Richardson: Narrative Patterns, 1700–1739*. Oxford: Clarendon Press, 1969.

Rickert, Edith. Introduction. *Early English Romances of Love*. New York: Cooper Square Publishers, 1966.

Ricks, Christopher. "Donne after Love." In *Literature and the Body: Essays on Populations and Persons*, ed. Elaine Scarry, 33–69. Baltimore: Johns Hopkins University Press, 1989.

Rivers, Isabel, ed. *Books and Their Readers in Eighteenth-Century England*. Leicester: Leicester University Press, 1982.

Robbins, Bruce. *The Servant's Hand: English Fiction from Below*. New York: Columbia University Press, 1986.

Roe, Nicholas. *John Keats and the Culture of Dissent*. Oxford: Clarendon Press, 1997.

Ruoff, Gene W. "1800 and the Future of the Novel: William Wordsworth, Maria Edgeworth, and the Vagaries of Literary History." *The Age of*

William Wordsworth, ed. Kenneth R. Johnston and Gene W. Ruoff, 291–314. New Brunswick, N.J.: Rutgers University Press, 1987.

———. "Anne Elliot's Dowry: Reflections on the Ending of *Persuasion*." In *Modern Critical Views: Jane Austen*, ed. Harold Bloom, 61–74. New York: Chelsea House, 1986.

Rzepka, Charles. *The Self As Mind: Vision and Identity in Wordsworth, Coleridge, and Keats*. Cambridge: Harvard University Press, 1986.

Samuels, Peggy. "Milton's Use of Sonnet Form in *Paradise Lost*." *Milton Studies* 24 (1988): 141–54.

Schellenberg, Betty A. *The Conversational Circle: Rereading the English Novel, 1740–1775*. Lexington: University Press of Kentucky, 1996.

Schlegel, Friedrich. *Dialogue on Poetry*. Trans. Ernst Behler and Roman Struc. University Park, Pa.: Pennsylvania State University Press, 1968.

Schoenfeldt, Michael C. *Prayer and Power: George Herbert and Renaissance Courtship*. Chicago: University of Chicago Press, 1991.

Shaftesbury, Anthony Cooper. *Characteristics of Men, Manners, Opinions, Times*. Ed. John M. Robertson. 2 vols. in 1. Indianapolis: Bobbs-Merrill, 1964.

Sherbo, Arthur. *English Sentimental Drama*. East Lansing: Michigan State University Press, 1957.

Sherwin, Paul. *Precious Bane: Collins and the Miltonic Legacy*. Austin: University of Texas Press, 1977.

Siskin, Clifford. "Eighteenth-Century Periodicals and the Romantic Rise of the Novel." *Studies in the Novel* 26, nos. 1–2 (1994): 26–42.

———. "The Lyric Mix: Romanticism, Genre, and the Fate of Literature." *Wordsworth Circle* 25, no. 1 (1994): 7–10.

———. *The Work of Writing: Literature and Social Change in Britain, 1700–1830*. Baltimore: Johns Hopkins University Press, 1998.

Sitter, John. *Literary Loneliness in Mid-Eighteenth-Century England*. Ithaca: Cornell University Press, 1982.

Smith, Adam. *The Theory of Moral Sentiments*. Indianapolis: Liberty Press, 1984.

Smith, Barbara Herrnstein. *Poetic Closure: A Study of How Poems End*. Chicago: University of Chicago Press, 1968.

Smith, Nigel. *Literature and Revolution in England, 1640–1660*. New Haven: Yale University Press, 1994.

———. *Perfection Proclaimed: Language and Literature in English Radical Religion, 1640–1660*. Oxford: Clarendon Press, 1989.

Spacks, Patricia Meyer. "The Eighteenth-Century Collins." *Modern Language Quarterly* 44, no. 1 (1983): 3–22.

———. *Imagining a Self: Autobiography and Novel in Eighteenth-Century England*. Cambridge: Harvard University Press, 1976.

———. *The Poetry of Vision*. Cambridge: Harvard University Press, 1967.

Sprat, Thomas. *History of the Royal Society.* Ed. Jackson I. Cope and Harold Whitmore Jacobs. St. Louis, Mo.: Washington University Press, 1958.

Stephenson, William E. Introduction. *Select Hymns, Taken out of Mr. Herbert's Temple, and Turn'd into the Common Metre* (1697). *Augustan Reprint Society* 98 (1962).

Stone, Lawrence. *The Family, Sex, and Marriage in England, 1500–1800.* New York: Harper, 1997.

Strauch, Gérard. "Dialogue intérieur et style indirect libre dans *Grace Abounding.*" *Bulletin de la Société de Stylistique Anglaise* 2 (1980): 33–48.

———. "Richardson et le style indirect libre." *Recherches Anglaises et Nord-Americaines* 26 (1993): 87–101.

Summers, Montague. Introduction. *The Works of Aphra Behn.* London: William Heinemann, 1915.

Targoff, Ramie. *Common Prayer: The Language of Public Devotion in Early Modern England.* Chicago: University of Chicago Press, 2001.

Tave, Stuart. "Jane Austen and One of Her Contemporaries." In *Jane Austen: Bicentenary Essays,* ed. John Halperin, 61–74. Cambridge: Cambridge University Press, 1975.

Taylor, Charles. *Sources of the Self: The Making of the Modern Identity.* Cambridge: Harvard University Press, 1989.

Thorne-Thomsen, Sara. "'Hail Wedded Love': Milton's Lyric Epithalamium." *Milton Studies* 24 (1988): 155–85.

Todd, Janet. Introduction. *The Works of Aphra Behn.* 7 vols. London: William Pickering, 1992.

———. *Sensibility: An Introduction.* New York: Methuen, 1986.

———. *The Sign of Angellica.* New York: Columbia University Press, 1989.

Townsend, Dabney. "Shaftesbury's Aesthetic Theory." *Journal of Aesthetics and Art Criticism* 41, no. 2 (1982): 206–13.

Tufte, Virginia. *The Poetry of Marriage: The Epithalamium in Europe and Its Development in England.* Los Angeles: Tinnon-Brown, 1970.

Tuveson, Ernest. "Shaftesbury and the Age of Sensibility." In *Studies in Criticism and Aesthetics, 1660–1800,* ed. Howard Anderson and John Shea, 73–93. Minneapolis: University of Minnesota Press, 1967.

Vendler, Helen. *The Art of Shakespeare's Sonnets.* Cambridge: Harvard University Press, 1997.

———. *The Poetry of George Herbert.* Cambridge: Harvard University Press, 1975.

Vickers, Brian. *Classical Rhetoric in English Poetry.* Carbondale: Southern Illinois University Press, 1989.

———. "The English Royal Society and English Prose Style: A Reassessment." In *Rhetoric and the Pursuit of Truth: Language Change in the Seventeenth and Eighteenth Centuries,* ed. Brian Vickers and Nancy S. Streuver, 1–76. Los Angeles: William Andrews Clark Memorial Library, 1985.

Wallace, Anne. *Walking, Literature, and English Culture: The Origins and Uses of Peripatetic in the Nineteenth Century.* Oxford: Clarendon Press, 1993.

Walton, Izaak. *Walton's Lives.* London, 1884.

Warner, William. *Licensing Entertainment: The Elevation of Novel Reading in Britain, 1684–1750.* Berkeley: University of California Press, 1998.

Warton, Joseph. *An Essay on the Genius and Writings of Pope.* 2 vols. London, 1806.

Wasserman, Earl. "The Inherent Values of Eighteenth-Century Personification." *PMLA* 65, no. 4 (1950): 435–63.

Watt, Ian. *The Rise of the Novel.* Berkeley: University of California Press, 1957.

Watts, Isaac. Preface to the *Horae Lyricae.* In *Eighteenth-Century Critical Essays*, ed. Scott Elledge. Vol. 1, 148–63. Ithaca: Cornell University Press, 1961.

Weinbrot, Howard. *The Formal Strain: Studies in Augustan Imitation and Satire.* Chicago: University of Chicago Press, 1969.

Weisman, Karen. "The Aesthetics of Separation: Collins's 'Ode Occasioned by the Death of Mr. Thomson.'" *Style* 28, no. 1 (1994): 55–64.

Wellington, James. Introduction. *Eloisa to Abelard.* Coral Gables, Fla.: University of Miami Press, 1965.

Wendorf, Richard. *William Collins and Eighteenth-Century English Poetry.* Minneapolis: University of Minnesota Press, 1981.

Wheeler, Roxann. *The Complexion of Race: Categories of Difference in Eighteenth-Century British Culture.* Philadelphia: University of Pennsylvania Press, 2000.

White, R. S. "Functions of Poems and Songs in Elizabethan Romance and Romantic Comedy." *English Studies* 68, no. 5 (1987): 392–405.

Wilcox, Helen. "Entering *The Temple:* Women, Reading, and Devotion in Seventeenth-Century England." In *Religion, Literature, and Politics in Post-Reformation England, 1540–1688*, ed. Donna B. Hamilton and Richard Strier, 187–207. Cambridge: Cambridge University Press, 1996.

Williams, Anne. *The Prophetic Strain: The Greater Lyric in the Eighteenth Century.* Chicago: University of Chicago Press, 1984.

Woodhouse, A. S. P. "The Poetry of Collins Reconsidered." In *From Sensibility to Romanticism: Essays Presented to Frederick A. Pottle*, ed. Frederick W. Hilles and Harold Bloom, 93–137. New York: Oxford University Press, 1965.

Worden, Blair. *The Sound of Virtue.* New Haven: Yale University Press, 1996.

Wordsworth, William. *Wordsworth's Preface to Lyrical Ballads.* Ed. W. J. B. Owen. Copenhagen: Rosenkilde and Bagger, 1957.

Wright, Walter Francis. *Sensibility in English Prose Fiction, 1670–1814: A Reinterpretation.* Urbana: University of Illinois Press, 1937.

Wu, Duncan. *Wordsworth's Reading, 1800–1815.* Cambridge: Cambridge University Press, 1995.

Young, Edward. "On Lyric Poetry." In *Eighteenth-Century Critical Essays*, ed. Scott Elledge. Vol. 1, 410–15. Ithaca: Cornell University Press, 1961.

Zimbardo, Rose. "Aphra Behn: A Dramatist in Search of the Novel." In *Curtain Calls: British and American Women and the Theater, 1660–1820*, ed. Mary Anne Schofield and Cecelia Machesky, 371–82. Athens: Ohio University Press, 1991.

Zimmerman, Sarah. "Charlotte Smith's Letters and the Practice of Self-Presentation." *Princeton University Library Chronicle* 53, no. 1 (1991): 50–77.

Index